THE MARITIME BOUNDARIES OF THE INDIAN OCEAN REGION

THE MARITIME BOUNDARIES OF THE INDIAN OCEAN REGION

Vivian Louis Forbes

SINGAPORE UNIVERSITY PRESS
NATIONAL UNIVERSITY OF SINGAPORE

ISBN 9971–69–189–2 (Paper)
9971–69–192–2 (Cloth)

Typeset by: Times Graphics, Singapore
Printed by: Photoplates Pte Ltd.

Dedicated to
Dawn, Andrew, Jennifer,
Mum Phyllis,
and the late Christopher Worth

CONTENTS

LIST OF FIGURES

LIST OF TABLES

LIST OF PLATES

LIST OF ABBREVIATIONS

AFZ	Australian Fishing Zone
BIOT	British Indian Ocean Territory
CP	Common Point
CS	Continental Shelf
CLOS	Convention on the Law of the Sea
DOSP	Dalhousie Ocean Studies Programme, Canada.
ECOSOC	Economic and Social Council of the United Nations
EC	European Community
EEZ	Exclusive Economic Zone
FZ	Fishing Zone
FAO	Food and Agriculture Organisation
GDS	Geographically Disadvantaged State
HAT	Highest Astronomical Tide
IOC	Indian Ocean Commission
IOMAC	Indian Ocean Maritime Affairs Committee
IOZP	Indian Ocean Zone of Peace
IHB	International Hydrographic Bureau
IHO	International Hydrographic Organisation
IMO	International Maritime Organisation
IMCO	Inter-Governmental Consultative Organisation
ISA	International Seabed Authority
ISLW	Indian Springs Low-Water
JDZ	Joint Development Zone
LLS	Land-locked States
LAT	Lowest Astronomical Tide
LTE	Low Tide Elevation
MSC	Malacca Strait Council
MLLW	Mean Lower Low-Water
MLWN	Mean Low-Water Neap
MLWS	Mean Low-Water Spring
PNG	Papua New Guinea
PREPCOM	Preparatory Commission on Deep Seabed Mining
SEAPOL	Southeast Asian Programme on Ocean Law and Management
TSS	Traffic Separation Scheme
UN	United Nations
UNCLOS	United Nations Convention on the Law of the Sea
UNEP	United Nations Environmental Programme
UNESCO	United Nations Educational, Scientific and Cultural Organisation
UKC	Under-Keel Clearance
VOC	Vereenigde Oostindische Compagnie (United Dutch East India Company)
ZOC	Zone of Cooperation
ZOPAN	Zone of Peace and Neutrality

FOREWORD

With the exponential increase in world population came a rapid growth in the demand for resources, both as foods and raw materials, while the use of ever more powerful and sophisticated equipment opened up new spaces for exploitation.

The latter half of the XIX century has witnessed extraordinary changes in the concepts of spatial political boundaries. The old concept of territorial waters has been fundamentally retained, but new, distinct jurisdictional rights have been defined with regard to the continental shelf and far beyond, to extensive fishing zones and economic zones, reaching long distances and greath depths.

A conspicuous consequence of these jurisdictional extensions has been the reduction of the areas that could be legally viewed as the high seas. A recent sentence of the High Court of the Commonwealth of Australia has placed in doubt the justification of the concept of *terra nullius,* at least with regard to a small island in Torres Strait. At the opposite extreme of the juridical and dimensional span, the concept of the High Sea as *mare omnium* has been steadily weakened and diminished, perhaps so far without full recognition of the vast consequences of the change.

International Law had always been of special interest because a large part of it was evolved and determined *inter pares,* between governments, whereas laws are usually established and enforced from above, by the governments and institutions that formulate them. But the rate of change in concepts relating to the sea (and especially to its resources) was so fast and the potential for conflict so great, that international bodies had to intervene by actively and systematically coordinating the formulation of the new Laws of the Sea by the many governments concerned.

Formulation, slow and laborious as it may be, can be completed soon enough, but the ensuing — and absolutely necessary — ratifications trickle in over many years, and in some instances never come.

In practice, some maritime zones may be formally and legitimately claimed, and assigned, but the claimant and titular states may be unable or perhaps unwilling to utilise them for some time. The claim has been made and the right has been established, but nothing seems to happen. Pressure may be put on the titular country for some action or a devolution of rights of exploitation to a better equipped (needier? greedier?) delegate. At this point one should stress that, no matter what users (exploiters?) of fishery or mineral resources may affirm, most resources which lie unused will be far more valuable in the future, when some other users active elsewhere may have exhausted their own supplies. Whether, and for how long, international bodies will allow single countries to let their resources lie dormant with a view to a future and perhaps slightly hypothetical utilisation remains to be seen, and may cause some concern. There is also the rather unlikely possibility that the unused resources may be rendered uneconomic by changes in the market forces, or superseded by technological or scientific changes, in which cases should take the long-term constructive view that the ultimate winner is the conservation of nature.

The author has restricted his field of research to the Indian Ocean, but had to examine the complex boundary issues of the Red Sea and Persian Gulf in the one direction, and the minutely complicated ones of the Malacca Straits in the other. The areas delimited by maritime boundaries 200 nautical miles or 370 km offshore may legitimately be claimed by two or more neighbouring countries, hence the lengthy negotiations that may be needed before treaties or conventions are barely initialled, let alone signed. Many maritime boundaries are wholly agreed on by the titular countries, some are accepted pending ratification, but some are still subject to negotiation or even, so far, to bare delineation.

The author's clear and steady guidance through this complex and multifarious, pluridirectional and three-dimensional field will be most welcome by students and practitioners of law, politics, navigation, fisheries and mining. The clarity of expression of the text and the precise delineations of the maps make the use of this book a rewarding pleasure.

Joseph Gentilli, Hon. DSc (W. A.)
Department of Geography
University of Western Australia
Nedlands, Western Australia

AUTHOR'S NOTE

INTRODUCTION

We encounter territories and boundaries in our everyday lives. This can be at the level of our own personal experience, or in dealing with local government authorities and at a much broader level, for example, in the case of international boundaries.

Political boundaries on *terra firma* have been in the news for many centuries, and in particular during the latter half of the 20th century. Maritime boundaries on the other hand have been elusive. They have not been "experienced" by mariners, who until recently and within reason, possessed the freedom of the high seas.

Ownership of the sea has become an increasingly important question in recent years. This has been prompted by discoveries of mineral wealth and oil and natural gas reserves on and below the seabed, as well as a desire by many countries to increase the limits of their exclusive fishing areas. For these reasons and many others ocean space has been bitterly contested in many geographical regions. The Indian Ocean Basin provides many classical examples of contested sovereignty to islands, rights to operate in "traditional" fishing grounds and exclusive claims to the marine biotic and mineral resources that lie in the waters and seabed adjacent to the marine coastal state.

Often it is difficult to find the relevant information and legal instruments — statutes, legal decisions, and international agreements. My task was made relatively easier by a network of contacts; through attendance at international meetings on boundary issues which provided opportunities to meet and discuss with policy-makers and negotiators from several countries and additionally through direct correspondence with diplomatic staff. An interdisciplinary approach has been adopted in the marshalling of the facts and in the collection of data.

My interest in maritime boundary determination has been fostered by an educational background in cartography, maritime studies and geodetic and hydrographic surveying.

UPDATING

This book describes the legal and political situation of the maritime boundaries of the Indian Ocean regional states as of October 1993. Further updating has been included where possible.

Such is the nature of the changing geopolitical scene in the Indian Ocean Region that, for example, the Republic of the Comoros deposited its instrument of ratification of the Convention on the Law of the Sea on 21 June 1994; in late July 1994 amendments to the Deep Seabed Mining regime were incorporated into the Law of the Sea document; new Australian maritime zones, namely, a 200-nautical mile Exclusive Economic Zone and a 24-nautical mile Contiguous Zone were adopted on 1 August 1994; Australia deposited its instruments of ratification of the Law of the Sea Convention on 6 October 1994; and about a week later (on 14 October 1994) Iraq announced that it was willing to accept Kuwait's sovereignty and recognise the common land and sea boundary that was demarcated under a United Nation's Commission in 1993. Also on that date, Malaysia and Singapore reached agreement in Kuala Lumpur on the demarkate of a boundary in the Straits of Johor.

To highlight the complexities of proving sovereignty to disputed islands: Bahrain and Qatar had sought in March 1994 the adjudication of the International Court of Justice on a ruling over the Hawar Islands in the Persian Gulf whilst Malaysia and Singapore agreed in August 1994 to take their case on the Pedra Branca Island, located at the eastern end of the Straits of Singapore, to the Honourable Members at The Hague.

ACKNOWLEDGEMENTS

Comments and suggestions from Patrick Armstrong, Francis Auburn, Bill Cooper, in particular Joseph Gentilli, Kenneth McPherson, Victor Prescott, Peter Reeves, Dennis Rumley and Alan Yardley are appreciated and taken into consideration. The views and shortcomings herein are, however, my own.

I am also grateful to many others. Access to primary sources and other publications was made possible thanks to Ambassadors, High Commissioners and their staff from numerous states in the region; friends at SEAPOL; the Office of the Geographer, United States; and to Mary Anne Schooling and Guy Foster.

For the opportunity to use the photographs in this book I am indebted to Jenni Forbes and Donald Froome. To Theresa Cruse, Halina Kobryn and the late Dr. Christopher Worth I offer thanks for access to their word processor on many occasions.

MAPS AND MAP PROJECTIONS

An atlas is a series of compromises in the choice of area, scale and projection of the maps included in it. Strict conformity in scales and projections, though desirable in theory, can produce undesirable results. The sheer bulk of the volume can be increased or decreased excessively; less populous geographical areas may receive over generous attention at the expense of the densely populated ones.

Whilst arriving at a standard range of scales for the maps in this publication, I departed from this principle when a special scale and/or projection best suited a particular area. Detailed large-scale case-studies are supplemented by smaller-scale regional surveys.

SPELLING OF PLACE-NAMES

Of the many problems associated with mapping few surpass the complexities of place-names. International standardisation has not yet resolved the manifold problems. There are alternative ways in which languages that use non-Latin alphabets are transcribed. An added difficulty is the widespread use of conventional names in one country for the names in another country.

The principles and practice of the British Permanent Committee on Geographical Names and the United States Board on Geographic Names are useful yardsticks to employ when faced with the dilemma of the nomenclature to use on maps.

Perth, 24 October 1994

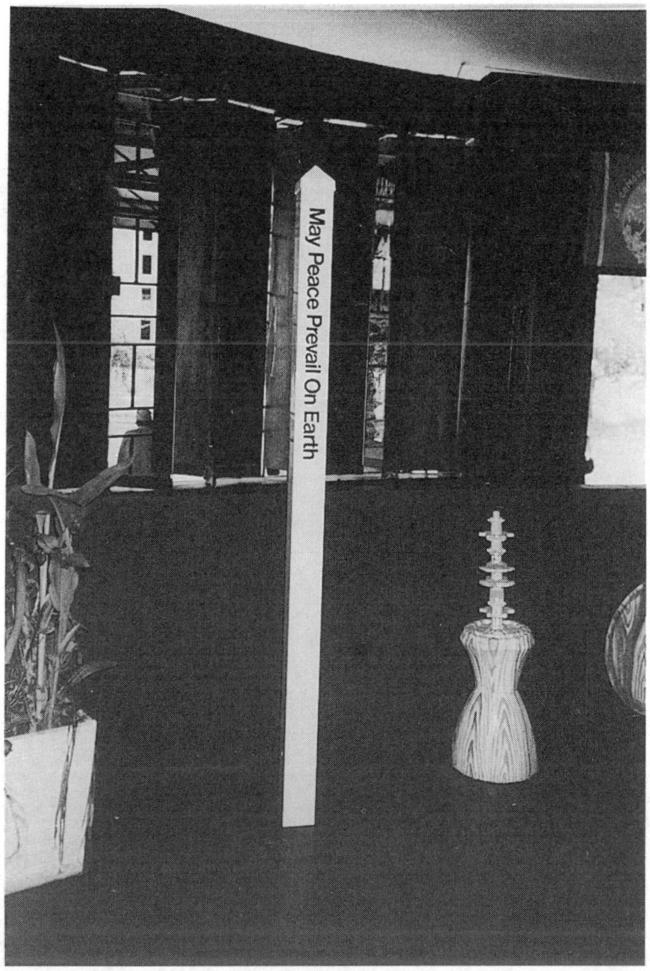

Plate 1 A gift to the people of Comoros from the government and people of Japan. (Photograph courtesy of Jenni Forbes, January 1992).

In a gesture of friendship and goodwill the Government of Japan which is a major user of the Indian Ocean presented to the people of Comoros a token gift which is housed in the Department of Tourism office, Moroni. Embossed on a white pole, in four languages, is the simple message: May Peace Prevail On Earth. Continuing progress, under the aegis of CLOS, in the forging of international agreements on Indian Ocean maritime boundaries, will contribute substantially to this aim.

Plate 2 The *Sanko Harvest* aground off Hood Island, Esperance Bay (Photograph courtesy of Department of Marine and Habours, W.A.).

Plate 3 The tanker *Kirki* off the Western Australian coast (Photograph courtesy of Department of Marine and Habours, W.A.).

Plate 4 Delegates attending SEAPOL's Second International Conference at Bangkok, 1987.

Plate 5 Panel of speakers discussing regional issues on marine pollution of SEAPOL's Third International Conference at Bali, May 1990.

Plate 6 Professor Mochtar of Indonesia in discussion on cooperative approaches to boundary determination with the author during the SEAPOL Conference, Bali, May 1990.

CHAPTER ONE

THE SCOPE OF THE STUDY

INTRODUCTION

One of the many problems in the demarcation of boundaries, and in particular maritime boundaries, is the complex issue of the ownership of the natural resources of the ocean — the water column, the seabed, and the substratum. Demarcation and delineation of maritime territorial claims and zones of national jurisdiction must be acceptable, not only to the negotiating states, but also to the international community of nations. Maritime boundary agreements, like those relating to terrestrial boundaries, are politically sensitive issues, and thus should be accorded the status of official recognition by all nations. As an example, the recently negotiated *Timor Gap Treaty* which permits the creation of a Zone of Cooperation between Australia and Indonesia for the exploitation of oil and natural gas in the Timor Sea region, came into force on 9 February 1991. The status of the treaty has been challenged by Portugal. Details of this challenge are covered in Chapter Four.

Although states are not compelled to delineate any maritime boundaries, most will eventually wish to do so when it is convenient to them, or on the insistence of their coastal neighbours. This study argues that there is a need for the early delineation of maritime boundaries between coastal states in the Indian Ocean region in order to settle the question of ownership of ocean resources, and to share the responsibilities for the care of the marine environment and for the conservation and careful exploitation of renewable and non-renewable resources. It is reasonable to expect that the increased utilisation of the oceans for purposes other than traditional fishing and navigation practices will create a greater need for regulatory control of national and international sea space.

Furthermore, although the extension of maritime jurisdiction by coastal states erodes the internationally accepted perception of the freedom of the high seas, such action will offer the coastal states the security they seek from any threatened naval attack by external forces, protect their resources and marine environment, and ensure their exclusive use of the ocean's resources within the proclaimed zones.

AIMS OF THIS STUDY

This study aims:

- to analyse the provisions contained in the deliberations of four Conventions held in Geneva during 1958, which were formally proclaimed as the first Law of the Sea;
- to analyse the provisions contained in the Articles and Annexes of the Third United Nations Convention on the Law of the Sea (CLOS), and their implications in the Indian Ocean context;
- to evaluate the national legislation of those Indian Ocean littoral states which have proclaimed their maritime limits over offshore waters;
- to evaluate the numerous bilateral and trilateral agreements among Indian Ocean states on maritime boundary delimitation as they relate to the continental shelf and exclusive zones, and to analyse these agreements in their regional setting;

- to analyse the maps of the agreed maritime boundaries of the Indian Ocean littoral states;
- to provide an up-to-date summary of the suite of maritime limits claimed by these littoral and island states and a status listing of the ratification and signature to the Third United Nations Convention on the Law of the Sea, 1982.

The mechanism and the guidelines for the establishment and formal recognition of national maritime limits of coastal states are contained in the as yet unratified Third United Nations Convention of the Law of the Sea, hereinafter referred to as CLOS. The Convention was concluded on 10 December 1982 after nearly a decade of negotiations. By October 1993, 56 nations had ratified the Convention. Of these, 11 were littoral states of the Indian Ocean basin. According to its own Article 308, the Convention will enter into force 12 months from the day of the deposit of the 60th instrument of ratification or accession (Appendix B).

Details of the negotiating processes and the final document of CLOS are given in Chapter Three, and a tabulation of the status of signatory nations of the region is in Appendix D.

RATIONALE

As the ownership of the landmass has more or less been determined, there has been, since 1945, a growing concern for the sharing out of maritime space. This process can be compared to the colonial era between the 16th and 19th centuries — a historical period of time which is all too familiar to the coastal nations and the island states of the Indian Ocean Basin. Such is the context of this study, which is probably the first attempt at an integrated approach to the political geography of the Indian Ocean. As such, it draws attention to the regional need for cooperation in fishery conservation and technology; for the establishment of joint development zones for the careful exploration and exploitation of mineral resources; and for the further development and enhancement of trading relationships among the littoral countries.

Political geography is the description, explanation and evaluation of the political organisation of space. In questioning how space should be organised and partitioned, Gottmann (1982: 345) asserts that "political geography exists because geographical space is politically partitioned".

Political geography is not merely a study of states, their boundaries and frontiers. It is also concerned with the growth of the state as a political unit, the welfare of its citizens, the relationships between states on local, interregional and international levels, the resources and the environment, and the geographical form that states assume. Past research in political geography has been concerned primarily with land-based issues. The need exists for a greater research effort on sea-based issues, following on from Prescott (1975), because of the increasing international interest in the oceans and their resources.

This study includes a synthesis of the literature on marine political geography as it relates to the laws of the seas and their application in the Indian Ocean context. It brings together the information available in the legislation of the coastal States and includes the bilateral and trilateral agreements on maritime boundary determination. The delineation of these agreed boundaries is portrayed both on maps for each case study and on maps designed for regional overviews. In almost all areas within this regional study of the Law of the Sea, boundaries have not been consolidated or approved by international law. There is, therefore, a lack of precise maps and descriptions of a number of negotiated maritime boundaries, for example, between Mauritius and Seychelles, and between Madagascar and Comoros.

All states who ratify CLOS and who wish to stake their maritime claims are, by the provisions of Articles 16 and 84, required to deposit with the UN Secretary for the Law of the Sea a copy of the relevant maps and/or charts and a listing of the geographical co-ordinates to such claims. Although a number of other states publish documents on boundary and frontier issues, these are mainly subjective interpretations of the Law of the Sea. Some states are also selective when it comes to providing information to researchers. In attempting an accurate presentation of the application of the Law of the Sea in a vast area such as the Indian Ocean region, it has been necessary, therefore, to consult a number of sources, especially the official documents, which were the primary sources for this study. The more important of these sources are referred to in the literature review and in the bibliography.

In a bid to obtain or control access to the use of the sea and the seabed, national claims on sea space have been steadily expanding to the point where the majority of coastal states have claimed offshore zones for distances varying from 200 to 350 nautical miles for their exclusive utilisation.

Such actions perhaps justify Gottmann's (1982: 345) observation that "even if geographical space had been perfectly uniform and homogenised, humankind would have partitioned it politically. . .". It is certain also, that all coastal states will strive for the largest possible sea area and the right to utilise the associated column of water, lateral surface, seabed, substratum, and to some extent, the column of air space directly above national jurisdiction. Agreements on the continental shelf of, for example, the North Sea, the Timor Sea and the Torres Strait and sections of the Persian Gulf (Chapter Four) demonstrate that the seas can be politically divided and regulated and in many instances the resources therein can be explored and exploited by cooperative ventures.

The provisions of CLOS ensure, however, that national claims to sea space will not unduly erode the acknowledged freedom of the high seas, for the seabed beyond national claims will come under the jurisdiction of the International Seabed Authority when it is established. The Authority will oversee the exploitation, development and marketing of the resources of the seabed and the final distribution of the profits from such ventures.

"The sea provides the general theorist of partitioning with an exciting field for reflection because it is a relatively uniform space which cannot be settled, fully occupied, or fenced off like land" notes Gottmann (1982: 346). Although the sea space cannot be settled permanently because of the elements of nature and the cost of the necessary infrastructure, the islands within it have played a pivotal role in gaining vast expanses of ocean space and continental shelf for the world's coastal states. For example, France has achieved vast gains to its ocean space in the Indian Ocean through its claims to islands and dependencies in the region. Australia acquired a substantial expanse of sea space surrounding its offshore territories of Ashmore, Cartier, Heard, McDonald and other Indian Ocean islands (Figure 1.1).

Lying some 1,300 nautical miles southwest of Tokyo in the Pacific Ocean at approximately Latitude 20°28′ N, Longitude 136°09′ E is a tiny coral islet that the Japanese call Okino Torishima (Offshore Bird Island). Apart from two rocky promontories this islet is under water at high tide. According to the 1958 Geneva Convention, any natural island which remains above the sea surface at high tide can be considered a country's territory, thus establishing the basis of a claim to territorial waters around it. Okino Torishima is at the centre of an area rich in bonito and tuna, and where it is believed that there are deposits of cobalt and manganese nodules on the ocean floor. Because the coral is being eroded by the forces of the sea, the island is in danger of disappearing. Efforts to save it began in April 1988 when a fleet of ships and a team of workers were despatched from the Japanese mainland to shore up the rocks by erecting 9,000 steel blocks in concentric circles around them. If Okino Torishima disappeared, Japan would forfeit its claim to mineral and fishing rights over about 815,000 sq km of ocean, an area larger than Japan itself (*Time*, 26 September, 1988). It must be emphasised, however, that the island status given to Okino Torishima will increase the area of Japan's maritime zone under the provisions of Article 121:3 of CLOS, only if these rocks can sustain human habitation or economic life of their own. If they cannot meet these criteria

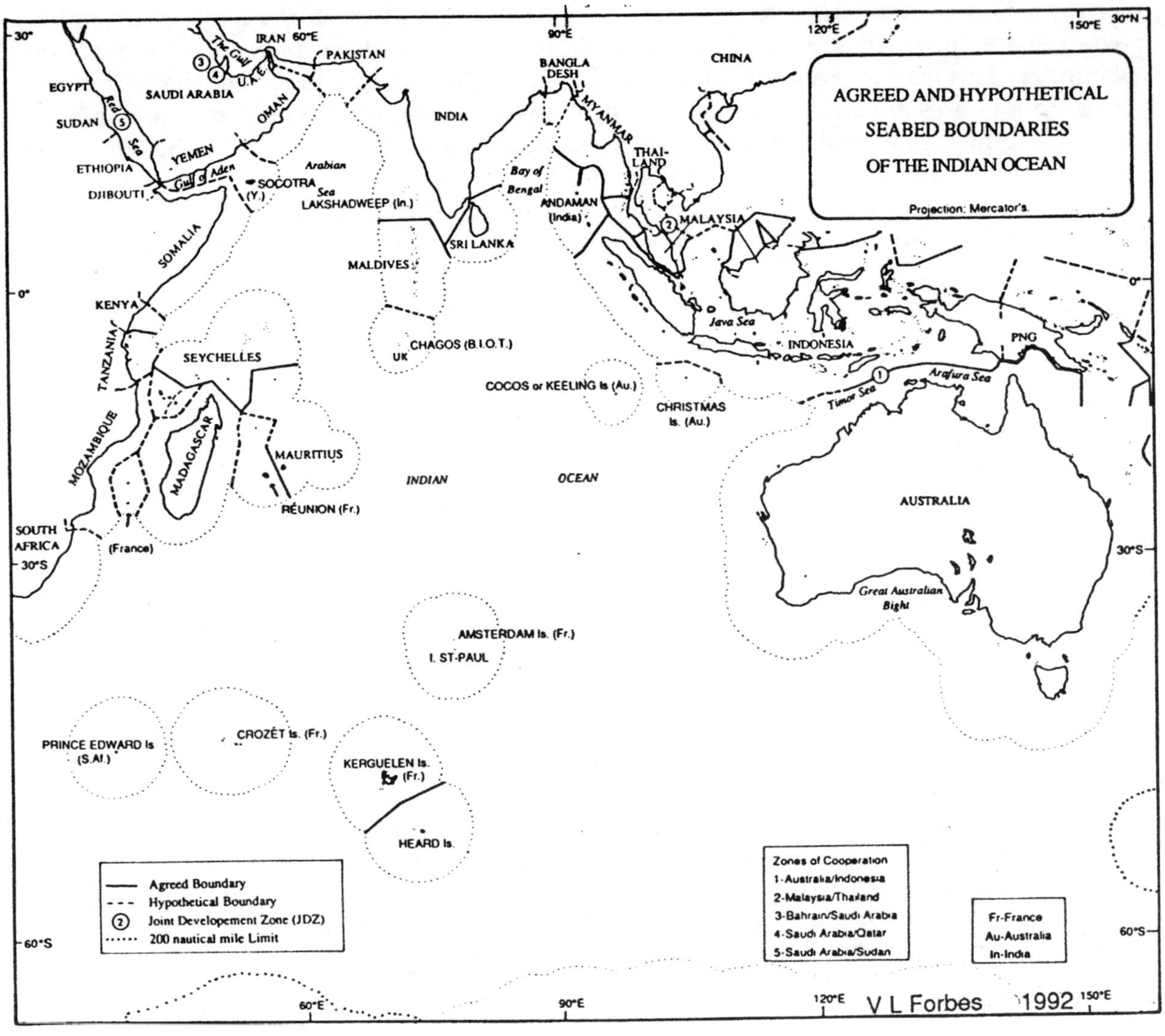

Figure 1.1 The extent of the 200 nm limit of coastal states of the Indian Ocean Region.

such natural features are not entitled to extended maritime zones. There is no equivalent example in the Indian Ocean basin.

The problem of maritime boundary determination is one of the most disputed questions in international law. Minghi (1963: 153) notes that "a maritime boundary, unlike a land boundary which directly affects only the two states it separates, marks the limits of the spatial encroachment of a state's sovereignty into the area of the high seas, and thus affects many states." Conflicting theories about the legal status of the surface, the water column of the ocean and the subjacent ocean floor have been voiced for many centuries. He notes that " little attempt has been made to treat offshore boundaries as part of the general complex of political boundaries".

As examples of the extent and complexity of continental shelf boundary determination, the following cases were deliberated upon extensively by international arbitrators: *The Anglo-Norwegian Fisheries Case*, 1951; *North Sea Continental Shelf (FRG/Denmark and FRG/The Netherlands*, 1969; *The Jan Mayen Continental Shelf* 1981; *Continental Shelf (Libyan Arab Jamahiriya/Malta*), 1985.

Out of the several hundred instances calling for maritime boundary delineation, no fewer than 100 have so far been settled. A recent case, *The Timor Gap Treaty*, establishes a Zone of Cooperation between Australia and Indonesia, to explore and exploit an area of seabed and substratum in the Timor Sea (Auburn and Forbes, 1991; Forbes 1991a; Forbes and Auburn 1991). Other negotiations are presently being undertaken, and several cases will eventually be placed before international tribunals over the next decade and perhaps beyond. A listing of the status of maritime boundaries determined between states of the Indian Ocean region is given in Appendix F.

The extent of the problems and the level of success associated with any attempt to make a political division of the sea vary with the political situation of the region, the potential wealth of the sea, seafloor and substratum, and the available technology to exploit this wealth. The hydrocarbon reserves that lie trapped in the subsoil structures of the Persian Gulf and its littoral states are one of the contributing factors that have assured the promptness in the determination of continental shelf boundaries between some of the littoral states in the Persian Gulf. For other Persian Gulf states, the problems of boundary delineation provide interesting case studies (Chapter Four).

In reviewing Indian Ocean maritime boundaries Prescott (1985: 179) concludes that the basin is "... a laboratory of case studies ... well equipped with proper extravagant baselines and claims to maritime zones." In support he quotes claims made by such coastal and island states as Burma (now Myanmar), Bangladesh and the Maldives. Despite Reitsma's (1983: 259) claim to the contrary, many writers do not anticipate that such claims to maritime zones in the region will hinder movement, stifle trade, and create conflict between the various political units (Buchholz, 1987: 103–104). On the other hand, the establishment of maritime jurisdictional zones by certain coastal states has created similar problems for their neighbours and for other states whose ships sailed through such zonal waters in the past. During the 1950s and early 1960s for example, Egypt forbade ships carrying cargo destined for ports in Israel from using the Suez Canal. There were similar problems in the Gulf of Aqaba for Israeli ships proceeding to the port of Elat. The 1979 *Treaty of Peace* based on the 1978 Camp David Framework following the 1967 Egyptian-Israeli war brought about the resolution of these issues (Lapidoth-Eschelbacher, 1982: 167).

Glassner (1986: 6–8) maintains that the study of the geography of sea space is one of the most difficult and challenging problems the political geographer faces. However, according to Alexander (1986: 19–24) the study of maritime boundary determination requires more attention from political geographers, for "if they fail to act, the lawyers surely will."

The lawyer-generated definition of the *Continental Shelf* (without consultation with geographers and geologists), is contained in Article 1 of the *Convention on the Continental Shelf* signed in Geneva on April 29, 1958 (and currently in force). It states that:

> For the purposes of these articles, the term continental shelf is used as referring (a) to the seabed and subsoil of the submarine areas adjacent to the coast but outside the area of the territorial sea, to a depth of 200 metres or, beyond that limit, to where the depth of the superjacent waters admits of the exploitation of the natural resources of the said areas; (b) to the seabed and subsoil of similar submarine areas adjacent to the coasts of islands.

This definition fails to avoid the very problem that the use of the continental shelf as a maritime boundary might have been expected to solve.

Any advantage of using a natural oceanographic boundary is overshadowed by an arbitrary numerical value. Unfortunately for the lawyers, the characteristics of the continental shelf vary considerably from place to place. Consequently the 200 metre isobath bears very little relation to the natural prolongation and geological extension of the land mass. As an example, under the current regime Australia can claim an area of about 662,000 square nautical miles as the legal continental shelf. As redefined in CLOS, however, Australia (Figure 1.2) may claim a shelf area of over 3,000,000 square nautical miles (Veenstra, 1984: 414).

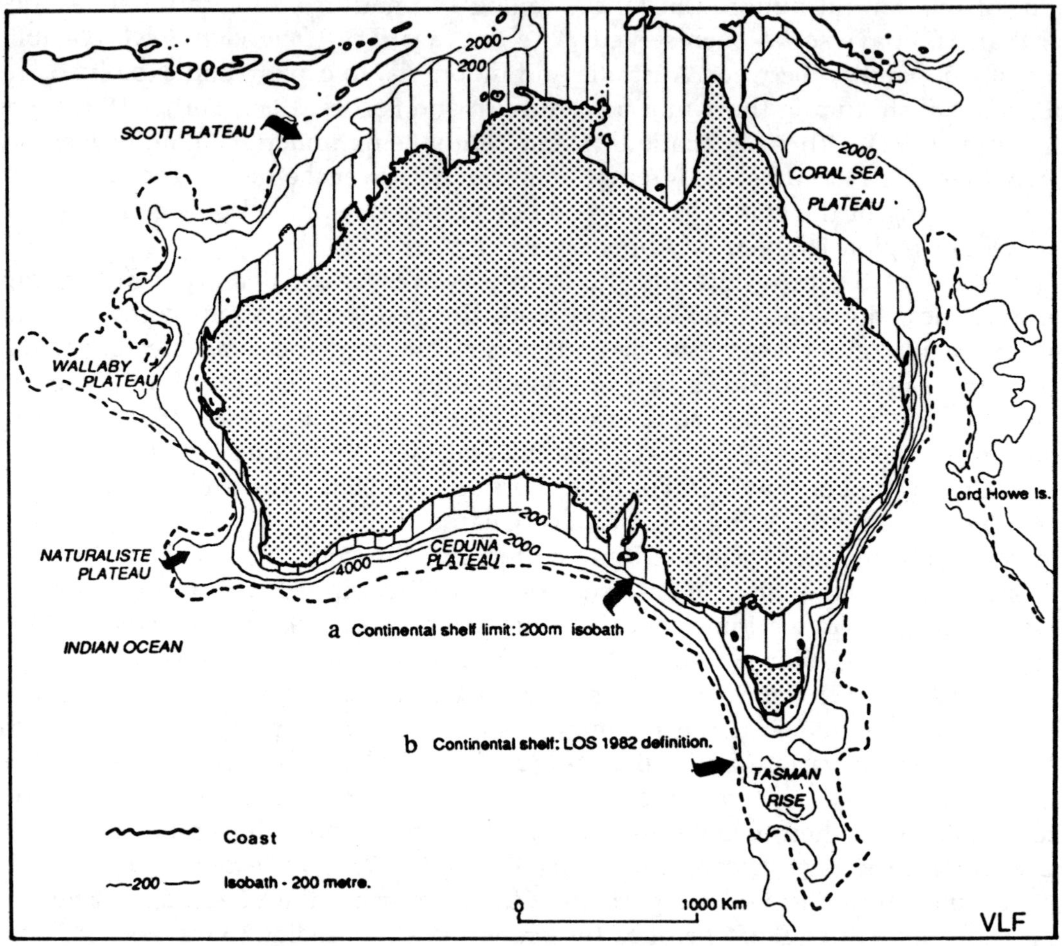

Figure 1.2 Defining the outer limits of the continental shelf; (a) the 200 metre isobath (1958 definition) and (b) an interpretation of CLOS, 1982.

The 1958 definition created an inequitable distribution of shelf area due to the variations in the shelf gradient. Coastal states with gently sloping continental shelves qualified for areas of maritime jurisdiction stretching hundreds of nautical miles out to the 200 m isobath whereas countries such as the East African littoral states, whose coasts have steep continental shelves, had extremely limited areal jurisdiction over the adjacent waters. As observed by Prescott (1975: 157), there "is no evidence to [suggest] that the term continental shelf is used in a geological sense". Indeed, the term was used only in a legal sense.

Furthermore, there are other difficulties with the 1958 definition. For example, the term 'exploitation' is ambiguous. May a state claim the sea-floor out to the limit capable of being exploited by the most advanced technology anywhere in the world or only by the technology available to the claimant state? If the latter concept was universally accepted, many of the less developed states would be at an obvious disadvantage. On the other hand, developed nations would stand to gain vast areas of sea-space by virtue of the advanced marine scientific technology available to them.

The continental shelf has been redefined in Part VI of CLOS in Article 76 (1) as follows:

> The continental shelf of a coastal State comprises the sea-bed and subsoil of the submarine areas that extend beyond its territorial sea throughout the natural prolongation of its land territory to the outer edge of the continental margin, or to a distance of 200 nautical miles from the baselines from which the breadth of the territorial sea is measured where the outer edge of the continental margin does not extend up to that distance.

More distant shelf areas may be claimed by the coastal state in certain circumstances as prescribed in the remaining paragraphs of Article 76. The new definition which is based on technical criteria, clearly reflects the current technological advances and technical feasibility to explore and exploit mineral resources from the seabed. Coastal states will need to undertake scientific surveys of their continental margins in order to ascertain and obtain the geophysical and geological data necessary for the determination of the outer limits of the continental shelf.

Continental shelves extend out from most of the continents and some of the large islands all around the world. They vary in width. From the shore they gradually tilt away to about depths of 110 to 200 metres on the average, although some drop to 800 metres. They meet a steeper slope, called the continental slope, down which the transition from shelf to deep sea is quite sudden (Figure 1.3).

The complex definition of the continental shelf was brought about by international concerns and fears that the strong and rich nations participating in the negotiating processes would gain an advantage over the weaker and poorer states whose total interests may not have been adequately represented at UNCLOS. In essence there was a greater input and a concerted effort by all concerned to produce a legal text and a political document for a new law of the sea.

In recent literature on the law of the sea with respect to maritime boundary-making and its implications to the coastal and island states, the strong contribution from the legal profession has continued. On the other hand there has only been a modest input from political geographers, and even less from publicists, diplomats and administrators, former mariners and hydrographers.

BACKGROUND TO THE STUDY

The oceans comprise over 70 per cent of the surface of the earth. They are a significant and critical part of our global ecosystem. By interacting with the atmosphere, they affect the climate of the planet. They also play a part in the biological, physical and chemical processes. The oceans are major suppliers of protein as fish and fish-meal, and fish-oil. All types of water transport move on or below the surface of the oceans. Much of the energy needs of future generations may well be derived from the harnessing of waves and tides to generate electrical power. By desalinisation processes sea water can be transformed into potable water. In the not too distant future the floor and the substratum of the seabed are likely to provide a wealth of minerals, in particular manganese nodules. The mining of such resources has proved to be feasible, although currently too difficult, dangerous and expensive to be practicable (Borgese, 1985).

The Indian Ocean basin is the third largest in the world. The ocean and the adjacent seas cover nearly 21,400,000 square nautical miles or about 14 per cent of the surface of the planet. Like the Pacific and Atlantic Oceans, this ocean makes a vital contribution to the welfare of the citizens of the littoral states, and to the international community in general. Like them also, it has been used and abused over a number of centuries.

From the thousands of millions of tonnes of raw material and fossil fuel consumed each year by society with its growing demands, a substantial proportion of the waste finds its way into the oceans. The resulting pollution has had a direct effect on the marine environment. At times this is not readily apparent as it is an ongoing process. The responsibility for the conservation of the resources of the ocean and the protection of the marine environment lies at local, national, and international levels and is of major global concern. International conventions on these issues within the past two decades have given the initative to all nations, and especially coastal states, to enact appropriate legislation.

A growing realisation that the oceans represent a responsibility and a source of wealth for our future needs has been the direct result of the upsurge of knowledge and understanding of them (Laughton, 1989: 91). In the last three decades, geographers,

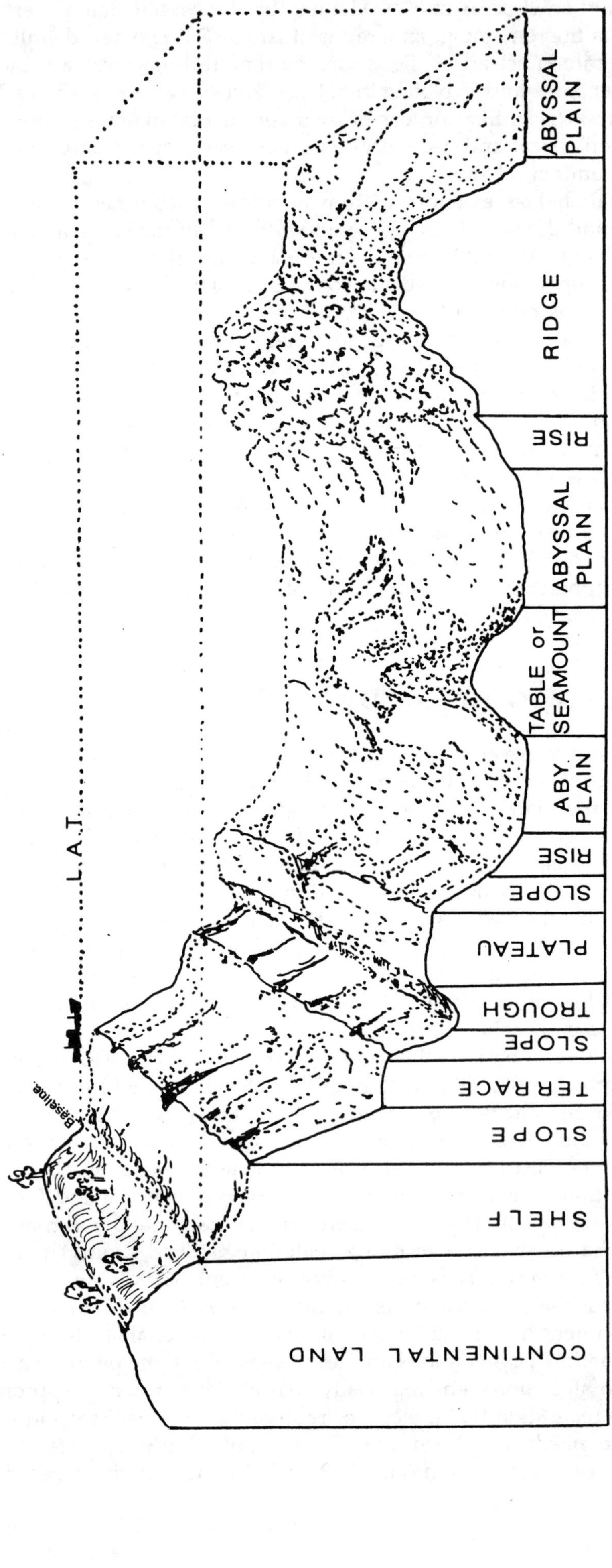

Figure 1.3 A diagrammatic representation of seafloor topography.

oceanographers, geologists, marine biologists, surveyors and cartographers have carefully examined such phenomena as: sea-floor spreading with the concept of continuous generation of oceanic crust; climatic change, global heating and depletion of the ozone layer in the atmosphere and their relationships to sea-level rise; and the effects of *El Niño* and the potentially catastrophic consequences associated with it. They have mapped, on a global scale, the bathymetry of the oceans and the age of basement rocks on land and below the seabed. They have verified: that tectonic plates carry the continents over the globe; that fast currents exist, even at the bottom of the oceans, which are capable of transporting sediments and that marine life is found at all oceanic depths even in deep trenches. They are studying the interrelationships between such phenomena and the ways in which they influence terrestrial life.

It is the responsibility of all nations, especially the coastal states, to ensure that the resources of the oceans are utilised in an environmentally acceptable manner. Sustainable development is being proposed on a global scale, in recognition of the problems of pollution, the rapid growth in population, and associated food shortages. National responsibilities extend to the atmosphere above the oceans, to the seabed below and to the coastal zone. They are clearly stated in Article 192 of CLOS which proclaims that: "States have the obligation to protect and preserve the marine environment".

Any discussion on the management and development of resources naturally raises the question of ownership and the problems associated with it, not the least of which is the demarcation of territorial claims and zones of national jurisdiction. Such questions, problems, and processes have unique characteristics in the context of the oceans. Until about 1930, fishing and marine transport and close inshore mining were the main human activities connected with the oceans. Fishing possibilities appeared to be constrained only by the physical limitations of the craft involved. The principle of the free use of the seas had existed for well over three centuries. Beyond the narrow limits of a coastal state's jurisdictional zone — its *territorial sea* — lay the high seas — *mare liberum* — upon and under which there was the freedom of navigation. A concept of a closed sea — *mare clausum* — existed, for a brief period during the 18th Century whereby a few maritime powers, such as Britain, Portugal and Spain proposed a seaward extension of the territorial sea, beyond the customary international law of three nautical mile limit and varying to as much as 100 or more nautical miles from their coastline.

During the second half of the 20th century, merchant shipping has undergone rapid development, especially with the introduction of larger, faster and more specialised vessels. Changes in design have occurred in the bulk carrier trade, with the introduction of ships capable of carrying oil one way and ore the other. Container ships, roll-on roll-off vessels and car ferries demonstrate how shipping has become part of a more closely integrated transport system. The increase in the size of ships poses navigational problems in restricted waters, related to the available depth of water and passage through confined space such as through the Malacca Strait and Straits of Singapore, the Strait of Hormuz and Bab el Mandeb (Couper, 1972: 151–155; Corlett, 1981: 26; Couper, 1986: 154). The increased use of oil and gas for heating, engine fuel and the petrochemical industries has led to a growth in the size and number of crude oil carriers and to the development of new types of tankers carrying liquefied petroleum gas and liquefied natural gas. To keep transport costs to a minimum, large tankers with 100,000 to 350,000 deadweight tonnes have been developed. Unfortunately larger vessels have been responsible for disasters of unprecedented magnitude.

Events such as the grounding of the tanker *Exxon Valdez* in April 1989, off Bligh Island in Prince William Sound, Alaska, the *Torrey Canyon*, the *Amoco Cadiz*, and the leaking of oil from the Norwegian tanker, *Mega Borg*, some 90 kilometres southeast of Galveston, Texas in the Gulf of Mexico, following a series of explosions aboard the ship during 10–14 June, 1990 are evidence that an urgent need exists for regulatory control of oil transportation by sea on a global scale. Within Australian territorial waters, on 14 February 1991, the *Sanko Harvest* ran aground on rocks off the port of Esperance (Plate

2). The subsequent oil spill and sinking of the ship resulted in a major environmental problem in the immediate waters and along the shoreline.

On 20 July 1991, another ecological catastrophe was in the making when about 10,000 tonnes of light crude oil spilled from the tanker *Kirki* as the ship headed towards Kwinana, Western Australia (Plate 3). The structural deterioration of the 21-year-old Greek registered ship had caused its bow section to shear away from the rest of the hull. Another 5,000 tonnes of oil was lost as the stricken ship was towed to calmer waters where the remaining cargo was transferred to another ship. A combination of a southerly flowing offshore current, a southeasterly breeze and the light consistency of the oil were factors which assisted in keeping the resultant oil slick away from the pristine beaches of the West Australian coast (Forbes, 1991: 14–18).

Whereas the offshore oil industry has brought substantial wealth to many coastal states there have been negative effects as well. The most important of these is the damage to the marine environment caused by blow-outs from drilling operations; accidental and intentional discharge of oil from ships at sea or in port and from land-based sources such as oil refineries and factories; discharge of sludge from the rigs and platforms; the use of sub-standard structures and the abandonment of these artificial islands. The environmental damage caused by offshore drilling is, however, less significant than that produced by the dumping of toxic wastes into the waterways that discharge into the North Sea (EC Environmental Conference, Dublin 1990). During 1988 large numbers of dead seals and other sea creatures were found washed up on North Sea beaches. They were presumably affected by pollutants discharged into the European river system. In the waters of the Persian Gulf masses of dead fish were found off Bahrain during 1991. They were victims of some bacterial infection, possibly as a result of the environmental pollution caused by the oil slick and the fires deliberately lit to the onshore oil-fields of Kuwait (Canby, 1991).

The need for comprehensive policies on coastal zone management, the sustained development of natural resources and the protection of the natural environment are issues facing administrators and governments of all political persuasions. Coastal erosion due to mining of beach sands along sections of the coast of Western Australia and off the coasts of Thailand and Malaysia in the Andaman Sea, the construction of an airport runway projecting out to sea on reclaimed land in Bali, and coastal zone development for tourists on islands of the Indonesian archipelago are examples that are of concern to policy-makers of coastal states in the region.

Many coastal states throughout the world, and especially those classified as developing nations, perceive a threat posed by the build-up of military strength and in particular the show of naval power on and below the surface of the oceans. Such naval strength has been witnessed in the Indian Ocean region during the past decade and with substantial evidence during 1987–1988 within and outside the Persian Gulf (Bruce, 1989; Tellis, 1989; Larus, 1989; Thomas, 1989). As a consequence of a border dispute and claims to offshore islands Iraq invaded and annexed Kuwait on 2 August 1990 (Forbes, 1990: 14–16). This action brought about a strengthening of military forces on and around the Arabian Peninsula in the four months to the end of 1990. An international force consisting mainly of Americans backed by U.N. Resolutions 660 and 661 (2 and 9 August, 1990), insisted that Iraqi occupying forces withdraw from Kuwait or face retaliation. All efforts to resolve the issue by diplomatic processes had failed by 15 January, 1991, the deadline imposed by the UN Resolutions. A 25-day war ensued. A cease-fire was declared after Iraq relinquished its claim to "its southern province called Kuwait". Somewhat ironically, despite the threat of conflict in the Middle East, the simmering antagonism between India and Pakistan on the issue of Kashmir, and the Tamil separatist terrorism on the Jaffna Peninsula in Sri Lanka, there exists a proposal by Sri Lanka to declare and develop the Indian Ocean region as a Zone of Peace.

Other controversial issues include: the legitimacy of traditional fishing grounds; the sovereignty and management of the reefs and uninhabited islands which lie within Australian jurisdiction in the Timor Sea; and the existence of historic fishing grounds in

Palk Bay, Gulf of Manaar and Andaman Sea and its adjacent straits. The trespassing of alien fishermen into a coastal state's declared territorial sea or economic zone either for fishing or to engage in other illegal activities, for example, drug trafficking and landing of persons on foreign soil, creates a nuisance and, in many instances, a financial burden to the coastal state. It is a problem that Australia, Hong Kong and the United States of America have experienced during the past decades. In this context two questions may be posed: to what extent are the traditional fishing activities of aliens to be permitted; and do coastal states have the right to prosecute offenders who stray — accidentally or intentionally — into waters claimed by such states for their exclusive uses? These problems are faced in the disputes between the following pairs of countries: Australia and Indonesia, Thailand and Malaysia, Thailand and Myanmar, and Indonesia and Thailand. Reactions to the problems vary greatly in severity.

STRUCTURE OF THE BOOK

This study is concerned not only with the demarcation of maritime boundaries, but also more particularly with the spatial structure of the Indian Ocean basin and its littoral and island states. Its regional context sets it apart from similar studies which have been undertaken in a global context (e.g. Prescott, 1985a; Jagota, 1985: Charney and Alexander, 1993) and on subregional sectors (e.g. Prescott, 1985b; Kriangsak, 1987; Ahnish, 1993). It consists of two parts: the study proper and appendices containing maps and lists of boundary agreements.

Chapter One provides an introduction to the aims, rationale and structure of the book and its relationship to the theory and literature of the political geography of the oceans.

The geopolitical setting is discussed in Chapter Two. Among the topics reviewed are: intra-regional issues such as ideology and the Zone of Peace concept; extra-regional issues such as the naval presence of the superpowers and the price-fixing of oil; fisheries and fishing agreements; the resources of the ocean and its seabed; conservation policies; and international conventions and national legislation for pollution control and the protection of the marine environment. Examples of all of the above, such as arose from the events in the Gulf region during the period 1970–1990, are reviewed, and the problems of ill-defined maritime territorial claims are highlighted and discussed.

Chapter Three presents a discussion of the concepts of maritime boundaries and an evaluation of the mechanism by which coastal states may legislate for sovereignty over the adjacent seas. It presents an examination of the problems that may be encountered by the utilisation of imprecise, out-of-date charts and maps, outmoded surveying practices and equipment, and data based on ambiguous wording in historical documents on land boundary demarcation. It highlights the practices and the problems of the states in the region in the negotiation and delineation of maritime boundaries. Although there have been coastal states such as India and Pakistan, India and Bangladesh, Madagascar and Mozambique eager to agree with their coastal neighbours on boundary delineation, many have yet to settle such issues. Concepts discussed include territorial sea baselines, historic rights on bays, claimed widths of territorial seas and contiguous zones, continental shelf boundaries and limits of the exclusive economic zone and other fishing zones. The chapter also examines the historical maritime claims in the region and the issues that relate to these claims.

Chapter Four contains an analytical and cartographical description of the maritime boundaries in the Indian Ocean that have been declared, both by unilateral proclamation and through bilateral and multilateral agreements. It also presents an analysis of the established and proposed joint development resource zones in the region, with special reference to bilateral fishing agreements.

The major issues relating to maritime boundary negotiations and delineations are discussed in Chapter Five. These include proposals on joint development zones, bilateral fishing agreements, technology information exchange, and the need for the delineation on charts of all maritime limits for the long-term benefit of mariners, fishermen, administrators, researchers and educators.

The second part of the book contains a series of maps which portray the present probable extent of national sovereignty over the waters of the Indian Ocean. It lists the official documents cited and tabulates the status of the International Conventions to 1994.

SOURCES, MAP COMPILATION, METHODOLOGY AND LIMITATIONS

Sources

It is a general rule of international customary law that terrestrial and maritime boundaries are established by negotiation between the nations concerned. Thus the main source for this study is the information contained in the official documents and legal instruments of the relevant coastal states. The proclaimed territorial sea baseline is the datum for measuring the seaward limit of the maritime zones of a coastal state. Proclamations such as the *Maritime Zones Act*, 1977 of Mauritius and the declaration on 14 February 1983 of the inner limit of a part of the territorial sea of Australia include a list of geographical coordinates utilised to determine the straight baselines of a coastal state. For the determination of the seabed boundary between coastal states it is necessary to gain access to the relevant bilateral or trilateral agreements made by the signatory states, such as the *Timor Gap Treaty* 1989, *The Torres Strait Treaty* 1979, the *Seabed Boundary Delimitation Between The Republic of France and Australia in the vicinity of Heard Island and Kerguelen Island* 1983.

Supplementing the authentic documents mentioned above are the published works of researchers and specialists in the disciplines of international law, political geography and the marine sciences. Other sources include the proceedings of conferences on maritime law and ocean development, reports produced by the various government and non-government authorities within and outside the Indian Ocean region, and related literature on maritime boundary delimitation. In particular, the writings of Boggs, Prescott, Johnston, Alexander, de Blij, Kent and Valencia, Buchholz, Kapoor and Kerr, Charney and Alexander and Weil, and the *Limits in the Sea* series prepared since 1970 by the Geographer of the State Department of the United States of America, are important secondary sources.

Map Compilation

Compilation of the maps delineating the maritime boundaries of coastal states as portrayed in this book was made possible from information gleaned from official sources, including national legislation, unilateral proclamations, bilateral and trilateral agreements, charts, maps, aerial photography and satellite imagery, and from the voluminous literature relevant to the determination of maritime boundaries.

In order to achieve some advantage in future negotations on maritime boundary delimitation, a few states exaggerate or perhaps even falsify their claims. In any case, their neighbours usually have a different opinion of their sea boundaries, as evident in the prolonged negotations over the settlement of the Timor Gap issue (Forbes, 1989). In such a study as this, therefore, it is essential to make a critical analysis and comparison of official documents and also to take into account the results of academic research, articles in scientific and economic publications, and reports in the news media.

The accuracy of depiction of various lines indicating the maritime jurisdictional limits on a map or chart is partly a function of the scale at which the map or chart is drawn. In plotting the limits of the declared zones and seabed boundary delineation, the list of geographical coordinates that are generally included in the declarations makes it possible to define limits and turning points with far greater accuracy. The problems inherent in maritime boundary delineation relate to the choice of map projection, the scale of representation of the surface area, and the chosen geodetic datum.

Because the maps used in this study were of necessity drawn at small scales, it was not possible to distinguish the low-water line from the high-water line, and details of various coastal features have been generalised. If larger scales had been chosen, it would not have been feasible to depict the maritime jurisdictional zones of the coastal states of the region. Such depiction is, of course, the main reason for the inclusion of the maps.

Methodology

This book adopts a deductive research methodology. It examines the general theory of maritime boundary determination, analyses the global and regional processes of delineation, and previews the potential demarcations in the region.

From the outset it must be stated that the study's structure, approach and methodology outlined above have limitations, which mainly pertain to the selection of the research period and the availability of the data.

Problems were encountered in collecting data on the maritime claims of coastal states from maps and charts delineating their proclaimed territorial sea baseline and the width of the territorial sea zone. Whereas states are required to deposit with the United Nations Office for the Law of the Sea copies of charts, maps and/or lists of the geographical coordinates, there is often a time delay for such action to be taken. Furthermore, delays occur in making the information public. A number of states are reluctant to forward information of this nature to researchers. In particular, countries like India, Pakistan, Malaysia, Saudi Arabia and Yemen, maintain that such documents relate to sensitive issues of the state. On the other hand, states such as Australia, Mauritius and South Africa have taken prompt action in meeting requests for the data on their respective limits of maritime jurisdiction. Indeed such material has, for the most part, been published and is available to the public.

Another important limitation of the study stems from the political issues that persist in the region, which result in delays in the negotiations of maritime boundaries. Such issues include the enduring Middle East conflict, the political instability in Sri Lanka, the Indo-Pakistani border dispute in the Kashmir region, and the reluctance of littoral and island states of the western margin of the Indian Ocean to settle their territorial differences.

PREVIOUS WORK IN THE FIELD OF MARITIME BOUNDARY DETERMINATION

A territory is an extent of water and land area that is defined by and is under the jurisdiction or sovereignty of a goverment. It should be governed, or be perceived to be controlled, by that authority or its representative. It may also be subject to change over time. For example, the demarcated territorial boundaries of the countries of India, Israel and Papua New Guinea have been altered several times. During the 1980s maritime boundary claims assumed greater prominence, and not always without dispute. For example, the Iraq-Iran eight-year war over territorial claims in the Shatt al Arab waterway at the head of the Persian Gulf and the Iraq-Kuwait dispute over the ownership of two islands and border demarcation (August to December 1990) prompted those states to attempt to settle the issues by military means. Nevertheless, it is not surprising that the centuries-old literature on boundary-making is largely devoted to terrestrial boundaries, which until recently dominated considerations relating to the delimitation of territories.

The geographical aspects of maritime boundaries were emphasised by the distinguished American geographer, S. W. Boggs (1961: 240–266) who was active in assisting lawyers to develop geographic methods of defining maritime boundaries during the years when the International Law Commission was preparing for the 1958 Geneva Convention.

By the 1960s the focus was changing. The sea was now being considered as possibly the last remaining frontier on the Earth's surface, whose "rational use will demand an extraordinary degree of intellectual effort and tolerance not only on the part of statesmen, but also of natural and social scientists throughout the world" (Alexander, 1968: 178). This view has been substantiated by the ever increasing literature that has subsequently been generated. Prominent among it is Prescott's (1975) study of the political geography of the oceans which came in the wake of the Law of the Sea Conference held in Caracas in 1974.

In the absence of any previously existing general survey which comprehended and related the many excellent individual studies already completed, Prescott presented an appraisal of the situation concerning the question of sovereignty of the oceans. In this benchmark study of marine political geography, he discussed the concept of the territorial sea, the contiguous zone and the continental shelf. Each maritime zone was analysed separately, current claims were fully described, and a few were illustrated by simple maps drawn by the author. He examined the evolution of the claims and the problems of measuring them, the contentious issue of the exclusive fishing zones claimed by coastal states on the South American continent and, with some foresight, emphasised the need for careful management of the world's resources. Prescott's studies have been important reference sources in the preparation of this book.

Bernaerts' (1988) guide to the 1982 Convention is a welcome addition to the literature that has been written on that subject. It provides a clear summary of the substance and structure of the contents of the Convention, and a comprehensive commentary on the numerous concepts and issues underlying CLOS. It supplements and indeed complements the continuous flow of journal articles and conference proceedings that have proliferated following the concluding session of UNCLOS III. The Official Text and Final Act follow the summary.

A serious study of maritime boundary demarcation requires an understanding of hydrographic surveying and marine cartography. In this context Langeraar (1984) and Johnston (1988) fill some serious gaps in the history and theory of maritime boundary-making and in the practicalities of carrying out the task. Whilst Langeraar emphasises scientific and mathematical components of maritime boundary delimitation, Johnston provides a preliminary review of the conceptual framework for the analysis and evaluation of all ocean boundary claims, practices, arrangements and settlements. He also notes (1988: 1) that "the problems of boundary-making in the ocean have not been a major preoccupation of governments until very recently".

Prescott (1985), Jagota (1985) and Charney and Alexander (1993) offer global overviews of maritime boundaries that have been delineated. Prescott reviews the state of international competition for control of the Earth's oceans and identifies those countries which have been most successful in their endeavours. He describes those situations where conflicting claims have created international tensions, and argues that the resolution of difficulties between countries is more often a matter of politics than of law. His first chapter, which deals with general principles, is well illustrated by numerous maps and diagrams. The remaining chapters treat in turn each of those oceans and seas in which national boundary claims overlap.

Jagota (1985) concentrates on an analysis of the development of international law relating to maritime boundaries since 1945, with greater emphasis on developments since 1958. Whereas Prescott takes a politico-geographical view, Jagota, adopts a politico-legal approach. Prescott reviews the issues of the maritime boundaries within the context of ocean basins, thus treating the Indian Ocean region in one chapter. Jagota, on the other hand, reviews the Asian and African perspective on boundaries from in less than three pages, devoting a mere paragraph to the agreed maritime boundary between Réunion and Mauritius Islands. It is not surprising, therefore, that Prescott's maps are much clearer and more detailed than those of Jagota.

Charney and Alexander (1993) as editors have brought together many contributors of international standing to analyse and comment upon various aspects of maritime boundary determination as well as to provide case studies and regional overviews in a two-volume set.

Other key reference works on the delineation of seabed boundaries and straight baselines on the global scale are by Conforti and Francalanci (1979) and Francalanci, Romano, and Scovazzi (1986). The latter publication contains 77 maps showing the coastal outlines and declared straight baselines of coastal states. Its text is limited to an acknowledgement of sources, and a brief statement on the number of segments and lengths of the baselines and the width of the claimed territorial sea of each of the coastal states. The maps are poorly presented, being hand-lettered and, in many cases, lacking a statement of scale.

The most important and useful tool for research in this field is the series *Limits in the Seas* produced by the Geographer, United States Department of State. The series was started by Hodgson in 1970. Although the studies are brief and concise, they are totally objective. Of the more than 100 booklets in the series, 23 are devoted to the analysis of the proclaimed straight baselines, continental shelf boundaries and other maritime jurisdictions of coastal states in the Indian Ocean and adjacent seas. This series is an authoritative secondary source, as each study is based upon the official documents on maritime boundary delimitation of the coastal states involved.

Whilst it is not easy to separate the legal from the technical, Kapoor and Kerr (1986) attempt to provide guidelines primarily for hydrographers. Their work also offers some guidance to geographers, cartographers and administrators concerned with the technicalities of maritime boundary determination. One chapter is devoted to a technical review of geodetic, hydrographical, cartographical and geological elements that are to be taken into consideration during the processes of boundary negotations, especially when determining the median line in the waters between opposing coastal states. Kapoor and Kerr provide ample illustrations, especially with reference to the establishment of baselines and the outer limits of the maritime jurisdictional zones. A summary of significant decisions made by the International Court of Justice and other international tribunals, and examples of state practice, are given in the appendices. By and large, however, the most important contribution of geographers, political scientists and international lawyers to the literature of maritime boundary, in terms of both volume and originality, is to specific regional studies.

Recent literature on the political geography of the Red Sea and the Persian Gulf, although not abundant, is important for this study. Earlier studies by Melamid (1947 and 1959) focus on the Red Sea. El-Hakim (1979) attempts to analyse the practices and policies of the Middle East States with regard to certain aspects of the International Law of the Sea. Attempting an equally difficult task and at a time when world interest was focused on the region, Ramazani (1979) offers the reader a politico-economic review of the Persian Gulf and Strait of Hormuz. He presents a detailed analysis of problems and issues in the region, scenarios of oil supply disruption, and a set of documents on shelf boundary delimitation. Lapidoth-Eschelbacher (1982) focuses on the Red Sea and the Gulf of Aden. MacDonald's (1980) perspective of the Law of the Sea as it relates to Iran and Saudi Arabia examines the political interaction and the legal development in the Persian Gulf. The recent atlas on the Middle East region edited by Blake *et al.* (1988) also provides a basis for studying the problems of conflicting maritime claims in the region.

There is a wide range of recent literature on the topic of maritime boundaries in the Southeast Asian region. Senftleben (1976), Lee Yong Leng (1978 and 1980), Prescott (1981, 1985a, 1985b), Tangsubukul (1982), Koh (1982), Morgan and Valencia (1983), Kent and Valencia (1985), Valencia and Miyoshi (1986), Johnston (1987), Kriangsak (1987) and Buchholz (1987), have all contributed to the better understanding of the complex issues of the region.

On the eastern fringe of the Indian Ocean, the Andaman Sea, the Timor Sea and the Torres Strait all provide an interesting setting for the study of boundary determination and the implementation of the new Law of the Sea. Discussions on these topical issues stemming from the many research papers (Burmester, 1982; Forbes, 1986 and 1989; Prescott, 1982 and 1985 b; Wilheim, 1989) on maritime boundaries in this region indicate the importance and urgency of boundary determination, especially in enclosed waters and narrow continental shelf areas. The common thread that binds the thoughts of such authors and of policy-makers of this subregion is that, if the implementation of the 1982 Law of the Sea is to be achieved, effective procedures for the settlement of maritime boundary disputes will be indispensable.

The regime of the 200-nautical mile exclusive economic zone in international law is presented in two separate studies. Attard (1987) and Kwiatkowska (1989) both explain how the exclusive economic zone (EEZ) regime can co-exist with the continental shelf (CS) regime, and analyse the particular implications of this new legal situation. The EEZ/CS regime parallelism is highlighted in the first chapter of Kwiatkowska's book, and studied in detail in the remaining five chapters which are devoted to the specific principles and rules that govern the various activities in the EEZ. Kwiatkowska examines the wide spectrum of rights and duties of states with regard to various activites such as fisheries and navigation, and evaluates the existing and potential impact of the EEZ upon the socio-economic development of states and the reduction of disparities between the developing and industrialised countries. Attard examines the process through which the concept of the exclusive economic zone entered the realm of customary international law, and the role of UNCLOS in that process. The concept of an EEZ has undergone a rapid and dynamic evolution since 1982.

In his study Johnston (1988: 286) concludes that the establishment and maintenance of jurisdictional zones " should be viewed as a beginning, offering a better hope for the world community". He notes that current maritime boundaries are the result of international negotiations and planning, and not necessarily the product of conquest or historic claim. This definitive contribution to ocean boundary-making is part of a series published under the Ocean Boundary Project of Dalhousie Ocean Studies Programme (DOSP) of Canada.

Other researchers associated with DOSP are Johnston and Saunders, and McDorman. McDorman *et al.* (1983) give an annotated bibliography on maritime boundary delimitation. Johnston and Saunders (1988) present seven regional studies written by specialists covering the Arctic, the Mediterranean, the Caribbean, the Persian Gulf, West Africa, East Africa and the Southwest Pacific. The contributors are for the most part lawyers but also include the geographer Prescott. The concluding chapter summarises the developments in these regions, and attempts to extract some generalisations which could give ocean boundary-makers a conceptual framework for the options they might choose.

As a professor of international law and counsel for a number of governments in international litigation including several maritime boundary delimitation cases, Weil (1989) argues convincingly in favour of equidistance as a basis for boundary delimitation, modified as necessary by equity considerations. He assesses the meaning and scope of the solutions already reached, and submits them to critical analysis. He reflects upon the problems and trends of the developing law of maritime boundary delineation, identifies the directions in which the law is heading and offers some suggestions as to desirable developments. Weil believes that the law of maritime delimitation has acquired a bad reputation. This well researched book unfortunately has no maps to illustrate the case studies. As noted by Tanja (1990: 290), Weil's terminology is not always consistent. Perhaps this defect is a consequence of the translation of the original French text.

Reference must also be made to the numerous agreements on the delimitation of the continental shelf. These are cited in Chapter Four and in the Bibliography and Appendix. The agreements between France and Mauritius, and between Australia and Indonesia are typical of the many bilateral accords. Trilateral agreements, which are few in number, include those involving India, the Maldives and Sri Lanka in one instance, and Indonesia, Malaysia and Thailand in another.

It is appropriate for a geographical approach to the study of the law of the sea to commence with an analysis of the uses which individual countries make of the marine environment, the historic and prevailing attitudes of their citizens toward the sea, the commitment they have in terms of financial investment in the sea, and their economic dependence upon it.

The following chapter sets the geopolitical scene, analyses the problems and the issues of the region, and examines the possibilities for future cooperation for peace and harmony, for the conservation of natural resources, and for legislation for pollution control of the adjacent seas.

CHAPTER TWO

THE GEOGRAPHICAL AND POLITICAL SETTING

INTRODUCTION

With the exceptions of a few enclaves such as Kashmir and the Ile Tromelin, the politico-geographical distribution of the land surface in the Indian Ocean Region seems to have been resolved and consolidated on a long-term basis after the colonial era of the last three centuries. In this chapter an appraisal is made of the geographical characteristics of the Indian Ocean States in the context of the physical geography of the ocean basin. The chapter then examines the historical background to the political geography of the region. It analyses the intra- and extra-regional issues and the geopolitical dynamics and balance. It appraises the fisheries and the associated maritime boundary problems, and the implementation of the new Law of the Sea.

The appraisal of the politico-geographical setting requires the study of maps and relevant literature. Emphasis on the map is necessary because it is through this cartographic medium that one can visualise the enormous distances involved. Modern technology provides access to up-to-the minute satellite imagery of portions of this planet from points beyond the Earth's atmosphere. Nevertheless, imagery of large and small sections of the Earth's surface displayed on a monitor is not an adequate substitute for a map. In a geographical study of the Indian Ocean and its relationships with the rest of the world, such physical features as area, distance, land and seabed forms, and such cultural features as political divisions, trading relationships and alliances are best conveyed by thematic maps. Because different projections distort sizes, shapes, distances, direction and relative locations to different extents, there can never be a total lack of bias in any map. The map user must, therefore, evaluate in each case the extent to which a map is either objective or deliberately biased.

For the purposes of this study the most appropriate map projection is the orthographic projection because it permits a relatively faithful representation of the spherical surface of the Indian Ocean basin. Gentilli (1948: 167) proposed that to view a map of the region drawn on an orthographic projection, ideally the point of projection should be taken as the intersection of Lat. 20° S, and Long. 80° or 90° E. Such a projection will convey to the map user the correct impression that this ocean is a semi-enclosed body of water with salient underwater physical features. Figure 2.1 drawn on an Equal-Area Azimuthal Projection centred on Lat. 20° S and Long. 80° E supports Gentilli's assertion.

THE OCEAN BASINS AND OCEANIC CRUST

Approximately 70 per cent of the Earth's surface is covered by water, but only about 60 per cent by deep ocean basins and oceanic (as distinct from continental) crust. The difference is mainly accounted for by the shallow shelves that lie between the coastlines and the continental slope. It is the continental slopes that define the true geological boundaries between the continents and oceans. The extent to which the oceans cover the continental margins has varied considerably throughout geological time, partly due to

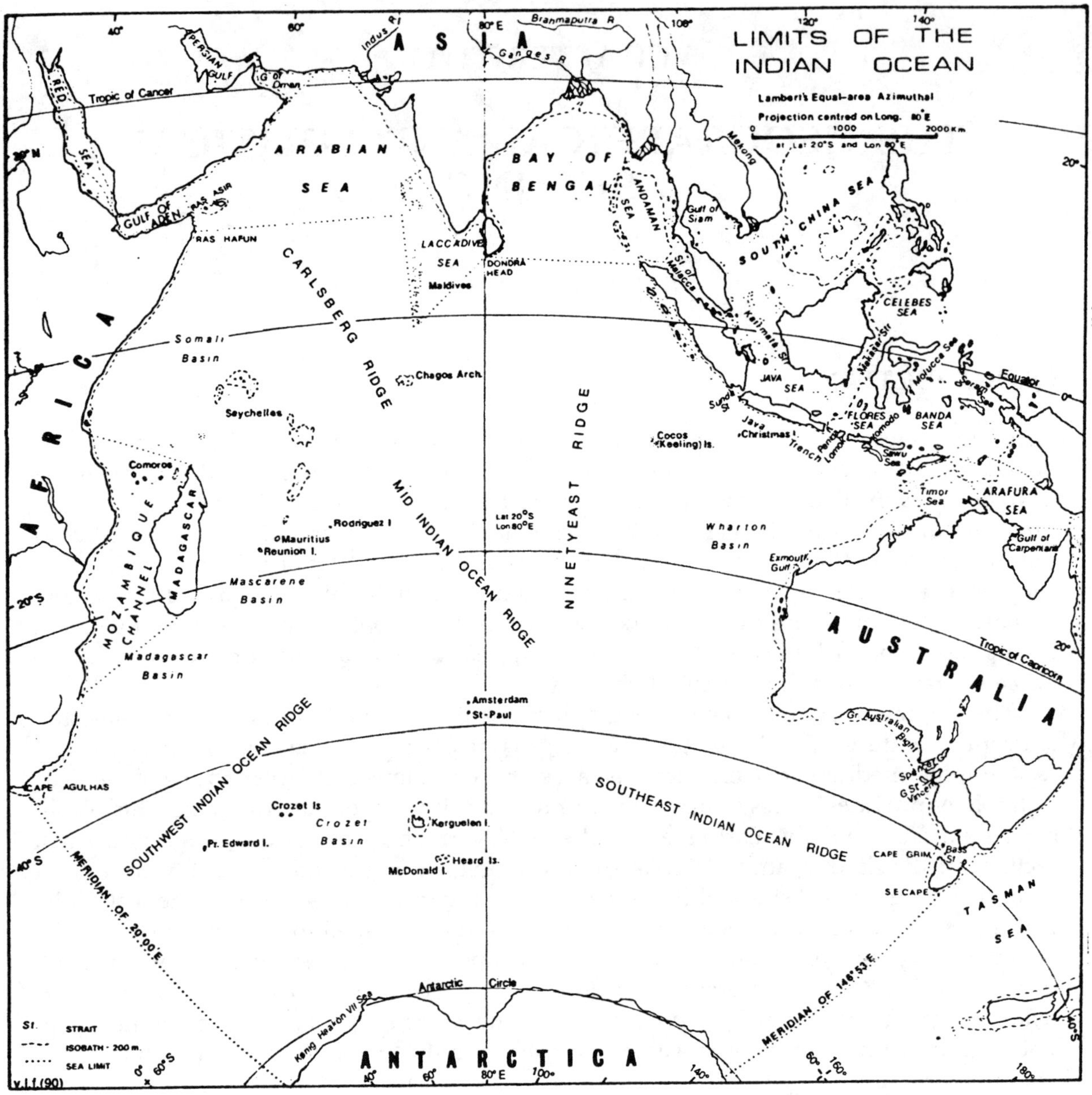

Figure 2.1 The limits of the Indian Ocean Basin as used in this study.

changes in the geometry and mean depths of the ocean basins, but primarily due to the amount of water stored in ice caps.

Intrigued by the puzzling distribution of the continents and oceans and in particular the parallelism of the opposing shores of the Atlantic Ocean, geologists and geophysicists (Snider-Pellegrini, 1858; Taylor 1910; Wegener, 1915; du Toit, 1937; Wilson, 1963) and oceanographers (Heezen, 1956; Heezen and Tharp, 1961) deduced that about 200 million years ago all the major continents of the Earth were linked together like a large jigsaw puzzle, which Wegener termed *Pangaea*. This super-continent (Figure 2.2) split in two at about that period, creating the super-continents referred to as *Laurasia* and *Gondwana*. Laurasia was the ancestor of the present-day continents of North America and Eurasia, and Gondwana the ancestor of South America, Africa, Australia, Antarctica and Peninsular India. The rifting of Pangaea was believed to have been initiated by the formation of a meridional sea named, by Wegener, *Tethys*. A crack in the seafloor subsequently opened to form the Atlantic Ocean. Further dispersion of the continents, through the process of seafloor spreading, enlarged the Atlantic Ocean. The Indian Ocean

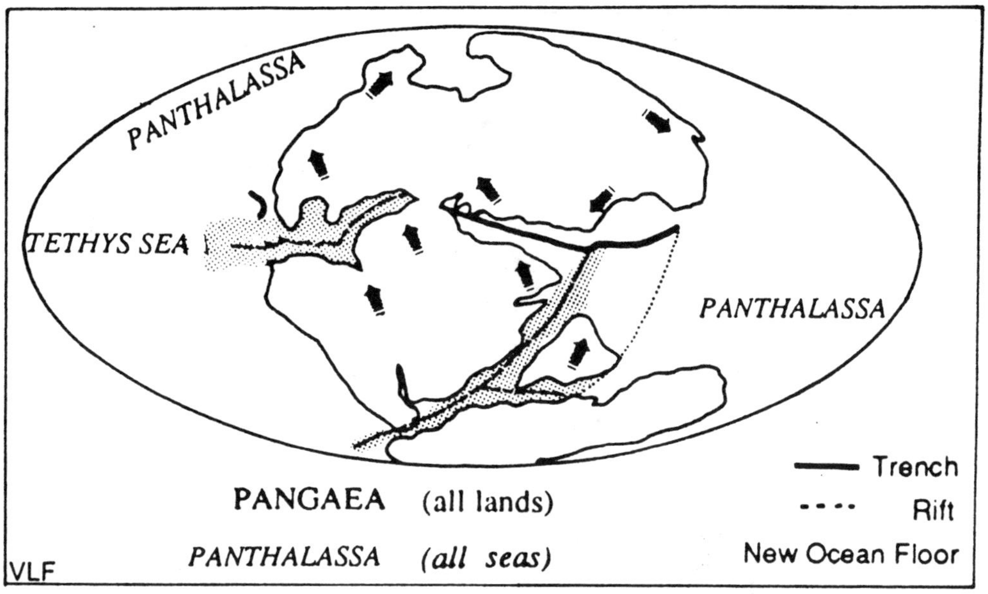

Figure 2.2 Pangaea and Panthalassa c. 200 million years ago.

evolved as a result of the breakup of East Gondwana. Peninsular India was borne northwards over Tethys into Laurasia.

Seafloor exploration over the last 20 years or so (Calder, 1972) has confirmed the theory of continental drift and seafloor spreading, and provided evidence to understand and explain, in part, their mechanisms. The basic explanation of continental drift, as proposed by geologists (McKenzie and Richter, 1976) is that the upper mantle is in a state of convection, associated with the release of heat of the earth from the asthenosphere. Where the hot rheid mantle material rises, divergence zones occur (Figure 2.3), breaking the crust into a mosaic of tectonic plates, which are borne apart on the low-viscosity plastic rock of the upper mantle (Figure 2.4a). Divergence zones are typified by rift valleys such as that along the crest of the Mid-Indian Ocean Ridge. This particular feature separates the African and Indo-Australian Plates (Figure 2.4b). Divergence zones are characterised by earthquake activity, volcanism and the generation of new lithospheric material.

One may expect that if plates separate in one place, they will converge somewhere else. When plates grind together head-on along convergence zones such as the Java Trench (Figure 2.5a and b) one plate usually buckles downwards and is ingested into the mantle. The overriding plate is crumpled and uplifted. Crumpled mountain ranges, deep-sea trenches, shallow and deep earthquakes and volcanoes are all associated with convergence (Figure 2.5c). Such regions of convergence, where the lithosphere on the edge of one plate is engulfed, are termed subduction zones. The major lithospheric plates

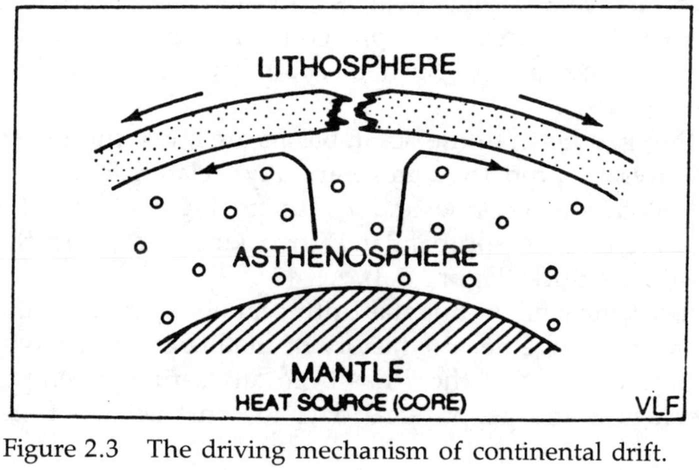

Figure 2.3 The driving mechanism of continental drift.

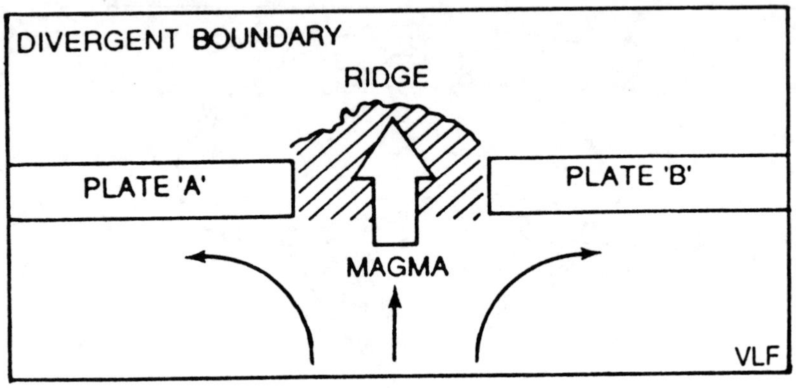

Figure 2.4(a) A divergent boundary.

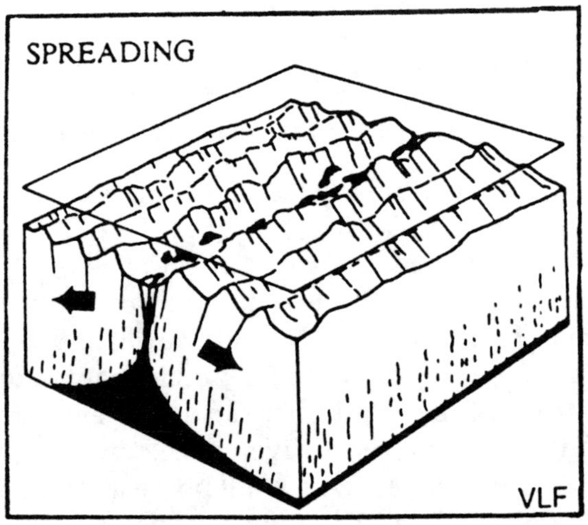

Figure 2.4(b) Example of a divergent boundary.

of the Indian Ocean Basin, their directions of movement, and the associated ridges and troughs are shown in Figures 2.6 and 2.7.

A new ocean basin may be formed when a continental area is rifted apart sufficiently for mantle material to well up into the gap and begin the process of creation of oceanic crust by seafloor spreading. The theory of seafloor spreading invokes a symmetrical process of lateral spreading about the ridges, and implies that the deep ocean floor is both young and renewable. Dewey (1972) suggests that the rate of sea floor spreading is between two and 18 centimetres per year. The age of the sea floor can be measured by the identification of magnetic anomaly bands and the stratigraphy of magnetic reversals, determined by research on land. This procedure has been verified and extended by deep-sea drilling. The outcomes of such measurements support the seafloor-spreading theory (Powell *et al.*, 1981).

The plates of the crust beneath the ocean basins are much thinner than the continental plates, and their physical properties are, naturally, related to those of the underlying mantle. Although both the oceanic and continental crusts are of relatively uniform thickness, the oceanic crust is approximately two kms thick, and the continental crust between 30 and 40 kms thick (Figure 2.8).

Within the substructure of continental drift, seafloor spreading and plate tectonics, it becomes possible to piece together the history of the life cycle of a typical ocean basin. It is only since 1968, however, that there has been any serious attempt by earth scientists to use marine geological and geophysical data to construct the tectonic history of the Indian Ocean.

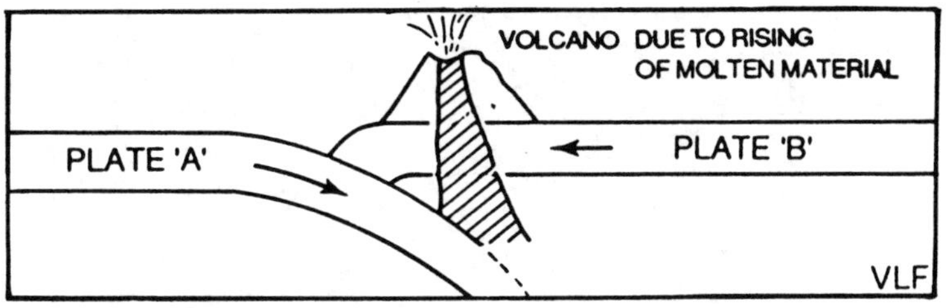

Figure 2.5(a) A convergent boundary.

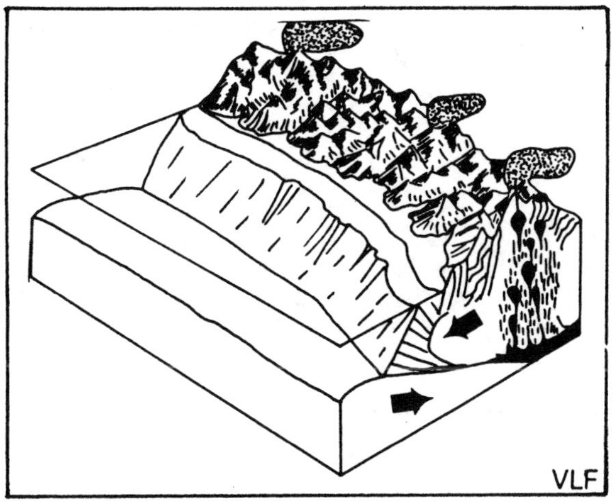

Figure 2.5(b) Example of subduction.

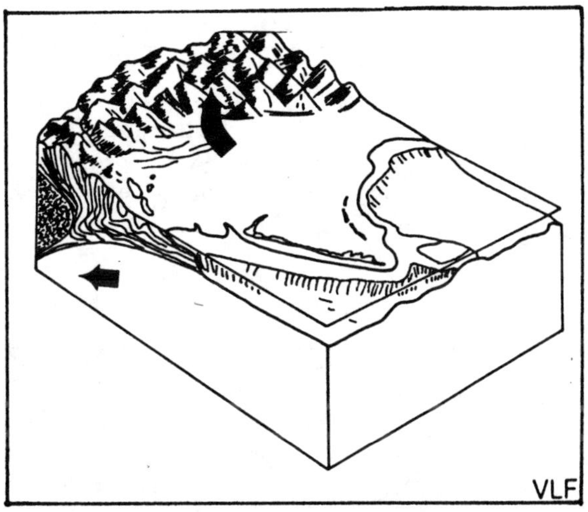

Figure 2.5(c) Example of plates colliding.

THE INDIAN OCEAN BASIN: ORIGIN, STRUCTURE AND RELIEF

During the early part of the Cretaceous Period, East Gondwanaland began to split, as India separated from a combined Australia/Antarctic land mass. By the Mid-Cretaceous the width of the Indian Ocean was greater than 1000 km. In the late Cretaceous, India was positioned between Lat. 20° and 40° S and moving rapidly northwards at rates that varied between seven and 16 cm per year (McKenzie and Sclater, 1974). About 55 million years ago the Indo-Australian plate crossed the Equator and collided with the southern margin of the Eurasian plate to form an intracontinental mountain range — the Himalayas — at the collision zone of the two plates. Antarctica at this time began to separate southward from Australia whose northern edge was at about Lat. 30° S. Arabia had not yet split off from Africa. During the Mid-Oligocene epoch Antarctica moved further southward.

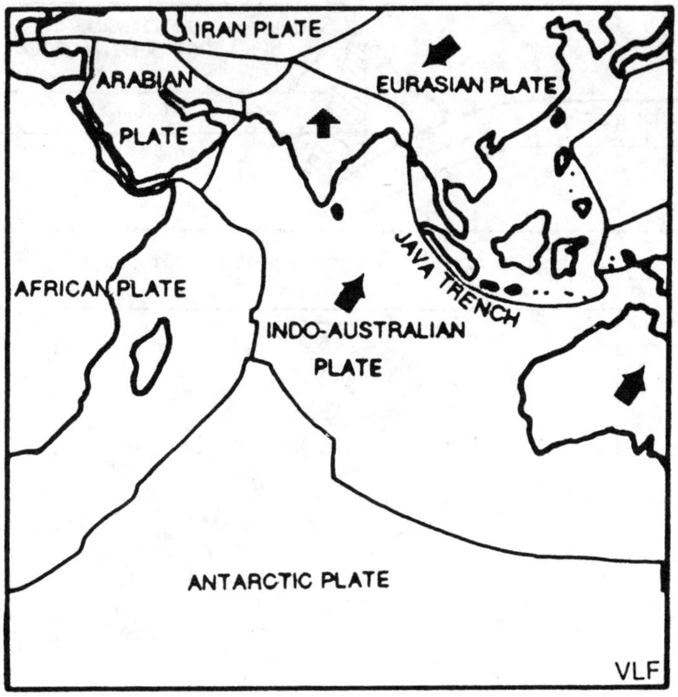

Figure 2.6 Major lithospheric plates of the Basin.

In the Mid-Miocene epoch, the Indo-Australian plate collided with the Sunda arc and the southern extremity of the Eurasian Plate (Figure 2.9a). Antarctica remained near the South Pole. At present India continues a slow convergence with Asia, and Australia continues to be propelled north towards the Equator (Figure 2.9b) at rates varying from two to four centimetres per annum (Powell *et al.*, 1981).

In contrast to the Atlantic Ocean, the shapes of the magnetic anomalies of the Indian Ocean are extremely complicated. McKenzie and Sclater (1973: 147) note, for example, that if the seafloor of the Atlantic Ocean resembled that of the Indian Ocean, "the verification of the concepts of seafloor spreading and plate tectonics might have been delayed for years".

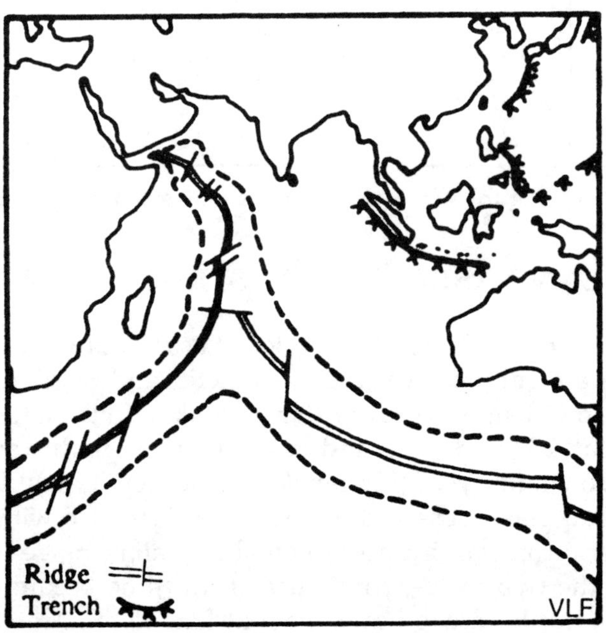

Figure 2.7 Ridges and trenches of the Basin.

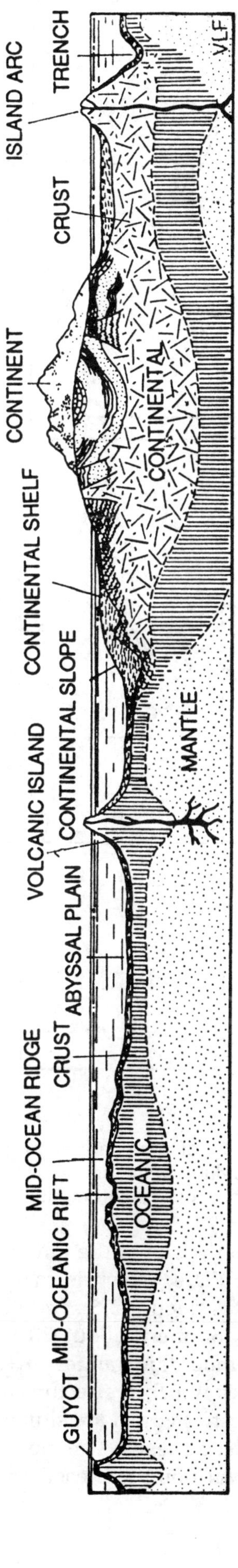

Figure 2.8 Cross-sectional view of the ocean floor showing relative thickness of the oceanic and continental crusts.

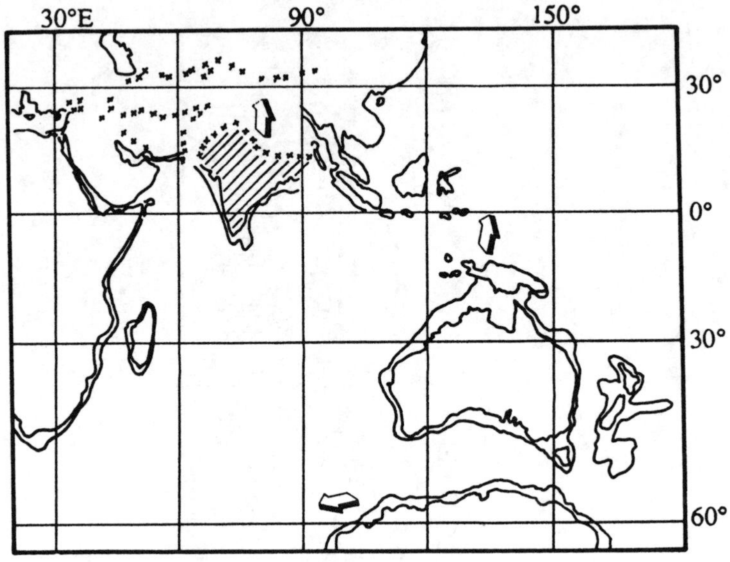

2.9(a)

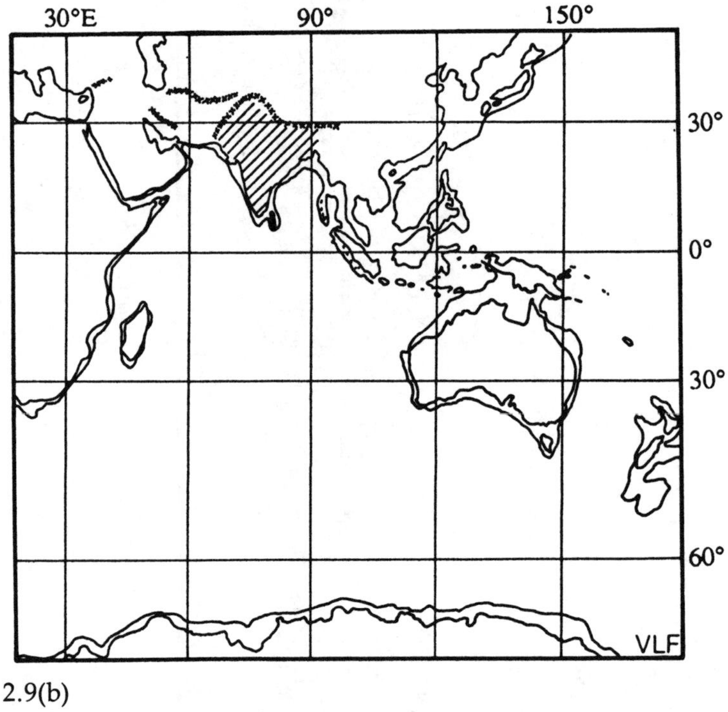

2.9(b)

Figure 2.9(a) The relative motions of the continental plates carrying India, Australia and Antarctica c. 10 million years ago.
Figure 2.9(b) The present position of the continental landmasses bordering the Indian Ocean.

The Indian Ocean basin is the site of the juncture of the African, Indo-Australian and Eurasian Plates. The Arabian Plate, which is comparatively smaller, is wedged between the African and Eurasian Plates (Figure 2.6). Present-day Iran and the Arabian Peninsula separated from the African Continent about 20 million years ago. The Indian Ocean's earthquakes, volcanoes and mountain ranges are mostly concentrated in fairly narrow interconnecting plate junctures which are tectonically active zones. Its deep-sea trenches are narrow, curved deeps, most of which are situated near and just on the landward edge of the structural limit of the deep oceans. The most notable of the deep-sea trenches is the Java Trench. Its deepest known point is measured at 7,125 metres.

The ridge lines that mark the plate junctures are the conspicuous ocean-bottom features (Figure 2.10). The Mid-Indian Ocean Ridge, which begins at the Vema Trench (Lat. 10° S, Long. 70° E) stretches for about 3,600 kilometres, and resembles an inverted Y. At about Lat. 23° S and Long. 70° E, it branches out into the Southwest Indian Ocean Ridge and, via the Amsterdam Fracture Zone, into the 8,000 km long Southeast Indian Ocean Ridge. The 4,000 km long Southwest Indian Ocean Ridge merges with the Atlantic-Indian Ridge at the Mozambique Fracture Zone. North of the Vema Trench, the Carlsberg Ridge extends 2,000 km to the Owen Fracture Zone. The Ninety East Ridge, which is about 4,500 km long and lies to the east of the Mid-Indian Ocean Ridge is named after the meridian of longitude which it most closely follows. It extends from a point in the Bay of Bengal at about Lat. 10° N to about Lat. 30° S and lies normal to the Broken Ridge and the Diamantina Trench, immediately east of Broken Ridge. The Ninety East Ridge is thought to provide the evidence of the Indian Peninsula's movement northward before its collision with Continental Asia.

South of Sri Lanka, there is geological evidence that the Indian Ocean plate is beginning to fracture (McKenzie and Sclater, 1974). Because Peninsular India cannot be pushed further north, subduction off its western coast is inevitable. In addition, there is evidence of differentiated movement of the Indian Ocean floor. Magnetic anomalies in the Arabian Sea south of Iran, aligned east-west, are about 2,500 km north of similar numbered anomalies that lie south of Sri Lanka. This differential indicates the existence of a large transform fault, the Chagos-Laccadive Fracture Zone, which divides the floor of the Indian Ocean into two large segments. About 55 million years ago Sri Lanka's southward movement slowed and possibly stopped in the Arabian Sea for approximately 20 million years before movement was resumed. The new direction was no longer parallel to the ancient transform fault. As new seafloor was generated in the vicinity, its boundary changed from a ridge oblique to the spreading direction, to a series of ridge segments, which were normal to the direction of motion (McKenzie and Sclater, 1974).

As well as the ridges which mark the plate junctures, the Indian Ocean Basin also possesses a series of oceanic uplands known as *aseismic ridges*. An aseismic ridge is not a volcanic site but may have been built up from volcanic products. There are several such ridge systems at varying depths mostly around 2,500 m in the Indian Ocean. These include the Agulhas, Kerguelen, Madagascar, Seychelles-Mauritius, Exmouth and the Naturaliste Plateaus (Figure 2.10).

Distributed throughout the ocean are a large number of islands: *continental islands* which are fragments of the adjacent continental landmass, and *oceanic islands* which are islands that rise from the ocean bed.

Madagascar, which is the largest island (587,000 sq km) in the basin, is a continental island that was once part of Africa. The Seychelles Islands are classified as largely consisting of continental fragments, because they contain granitic rocks which do not occur in the oceanic crust. Other continental islands in the basin include Socotra, Sri Lanka and the Andaman and Nicobar Groups. The Indonesian Archipelago is also a continental fragment.

Oceanic islands may be classified into volcanic islands and coral islands. Volcanic islands of the Indian Ocean Basin include Réunion, Mauritius, the Comoros Group, Rodrigues, Kerguelen, Crozet, Prince Edward, Amsterdam, Saint-Paul and Heard Islands. Coral islands, islets and sand cays include the Maldives, Laccadives and Cocos (Keeling) Islands, Ashmore Reefs and Cartier Island and several islands and reefs of the Seychelles group.

THE LIMITS OF THE INDIAN OCEAN

The Indian Ocean is the third largest of the world's oceans. It and its adjacent seas cover about 14 per cent of the Earth's surface and wash the shores of 37 independent nations.

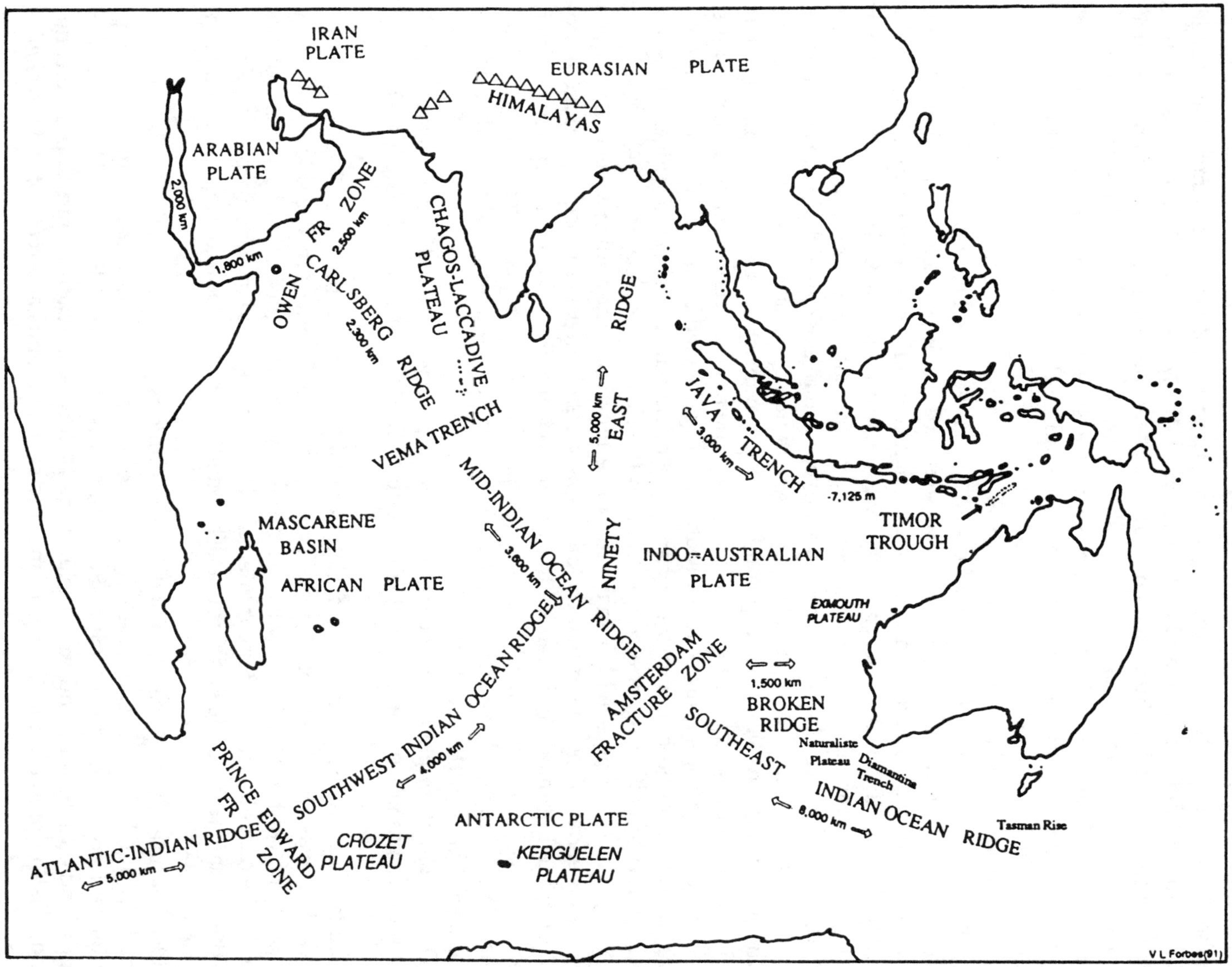

Figure 2.10 Seafloor features of the Indian Ocean Basin and approximate lengths of the features.

Its volume is about 292 million cubic kilometres. Its littoral comprises the coastal regions of southern and eastern Africa, northeastern Africa bordering the Red Sea, the Arabian Peninsula, the Persian Gulf states and emirates, South Asia, Southeast Asia including the Indonesian Archipelago, and northern and western Australia.

The precise location of the southern, southwestern, and northeastern boundaries of the Indian Ocean has been debated in the literature of oceanography for almost two centuries (Fleurieu, 1798–1800; Herschel, 1875; Krümmel, 1897). It is therefore appropriate to introduce here the historical arguments in order to justify the choice of geographic limits for this study as outlined in Figure 2.1.

There are two general trends of thought regarding the definition of the limits or boundaries of oceans and seas. On the one hand, cartographers, hydrographers and mariners would prefer such limits to be delineated by a series of rhumb lines ruled on a Mercator's Projection chart, with their extremities expressed as geographical coordinates of latitude and longitude. On the other hand, earth scientists favour the concept of using as boundaries the projection to the surface of the approximate crests of the major seabed features (Vaughan, 1940). Where such natural features are not known to exist, arbitrary bounaries must be used (Sewell, 1940).

The employment of geographical coordinates provides limits that can be easily plotted and clearly understood by mariners, who are the prime users of the oceans. Oceanographers would argue, however, that such a method of arbitrary limits is of little or no value to their research and may even produce serious anomalies. The method of relating seabed features to ocean surface divisions is, however, less simplistic. Such boundaries are often curvilinear, frequently approximate and occasionally hypothetical (Figure 2.1). There is, nevertheless, a considerable measure of agreement amongst the global scientific community as to the principal seabed features involved.

In the late 19th Century Krümmel (1897) attempted a comprehensive classification of the oceans. He concluded that there were three distinct oceans — the Atlantic, the Indian and the Pacific. He set the southwestern limit of the Indian Ocean as Long. 20° E which is the meridian of Cape Agulhas, South Africa. His southeastern limit was Long. 146°53′ E which is the meridian of Southeast Cape, Tasmania. He admitted that boundaries coinciding with submarine ridges might be selected when more data became available. These two limits proposed by Krümmel are adopted for this study.

A decade or so earlier, Murray (1888) on the basis of data collected during the voyage of the *Challenger* in 1876, had identified Lat. 40° S as the southern boundary of the Indian Ocean. He named that stretch of water between Lat. 40° S and the Antarctic Circle the Southern Ocean, and the waters further south the Antarctic Ocean. He included the waters of the Red Sea and the Persian Gulf in the Indian Ocean, but excluded the Arafura Sea and the waters of the East Indonesian Archipelago. Ratzel (1901) also argued that the natural northern limit of a Southern Ocean should be Lat. 40° S as this parallel closely corresponds with the northern limit of the West Wind Drift of the Southern Hemisphere.

Many subsequent authors (Murray and Hjort, 1912; Kossinna, 1921; Joerg, 1930; Schott, 1935; Vaughan, 1938) attempted to distinguish a Southern and an Antarctic Ocean. They failed to heed Krümmel's (1897) observation that it was easy to be misled about the size and distinctiveness of the southern waters because of the navigator's preference for the Mercator's Projection which massively exaggerates areas in the high latitudes. Figure 2.11 demonstrates the differences in the appearances of the Indian, Southern and Antarctic Oceans on a Mercator's and an equal-area projection.

The whole question of the precision of the limits of oceans and seas was extensively discussed at the International Hydrographic Conferences held in London in 1919 and in Monaco in 1926. In an endeavour to reconcile the various conflicting opinions, the International Hydrographic Bureau (1928) defined the southern limit of the Indian Ocean as a line on the map joining Cape Agulhas, South Africa (Lat. 35°30′ S, Long. 20°00′ E) and Cape Leeuwin, Western Australia (Lat. 34°25′ S, Long. 116°30′ E) It also defined the northeastern limit as a series of lines on the map joining Cape Bougainville, Western

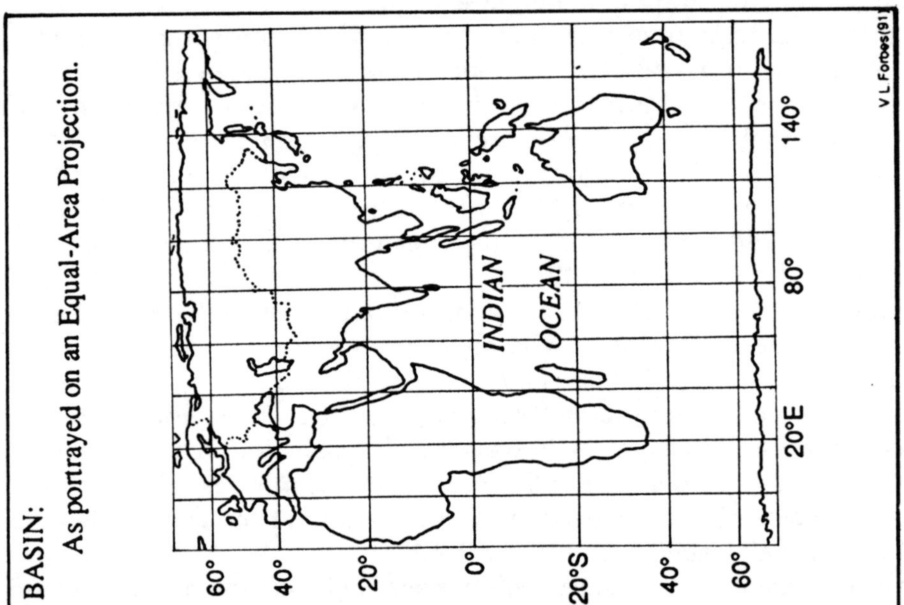

Figure 2.11 Cartographical portrayal of the Indian Ocean Basin.

Australia (Lat. 13°54′ S, Long. 126°30′ E) to Poe Loe Dana on the southern coast of Roti Island (Lat. 11°00′ S, Long. 122°52′ E) and thence along the southern and southwestern coastlines of the Sunda Islands and Sumatra Island. The waters of the Arafura Sea, Timor Sea, Bay of Bengal, Arabian Sea, Red Sea, Gulf of Aden and Persian Gulf were not considered integral parts of the Indian Ocean.

The Bureau subsequently modified its definition on two occasions. It acknowledged that the above-mentioned water bodies were part of the ocean in which they lie, but excluded the Bass and Torres Straits from the Indian Ocean. The limits adopted by the Academy of Science of the Soviet Union in the *Geological-Geophysical Altas of the Indian Ocean* (1975) and by Wyrtki (1988) on behalf of the National Science Foundation in the *Oceanographic Atlas* were largely compiled from data obtained during the 1965 International Indian Ocean Expedition, differ slightly from those of the International Hydrographic Bureau in that they exclude the waters of the Bass Strait from the Indian Ocean. On the other hand they retain the prescribed meridians of longitude for the southwestern and southeastern limits of the Indian Ocean, and exclude any recognition of a generic Southern Ocean or Antarctic Ocean (Figure 2.12). These authorities, however, exclude the waters within the Indonesian Archipelago from the Indian Ocean.

In direct contrast, a chart of the limits of the oceans and seas around Australia produced by the Hydrographic Service of the Royal Australian Navy in 1978 implies the existence of a Southern Ocean by delimiting the Indian Ocean to the south with a line

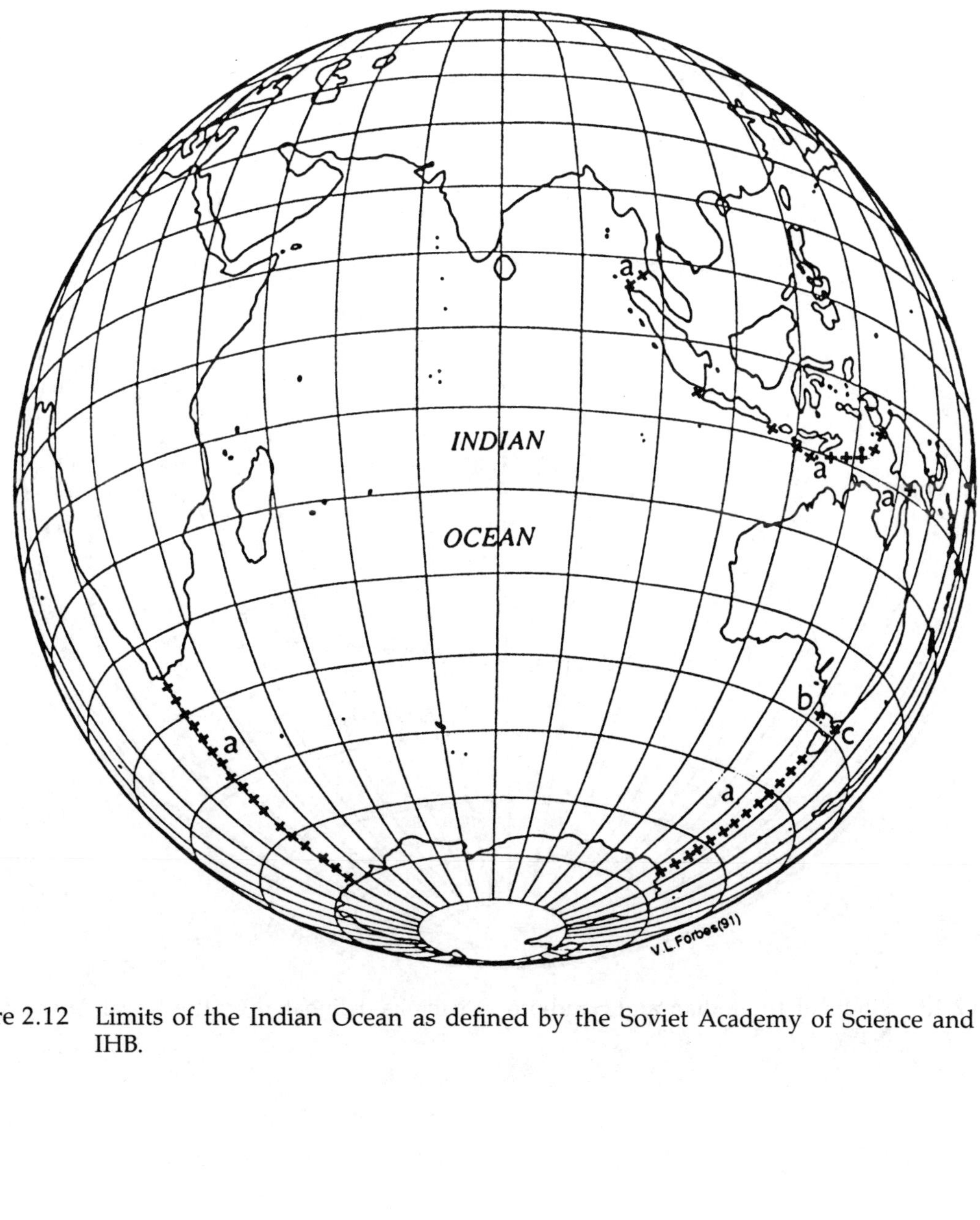

Figure 2.12 Limits of the Indian Ocean as defined by the Soviet Academy of Science and the IHB.

from Cape Leeuwin on an azimuth of 256°. A western terminating point is not defined. It is assumed, however, that the limiting line extends to Lat. 41° S, Long. 77° E on the edge of the map and perhaps beyond. Furthermore, the map implies that the waters of the Indonesian archipelago south of the Equator are indeed part of the Indian Ocean (Figure 2.13). A disclaimer concedes, however, that the delineation of the limits of the seas on the map is solely for the convenience of Australian mapping authorities and therefore has no political significance. Other maps and charts produced by the Australian and Western Australian mapping agencies limit the Indian Ocean to the area north of the latitude of Cape Leeuwin.

This convention conforms with the reasoning of Vallaux (1933) who claimed that there were significant hydrological and meteorological differences in the waters north and south of Lat. 35° S. Others, however, objected (Sverdrup *et al.*, 1942) to this idea of a limiting line associated with a subtropical divergence, which is subject to movement with the seasons and to marked variations in intensity of atmospheric pressure. Vallaux also defined the northeastern boundary of the Indian Ocean as the meridian of Long. 123° E from Roti Island, Indonesia, to Cape Leveque, Western Australia (Lat. 16°24′ S, Long. 122°56′ E). Such a definition places part of the Timor Sea in the Indian Ocean and part elsewhere. It is therefore unacceptable for the purposes of this study.

The definition of the limits of the Indian Ocean given by Schott (1935) indicates his preference for using natural seabed features, such as submarine ridges, as boundaries. He

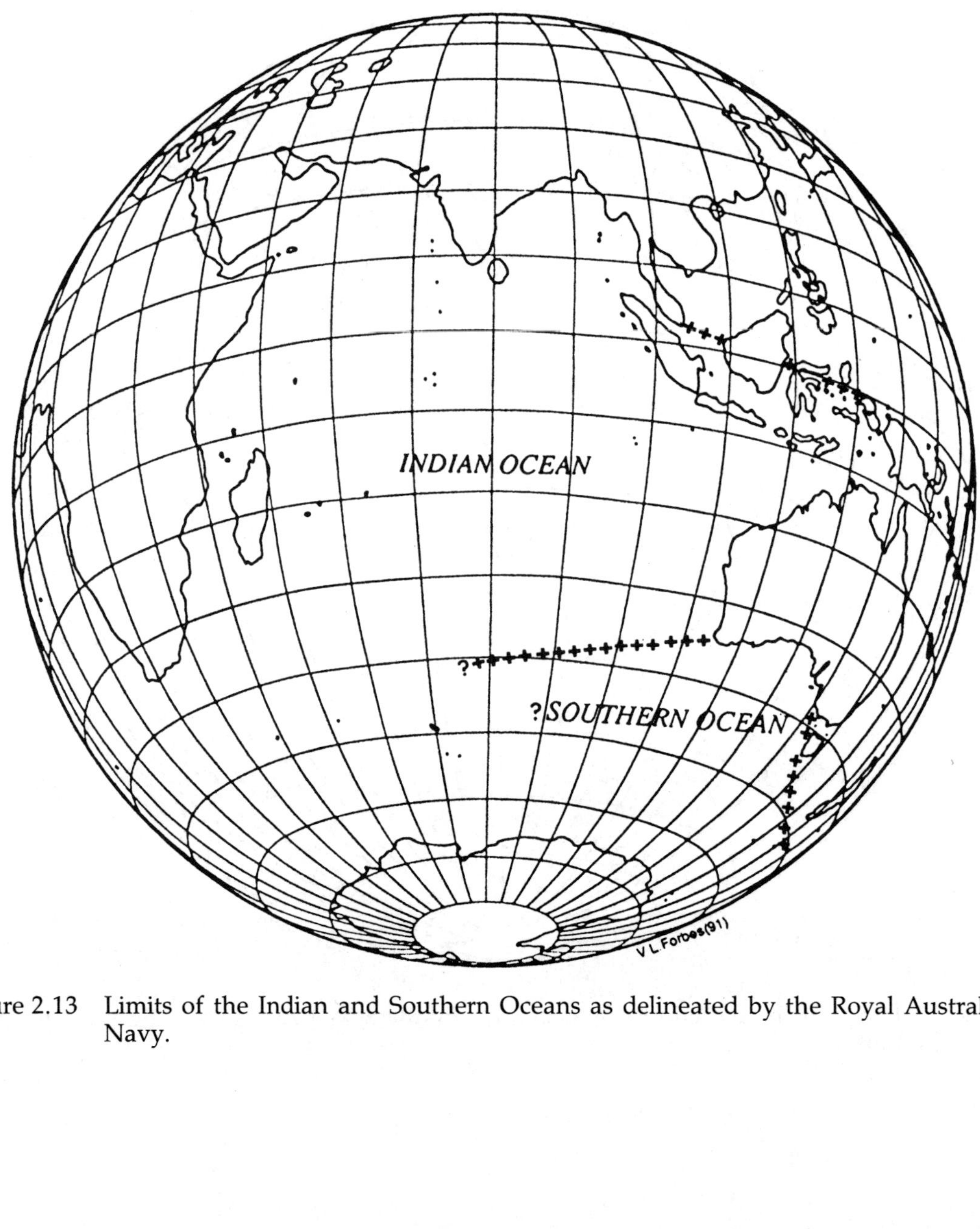

Figure 2.13 Limits of the Indian and Southern Oceans as delineated by the Royal Australian Navy.

refers to geographical coordinates only when there is no alternative. Thus, whilst accepting the southwestern limit as the meridian of Longitude 20° E from Cape Agulhas, in the absence of any natural feature, he defines the southeastern limiting line as the projection to the water surface of the Macquarie Ridge, which extends southwards from Tasmania via the Mill Bank Rise, Macquarie Island and Balleny Islands to Cape Adare on the Antarctic Continent. Furthermore, Schott differs from Kossinna, Krümmel and Vallaux by including the waters of the Arafura Sea, the Timor Sea and Bass Strait in the confines of the Indian, rather than the Pacific Ocean.

The geographical setting for this study on the determination and delineation of maritime boundaries of the Indian Ocean region employs an amalgam of those limits defined or proposed by Murray (1888), Krümmel (1897), Schott (1935), the International Hydrographic Bureau (1953) and the Academy of Sciences of the Soviet Union (1975). It adopts the southwestern and southeastern limits defined by Krümmel; it includes the Red Sea and Persian Gulf in the Indian Ocean as proposed by Murray; it considers the Bass Strait, Timor Sea and Arafura Sea to be parts of the Indian Ocean. The limits of the Indian Ocean for this study are extended to include the Torres Strait, the Malacca Strait, the Straits of Singapore and the Indonesian archipelagic waters south of the Equator. This study accepts that the waters of the Indian Ocean extend south of the Antarctic Circle. It does not recognise the existence of a generic Southern Ocean or Antarctic Ocean (Figure 2.14).

Having established the limits of the ocean basin, it is necessary to examine the importance of the configuration of the coastline as a datum for maritime boundary determination.

THE COASTAL CONFIGURATION OF THE INDIAN OCEAN BASIN

The islands, the peninsular projections of the Asian continent, such as the Malay and Indian Peninsulas, which penetrate into the ocean for hundreds of kilometres from the north, and the general configuration of the coastline all play an important role in the determination of the extent of the jurisdiction that a coastal state may legally claim.

Within the context of coastal geomorphology the term *coastline* is considered as the seaward margin of the land. This is not to be confused with the term *shoreline* which denotes the water's edge. The shoreline moves to and fro as the tides rise and fall. The coastline, as defined, is usually synonymous with the high spring tide shoreline (Figure 2.15). Where the tidal range is large, say five metres or more, as off the Kimberley coastline of Western Australia, there is considerable variation between the positions reached by the sea at high and low spring tides. Further complications such as storm surges, and other unusual phenomena such as tsunami waves generated by earthquakes or volcanic eruptions, result in the temporary submergence of coastal land margins. Within the intertidal zone it is possible for low-tide shorelines to retreat at the same time as high-tide shorelines advance, as the shore profile is flattened over time by coastal processes. Conversely, if the shore profile becomes steeper, the distance between the shorelines is likely to decrease.

Coastlines are usually accurately depicted on large-scale topographical maps, which may, however, be unreliable in showing the intertidal features, especially low-tide shorelines, which are generally submerged and less easily accessible to surveys and revision than features landwards. Hydrographic charts are even less accurate in portraying the coastline, for their primary purpose is to delineate the pattern of navigable waters and the accurate locations of hazards to ships and boats.

The configurations of territorial coasts, their lengths and their geographical relationships to one another, are the factual elements which must be considered when defining a datum for the purpose of delineating maritime boundaries. The International Court of Justice in its judgement in the 1969 *North Sea Continental Shelf Case (Federal Republic of*

Figure 2.14 Limits of the Indian Ocean as defined for the purpose of this study.

Germany/Denmark and Federal Republic of Germany/The Netherlands) stressed that, in any maritime delimitation process, the general configuration of the coasts of the parties involved must be taken into account as a matter of principle (ICJ, 1969; Weil, 1989).

There have been a number of attempts at coastal classification by geomorphologists, including Suess (1906), Johnston (1919), McGill (1958), Bird (1964), Inman and Nordstrom (1971), Davies (1972) and Bird and Schwartz (1985). It has been argued that no classification has been entirely successful (Bird 1964: 170). Indeed, Rice (1977) maintains that, until a better factual knowledge is gained, any attempt at coastal classification is premature. Notwithstanding such opinions, any such undertaking is of value to the researcher and scholar of marine geography, because it offers a datum for further research and investigation.

Johnston (1919) introduced a fourfold genetic classification of coasts as submergent, emergent, neutral or compound. A submergent coast is found where the submergence of the land relative to the sea is the dominant agent in shaping the coastline. The Kimberley coastline of Western Australia is a typical example. Along the Gulf of Kuchh also, in 1819 and 1845 earthquake-induced submergences were evident (Bird, 1985). An emergent coast is one where the uplift of the land relative to the sea is the dominant factor in shaping the coast. The Swan Coastal Plain, Western Australia, is a typical example. At Pasni, Pakistan, the coastline was raised 4.6 metres during an earthquake in 1945 (Bird,

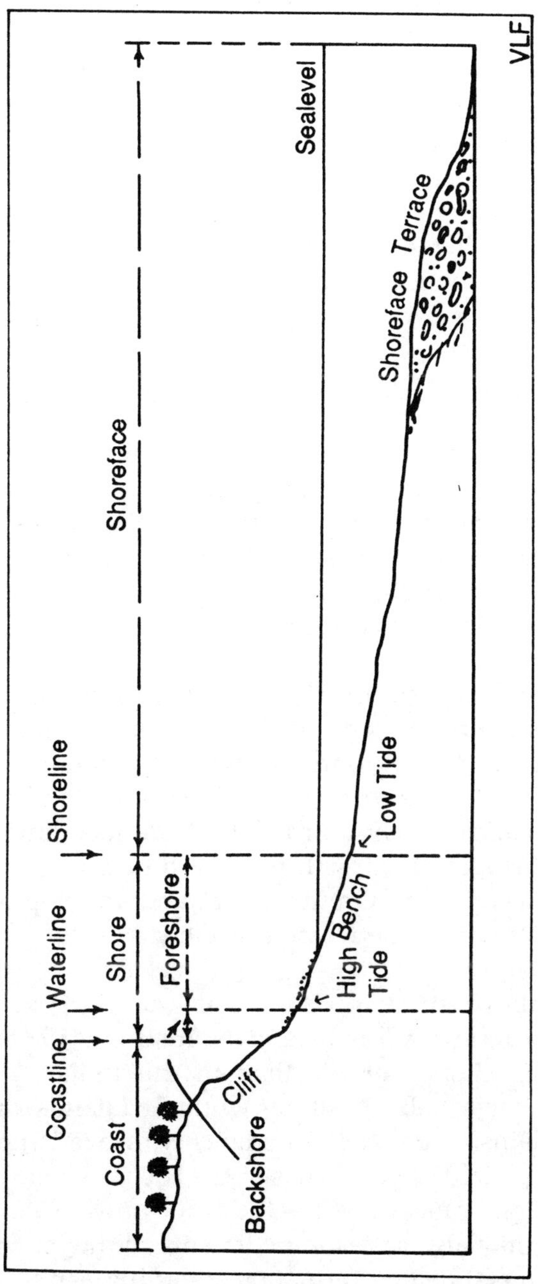

Figure 2.15 Defining the shoreline.

1985). A neutral coast is formed essentially by non-marine processes and is not due to sea-level change. Typical examples in the Indian Ocean basin are Cheuba Island in the Bay of Bengal and the Ganges Delta, which is the result of alluvial deposition. A compound coast is one which may involve some combination of all three processes. Johnston (1919) also theorised that the sequence of changes, after a rise in sea-level and after a fall in sea-level were different. Figure 2.16 depicts Indian Ocean examples of Johnston's classification of coastlines.

Davies (1972) advocated a dynamic classification, based on coastal forms being shaped by wave action. He distinguished four contrasting wave environments, namely, storm wave coasts; protected coasts; west coast swell coasts; and east coast swell coasts (Figure 2.17a). A storm wave coast, for example, experiences a significant proportion of the waves generated by local gale-fore winds which are common in the temperate storm-belts of mid-to-high latitudes. The waves generated by such storms are of high energy and therefore are capable of producing prominent cliffs and shore platforms. In the Indian Ocean Basin only the west coast swell and east coast swell are to be found.

A coastal classification scheme by Inman and Nordstrom (1971), based upon the concept of plate tectonics, produced three primary classes of coastlines: marginal sea coasts, separated from the deep ocean basins by island arcs such as the Indonesian archipelago; trailing-edge coasts where continental blocks are diverging; and collision coasts at the margins of the converging plates. The trailing-edge coasts were further classified into three types: *neo-type,* where continental separation is geologically recent; *afro-type,* when both margins of the continent are trailing edge coasts; and *amero-type,* where one margin of the continent is a trailing-edge coast and the other a collision coast (Figure 2.17b). This tectonic classification, note Inman and Nordstrom (1971), is not easy to apply, as there are times when a coast might be reclassified without undergoing any morphological change. Carter (1988: 16) cites the example of the afro-trailing-edge of India becoming an amero-trailing-edge coast when India tectonically collided with the Asian Plate.

Furthermore, Inman and Nordstrom (1971) identify three coastal morphological scales. A first-order scale has minimum dimensions of 100 km in length, 100 km in width and 10 km in height from the ocean floor to the continental summit. A second-order scale has minimum dimensions of 100, 10 and one km respectively and may include submarine canyons, estuaries and rock cliffs. The third-order scale has dimensions of one, 0.1, and 0.01 km respectively and is associated with wave and tide action. For the purpose of this study the first-order scale is relevant. On the other hand, in the practical application to the detailed boundary determination between coastal states the third-order scale would naturally be drawn upon.

The most meaningful coastline division, for the purpose of this study, is the geomorphological classification by Inman and Nordstrom (1971) as depicted in Figure 2.17. It identifies eight categories of coastline in the Indian Ocean Basin. These are mountain coastlines; narrow shelf coastlines with headlands and bays; narrow shelf coastlines with coastal plains; wide shelf coastlines with headlands and bays; wide shelf coastlines with coastal plains; deltaic coasts; reef coasts and glaciated coasts. This classification identifies geographical features that not only profoundly influence human activity on the land, but may also act as impediments to movement by sea. For example, coastlines with fringing reefs, deltaic formations, shifting sands, or opposing headlands that create narrow straits are all restrictive to the safe passage of ships in coastal waters.

STRAITS AND SEA LANES

Each of the entrances at the four corners of the Indian Ocean is of immense strategic importance, not only to the littoral states but also to users. Each constitutes a geographical choke-point, where the major shipping channels are constricted because of landmasses,

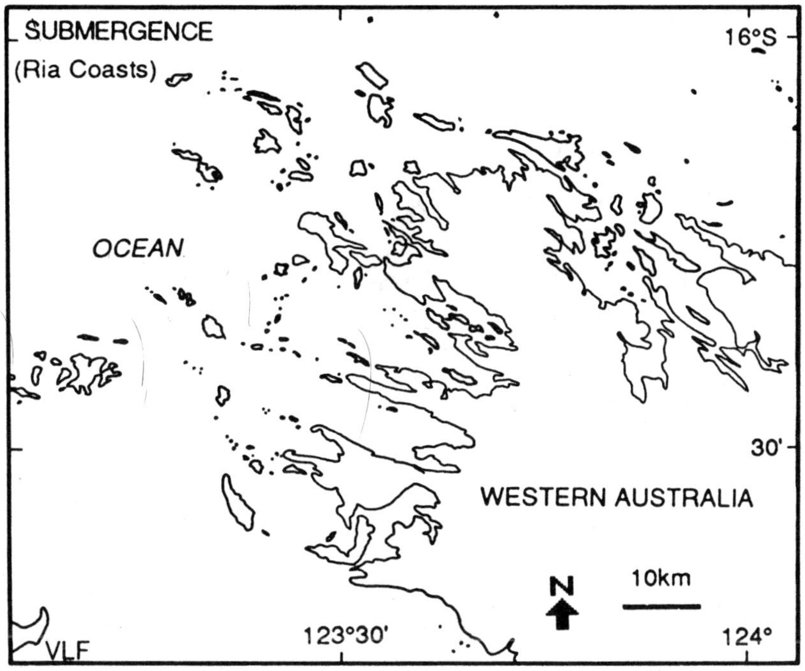

(a) Coastline of submergence Kimberley, Western Australia.

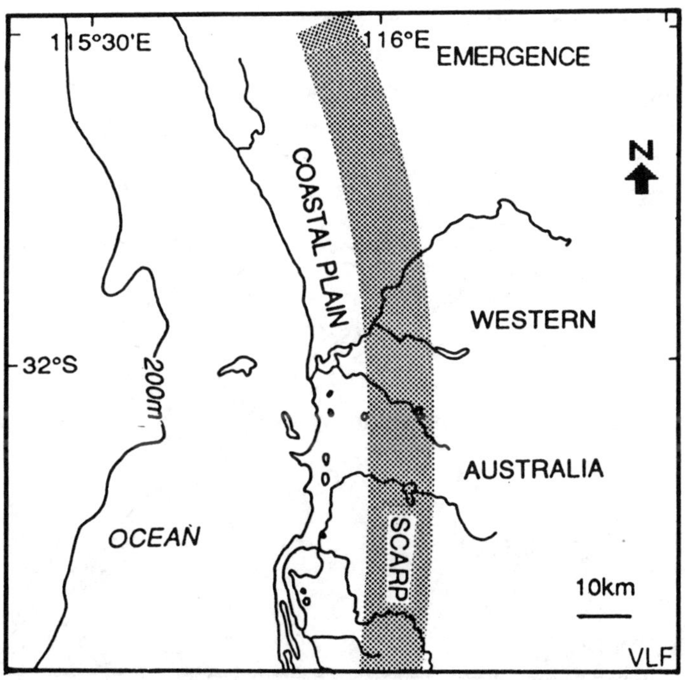

(b) Coastline of emergence: The Swan Coastal Plain, Western Australia.

Figure 2.16 Johnston's (1919) classification of coastlines.

underwater dangers, adverse weather or contrary ocean currents.

Entry into the Indian Ocean from the Mediterranean Sea entails navigating the waters of the Suez Canal, the Strait of Jubal, the Red Sea, the Bab el Mandeb, the Gulf of Aden and possibly the Socotra Channel. Entry from the Persian Gulf involves passing through the Strait of Hormuz which is both a strategic chokepoint and a navigational hazard. Entry

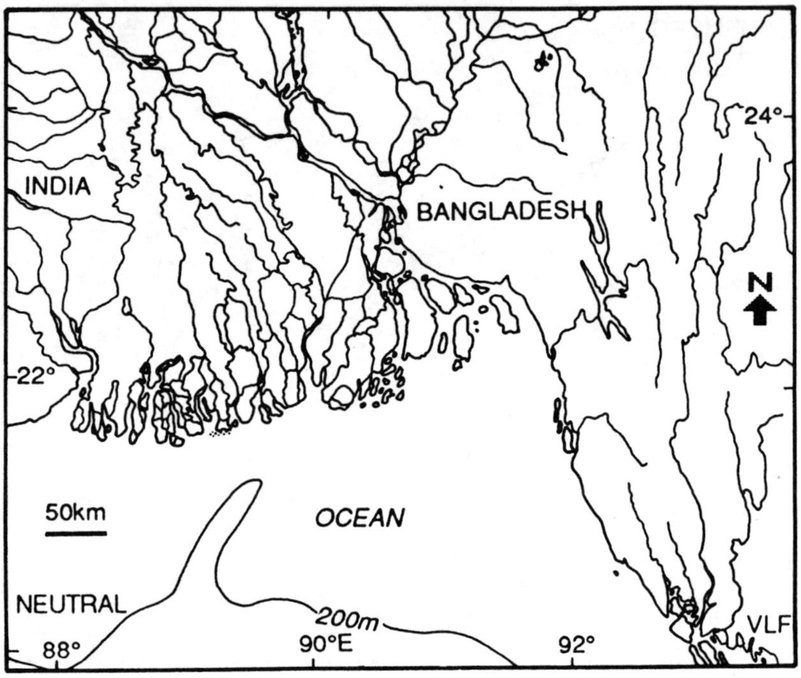

(c) Neutral coastline: Ganges Delta.

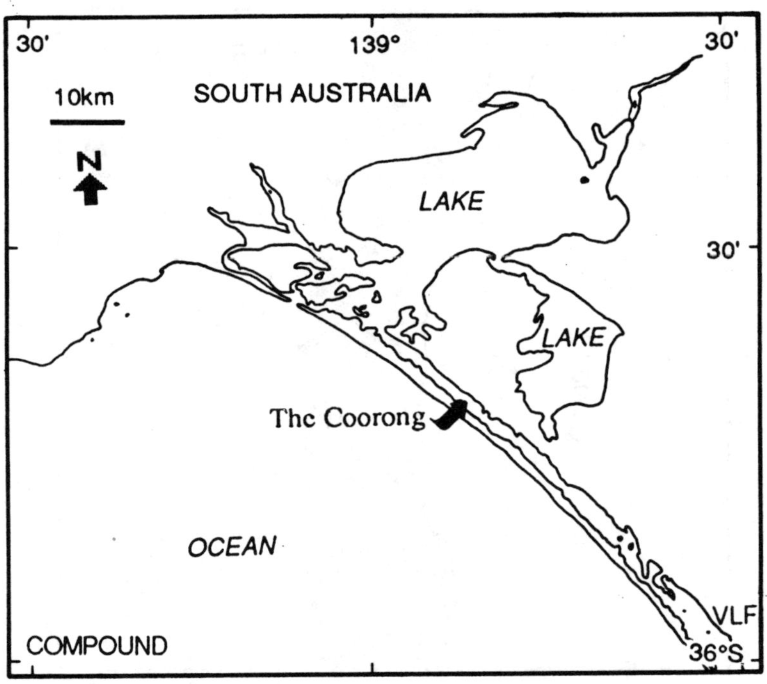

(d) Compound coastline: The Coorong, South Australia.

Figure 2.16 *(continued)* Johnston's (1919) classification of coastlines.

from the North Pacific Ocean and the South China Sea may be through the Straits of Singapore and the Malacca Strait, through one of the major deep water straits of Makassar, Lombok or Sunda, or via the Torres Strait. Ships with comparatively shallow draught may choose to negotiate any number of narrower and shallower straits of the Indonesian archipelago in order to enter the Indian Ocean from the northeast. Ships

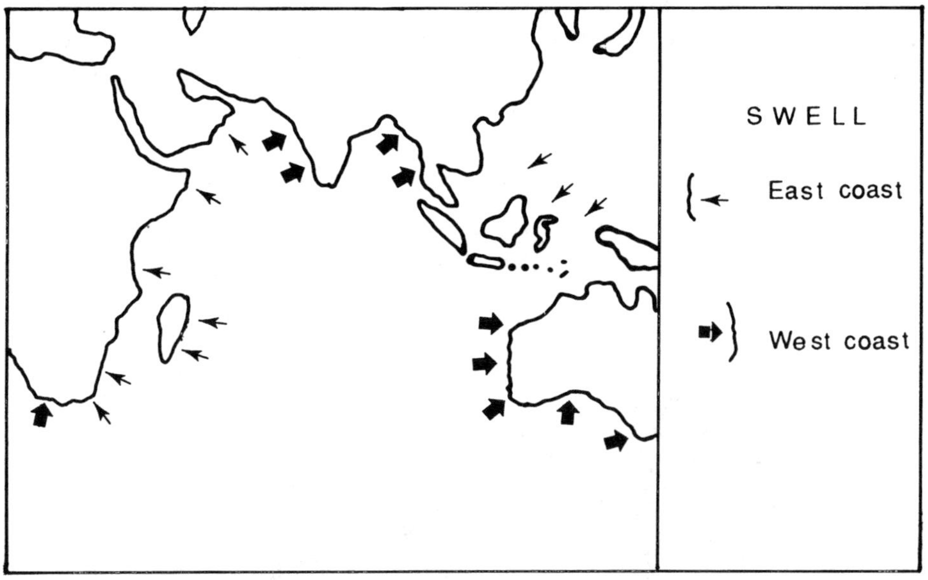

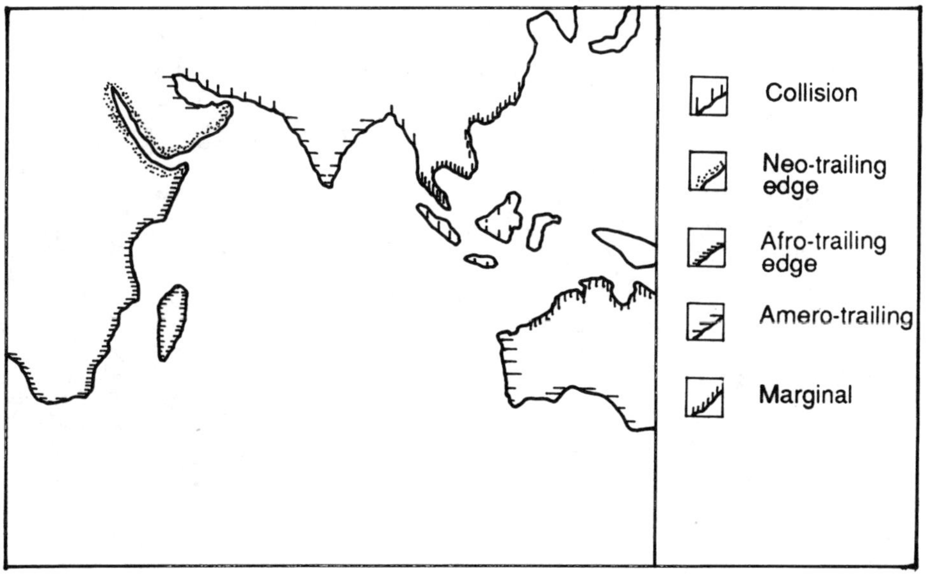

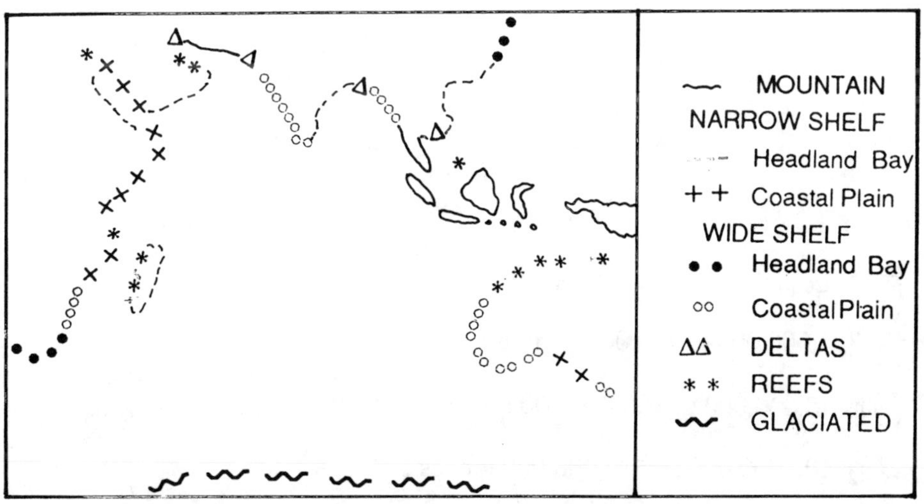

Figure 2.17(a) Coastal classification by wave environment.

Figure 2.17(b) Coastal classification by tectonic type.

Figure 2.17(c) Coastal classification by geomorphology.

entering the Indian Ocean from the southeastern quadrant may use the Bass Strait or pass to the south of Tasmania. The entrance into the Indian Ocean from the Atlantic Ocean lies south of the Cape of Good Hope. Although there are broad expanses of ocean south of Africa and Australia, the most direct and comfortable sea routes lie close to the continental margins (Figure 2.18).

The Suez Canal, the straits, channels and other points of entry are not only

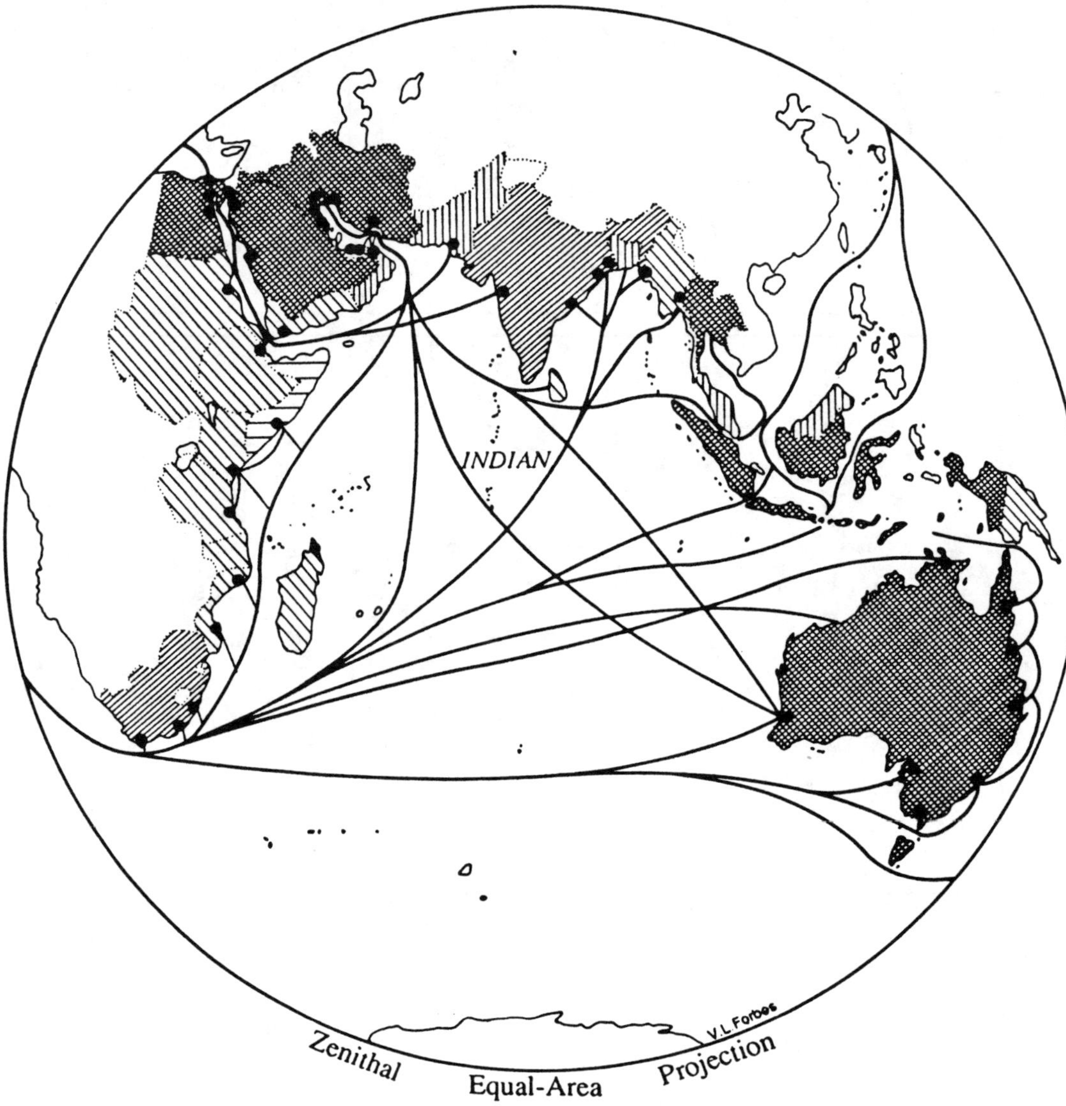

Less than 1,000,000 tonnes

1,000,000 to 10,000,000 tonnes

10,000,000 to 100,000,000 tonnes

100,000,000 to 500,000,000 tonnes

More than 500,000,000.

Sealanes linking principal ports

Source: Author's research. Various annual reports of Port Authorities in the Region. World Trade Figures.

Figure 2.18 Annual cargo turnover in tonnes.

strategically significant to their respective coastal states, but also play an important role in the geopolitical balance in the region. Therefore their importance cannot be overlooked. Through these constrictions pass the ships of maritime states to ply the sealands of the Indian Ocean. Such routes not only connect the trading centres of the coastal and island states of the region but are also linked to the ports of East Asia, Europe and, to a lesser extent, the eastern and western seaboards of the Americas.

Since 1945 a number of political and economic issues have focused interest upon the Indian Ocean region. Significant amongst them are internal political upheavals, such as those in Madagascar and Sri Lanka, the decolonisation of many littoral and island states, shifting international political allegiances, and localised infighting in countries such as Ethiopia, Sudan and Yemen. In addition, the industrial needs of countries within and outside the region have created an extraordinary reliance on the production and transportation of petroleum and other commodities. Maritime trade in the region has, however, been in existence for over 4000 years.

McPherson (1991b: 7) observes that "before the advent of modern communication technology trade across the high sea and land was the major means of contact among the peoples of the Indian Ocean". In a sense, organised trade in the Mediterranean littoral marked the beginning of modern exploration and subsquent trade practices. Indeed, the extent of human contact and communication would have been greatly restricted without these trading links. History's first recorded voyage into the unknown seas was a four-year expedition that set out from Egypt to the mysterious land of Punt in 2500 BC to obtain incense, gold, ebony and myrrh. Phoenician claims of penetrating the Indian Ocean waters via the Cape of Good Hope have been documented.

Mariners and merchants of many nations have navigated the sealanes of the Indian Ocean for many centuries. They mastered the monsoon winds of the Indian Ocean which provided them with regular passage across the Arabian Sea and the Bay of Bengal. Men from Greece, Egypt, and the Red Sea and Persian Gulf countries converged on and jostled for trade with their counterparts in the ports along the western coast of India and also sailed past the Horn of Africa as far south as the Comoros Archipelago and Tanzania. The Arabic culture and influence is evident today in the islands of Comoros, Pemba and Zanzibar.

Inasmuch as maritime trade in the western half of the Indian Ocean was dominated by the littoral states of the Red Sea, Persian Gulf and Arabian Sea, maritime trade in the eastern half of the basin, focused on the Bay of Bengal, was controlled by the merchants from South and Southeast Asia dealing in cargoes from China and the Indian Ocean littoral. Free-trade ports were established in southern India and Sri Lanka, enabling an extension of the maritime network in the Indian Ocean basin. McPherson (1991b: 7) suggests that to "understand the maritime trade network of the Indian Ocean is to understand how the disparate parts of the Indian Ocean littoral became integrated into a world based on economic and cultural commonalities".

Direct European involvement in the region is of long standing. By establishing bases and trading posts at strategic locations in ports on the periphery of the Indian Ocean, European maritime states maintained a presence in the region for almost 500 years, seizing territories and dominating trade within and outside the basin. To safeguard territorial interests and to keep the sealanes open, the stronger European states also established naval bases and maintained a naval presence there. The legacies of the influence of these external powers are evident in the political, judicial and legal systems adopted by many of the emerging littoral and island states in the region.

EUROPEAN PENETRATION INTO THE INDIAN OCEAN

During the 15th century European maritime powers became increasingly interested in and capable of penetrating the Indian Ocean. It was a critical period for Europe in several ways

(Parry, 1966; Doyle, 1978). Four developments, in particular, affected that continent's subsequent relationship with the rest of the world. Firstly, the Ottoman Empire gained control of the overland trade routes between Europe and Asia established by Marco Polo during the 13th century, virtually cutting off the flow of commodities from Asia to Europe. Secondly, within Europe a number of states, some of which had already been in existence for a considerable time and some of which were just emerging, were achieving a consciousness of their nationhood. Thirdly, there was a curiosity about the world afar, motivated by the desire to expand trading links and, in the case of Portugal, Spain and France, to Christianise the local inhabitants. Fourthly, there was the development of shipping, charts and navigation instruments that enabled seamen to venture with confidence beyond the boundaries of the known world. These four apparently unconnected developments together were instrumental in the process of Europeanisation of the littoral states of the Indian Ocean basin.

The first two developments mentioned above, whilst of significance to the maritime explorations of the Indian Ocean region, are beyond the scope of this study. The other two, however, had a direct impact on the decisions that were to be made in future exploration of the lands beyond the Atlantic Ocean.

The countries bordering the seas of western Europe greatly improved the design of the ships that were to carry their sailors on voyages of discovery. Between the 15th and 18th centuries there were two great developments in marine technology. The first was the development of the three-masted ship which made possible voyages from Europe to the New World and the Indies, creating trade routes that were independent of the goodwill of the peoples of the Eastern Mediterranean. The second was the adaptation of the three-masted ship for both military and commercial purposes. An example of the former was the 100-gun First Rate of the mid-17th century, which was a mobile artillery platform of considerable potency. At the same time specialist cargo-carrying ships were being introduced. Their efficiency was measured, then as now, by the relationship between deadweight and running costs.

During the 15th century, however, there was an initial need for a very special type of ship that would be capable of sailing southward along the west coast of Africa, around the Cape of Good Hope and into the Indian Ocean. The vessel had to be able to accommodate the explorer and crew, together with enough supplies to last through many months of sailings. It had to be seaworthy and strong enough to withstand the elements of the southern waters. The Portuguese carrack (Figure 2.19) was the first European ship to meet such requirements.

THE EUROPEAN MARITIME POWERS

The Portuguese Venture

Portugal, a small agricultural nation on the western edge of the European continent had, during the 15th century, became a leading maritime nation in Europe. A moving force for exploration and the expansion of maritime trade was Prince Henry the Navigator, younger son of Portugal's King John (Parry, 1966: 11) who wished to convert the inhabitants of Western Africa to Christianity, control the rich Moorish caravan trade of Northwest Africa and discover the land that lay beyond Cape Bojador on the northwest coast of Africa. To further these aims, he founded a school of navigation and pilotage at Sagres, near Cape St. Vincent and promoted a Portuguese school of cartography by importing Catalan cartographers from Majorca.

Portuguese shipping was also rapidly improved. For the early journeys seamen used the caravel, an adaptation of the fishing boat — probably without a deck — which was used in the waters closer to the home ports. The caravel was a low-profile broad-beamed ship, about six meters in width, capable of carrying ample supplies of provisions and

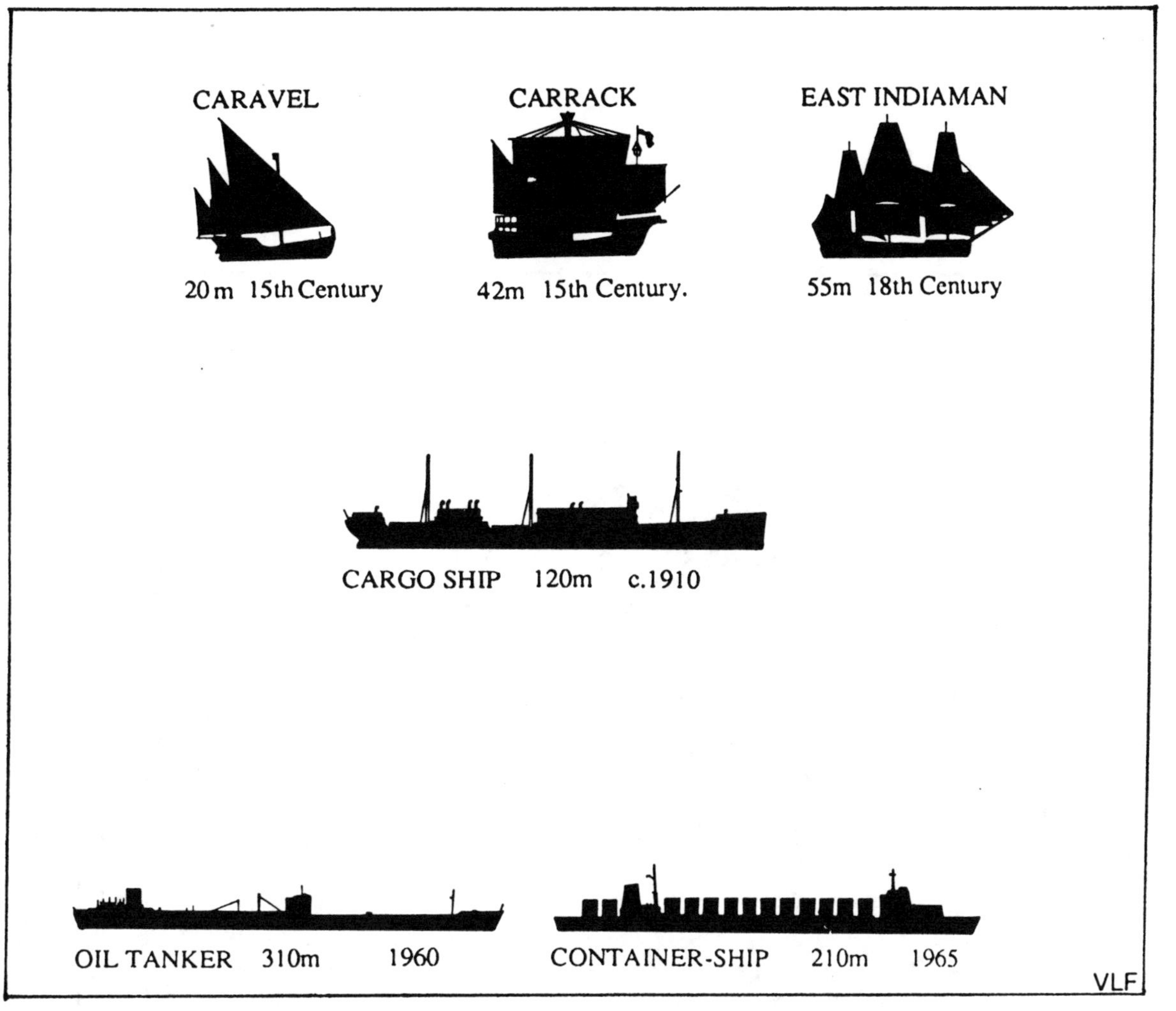

Figure 2.19 Principal commercial ships plying the Indian Ocean sea lanes during the past five centuries.

water (Figure 2.19). It was enlarged to a maximum length of 20 metres and fitted with a deck and two masts. The vessel was lateen-rigged, with triangular sails on tilted masts (Parry, 1966: 21). This combination of hull and rig was a significant factor in the successes that these slow-moving ships achieved in their very difficult task of coastal navigation. They were designed to sail within five points (56°15′) off the wind, affording the navigator a wide range of options in choosing his intended course.

For voyages on the high seas the Portuguese employed the carrack (Figure 2.19) which was a three-masted ship with a broad beam and deep hull, capable of withstanding the battering of storm waves and of carrying a large volume of cargo. The ratio between beam, keel length and length on the deck was commonly 1:2:3. The hull was skeleton-built with a curved stem and a curved stern-post. The propulsion was derived from the square sail on the main mast with the fore and mizzen sails being mainly aids to steering. During the 15th century the carrack was increased progressively in size, and its deadweight increased to approximately 200 tonnes. It was a fleet of four such ships which, under the command of Vasco da Gama, completed a 10-month voyage from Lisbon to Calicut, on the west coast of India, in May 1492 (Jacob and Vellios, 1987).

Although the Portuguese had seaworthy ships, their limited navigational ability made them reluctant to venture too far away from the coast. Nevertheless, their superiority in technology and weaponry enabled them to solve the problem of reaping the riches of the Spice Islands by creating a garrison empire along the littoral of the Indian Ocean (Figure 2.20). By the early 16th century they had established a number of fortified trading

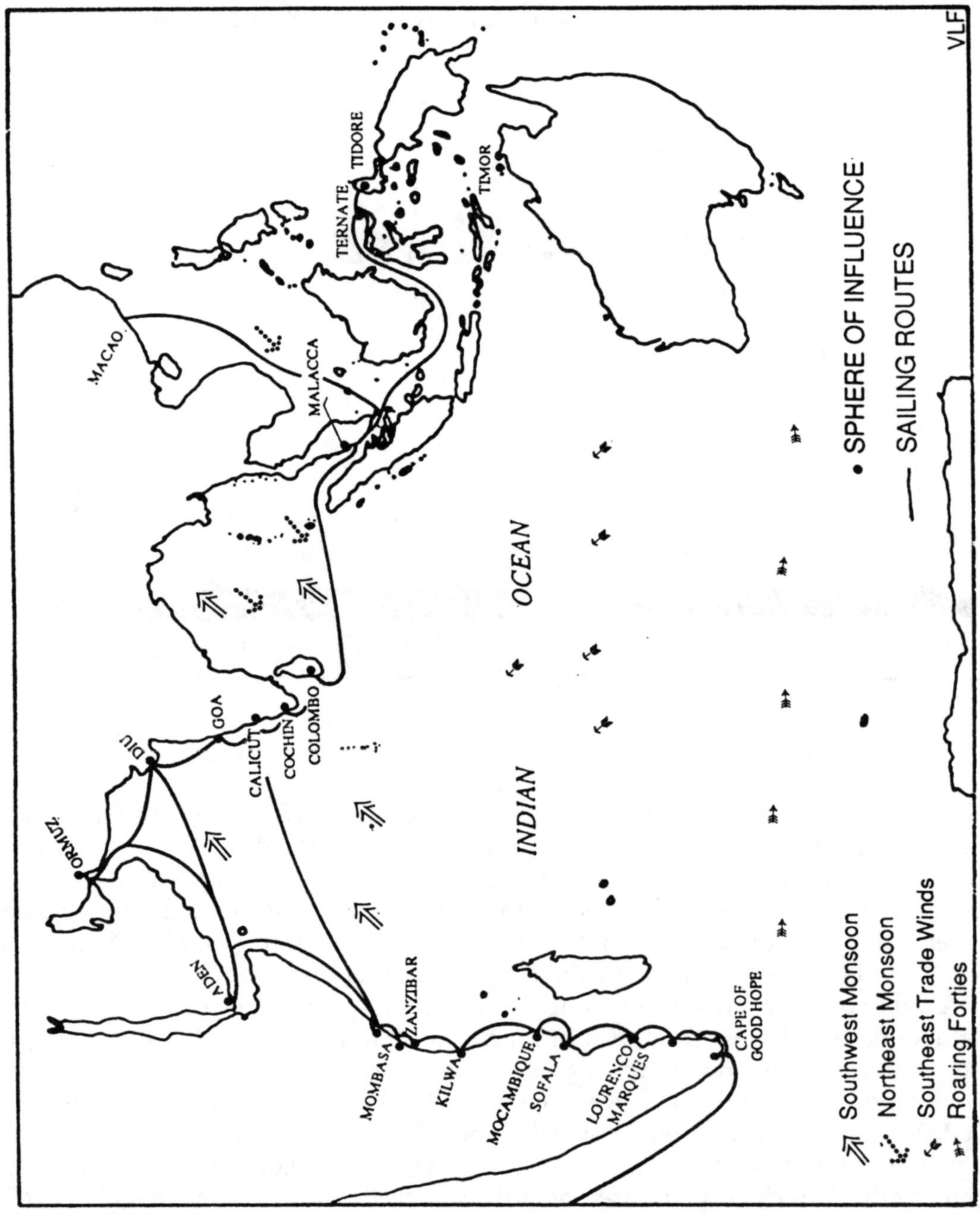

Figure 2.20 Portuguese garrisons and trading posts in the Indian Ocean Basin c. 15th century.

settlements along the coasts of East Africa, the Persian Gulf, India, Sri Lanka, Indonesia, including Diu (1505), Goa and Malacca (1511), Hormuz (1515) and Colombo (1518), and a network of commercial ports in southeast Asia as far east as Timor Island and in the South China Sea (Harrison, 1954: 84; Fisher, 1966: 130). Unfortunately for the Portugese, the maintenance of such a complex and extended operation was beyond their capabilities. It lasted a mere 100 years.

The *Treaty of Tordesillas* of 7 June 1494 endorsed the Portuguese and Spanish monopoly of the New World and its resources. The agreement was a modification of the 1493 decree by Pope Alexander VI who established a line of demarcation 100 leagues west of Cape Verde Islands, giving Portugal exclusive rights to new lands and seas east of the line, and Spain the same rights west of the line as far as the corresponding meridian in the Western Pacific (Figure 2.21). This line was the first recorded international maritime boundary. Although the treaty was given papal sanction in 1506, it cut no ice with Dutch and British interests.

The Dutch Venture

Despite the attempts of the Portuguese to keep their operations secret, the Dutch were familiar with their sailing routes and ports of call. Indeed Fisher (1966: 134) notes that by 1601 a total of 65 Dutch ships had visited the Moluccas and Bantam. In addition a provisioning base was established on the former Portuguese island of Mauritius in 1598. The newcomers subsequently became the most formidable trading force in the East, quickly reducing the Portuguese presence in the Indian Ocean basin to Mozambique, three enclaves (Goa, Damao and Diu) on the west coast of India, and the enclave of Occussi on Timor Island (Osborne, 1990).

The superior seamanship of the Dutch, who were prepared to sail across the Indian Ocean instead of coasting along its littoral, and the desire of the Netherlands to be commercially independent of the Iberian powers were factors that contributed to the Duch enterprise in the Indies. The Dutch were technologically well equipped for the task. They have been credited with the development of the spritsail, which enabled their vessels to sail efficiently close to the wind. It was a true fore-and-aft sail, rectangular in shape, set abaft the mast and spread by a diagonal sprit extending from the heel of the mast to the peak of the sail. Dutch ships were also strong and seaworthy, capable of carrying great loads, and with a shallow draught that enabled them to negotiate the sandbanks that lay across the entrance to estuaries (Phillips-Birt, 1971). Although their navigational instruments were limited in both accuracy and scope, ship's masters had access to charts produced by such outstanding cartographers as Ortelius (1527–1598), Mercator (1512–1594), Blaeu (1571–c.1646), Jansson (1596–1664) and Doncker (1629–1699). Most significant from the mariner's point of view was the publication by Mercator a *World Chart of 1569* in 18 sheets. He devised for his world chart a grid system which was of enormous benefit to navigators because it depicted rhumb lines as straight lines.

The Dutch overseas enterprise was backed by an aggressive commercial attitude and a sophisticated banking and financial system in the form of a chartered joint stock-holding company, formed after Portugal's hold over the Indies was destroyed by the Dutch naval victory off Bantam Island in 1602. The Dutch-owned Vereenigde Oostindische Compagnie or VOC (United East India Company) rapidly became the largest corporation in Europe. In 1619 it established its eastern headquarters at Batavia (now Jakarta), Java, from where the Dutch could dominate the trade in the region. The Dutch commercial interests rapidly extended throughout maritime Asia from the Persian Gulf to Japan. In 1642 they took over Malacca, which was a strategically important trading centre at the time. In 1652 the Company also set up a provisioning station at the Cape of Good Hope (Figure 2.22).

The decline of Dutch domination in the region may be said to have begun with the abandonment of their base at Mauritius in 1710. A subsequent contributing factor was the

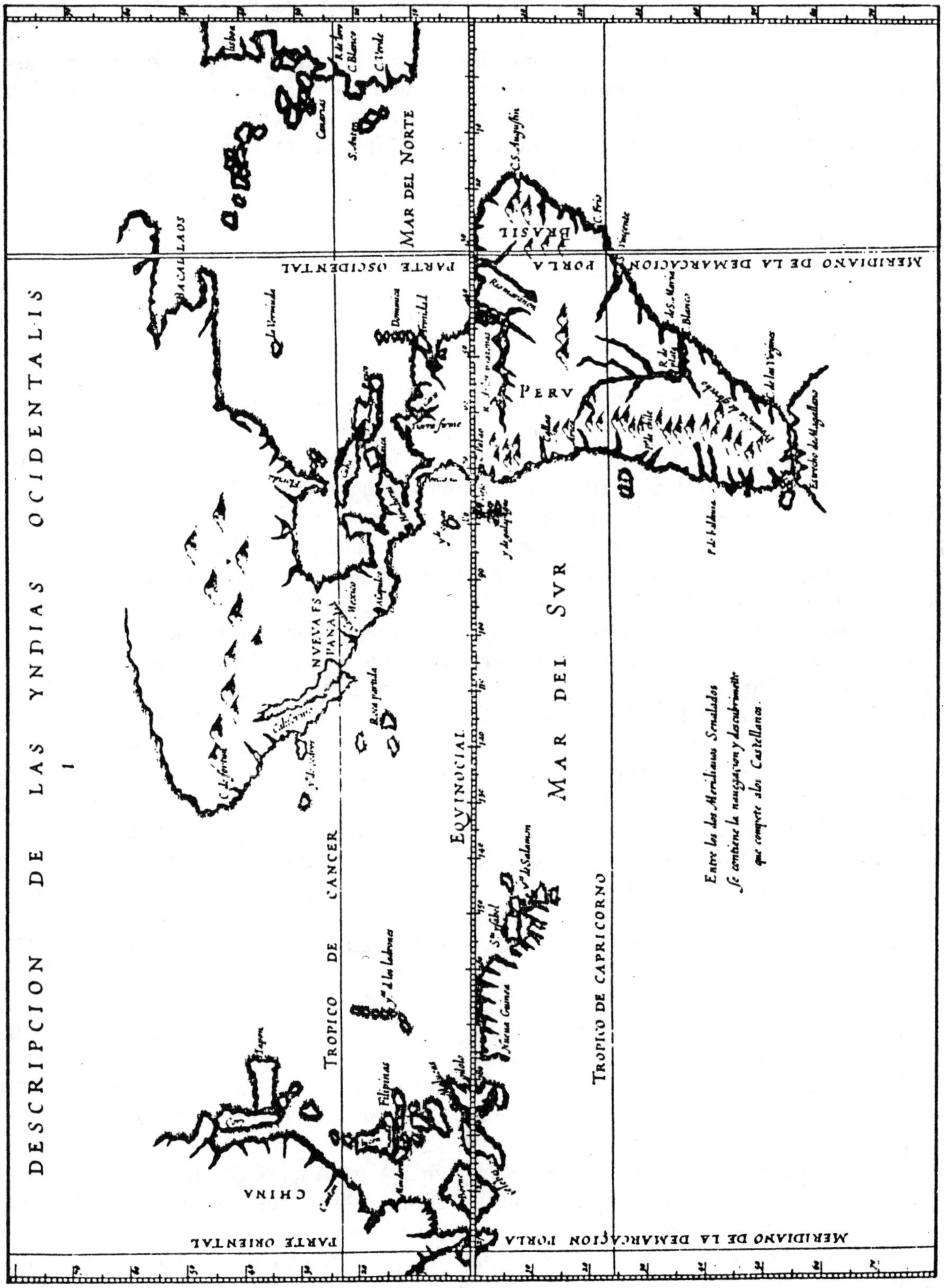

Figure 2.21 Meridian of Demarcation in the Atlantic Ocean (1493–1529).

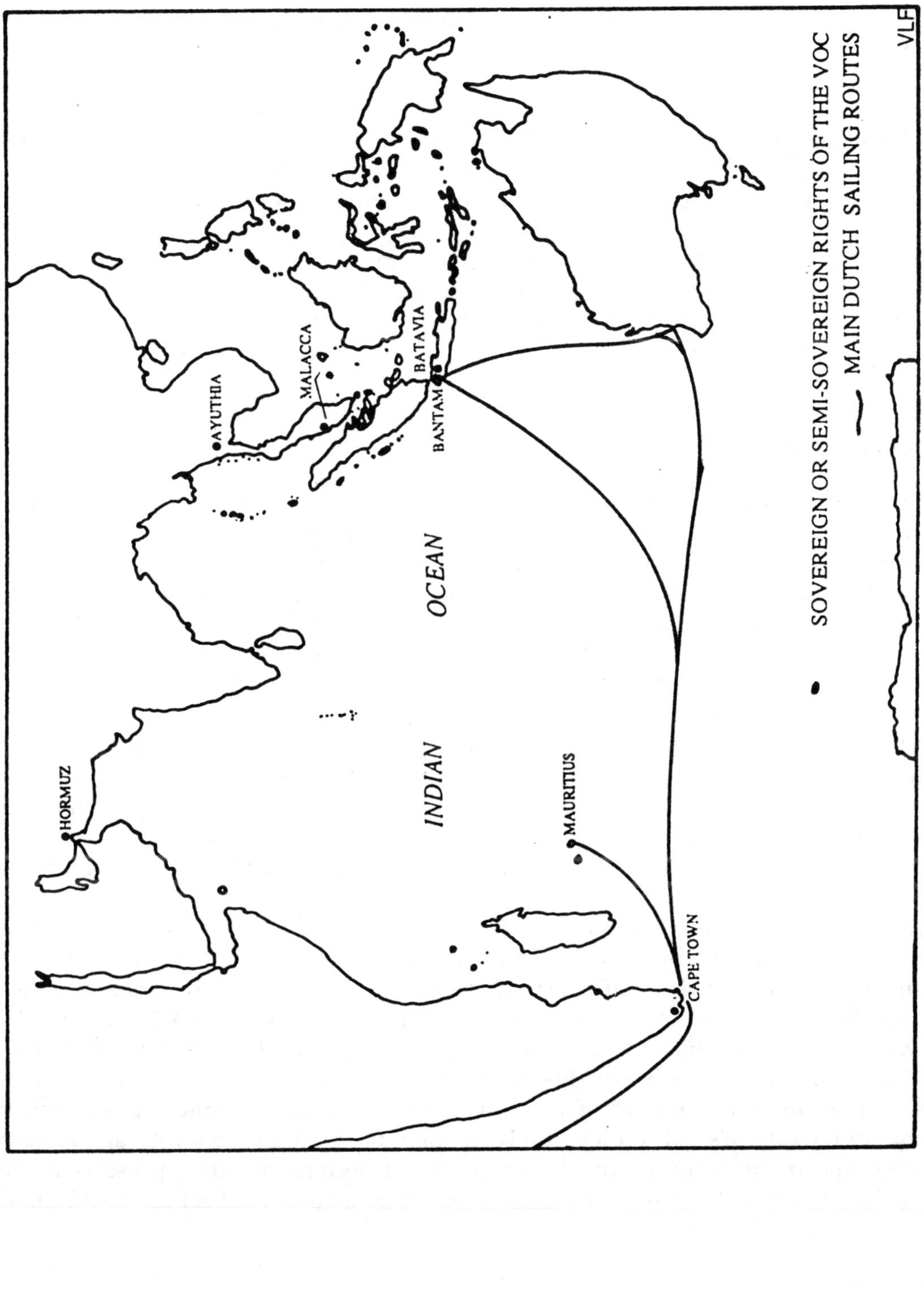

Figure 2.22 Seventeenth Century Sovereign and semi-sovereign rights of the Dutch VOC in the Indian Ocean Basin.

bankruptcy of the VOC. Also, during the Napoleonic Wars the Netherlands was occupied by French forces, and the Dutch lost the provisioning and trading base at the Cape of Good Hope to the British. However, in order to protect India from the threat of a French invasion, the British occupied Java and Malacca. Both territories were subsequently returned to the Dutch. By the provisions of the *Treaty of London* of 1824, however, Malacca was exchanged for the British base at Benkulen and the Dutch gave an assurance that they would respect the territorial sovereignty of Atjeh at the northern tip of Sumatra, thus ensuring British control of the Malacca Strait.

Dutch commercial activity in the basin was restricted geographically to the East Indies. The riches of the Spice Islands were a means of reviving the war-damaged Dutch economy. The development of an increasingly oppressive system of forced cultivation before 1870, the introduction of the plantation system to the uplands and outer islands in the late 19th and early 20th centuries, and the failure to contain the nationalist movement in Java resulted in the gradual expansion of Dutch territorial control over the whole of the future Republic of Indonesia. The colony became known as the Netherlands East Indies (NEI).

By the 1930s the Netherlands was one of several European nations with colonial interests in the Indian Ocean Basin. Each was motivated, to a greater or lesser extent, by commercial interest, national prestige and strategic considerations, and each evolved its own form of colonialism in the region.

The French Venture

France, notes Marchant (1982: 24), was disadvantaged in her quest for colonial expansion by the provisions of the *Treaty of Tordesillas.* On the other hand, Catholic France tried to have the provisions of the treaty altered. When the Pope proved obdurate, King Francis I (1515–1547) who refused to recognise the political supremacy of the Church, gave his subjects his full support to trade overseas. The Company of New France, established in 1627, concentrated on trade and colonisation in North America. The French East India Company, which was founded in 1664, during the reign of Louis XIV, aimed to secure a series of bases around the Indian coast and a number of island outposts in the Indian Ocean. The first French trading centre on the Indian Subcontinent was established at Pondicherry in 1674 (Figure 2.23). Almost a century of Anglo-French struggle for the control of southern India followed. French dreams of an Indian Empire ended with the fall of Pondicherry to the British in 1761. Furthermore, Britain's decisive naval victory over the French at the Battle of the Nile in August 1798 ended France's aspirations for an Eastern Empire.

French island conquests, which began with Bouvet de Lozier's annexation of Mauritius in 1739, were more successful. The Comoros, Madagascar, Reunion, the Seychelles and numerous other islands in the southwestern and southern sectors of the basin all passed into French hands. Djibouti, shown as Obock in Figure 2.24, at the head of the Gulf of Aden, was France's sole Indian Ocean mainland possession after her expulsion from India (Figure 2.23). Although French expeditions were despatched to Australian waters, there was never any formal annexation of territory. Contrary to the argument postulated by Marchant (1982), France's interest lay purely in scientific research. As with Canada in the New World and India to the north, Australia was to become a British possession. The current political status of the former French colonies is detailed in Section 2.10 below.

The British Venture

Early British interests in the Indian Ocean were dominated by the desire of the British East India Company to tap the wealth of the Indian Subcontinent. Decisive victories over the

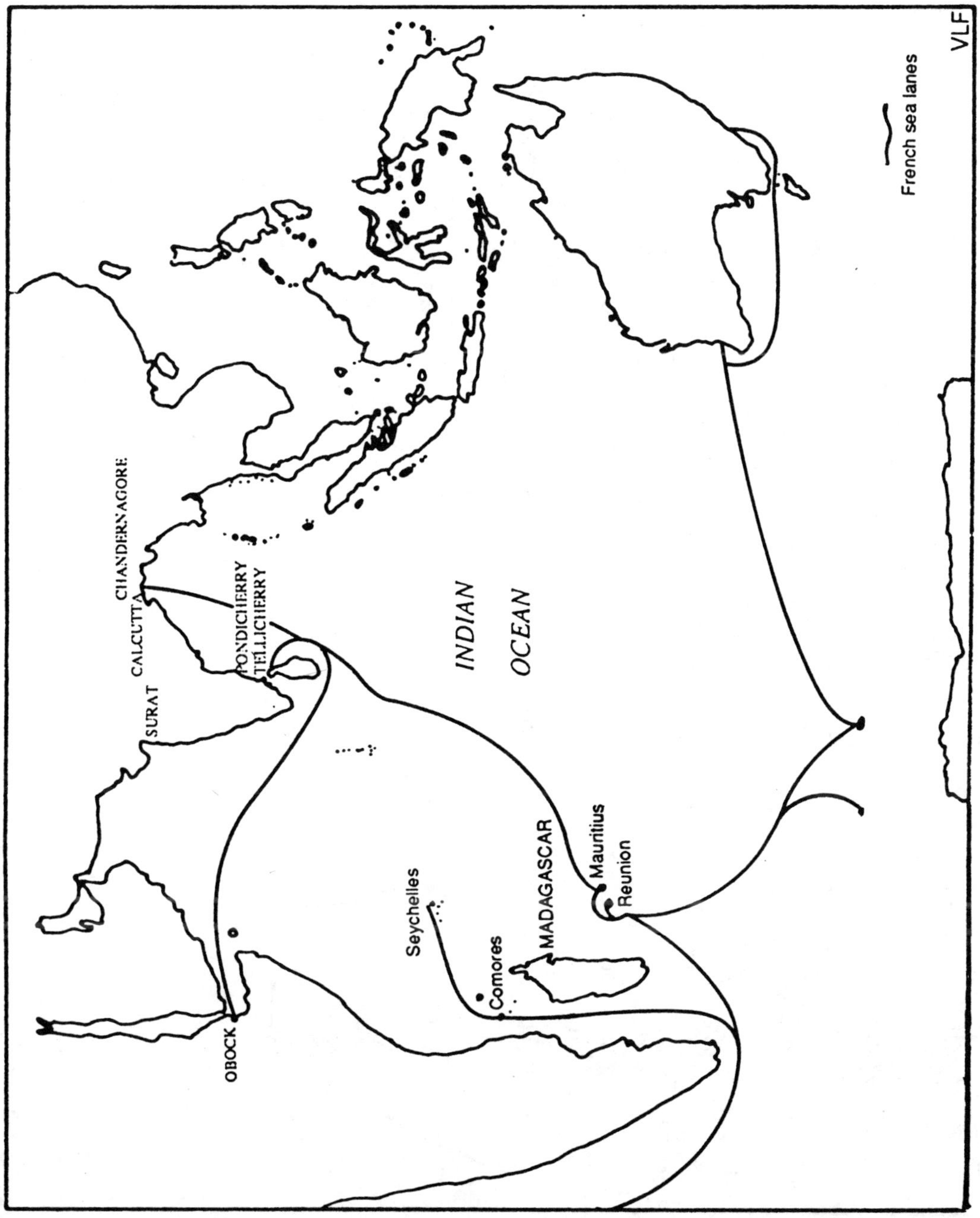

Figure 2.23 French possessions in the Indian Ocean Basin, 18th century.

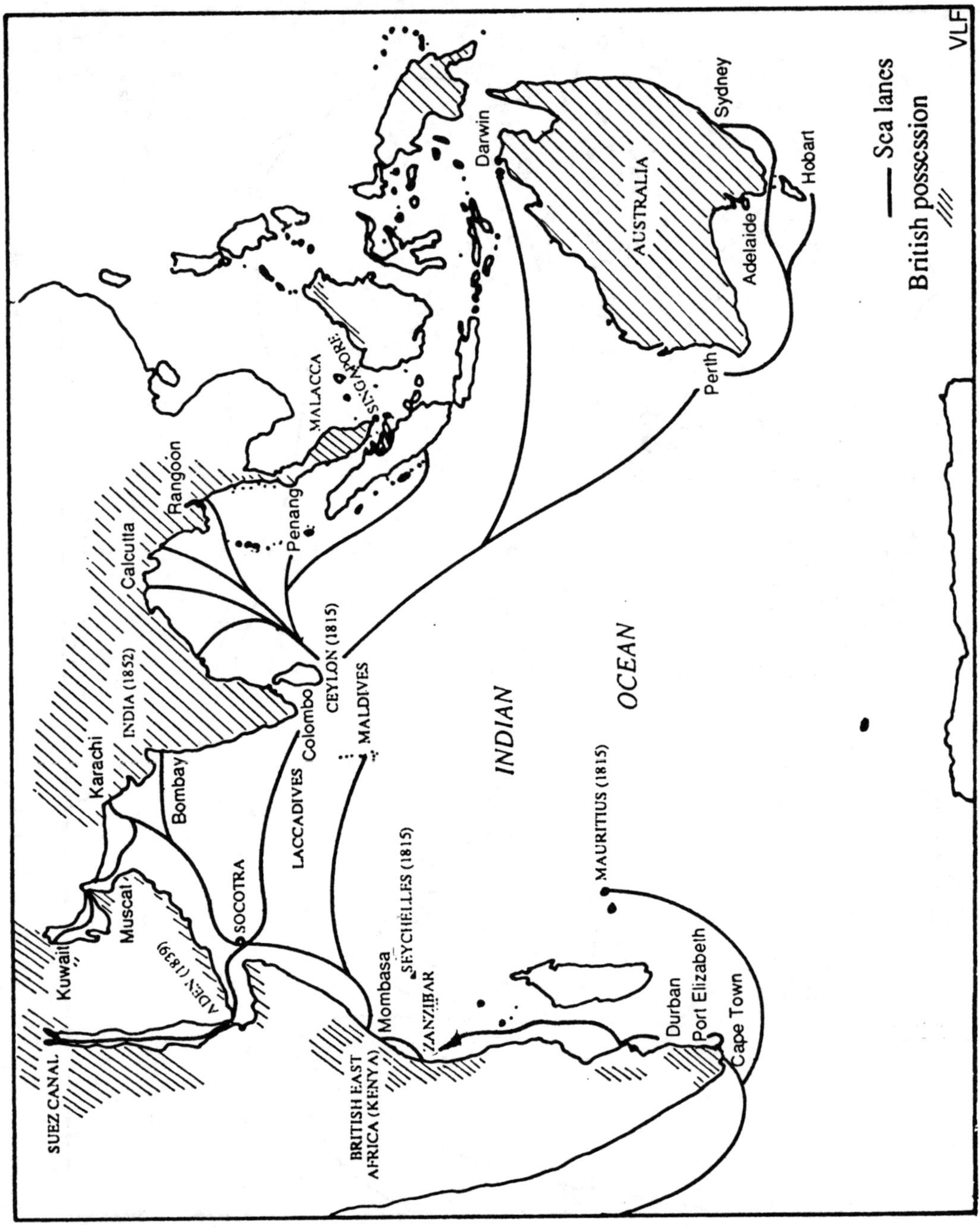

Figure 2.24 British possessions in the Indian Ocean Basin during the 19th and early 20th centuries.

French at Plassey in 1757, and at Pondicherry in 1761 consolidated British control, whilst French interest in South Asia languished for over half a century. Initial British interest in the Malaysian archipelago stemmed from the need to protect the Coromandel Coast during the northeast monsoon, and to safeguard the navigation rights of British ships passing through the Straits of Malacca in pursuit of the lucrative China trade. In 1786 the British East India Company took possession of the island of Penang (Osborne, 1990: 69), situated at the northern approaches of the Malacca Strait (Figure 2.24).

British control of Burma was also motivated initially by the need to protect India. In 1746 the British seized the island of Negaris at the mouth of the Bassein river on the western fringe of the Irrawady Delta, in retaliation for French support of the Mon rebellion in Burma. When the Burmese were foiled in their attempt to conquer Siam, they concentrated their efforts to the northwest. Fearing for the security of Bengal, the British intervened once again. This resulted in the first (1824–1826) of three wars with Burma and the British annexation of Assam, Arakan and Tenasserim. By 1886 Upper Burma was brought under British control.

Although the Australian coast had been progressively delineated since about 1600 AD, colonisation of the country only began with the establishment of a penal colony in New South Wales in 1788. Fear of France's ambitions in the region prompted the settlement of King George Sound in 1827. Finally, with the establishment of the Swan River Colony in 1829, Britain laid claim to the whole Australian continent.

As Fisher observes (1966: 144), colonial policies in Southeast Asia during this period were largely determined by events in Europe. Britain was in the forefront of the Industrial Revolution and had emerged from the Napoleonic Wars as a major sea power. Its vast gains in overseas territories in the Indian Ocean Basin were at the expense of the Dutch and French. The British formally gained the Cape Colony and Ceylon from the Dutch at the Congress of Vienna in 1815. Other territorial gains in that year included the Laccadive, Maldives, Mauritius and Seychelles islands and the Chagos archipelago.

Britain's sphere of influence on the Indian subcontinent extended along the Indo-Gangetic Plain and the eastern seaboard of India. It not only built up its power in India, but also acquired Singapore and Malacca. Peninsular Malaya progressively came under British control during the 19th century. The British North Borneo Company controlled Sabah, and Sarawak became the personal territory of the Brooke family (Figure 2.24).

THE DECLINE OF EUROPEAN IMPERIALISM IN THE INDIAN OCEAN REGION

The opening of the Suez Canal in 1869 was a milestone for Britain's maritime domination of the basin. By now it claimed virtual control of the approaches to the basin: from the northwest by possession of the Canal; from the southwest by occupation of the Cape; from the southeast by the formal colonisation of Australia; and from the northeast by the establishment of the base at Singapore.

Between 1815 and 1914, under the impact of the Industrial Revolution and of emerging nationalism, the character of European imperialism changed. Whereas historically the search for the riches of the Orient had led to the establishment of trading bases and strategic outposts, it was the quest for territory that opened the door for late 19th century European penetration into the basin. By 1914 the major European powers had seized nearly 90 per cent of Africa and a greater part of Southwest, South and Southeast Asia, either through direct or indirect rule. The partition of East Africa began when that part of Somalia which fronts onto the Gulf of Aden became British Somalia in 1884.

Tanganyika was occupied by Germany in 1886, whilst the British East Africa Company gained possession of Uganda and Kenya in 1888. The British South Africa Company took possession of Rhodesia in 1896. British also occupied Ottoman Egypt in 1882 and Sudan in 1898. Italy took possession of Italian Somaliland in 1883, and of Eritrea in 1889. France took Obock in 1894, the territory being commonly referred to as French Somaliland.

As a result of the *Treaty of Versailles* after World War I, Tanganyika and parts of the former Ottoman Empire, including present day Israel, Jordan, Iraq, and the coastal strip along the western seaboard of the Red Sea, Kuwait, Bahrain, Oman and Aden became British protectorates. These gains were strategically significant, for Britain now had important coaling bases at Simonstown, Mombasa, Aden, Bombay, Colombo and Calcutta, and a provisioning base at Singapore.

World War II precipitated the rapid decline of colonial power in the Indian Ocean Region. By exposing the fragility of the colonial regimes in the early 1940s, Japan gave an impetus to the anti-imperial revolt in Asia which was to be the dominant feature of the postwar world. Europe emerged from the war devastated and politically divided. Under such circumstances the pre-war colonial empires had no prospect of surviving. Not surprisingly therefore, the contemporary Indian Ocean political map is in sharp contrast to those of the previous four centuries. For the purpose of this study it is therefore necessary to review the changes that brought about the redrawing of the terrestrial and administrative boundaries in the geopolitical context.

THE POLITICAL ENTITIES OF THE REGION

The history of the African and Asian states of the basin since independence is one of chronic instability on the one hand, and of varying rates of economic progress on the other. There have been four major contributions to political instability. The first was seizure of power by military leaders in Egypt (1952), Pakistan (1958), Indonesia (1967), Iraq (1968) and Uganda (1971), with the stated aim of abolishing corruption and stabilising wayward economies. The second was the resurgence of long-standing regional, tribal and religious conflicts, such as Kurdish revolts in northern Iraq, Turkey and Iran, Naga unrest in Northeast India, Hindu–Muslim and Hindu-Sikh bitterness in Northwest India and nationalist uprisings among the ethnic minorities and hill peoples in Thailand and Burma. Ethnic violence in Ethiopia, Sudan and more recently in Somalia has resulted in mass movements of people seeking refuge in neighbouring states, and in a breakdown in the government systems, particularly in Somalia. The third was the onset of guerrilla activities in Oman (1965–1975), Israel (since 1967), Sri Lanka (since 1971) and periodically in Iran, Iraq, Burma and Pakistan. The fourth was the persistent intervention by the superpowers particularly in the Middle East region.

The retreat of colonial influence in the region began when responsible government was established in the Colony of Western Australia in 1891. A decade later a federation comprising the Australian States and Territories was formed, with its own constitution but under the nominal sovereignty of British. South Africa gained independence in 1910. Elsewhere, independence was only achieved after World War II, and after struggles involving varying degress of violence and civil disobedience. Resistance to independence was strongest in the colonies with substantial white minority settler populations, or with considerable European investment.

Continuous unrest forced the British to grant independence to India and Pakistan, formerly the Indian Empire, in 1947 and to Burma and Ceylon in 1948. The final processes of decolonisation in the region and indeed in the rest of the world can be attributed to the UN Declaration on the granting of Independence to Colonial Countries and Peoples, which was adopted on 14 December 1960. It proclaimed the "necessity of bringing a speedy and unconditional end to colonialism in all its forms and manifestations".

A special committee on the implementation of this declaration, known informally as the Special Committee of Twenty-four, maintained continuous pressure for its application to the remaining non-self-governing territories.

Britain clung to its strategic base of Singapore until 1965, fought a long war against insurgents before granting independence to Malaya in 1963 and resisted Indonesian attempts to annex Sarawak and Brunei. Sarawak and Sabah were incorporated into the Malaysian Federation in 1963, and Brunei was given internal self-government in 1971. Also in 1971 Bangladesh, formerly East Pakistan, became independent.

Kenya, the Rhodesias and Nyasaland witnessed many bloody conflicts in their efforts to gain self-government. The British attempted to save the situation by creating federations such as that between the Rhodesias and Nyasaland (1953) and granting independence to some states: Tanganyika (1961), Kenya (1963). Northern Rhodesia (Zambia) was granted independence in 1964 whilst its sister state declared unilateral independence in 1965. South Africa, which had gained independence in 1910, left the British Commonwealth in 1961 over criticism of its policy of apartheid.

The three parts of Somalia had been controlled until 1960 by Britain. France and Italy. In that year, the British and Italian sectors were reunited to form the Republic of Somalia which came under a military regime in 1969. The French sector was claimed by the Republic of Somalia but a referendum decided in favour of retaining links with France. This sector was now called the Territory of the Afar and Issas. On gaining its independence in 1977, it took the name of Djibouti. Its economy, like that of the Comoros, remains reliant on France.

Its western neighbour, Ethiopia, was historically a monarchy until it was invaded by Italy, but was liberated by the British in 1941. Eritrea was incorporated into a federation with Ethiopia, in 1952 with formal recognition in 1962. This action fanned separatist sentiment, which generated protracted guerilla warfare for nearly three decades. Settlement was reached in July 1991, leaving Eritrea free to remain or to leave the federation according to the wishes of its citizens in a UN-sponsored referendum on independence. This was held on 23–24 April, 1993. Two months later, Eritrea was declared an independent state.

Until 1956 Sudan was an Anglo-Egyptian condominium. In 1991 it was a democratic republic with a revolutionary military regime. Its northern neighbour, Egypt, had treaty relations with Britain and a British military presence until 1956, when the Suez Canal was nationalised by Egypt.

By 1971 British influence in the Arab countries in the Middle East had greatly diminished. Iraq, a British mandated territory under the League of Nations, was granted independent status in 1932. A constitutional monarchy was established in Jordan in 1946; the State of Israel was formed in 1948; Britain granted Kuwait independence in 1961; Southern Yemen, which was a British protectorate, became a People's Democratic Republic in 1967; and the British protectorates in the Persian Gulf were granted independent status during 1971.

The islands of the basin were equally involved in their fight for freedom to guide their own destiny. Independence from France was gained by Madagascar in 1960, Comoros (excluding Mayotte) in 1975. Britain for its part, also granted independence to the Maldives in 1965, Mauritius in 1968 and the Seychelles in 1976.

The remnants of colonial links remaining in the region in 1991 were the territories held by Britain and France. The former possessed the Chagos Archipelago, which is referred to as the British Indian Ocean Territories. The latter claimed Mayotte, Réunion, Tromelin, numerous small islands in the Mozambique Channel and others in the southern sector of the basin (Figure 2.1).

Thus, with the exception of Saudi Arabia, Iran, Thailand, and Ethiopia (other than for the brief time it was occupied by Italians) which continued to enjoy some semblance of independence, the entire Indian Ocean littoral came under the colonial domination of the European powers in the years before World War II. Since 1945, however, nearly all Indian Ocean coastal states have won their independence.

GEOPOLITICAL ISSUES

Politically therefore, the Indian Ocean countries are independent states of recent origin. Many of them, like Indonesia, Malaysia, Singapore and Thailand, have achieved substantial economic development. The Persian Gulf States found wealth as a consequence of the Arab Oil Embargo of 1973. Countries like Sudan, Ethiopia and Somalia have, however, a never-ending battle with the vagaries of weather, drought and soil erosion, resulting in famine and low levels of health. Many of the Indian Ocean states are also politically unstable. Internal rivalries and contradictions in South Africa and Sudan; political instability and upheavals in Ethiopia and Somalia; insurgency in Iran and Iraq; frequent changes of government in Yemen; and border and frontier troubles in the Indian Subcontinent and Southeast Asia all have national, regional and global implications.

Despite these problems there are certain positive trends and cooperative ventures at the subregional scale such as the *Torres Strait Treaty* between Australia and Papua New Guinea, the *Timor Gap Treaty Zone of Cooperation* between Australia and Indonesia in the Timor Sea, and the Saudi Arabian and Sudanese *Common Zone of Exploitation* in the Red Sea. Many of the states in the Indian Ocean including Pakistan, India, Malaysia, Singapore, Tanzania, Somalia and the Arab States in the Middle East also support the non-aligned movement. In practice, however, states such as Pakistan and Somalia have re-aligned themselves politically with the superpowers when an external threat to their security has been perceived.

In order to introduce unity, create a sense of identity and establish zones of security, regional organisations such as the Association of Southeast Asian Nations, the Arab League and the Organisation of African Unity have evolved in the last few decades. Concern on marine issues that may create conflict played a part in the establishment of the Gulf Cooperation Council, and was responsible for the establishment of the Southeast Asian Programme on Ocean Law and Management and the Indian Ocean Marine Affairs Committee. Nevertheless, despite a general regional and global desire for peace, manufacturers of armaments and international financial institutions have continued to supply arms and money to those states that wish to be militarily prepared for any eventuality, or indeed, to overpower and absorb their neighbours. In addition, some of the regional states are known to allocate more money in their annual budget to defence spending than they do to education (Table 2.1).

In orders to ensure, therefore, that states can live in harmony and free from fear of their neighbours and of external threat, there are three basic geopolitical issues that require urgent attention. These are: the establishment of a zone of peace and neutrality; the equitable sharing and conservation of the marine living resources; and the careful exploitation and management of the non-living resources of the ocean.

Table 2.1 Selected Indian Ocean States: Comparison of Annual Expenditure on Defence and Education as a Percentage of Gross National Product (GNP).

COUNTRY	Per Capita GNP $US	Defence Exp. as % GNP	Education Exp. as % GNP
EGYPT	1,370	9.2	5.5
INDIA	307	3.9	3.4
INDONESIA	365	2.1	2.0
MALAYSIA	1,803	3.2	7.0
PAKISTAN	327	6.5	2.1

Source: US Bureau of the Census, *Statistical Abstract of the United States: 1990,* 110th Edition, Washington, 1990, pp. 839, 840 and 862.

Zone of Peace and Neutrality

The build-up of military bases and communication facilities in the Indian Ocean Basin by the Soviet Union and the United States in the 1960s and 1970s prompted Sri Lanka to propose, in 1971, the creation of the Indian Ocean Zone of Peace (IOPZ). A separate initiative by Malaysia in 1972 suggested that Southeast Asia through ASEAN be declared a Zone of Peace, Freedom and Neutrality (ZOPFAN). Despite a UN resolution in favour of IOPZ and of the associated neutralisation and demilitarisation schemes, the lack of implementation by Indian Ocean states was disappointing. Of the great powers, the Soviet Union, weakened by internal unrest and the collapse of Communism, demonstrated during 1991 that it could no longer maintain its military strength at home, let alone keep up a presence in the basin. France retained a marginal naval presence in Djibouti and Réunion to preserve its overseas dependencies and territories. The United States' naval presence was located at Diego Garcia, an island in the Chagos Archipelago, with a communications base at Exmouth in Western Australia (Figure 2.25).

The arguments used in the 1970s and 1980s by littoral and island states to maintain or increase their military strength related to the protection and exploitation of the resources of the ocean. If these countries were not successful in ensuring their own security, in defining their own interest and in cooperating economically, militarily and politically, the initiatives proposed for IOPZ and ZOPFAN could leave the way open for the domination of the Indian Ocean Basin by the People's Republic of China. Such domination might not only be political, but might also extend to the exploitation of the ocean's biotic and mineral resources.

Biotic Resources of the Indian Ocean

In comparison with the Atlantic and Pacific Ocean Basins the Indian Ocean Basin is not rich in biotic resources. There are a number of factors that contribute to this relative discrepancy (Fagoone, 1983; UNEP, 1985; Study No. 60). A greater portion of the waters of the Indian Ocean Basin lie between Lats. 23° N and 35° S thus averaging comparatively high water temperatures and correspondingly low oxygen content. There is limited nutrient discharge from land surfaces as a result of desertifications and of the extreme age of rocks surrounding the basin. On the other hand Krey (1973) recognised the following plankton-rich regions characterised by ocean upwelling: the coastal upwelling areas along the southern Arabian peninsula and between Australia and Indonesia; the Central Arabian Sea and Bay of Bengal; the Somali Current region; the Mozambique Current region; the Equatorial Current region and the Southern subtropical gyre.

In any ocean basin the continental shelves are the most productive fishing areas. The surface area of the continental shelf of the Indian Ocean is about 3,000,000 sq km, only 35 per cent of that of the Pacific Ocean's shelf and 37 per cent of that of the Atlantic Ocean's. The largest shelf areas in the Indian Ocean are found in the Arabian Sea, the Bay of Bengal and off the northern coastline of Australia. Much of the shelf area lying off the the coast of eastern Africa cannot be harvested by net fishing because of extensive coral growths within inshore waters.

For statistical purposes, the United Nations Food and Agriculture Organisation has delineated three marine zones (Figure 2.26 — Areas 51, 57 and 58). The combined total landing of fish, crustaceans and molluscs in these three zones during 1988 was 5,348,259 tonnes (FAO, 1990). Although this value represents only about 5.45 per cent of the world total for the same period, it compares favourable with those of the 1950s (1.3 per cent) and early 1980s (3.3 per cent) (FAO *Fishery Yearbook* 1990; Forbes 1987a).

Generally speaking, the fisheries throughout the basin can be classified as artisanal. Methods have changed little over the centuries, and fishing is largely conducted in close proximity to the coastline. The work is labour-intensive, and yield per unit surface area is

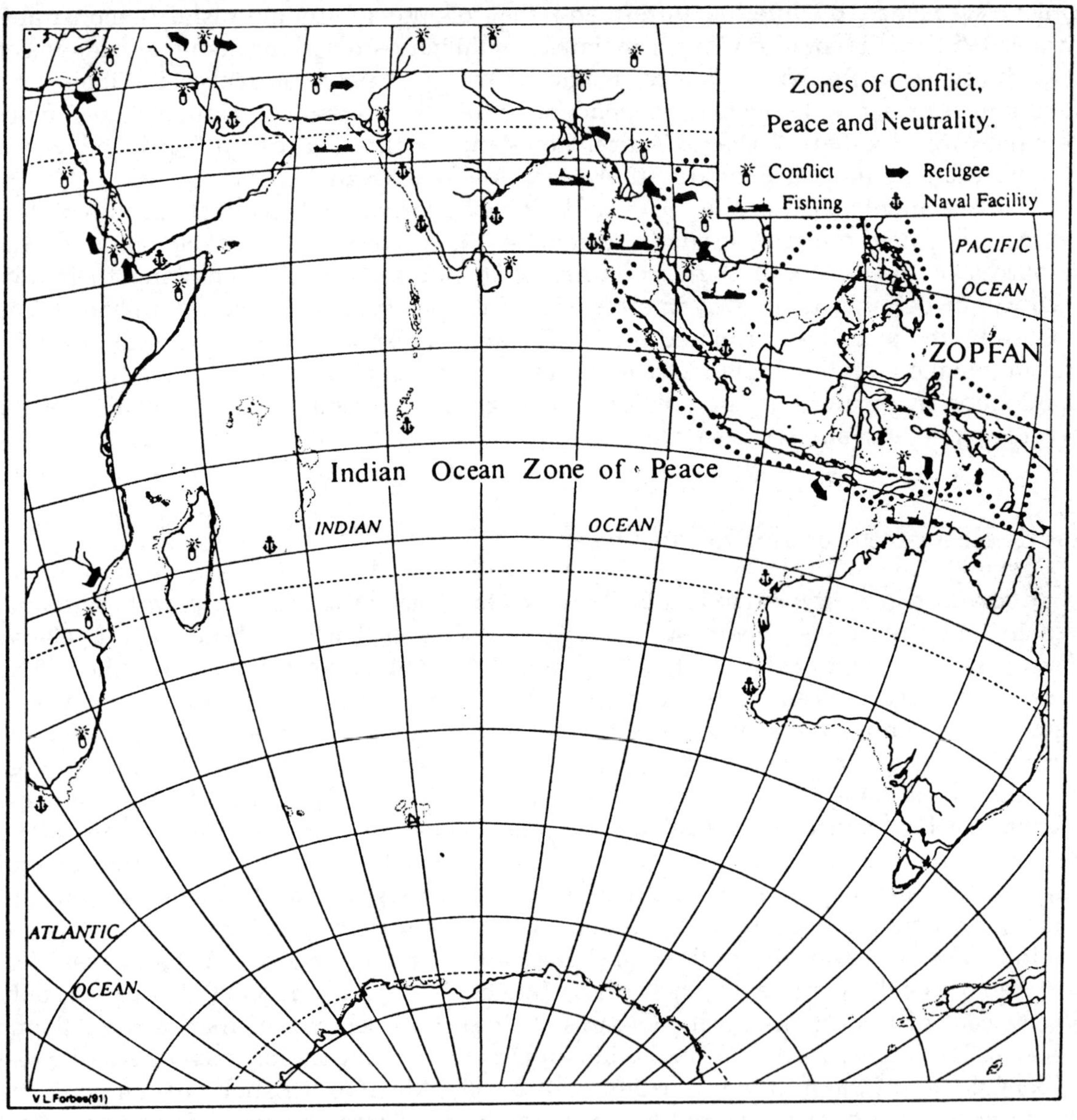

Figure 2.25 Zones of Conflict, Peace and Neutrality.

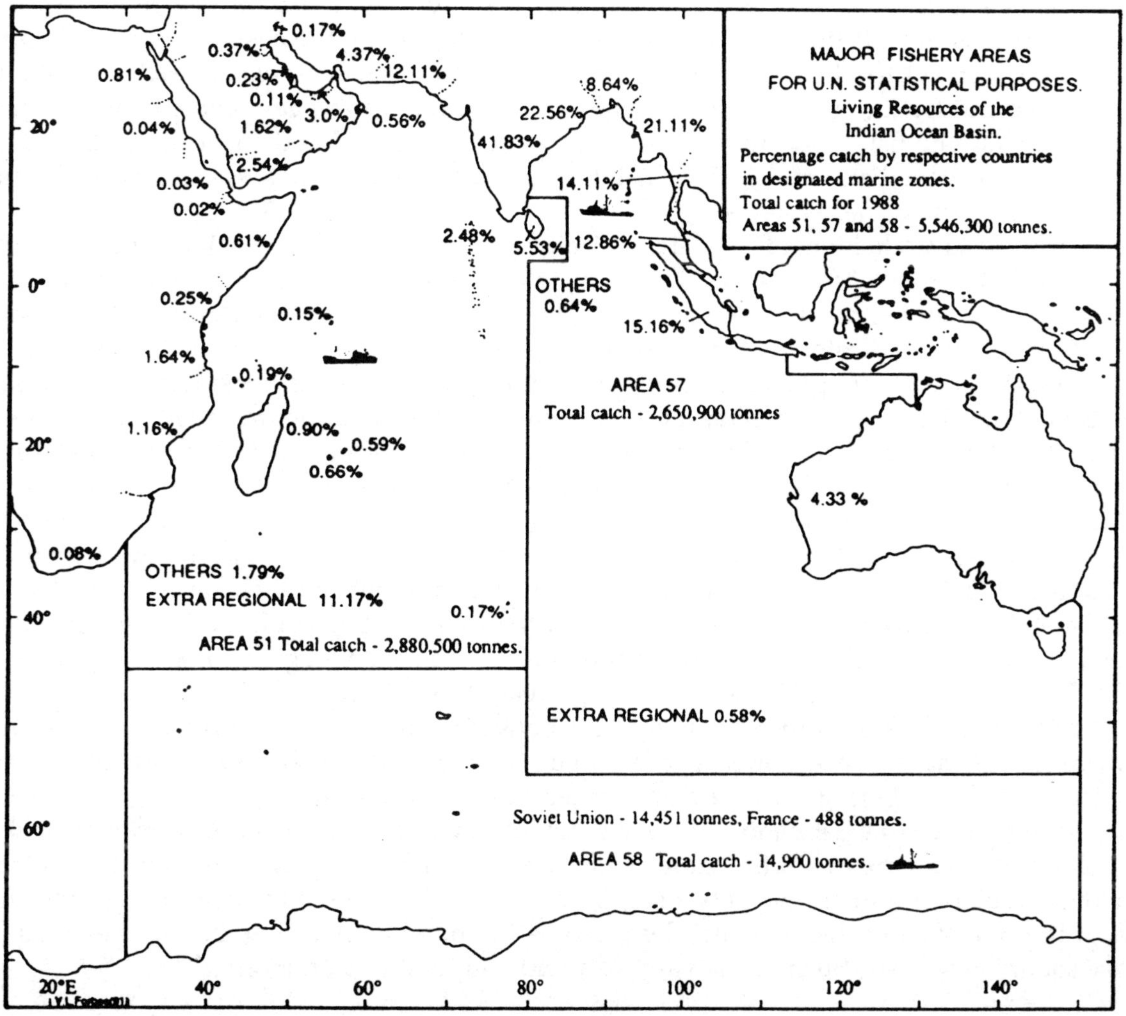

Figure 2.26 Biotic resources of the Indian Ocean Basin.

small when compared with fisheries in either the Atlantic or Pacific Ocean (Forbes, 1987a; FAO Annual Statistics). Pearl fishing was once one of the most important industries in the Indian Ocean Basin, but has now declined and is restricted to the shallow waters of the Persian Gulf, Palk Bay and off the northwest coast of Australia in the vicinity of Broome.

Whaling was another important industry in the southern waters and regions of the ocean basin. The International Whaling Commission has exerted a measure of control on the taking of whales. Countries like Japan are permitted to catch whales for scientific research purposes. This practice, however, has not met with the approval of conservation and environmental lobby groups.

The ocean fishery resources of the region represent an important factor in the lives of many coastal communities, who rely on fish to provide much-needed animal protein. Small-scale subsistence fisheries are particularly prevalent in the Bay of Bengal and off the west coast of India, off the coast of some Arabian states, along the east coast of Africa and off the coastline of the Malay Peninsula and the Indonesian archipelago. Such operations are carried out from a great range of small craft including outrigger canoes, dugouts and Arab dhows. The fishermen harvest a wide variety of tropical and sup-tropical fish. The fishing gear is varied and may include fish traps, handlines, drift nets, spears, longline gear and a variety of set net systems.

With the introduction of modern techniques, industrial fisheries have been established, notably trawl fisheries for shrimp in the waters off the coasts of Southeast Asia, northern Australia, India, the Red Sea, the Persian Gulf, and the East African littoral, and the Western Rock Lobster industry off the Western Australian coastline. In some areas commercial development has been very limited; in others, there is considerable potential, especially in the northern sector of the basin and the continental shelf off Western Australia. Rapid growth in fisheries had been experienced off Indonesia, Malaysia, Thailand and the Seychelles. Major efforts are being made by India, the Maldives and Myanmar to develop their coastal fisheries. Bilateral cooperation has been then linked to such initiatives. Exploitation by extra-regional fishing fleets is significant. In 1988 they accounted for 11 per cent of the catch in Zone 51 and about one-half of one per cent of the catch in Zone 57. Ninety-seven per cent of the total landings in Zone 58 were by such vessels, with Soviet fishing fleets predominating. Overall, extra-regional boats landed over 350,000 tonnes of Indian Ocean fish in that year (FAO, 1990).

A number of states in the region are both conscious of the need to protect, control and effectively manage the fisheries within their jurisdictional zone, and aware of similar needs outside it. Perhaps the greatest threat to a coastal state's fishery comes from encroachment and illegal fishing by one's neighbours. Such actions are prevalent in the waters of the Andaman, South China, Timor and Arafura Seas and in the northern sector of the Arabian Sea in the vicinity of India and Pakistan. It is difficult to determine the magnitude of such problems, much less resolve them, while maritime boundaries remain inadequately defined. Such is the case also with mineral exploitation.

Mineral Resources of the Indian Ocean

Although the continental margin covers only about one-fifth of the whole seafloor, its mineral resources constitute the most important submarine resource (Figure 2.27). The continental shelf, and to a lesser extent the continental slope, are rich in oil and gas. Fossil fuels continue to be the main source for energy consumption, although the global demand for oil slowed down as a consequence of the Arab Oil Embargo of 1973 (Beazley, 1981).

The major areas of oil and gas extraction in this region are the Persian Gulf, the Gulf of Suez, Bombay High off the Gulf of Cambay, the Gulf of Martaban, the Java Sea off the coast of Java, the Northwest Shelf of Western Australia, the Timor Sea and the Bass Strait. Exploration in areas with geological potential continues as new fields come on stream, especially in the Timor Sea basin.

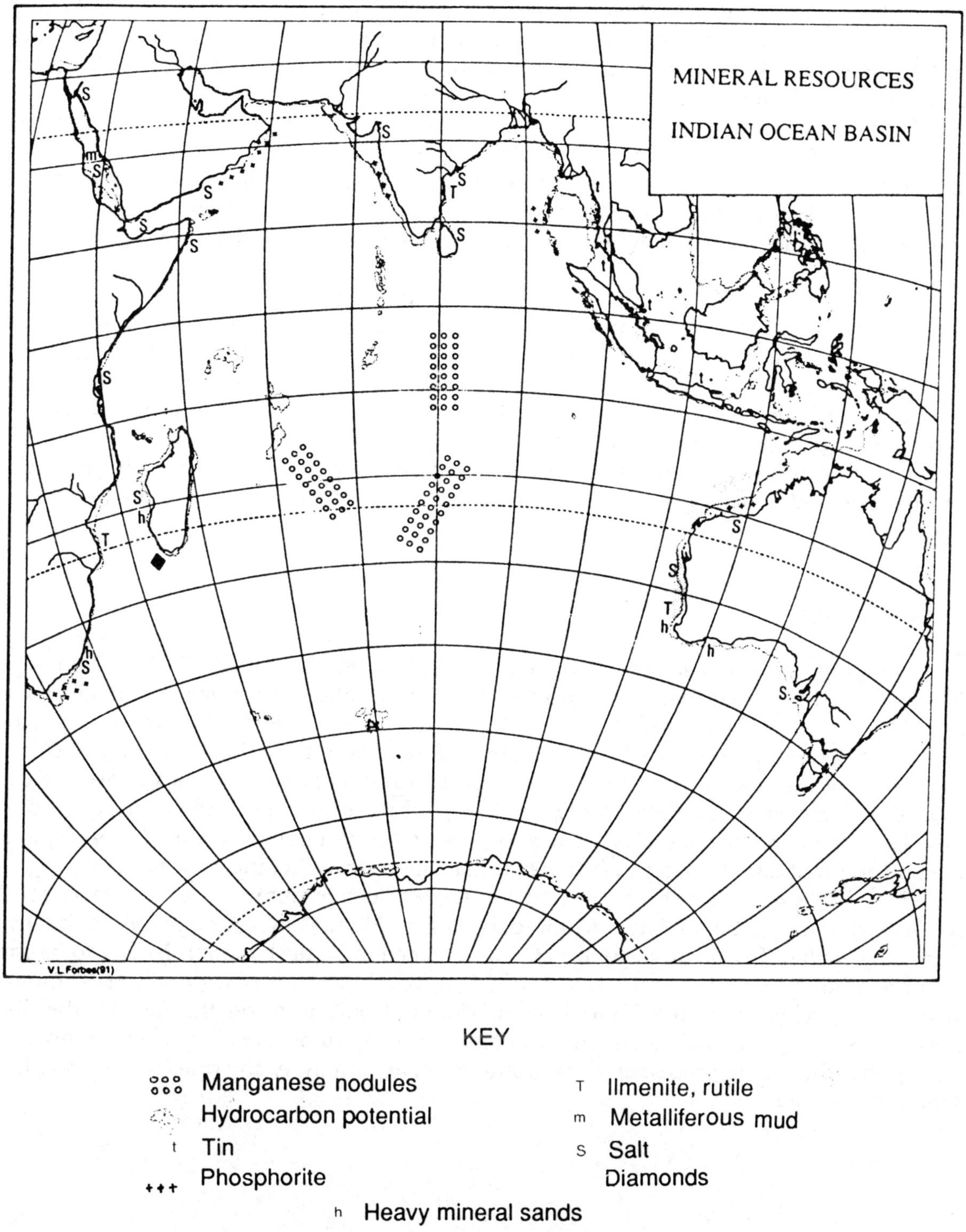

Figure 2.27 Mineral resources of the Indian Ocean Basin.

Certain parts of the deep ocean floor are strewn with millions of tonnes of polymetallic nodules containing iron, manganese, nickel, cobalt, copper, vanadium and molybdenum. Metalliferous ore deposits have also been identified on the ocean floor, and their locations have been related to past and present tectonic plate boundaries. Several geological investigations during the 1960s reported finding enrichments of manganese and iron in the sediments over wide areas of the ocean floor and in particular along the plate boundaries in the vicinity of the Mid-Indian Ocean Ridge.

Deep-sea drilling in the Red Sea during the early 1960s uncovered several metalliferous deposits associated with hot brines. Such deposits are located generally in the northern sector of the Red Sea and in water depths greater than 1000 m. The Atlantis II Deep (Lat. 25° N, Long. 40° E) brine pool is of current commercial interest. Covering an area of about 60 sqkm, its metalliferous mud lies about 2000 m below the sea surface and varies in thickness from two to 25 m (Borgese, 1985).

Placer deposits are concentrations of heavy, resilient and chemically-resistant minerals separated from existing ore bodies by weathering. These minerals either remain *in situ* on the land, or are transported and concentrated in sands and gravels found in river deltas and on beaches. Sections of the coastlands of Sri Lanka, Southwest India, Southeast Asia and Western Australia have deposits of ilmenite, monazite and zircon ores.

Rocks and unconsolidated sediments of marine origin in which the phosphate mineral apatite occurs in significant quantity are termed phosphorites. Apatite is used in the manufacture of phosphate fertilisers and certain phosphorus-based chemicals. In the Indian Ocean basin phosphorite deposits are found along the Agulhas Bank off the coast of southern Africa, and along the continental margin south of the Arabian Peninsula. Lesser quantities have been deposited along the west coast of India, the Andaman Islands and off the coast of northwestern Australia.

Marine aggregates comprising sand, gravel or shell deposits are used primarily in the construction industry. They are, at present, quantitatively the most important marine mineral deposit mined.

CONCLUSION

This chapter has outlined the geographical and political setting of the basin and highlighted the issues that call for urgent action in the settlement of jurisdictional maritime zones. It has demonstrated that the conditions, standards and concepts of exploiting the resources on the land are often different from those for the oceans and that the wealth of the oceans has eluded the terrestrial concepts of boundaries and ownership. Indeed, the controlled utilisation of the resources of the sea requires the codification of a new law for the management of such resources and for the penetration of ocean space, beyond the traditional concept of the territorial sea of three nautical miles.

This issue was brought to the attention of the world community on 1 November 1967 by Dr Arvid Pardo, Malta's Ambassador to the United Nations, when he proposed that the mineral wealth of the ocean beyond national jurisdiction be declared by the UN to be the "common heritage of mankind" (UN, 1967). This revolutionary concept was the stimulus which eventually led to the Third United Nations Conference on the Law of the Sea (1973–1982). The following chapter examines the maritime zonal concepts proposed during the negotiating processes of the Conference, and analyses the rules for defining the limits of the zones.

CHAPTER THREE

REGULATING THE USE AND MANAGEMENT OF THE OCEANS

INTRODUCTION

This Chapter examines the contribution of the Third United Nations Conference on the Law of the Sea (UNCLOS III), explains the definitions and significance of the terms associated with the determination of maritime boundaries, and examines the legal relationship of the various maritime jurisdiction zones with the Baseline and the apparent overlap of the Exclusive Economic Zone with the Contiguous Zone and the Continental Shelf. It also analyses the differences between the rights of the coastal states and those of aliens within these jurisdictional zones.

UNCLOS III

The first session of the Third United Nations Conference on the Law of the Sea was held in Caracas in 1973, after lengthy preparations following the historic address to the United Nations General Assembly by Dr Pardo in 1967. Subsequent negotiations were spread over 11 sessions in the following nine years. During the 93 weeks of negotiations, 157 states and many non-government organizations were involved in the drafting of the Convention of the Law of the Sea (CLOS). The final product was a compendium of 320 articles covering every aspect of the law of the sea, with nine very complex annexes and a number of conference resolutions, some of which are just as important as the Convention itself.

It was the final day of the Eleventh Session of UNCLOS III, at Montego Bay, Jamaica, when 119 states signed the Convention. This event, on 10 December 1982 marked both the end of more than a decade of negotiations and the beginning of the important task of implementing a new regime for the regulation of the use and management of the oceans. Conspicuous by their absence were signatories from those states who held some reservations over the provisions of CLOS. These included Italy, Belgium, the Federal Republic of Germany, the United States of America, Japan, and the United Kingdom, although Japan did sign later. Details on international alignments during this period are documented in the files of the United Nations (Churchill *et al.*, 1973, Forbes, 1987a).

In April 1987, 159 States had signed the Convention. By October 1993 the number of states that had ratified it was 56. Under the provisions of Article 308, the Convention will enter into force 12 months after the date of deposit of the 60th instrument of ratification or accession, both being instruments which formally signify a state's consent to be bound by CLOS (see Appendix B). Signatory states are entitled to participate with voting rights in the Preparatory Commission (PREPCOM) for the International Seabed Authority (ISA) and for the International Tribunal for the Law of the Sea.

This new Convention is expected to replace the four 1958 Geneva Conventions. In addition to the Internal Waters, the Territorial Sea and the Contiguous Zone, five additional jurisdictional zones are in the course of attracting general recognition. These are: the Continental Shelf, the Exclusive Economic Zone (EEZ), the Exclusive Fishing

Zone, Archipelagic Waters and the Area (Figure 3.1). Their existence permits coastal states to claim rights over the adjacent seas for a variety of purposes and over varying distances from an established datum.

BASELINES

The starting point for measuring the breadth of the various jurisdictional zones extending from the coast seaward is the Baseline. Naturally, until a coastal state establishes its baseline, it is unable to define its maritime boundaries.

Article 5 of CLOS states that "the normal baseline for measuring the maritime zones is the low-water mark along the coast which is marked on large-scale (hydrographic) charts officially recognized by the coastal state". The datum for the low-water mark or low-tide elevation (LTE) has been defined in different ways (Article 13). For example, in determining its baselines from which the territorial sea is measured, the Kingdom of Saudi Arabia, in Article 5 (a) of Decree No. 33, 1958 declared that the datum will be "the lowest low-water mark on the shore". The Yemen Arab Republic also adopted this datum. The advantage of selecting a low-water mark is that the coastal state secures thereby the widest possible area of the sea. On the other hand, the Imperial Ethiopian Government stated in Maritime Proclamation No. 137, 1953 that:

> Territorial waters of Our Empire are defined as extending from the extremity of sea-board at maximum annual tide of the Ethiopian islands.

Different countries thus use different data based on a range of low-water marks, such as Lowest Astronomical Tide (LAT), Indian Springs Low Water (ISLW), Mean Low-Water Springs (MLWS), Mean Low-Water Neaps (MLWN) and Mean Lower Low-Water (MLLW). The MLWS was advocated by delegates at an international conference at the Hague in 1930. The MLWS, also called springs low-water, is defined in the Hydrographic Dictionary as being "the average height of the low waters of Spring Tides", measuring successive low-waters during the period when the moon's declination is at its maximum of 23°30′.

Along the west coast of Australia, the official large scale charts have adopted ISLW, an arbitrary tidal datum which approximates to the level of the MLLW. This datum is also called Indian Tide Plane. There have also been moves to use the LAT, a level which can be predicted to occur under average meteorological conditions, and under any combination of astronomical conditions. In this connection, the Western Australian Department of Land Administration has been using Landsat Imagery and infrared sensing photography to determine LTE off the Kimberley coastline, because conventional aerial photography can only be used during daylight hours. The LTEs fringing the Ningaloo Reef complex off the northwest coast of Western Australia are depicted in Figure 3.2.

In case of islands comprising parts of atolls, or of islands having fringing reefs, the baseline is determined by the LAT (Article 6). Where a coastline is deeply indented or there is a fringe of islands along the coast, straight baselines joining appropriate points on the coastline may be used in drawing the baseline from which the breadth of the maritime zones is measured (Article 7). These lines must not deviate to any appreciable extent from the general direction of the coast. The sea areas lying within the lines must be sufficiently closely linked to the land to be subject to the regime of internal waters.

Article 7 (4) of the Convention stipulates that straight baselines may not be drawn to and from LTE, unless they pass under structures (lighthouses or similar installations) which are permanently above sea level. An exception exists in instances where the drawing of the baselines to and from such elevations has received general international recognition. On the other hand, Article 13 provides that, if the LTE lies within the territorial sea claimed from the coast of the mainland or an island, the low-water line on that elevation may be used as a point for a baseline system. However, if the LTE, which is located on a naturally formed area of land and which is exposed at low-tide level, lies

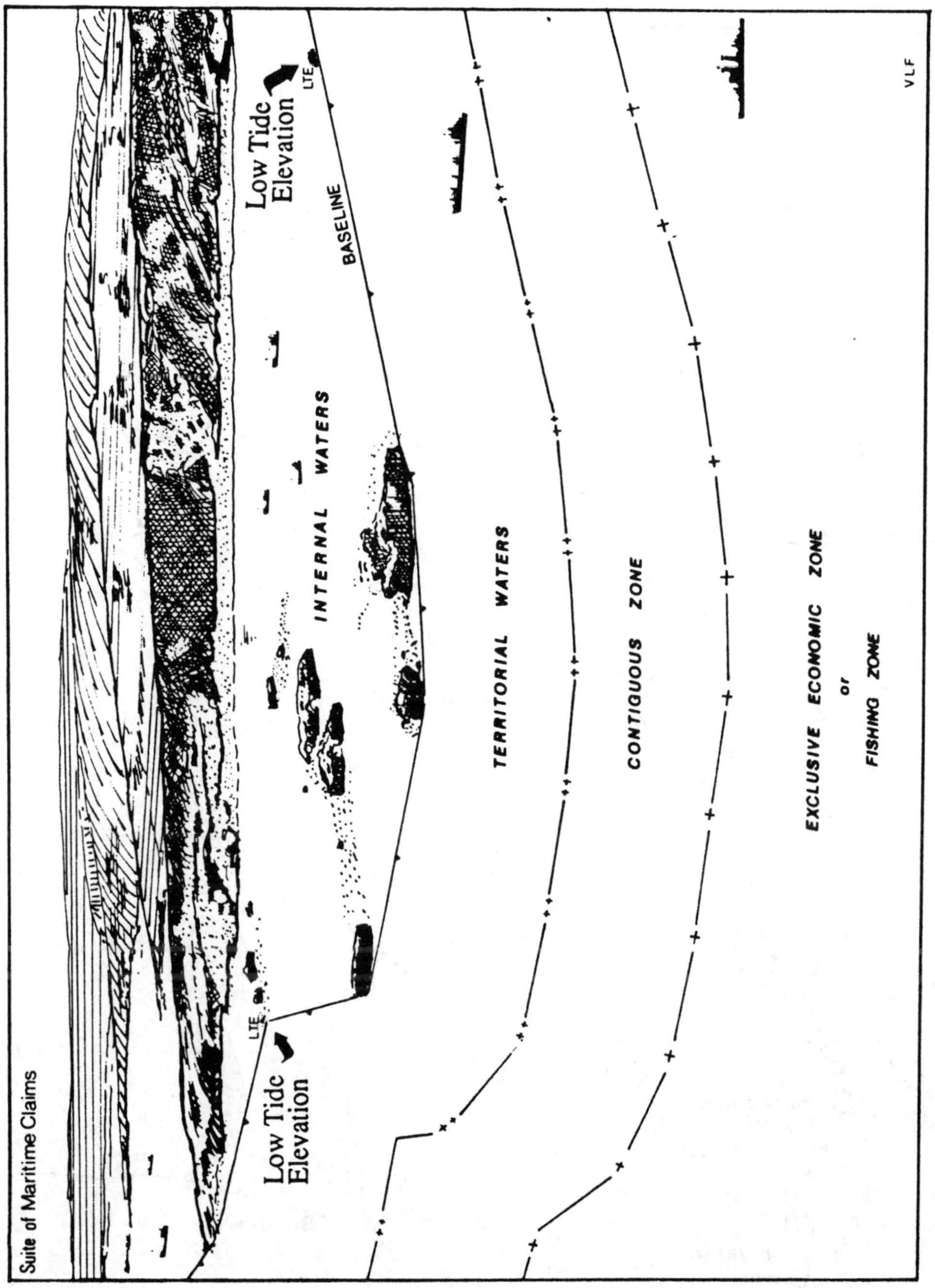

Figure 3.1 Maritime jurisdictional zones a coastal state may claim.

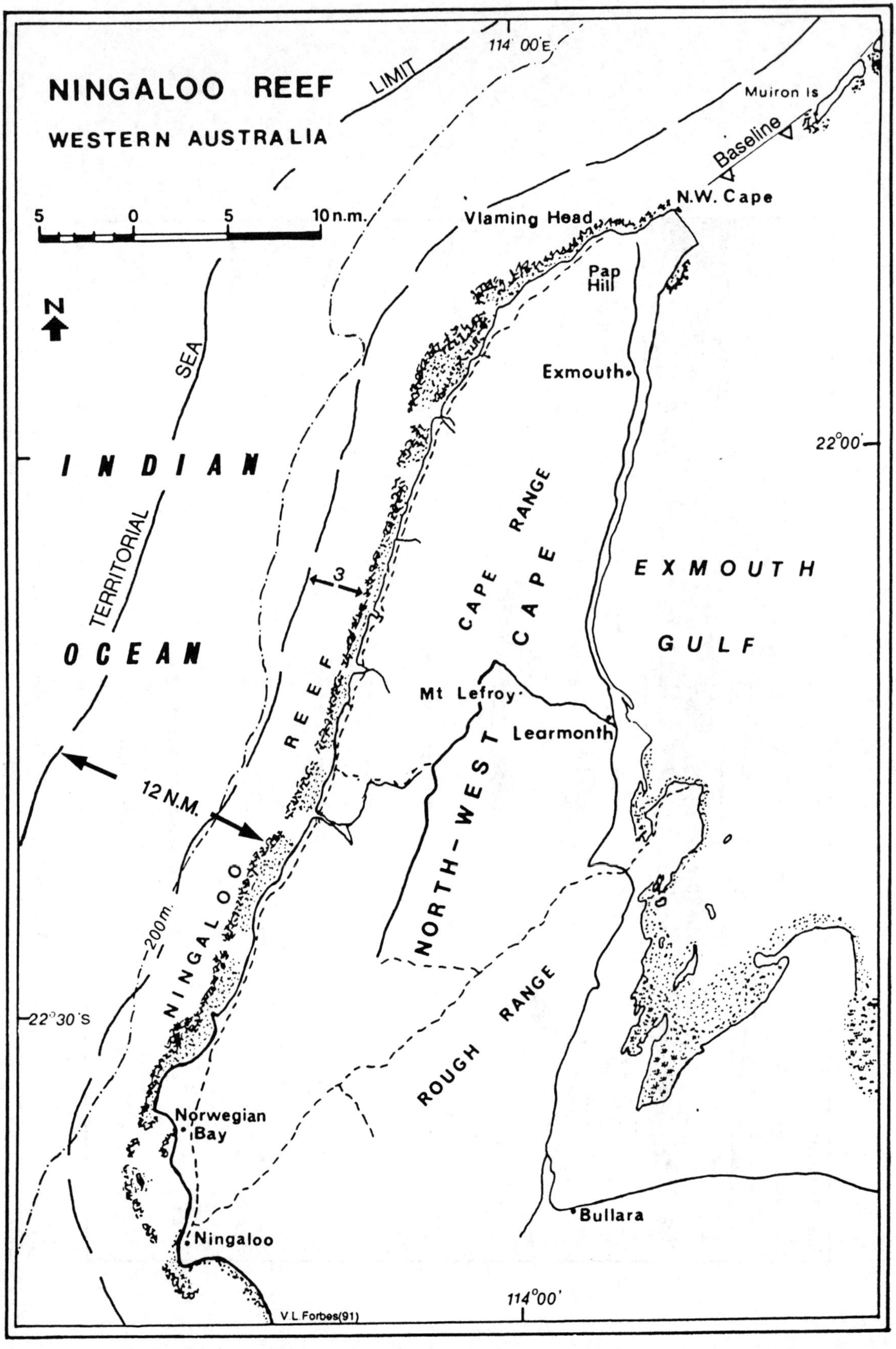

Figure 3.2 Low tide elevations of Ningaloo Reef, Western Australia. Australia's Territorial Sea belt of 3 nm (Pre-November 1990) and revised 12 nm belt (Post-November 1990) are delineated using the outer edge of Ningaloo Reef as a datum.

at a distance that exceeds the breadth of the territorial sea from the mainland or an island, it may not be used to generate a further territorial sea of its own (Figure 3.3). A coastal state may not apply a system of straight baselines in order to cut off the territorial sea of another state from the high seas or from an exclusive economic zone.

Coastal states may determine baselines by any method, or a combination of methods as provided for in Articles 5–14, and these baselines must be shown on charts of a scale or scales adequate for ascertaining their position. Alternatively, a list of geographical coordinates, specifying each geodetic datum, may be substituted. Either of these types of

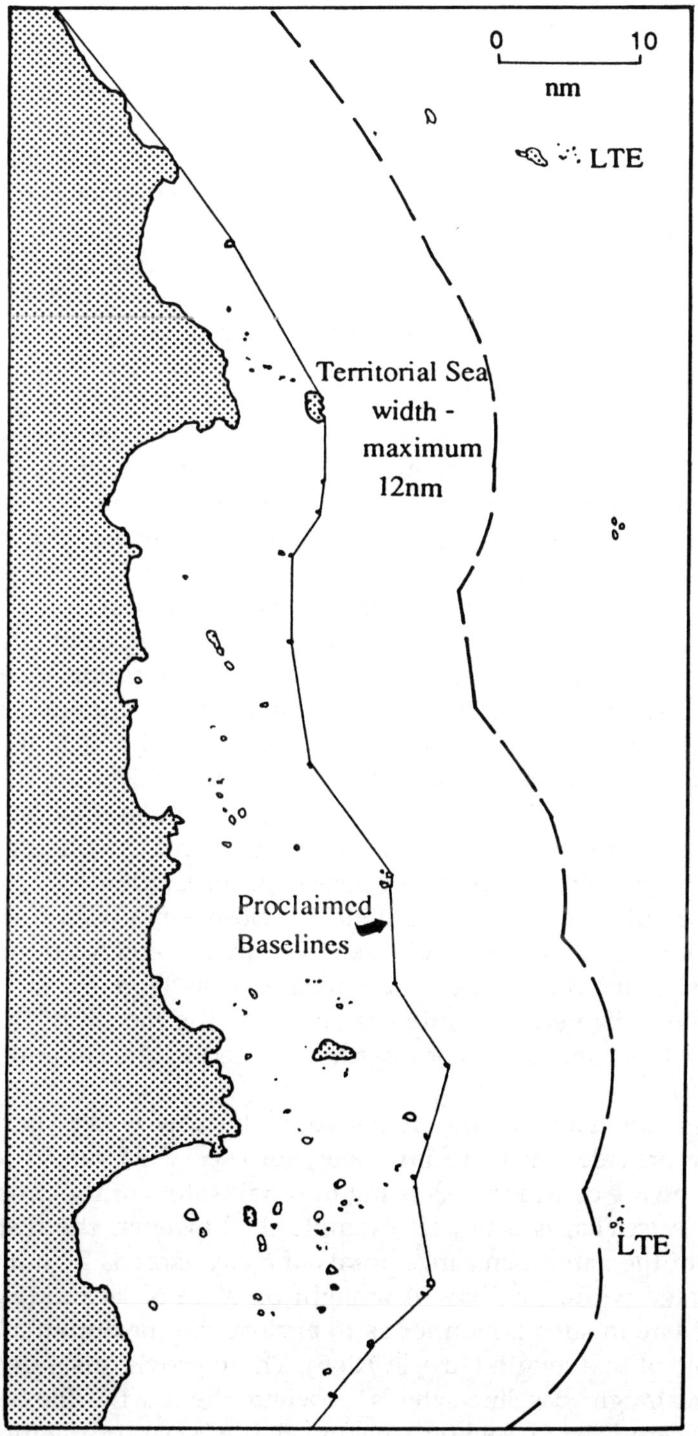

Figure 3.3 Low tide elevations lying at a distance that exceeds the maximum breadth of the Territorial Sea.

information must be given due publicity and a copy of each chart or list must be deposited with the Secretary-General of the United Nations (Article 16). Australia's first attempt to define a set of baselines was made on 31 March 1974, with the issuing of two proclamations. One proclamation dealt with the island of Tasmania and the other with parts of the coast of New South Wales. Finally, on 9 February 1983 the nation identified 297 points for its baseline around the mainland (Attorney-General's Dept., Aus., 1983; Prescott 1985). Figures 3.4 and 3.5 depict the straight baselines and some bay-closing lines which constitute part of the inner limit of Australia's Territorial Sea in the vicinity of the Northern Territory and South Australia respectively.

An analysis of the methods employed by coastal states in the Indian Ocean region to determine their baselines is presented in Chapter Four.

Archipelagic states have a special set of rules (Article 47) for the establishment of baselines. For the purpose of the Convention such a state is defined as a state composed "wholly by one or more archipelagoes and may include other islands" (Article 46: a). An archipelagic state is permitted to draw straight archipelagic baselines joining the outermost points of the outermost islands and drying reefs of the archipelago, provided that within such baselines are included the main islands and an area in which the ratio of the area of the water to the area of the land, including atolls, is between 1:1 and 9:1.

The length of such baselines must not exceed 100 nm, except that up to three percent of the total number of baselines enclosing any archipelago may exceed that length, up to a maximum length of 125 nm. The drawing of such baselines must not depart to any appreciable extent from the general configuration of the archipelago. Such baselines may not be drawn to and from low-tide elevations, unless they pass under lighthouses or similar installations which are permanently above sea level or where a low-tide elevation is situated wholly or partly at a distance not exceeding the breadth of the territorial sea from the nearest island. Figure 3.6 depicts a typical archipelagic baseline system adopted for the Houtman Abrolhos Islands which are located about 22 nm west of Geraldton.

In February 1960 before the rules were codified, Indonesia proclaimed archipelagic baselines which satisfied the provisions of Article 47 of the Convention. On the other hand, the Maldives territory was defined in its 1964 Constitution as the islands and the sea and the air surrounding and in between the islands, contained within a rectangle formed by parallels and meridians. The size and shape of the rectangle was amended in 1972, when the boundaries were set at Lat. 0°45'15" S and 7°9'30" N, Long. 72°30'30" W and 73°48'00" E (Figure 3.7). Prescott (1985: 161) notes that "there is no evident historic justification for these meridians and parallels", and the Maldives could well have defined archipelagic baselines in terms of Article 47 of CLOS.

The special formula for drawing baselines to close a bay was first prescribed in the Geneva Convention of 1958, and was retained in an amended form in CLOS. An indentation is not regarded as a bay unless its area is as large as, or larger than, that of the semi-circle whose diameter is a line drawn across the mouth of that indentation. On the other hand, in this context a river mouth is treated in the same way as the entrance to a bay (Article 9).

A bay-closing line may be drawn between the low-water marks of the natural entrance of a bay provided that the line does not exceed 24 nm in length. The waters enclosed by this line are considered as being internal waters of the coastal state. Exmouth Gulf, in Western Australia, is a typical example. If, however, the distance between the low-water marks of the natural entrance points of a bay exceeds 24 nm, a different closing line must be adopted within the bay. A straight baseline of 24 nm (Figure 3.8a) may be drawn within the bay in such a manner as to enclose the maximum area of water that is possible with a line of that length (Article 10: 5). These provisions, however, do not apply to historic bays, in straight-baseline sytems, or where the coast of the bay is shared by two or more states. A historic bay based on a historical title is part of the internal waters of the coastal state (Article 15). Encounter Bay in South Australia is a historic bay within the meaning of the law (Figure 3.5).

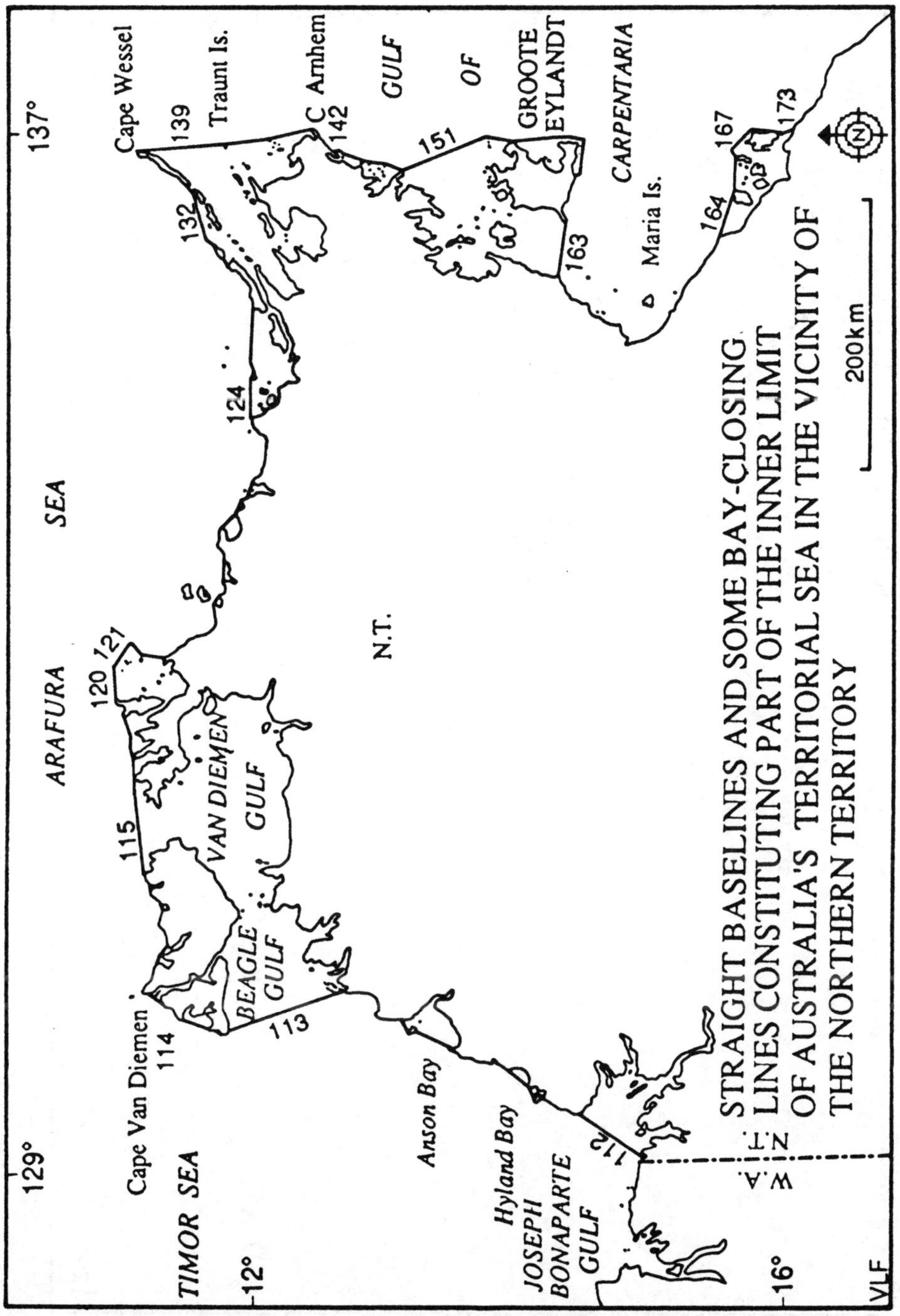

Figure 3.4 Territorial Sea Baseline system along the Northern Territory Coast, Australia.

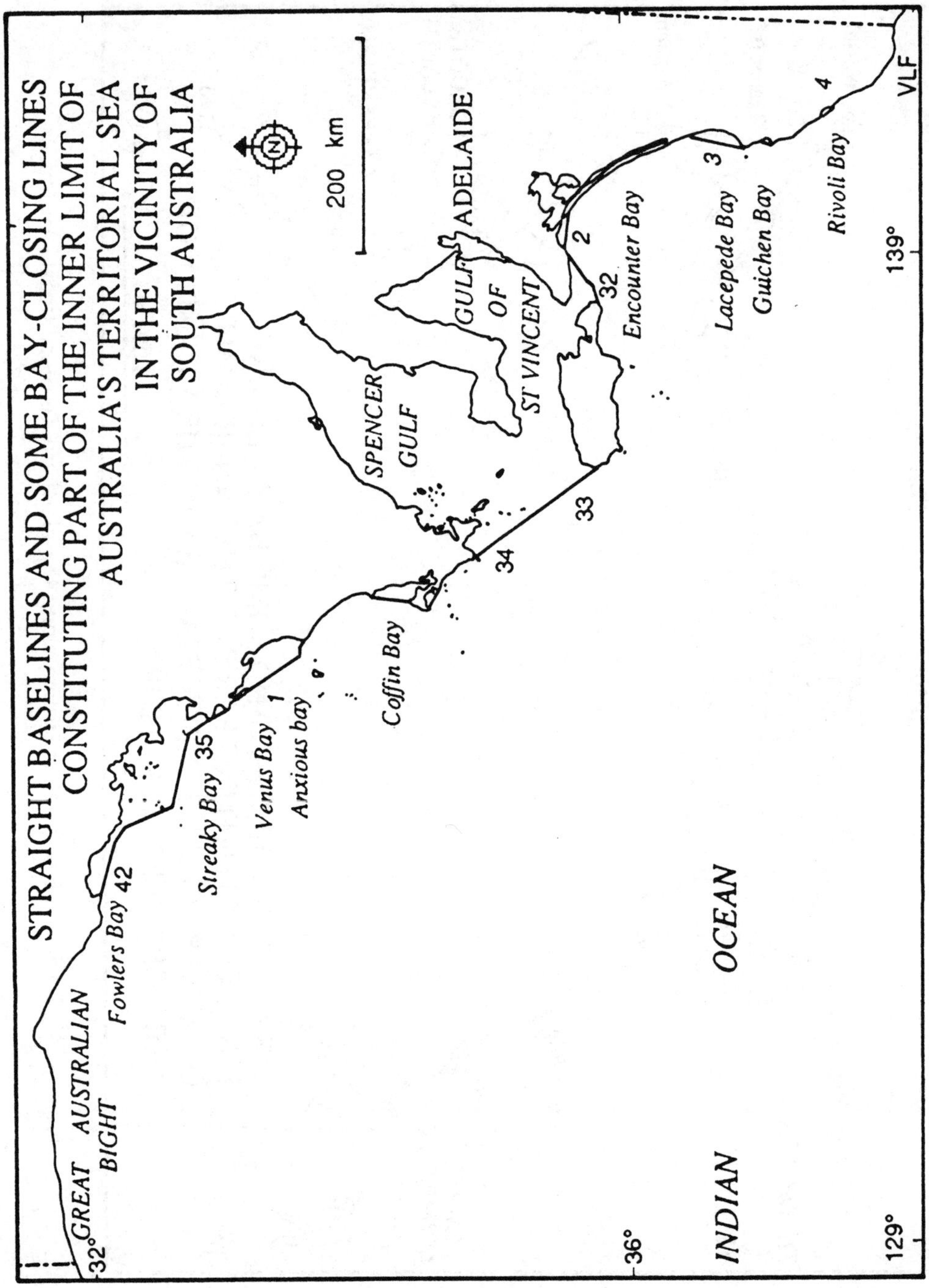

Figure 3.5 Territorial Sea Baseline system along the South Australian Coast, Australia. Encounter, Anxious Lacepede, Rivoli and Fowler Bays are proclaimed historic bays by Australia.

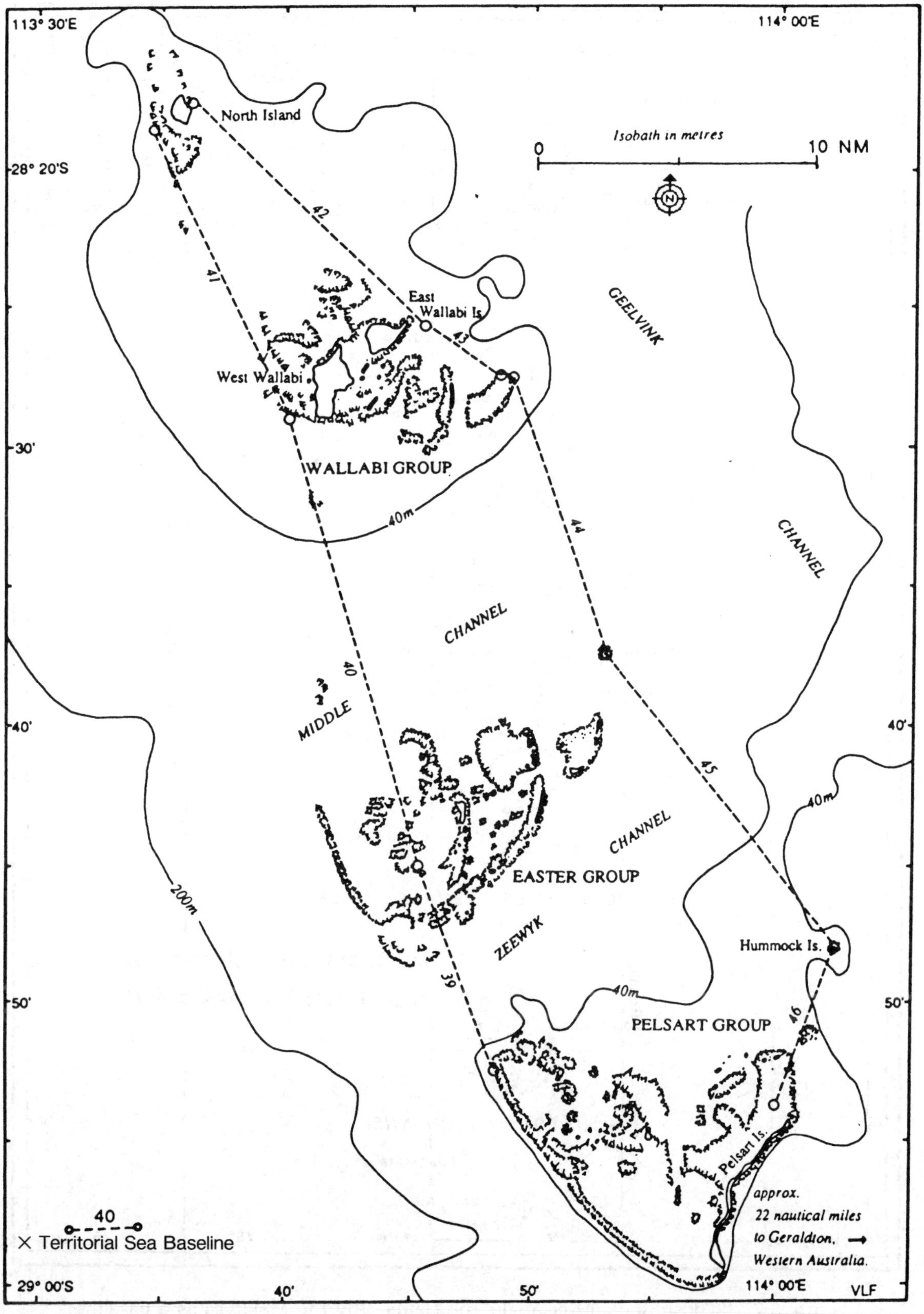

Figure 3.6 Archipelagic Baselines: Houtman Abrolhos Islands.

Finally, whereas offshore installations and artificial islands are not considered as permanent harbour works within the context of the Convention, the outermost permanent harbour works which form an integral part of the harbour system, may for the purpose of delimitation of the width of the territorial sea be regarded as forming part of the coast (Article 11).

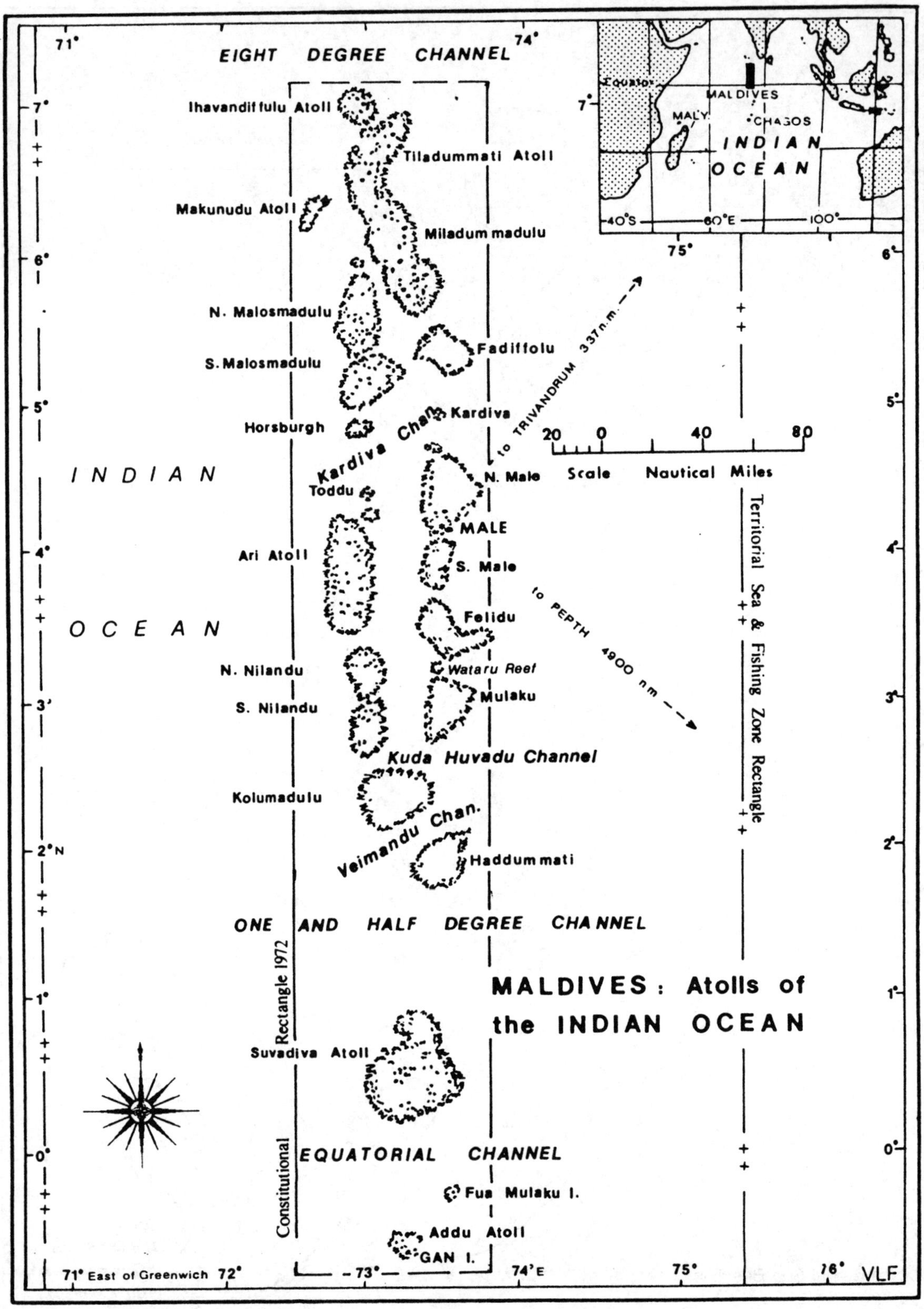

Figure 3.7 "Constitutional Rectangle" proclaimed by the Maldives as a Baseline.

INTERNAL WATERS AND TERRITORIAL SEAS

Except as provided in Part IV (Archipelagic States) of CLOS the waters on the landward side of the proclaimed baseline of a coastal state form a part of the Internal Waters of that state (Article 8: i). Such waters are created when baselines other than the natural

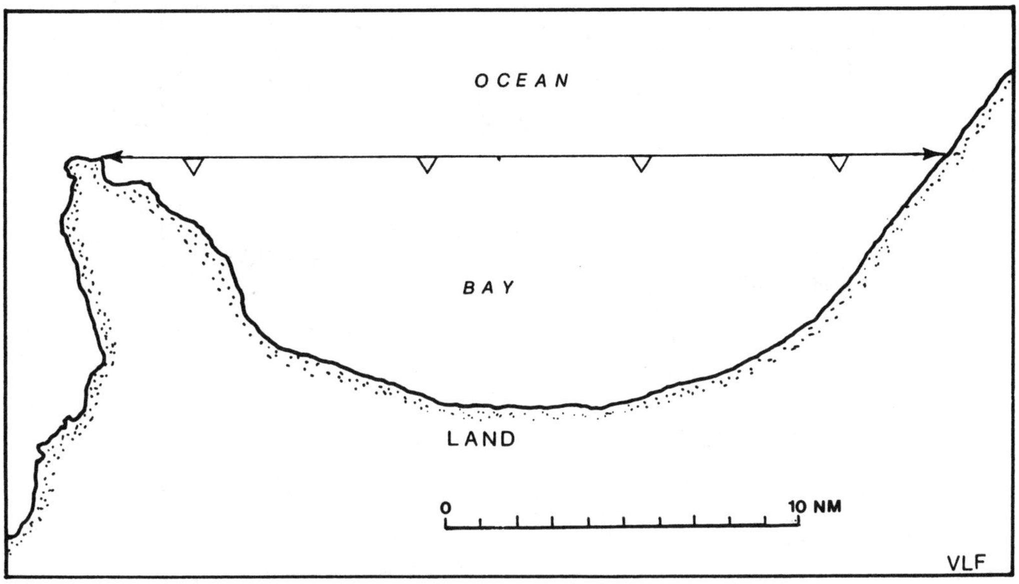

(a)

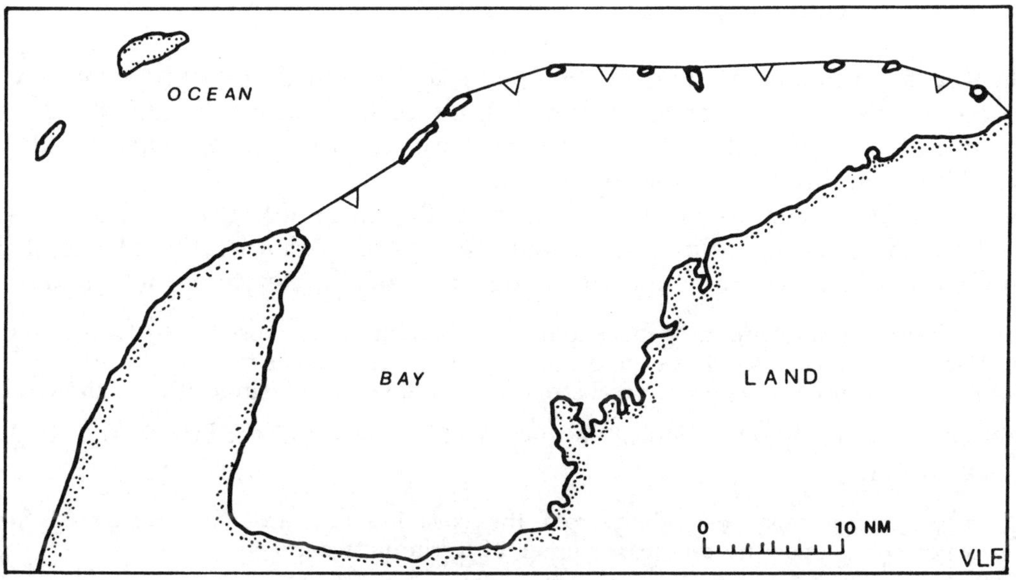

(b)

Figure 3.8 Rules for defining Bay-closing Baselines:
(a) a bay-closing line may not exceed 24nm;
(b) islands conveniently situated across the mouth of a bay may be connected by a series of straight lines.

low-water mark are selected. It must be noted, however, that where a straight baseline has the effect of enclosing as internal waters areas which had not previously been considered as such, the right of innocent passage exists in those newly created internal waters.

Shark Bay, Western Australia, is a fine example of the internal waters of a coastal state (Figure 3.9). Within the bay aliens have no rights with reference to fishing, carrying out scientific research, mining the seabed, laying submarine cables, overflight and navigation, except as provided by Article 8, which allows for the right of innocent passage. Australia also has complete authority as to the imposition of environmental legislation over the bay.

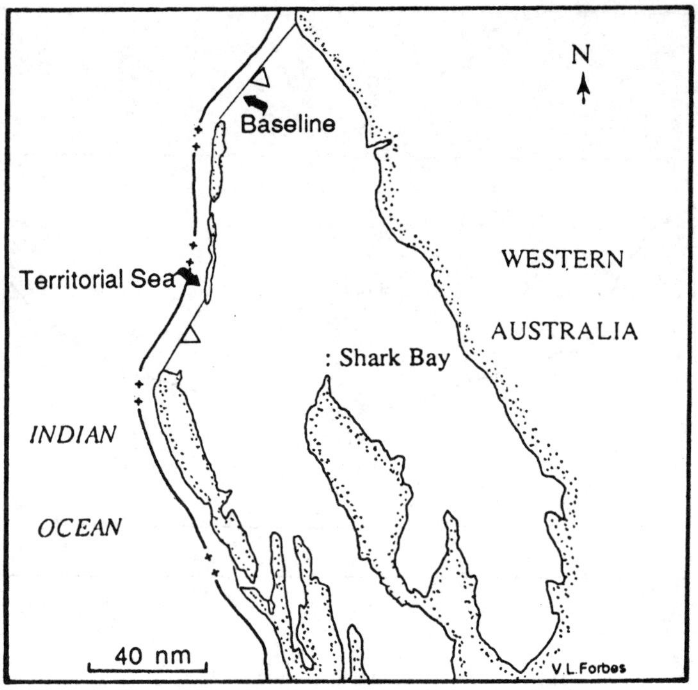

Figure 3.9 Bay-closing lines: Shark Bay, Western Australia.

The Territorial Sea is that part of the open sea over which a coastal state may claim jurisdiction for its own protection. Although traditionally one league (3.5 statute miles), the breadth of the territorial sea has been a matter of controversy for many decades, with seaward limits varying from three to 200 nm.

In a decision handed down in September 1910 (van Zandt, 1976: 44) over a special case submitted to it regarding fisheries in the North Atlantic, the Hague Tribunal determined that for bays contiguous to the territory of the Dominion of Canada

> the three marine miles are to be measured from a straight line across the body of water at the place where it ceases to have the configuration and characteristics of a bay. At all other places the three marine miles are to be measured following the sinuosities of the coast.

Section 1 of a treaty signed on 23 January 1924 between Great Britain and the United States stated that:

> the three marine miles extending from the coastline outwards and measured from low-water mark constitute the proper limits of territorial waters.

The interest in the sovereignty over offshore areas has greatly increased with the spread of extensive fishing operations and the extraction of hydrocarbons from beneath the ocean floor. The Geneva Convention on the Territorial Sea and Contiguous Zone which formally defined the territorial sea on 28 April 1958, set no outward limit for the territorial sea. Subsequently many Central and South American states laid claim to a territorial sea width of 200 nm. In the Indian Ocean region, Somalia claimed a width of 200 nm whilst Tanzania and Malagasy claimed a more modest width of 50 nm.

In 1982, however, Article 3 of CLOS reserved for every coastal state the right to establish the breadth of its territorial sea up to a limit not exceeding 12 nautical miles, measured from the baselines determined in accordance with the Convention.

It is therefore likely that most states will claim this maximum width, in conformity with international standards. Indeed, Nelson (1987) suggests that, as states ratify the Convention, they will adapt their maritime limits to the provisions of the Convention, either by extending their present limits or pegging back their previously excessive claims.

In the Indian Ocean region, in mid-1991, for example, while seven states still claimed a territorial sea of three nm breadth, 36 other states claimed a width of 12 nm. For this summary, each of the six Emirates within the United Arab Emirates has been included as a single state as five had declared a three nm and one a 12 nm limit. Israel which initially claimed a six nm limit, later extended its claim to the international norm. Likewise, Australia extended its claim from three to 12 nm on 13 November, 1990 (Figures 3.2; 3.9).

The territorial sea, the airspace above it, its bed and substratum remain under the sovereignty of the coastal state (Article 2), which, however, has an obligation to accord the right of innocent passage to foreign shipping (Article 17). Although a signatory to CLOS, the Republic of Iran in 1982 reserved the right to require prior authorization for warships to exercise right of innocent passage through its territorial sea, and to limit the right of transit passage through straits used for international navigation to the shipping of those states which had signed CLOS. The United States protested against this declaration (Smith, 1990: 75).

The increase to 12 nm in the breadth of the territorial sea means that many waterways such as the Malacca Strait, the Straits of Singapore and the Strait of Hormuz through which there was previously a belt of high seas, will become territorial sea straits. Provision for the passage of commercial and military ships and aircraft through and over such straits (Articles 37–44), along similar lines to the right of freedom of navigation on the high seas, was a concession that the principal maritime powers secured during the negotiations.

Nevertheless, attempts have been made by some nations in the region to block or hinder the passage of foreign vessels through some straits, most notably the Strait of Hormuz and Bab-el-Mandeb. Events between April and November 1987 in the Persian Gulf region and later during the Gulf War of 1990–1991 demonstrated the vulnerability of unarmed merchant ships plying these international waters. Such events make a mockery of provisions of CLOS relating to the freedom of navigation of the high seas.

As matters now stand, aliens have no rights to fishing, mining, or laying of submarine cables within the territorial sea. Scientific research can only be conducted with the express consent of the coastal state. Aliens do, however, have the right of innocent passage provided they comply with legitimate laws and regulations adopted by the coastal state and with accepted international regulations to prevent collisions at sea. They also have the right of transit passage through straits used for international navigation, but when doing so must follow designated sea lanes and traffic separation schemes. Aircraft of alien states may overfly straits used for international navigation.

The coastal state has complete authority to impose environmental legislation over its territorial sea, provided it does not hamper innocent passage. Some states may also impose strict guidelines for ships operating in narrow seaways. The grounding of the Showa Maru in the Straits of Singapore in 1975; the grounding of and subsequent oil-spill from the tanker Exxon Valdez in Prince William Sound, Alaska, in 1989; and the grounding and subsequent sinking of the bulk carrier Sanko Harvest in waters off Esperance, Western Australia in February 1991 prompted the coastal states concerned to review their shipping regulations with the aim of issuing more stringent requirements (Joint Statement, 19 February 1975, Malacca Strait Council).

THE CONTIGUOUS ZONE

Article 24 of the 1958 Geneva Convention on the Territorial Sea and Contiguous Zone entitled a coastal state to claim as a Contiguous Zone waters extending out to 12 nautical miles from the baseline; to operate in such waters in order to prevent infringement of its customs, fiscal, immigration or sanitary regulations within its territory or territorial sea; and to punish infringement of the above regulations committed within its territory or territorial sea. In other words the coastal state was given partial jurisdiction over a limited area of what were conceived as international waters.

Article 33 of CLOS contains a similar provision except that the width of such waters has been extended to 24 nm measured from the baseline, and the words, "in a zone contiguous to its territorial sea, described as the contiguous zone" have been used, to indicate that this zone is no longer a part of the high seas.

This concept of the contiguous zone could be linked to the 18th Century British Hovering Acts which were enacted to contain the activities of smugglers on the high seas who hovered beyond the legal range of the authorities. Faced with the prospect of heavy revenue losses through illegal imports and exports of various commodities such as wool, liquor, tobacco and tea, the government resorted to drastic legislation. The Act of 1790 extended the jurisdiction of Great Britain to marine areas ranging from one league to one hundred leagues from the shore. The extent of the operation of this and succeeding Acts was determined on the basis of several factors, including the distance from which the smuggler operated, the type of craft used, the extent to which the smuggling was carried on and the commodity smuggled. The Hovering Acts remained in the statute book until 1876 (Johnston, 1988).

Within the contiguous zone of a coastal state, aliens have full navigation rights provided they do not infringe regulations relating to the territorial sea. By contrast, overflight rights may be restricted. Aliens also possess the rights to conduct scientific research in the water column and to fish for all but sedentary species, if the coastal state has not proclaimed a fishing zone or an exclusive economic zone extending beyond the seaward limit of its territorial sea. They may also lay submarine cables within this zone, but do not possess any mining rights.

A coastal state may impose environmental legislation on the contiguous zone provided it is overlapped by an exclusive economic zone or underlain by a continental shelf. In the first instance, the coastal state has authority over the seabed and the water column; in the second, it can only legislate for the seabed (Article 194).

CLOS is to be commended for granting special status to the contiguous zone with reference to the control of traffic and trade in archaeological and historical objects. A coastal state may presume that the removal of any such objects from the contiguous zone without the state's approval violates the laws provided in Article 33. On 9 February, 1991 Thai naval authorities forced an Australian salvage vessel *Australia Tide* to hand over treasure taken from a 12th century shipwreck in the Gulf of Thailand. The vessel was eventually escorted out of the Gulf after being surrounded by Thai naval and water police vessels for two days. It was alleged that the Australian vessel had violated the maritime jurisdiction of Thailand and the cargo was worth millions of dollars. This claim was rejected by the ship's owners who stated that the position of the wreck was in international waters (The West Australian, 10 February 1991: 5).

The contiguous zone thus enjoys specific legal status only as long as the coastal state has not proclaimed an exclusive economic zone (Article 57) exceeding the outer limits of the contiguous zone.

THE CONTINENTAL SHELF

According to CLOS, the regimes of the Territorial Sea and the Contiguous Zone take precedence over the regime of the Continental Shelf in that part of the seabed that underlies the water columns of the territorial sea and contiguous zone. Geomorphologically, the continental shelf is defined as the zone around a continent extending from the low-water line to a depth at which the ocean bottom slopes markedly downward, and away from the continent. Conventionally, the edge of the shelf was taken to lie at 200 metres, or 100 fathoms. A more accurate average depth is about 130 metres. Continental shelves underlie about eight percent of the total ocean area. Figure 3.10 depicts the approximate location of the 200 m isobath in the Indian Ocean Basin.

Coastal states have increasingly tended to regard the continental shelf as a natural continuation of their land area, and therefore as part of their national territory. In what

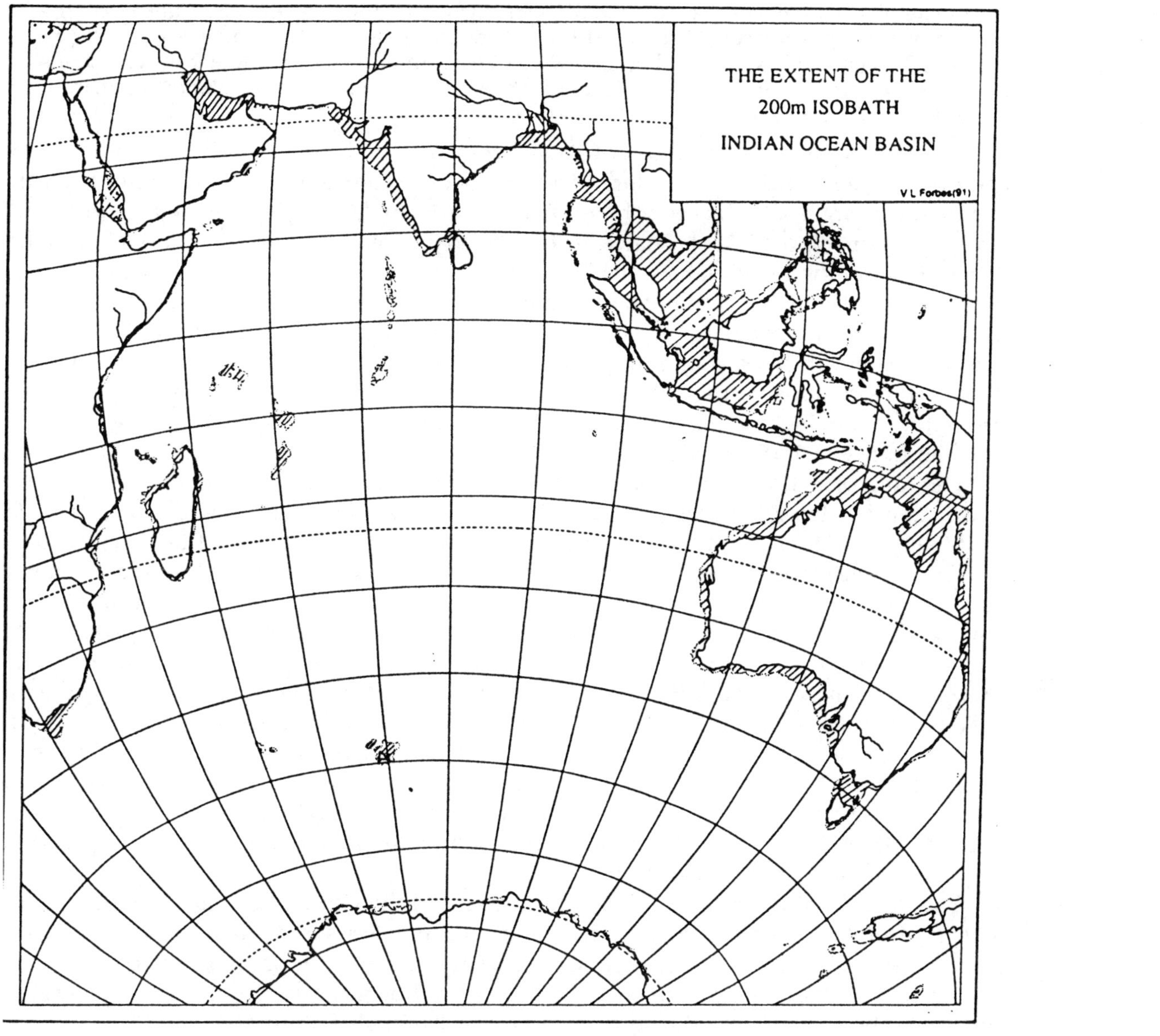

Figure 3.10 The extent of the 200 m isobath — the edge of the continental shelf as defined in the 1958 Geneva Convention on the Continental shelf.

is regarded by historians of sea law as a landmark decision United States President Harry S. Truman, in an executive order on 28 September 1945, proclaimed that:

> the natural resources of the subsoil and seabed of the continental shelf beneath the high seas but contiguous to the coast of the United States [are] declared to appertain to the United States and subject to its jurisdiction and control.

In what became known as the Truman Doctrine the United States had declared dominion over "land beneath the sea". Other states followed suit.

In 1958 the Geneva Convention on the Continental Shelf confirmed that the mineral resources of the seabed and subsoil and the sedentary living resources on the continental shelf were the property of the adjacent state. States which had the necessary technology were also permitted to exploit the continental slope beyond 200 metres.

The complexity of fixing the outer limit of the continental shelf has been a problem for coastal states since 1945. The situation was not improved by the definition incorporated in Article 1 of the Geneva Convention on the Continental Shelf 1958, which stated that:

> the term continental shelf is used as referring (a) to the sea-bed and subsoil of the submarine areas adjacent to the coast but outside the area of the territorial sea, to a depth of 200 metres, or beyond that limit, to where the depth of the superadjacent waters admits to the exploitation of the said areas; (b) to the sea-bed and subsoil of similar areas adjacent to the coasts of islands.

The 1958 legal definition thus bore no resemblance to the geomorphic definition of the continental shelf and only a rough resemblance to the geomorphic definition of the continental margin. On the other hand, Article 76:1 of CLOS redefines the area of seabed sovereignty of adjacent coastal states as the seabed and subsoil of the submarine areas that extend beyond the territorial sea throughout the natural prolongation of its land territory to the outer edge of the continental margin, or to a distance of 200 nm from the baseline from which the territorial sea is measured where the outer edge of the continental margin does not extend to that distance. In paragraph 3 of the same Article the continental margin is defined as comprising the submerged prolongation of the land mass, the slope and the rise but does not include the deep ocean floor with its oceanic ridges. Its average gradient must lie between 1:10 to 1:50 (Article 76).

The area of natural land prolongation over which Australia is now entitled to claim jurisdiction by this definition is about 10 million square kilometres (Veenstra, 1984). Its limits will, no doubt, be subject to negotiations between Australia and her neighbours.

The establishment of a definition of the continental margin required the development during the negotiating processes of UNCLOS III of detailed and precise formulae as to how the limits of such margins were to be determined. One approach, which came to be known as the Irish Formula because it originated from the Irish delegation, provided alternative means of establishing the outer limit of the continental shelf in cases where the continental margin extended more than 200 miles from the baseline. One alternative was to construct straight lines joining fixed points, at each of which the thickness of sedimentary rock was at least one percent of the shortest distance from such point to the foot of the continental slope. The other was to construct straight lines joining fixed points not more than 60 nm from the foot of the continental slope. Figure 3.11 interprets the definition of the continental margin.

The Soviet Union proposed that in no case could the continental shelf extend beyond 300 nm from the baseline. Where the margin terminated somewhere between 200 and 300 nm, the outer limit of the shelf would be the edge of the margin, which would be determined on the basis of geological and geomorphological data and, in the absence of such data, by reference to the second variant of the Irish Formula.

In the case of narrow continental margins the 200 nm formula as put forward by a group of Arab States has been recognised and generally accepted. A number of coastal states had by that time implemented an exclusive zone of a width of 200 nm.

Article 76 also authorised the creation of a Commission on the Limits of the Continental Shelf, whose function was to provide competent advice to states on the establishment of the outer limits of their continental shelves. The composition, functions and workings of the 21-member Commission are specified in Annex II of the Convention.

The Commissioners were directed to the Statement of Understanding Concerning a Specific Method to be used in Establishing the Outer Edge of the Continental Margin, when making their recommendations on such matters relating to the southern region of the Bay of Bengal. This request was in direct response to the argument put forward by Sri Lanka's delegates that the Irish formula was based on a configuration common to most, but not all, continental margins. In such cases the formula resulted in a limit of coastal state jurisdiction which coincided with the limit of the margin's significant resource potential. Where the geological and geomorphological characteristics of the continental margin were quite different, however, the Sri Lankans claimed that this result was not achieved.

The continental margin off Sri Lanka has two characteristic features. Although the foot of the slope occurs close to the coast it is followed by an extensive rise beneath which lies

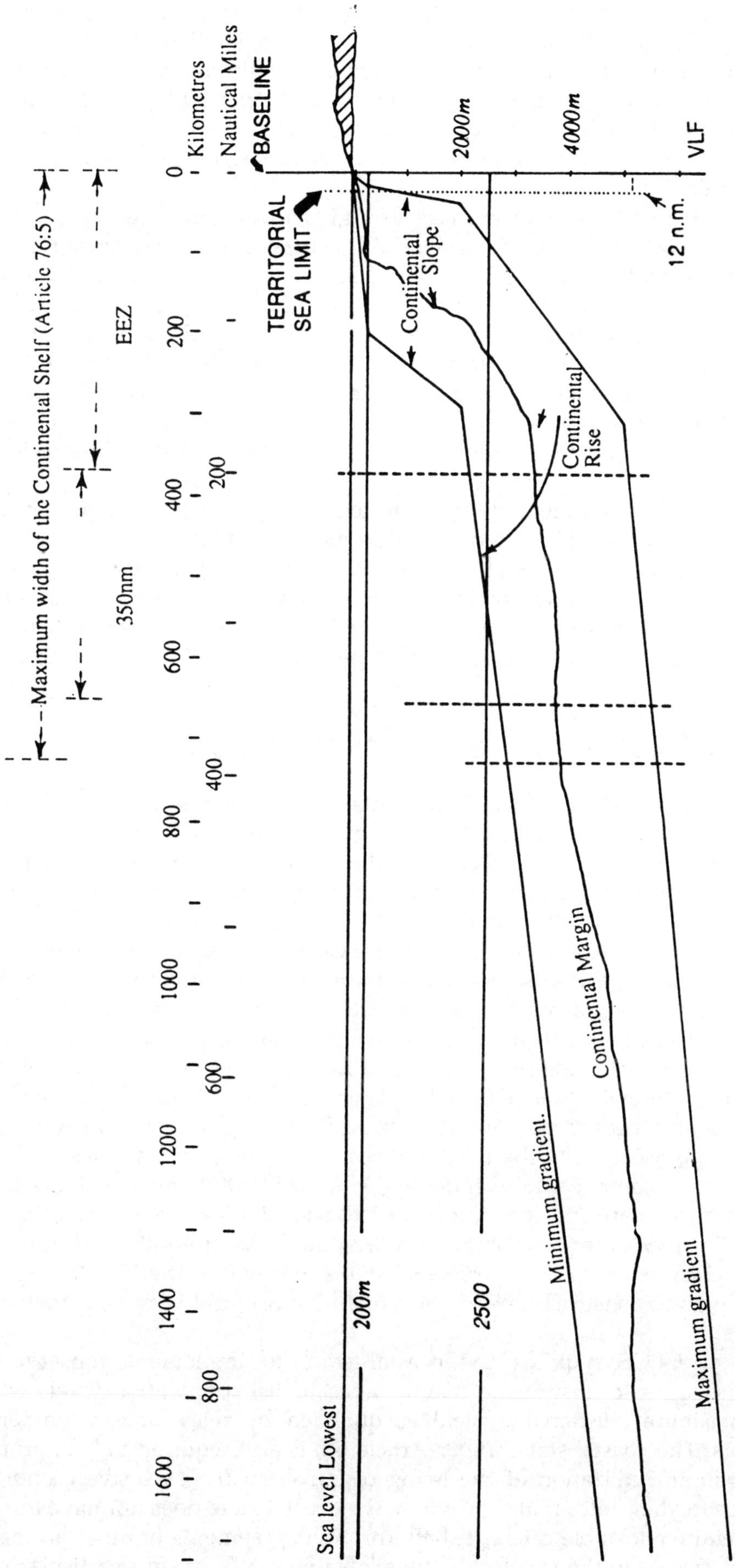

Figure 3.11 Two extreme cases of hypothetical continental margin, one with maximum gradient from the continent to the abyssal ocean floor, the other with minimum gradient. Between the two extremes is a fictitious sea floor.

the greater portion of the margin's valuable sedimentary rocks. The Sri Lankans argued that to apply the Irish Formula in this case would be to deprive their country of about half of its continental margin. They therefore suggested a third alternative to the Irish Formula, proposing that, in situations where such geological and geomorphological characteristics were displayed, the boundary line be delineated by reference to points where the sedimentary thickness reaches the minimum by either variant of the Irish formula in areas where that formula applies.

Whereas the coastal state may exercise its rights to explore and exploit its natural resources over the continental shelf (Article 77: 1), these rights "do not affect the legal status of the superjacent waters or of the air space above those waters" (Article 78: 1). Furthermore, the rights of the coastal state over its continental shelf should not infringe or interfere with safe navigation and freedom of the seas. In addition, within this zone, aliens have full navigation rights provided they observe the rules and safety zones designated by the coastal state. They also possess the rights to lay submarine cables; conduct research in the water column, but with consent from the coastal state if the research is of the seabed; fish in the water column, but not catch sedentary species (Article 77: 4).

The coastal state has complete authority to legislate for the protection of the seabed environment (Articles 194 and 200) provided that such regulations do not unduly interfere with the rights and duties of aliens. The Convention also permits aliens to conduct research in those areas of the shelf which are more than 200 nm from the baseline of the coastal state and which have not been designated by that state as areas within which exploration "... will occur within a reasonable period of time." (Article 246: 6).

EXCLUSIVE ECONOMIC ZONES AND FISHING ZONES

Although the Truman doctrine of the Continental Shelf provided for dominion over the land beneath the sea, it was not sufficiently specific about the exploitation of living non-sedentary marine resources. Concern over this issue during the 1960s and 1970s gave rise to the concept of an Exclusive Economic Zone (EEZ) which became a specific legal regime created by CLOS. Initially proposed by Kenya at Lagos in 1972, the concept of the EEZ had its origins in the claims of Chile, Peru, Costa Rica and El Salvador to 200 nm fishing zones in their respective adjacent waters in the late 1940s (Attard, 1989). Article 57 of the Convention gives a coastal state the right to establish an EEZ extending up to 200 nm seawards from the baseline and requires the state to provide details of its outer limits. Within the zone the State has preferential fishing rights and exclusive control over the exploitation of mineral resources. Archipelagic states and many coastal states would gain substantial advantages in claiming the full width of such a zone which is defined as an area beyond and adjacent to the territorial sea. Two exhaustive studies of the regime of the EEZ have been compiled independently by Attard (1989) and Kwaitkowska (1989).

If a conflict arises between the interests of the coastal state and any other state or states, Article 59 provides for a resolution on "... the basis of equity and in the light of all the relevant circumstances ...". Article 60 states that within the EEZ the coastal state has exclusive rights to construct, operate and maintain artificial islands, installations and other structures.

Article 61 of CLOS requires the coastal state to implement conservation and management measures to ensure the maintenance of fish population levels which can produce the maximum sustainable yield as qualified by relevant environmental and economic factors. The coastal state, under Article 62, is also required to "... promote the objective of optimum utilization of the living resources in the exclusive economic zone ...". The Article further notes that "... where the coastal state does not have the capacity to harvest the entire allowable catch, it shall, through agreements or other arrangements, give other states access to the surplus of the allowable catch, having particular regard to the provisions of Articles 69 [Rights of landlocked states] and 70 [Rights of geographically disadvantaged states], especially in relation to the developing states mentioned therein". CLOS, however, does not attempt to elaborate on the meaning of the objective "optimum utilization", the definition of which is likely to change with technological development and is left to the discretion of the coastal state.

Provisions for the enforcement of a coastal state's laws and regulations within the EEZ are contained in Article 73, which indicates that the penalties for violation may not "include imprisonment, in the absence of agreements to the contrary by the states concerned", or other forms of corporal punishment, but that offenders may be required to post a reasonable bond or other security, to obtain release after being arrested. The consequences of not posting a bond are, however, not clear. Most trespassing fishermen, for example, could ill afford to pay a bond. State practice in the region is varied. Thai fishermen have been apprehended and jailed by Malaysian authorities, being required to pay between US$ 12,000 and 40,000 to redeem their seized boats and about US$ 800 per head for their release from Malaysia's authorities (Bangkok Post, 8 June, 1991: 5). Pakistani fishermen operating off the Iranian coast in the Arabian Sea have had their vessels escorted into the Persian Gulf and confiscated. Indonesian poachers in Australian waters have been jailed and their fishing boats set alight by Australian quarantine and customs officials. Japanese and Taiwanese commercial operators illegally fishing in Australian waters have been fined in accordance with Australian laws.

Perhaps the most vexing question concerning the EEZ is its delimitation between states with opposite or adjacent coasts. In order to achieve an equitable solution, Article 74 proposes that the delimitation "be effected by agreement on the basis of international law", and cites Article 38 of the Statute of the International Court of Justice, in order to achieve such a solution. A provisional arrangement of a practical nature, without prejudice to the final delimitation, would be preferable to failure to proclaim the outer limits of an EEZ. However, where there is an agreement in force between the coastal states, the delimitation issue should be determined in accordance with the provisions of the existing agreements (Article 74, para. 4).

The expanse of each nation's EEZ varies with the length and configuration of its coastline. India, with its long coastline and numerous island territories, could claim a zone of about 588,000 sq nm, whereas Kenya, with the shortest coastline of Africa's Indian Ocean littoral states, could claim a zone of about 34,000 sq nm. The island state of Singapore, being zone-locked by its coastal neighbours of Indonesia and Malaysia has, not surprisingly, consistently opposed the establishment of the EEZ, for it could only claim a very modest area of the seas beyond its territorial jurisdiction.

Coastal states that fringe the Andaman Sea and the Persian Gulf likewise maintain that, by the very proximity of their neighbours, they cannot claim the maximum allowable width. Nevertheless such states are more fortunate than those that are landlocked, even though provisions in the Convention have been made for the landlocked and the geographically disadvantaged states to have access to coastal states' zones. Figure 3.12 sets out the limits of the Exclusive Economic Zones in the Indian Ocean. The archipelagic states of Indonesia, Maldives, Mauritius and Seychelles appear to have the most to gain by the establishment of such zones when the Convention is finally ratified.

The Republic of Indonesia, with its islands stretching over about 15° of latitude and 46° of longitude, may claim a zone of about 1,577,300 sq nm. Likewise, the Seychelles with a land surface area of a mere 453 sq km, composed of 115 islands, claims a zone of about 13,150 sq nm. France, through its overseas territories, also claims a vast area of the Indian Ocean.

The establishment of the 200 nm EEZ of the 36 coastal nations bordering the waters of the Indian Ocean would collectively place approximately 7,000,000 sq nm or approximately one-third of its total surface area under some degree of national jurisdiction. Whilst a number of coastal states in the region had proclaimed jurisdiction over their zone by 1991, many had not yet ratified the Convention or deposited the charts

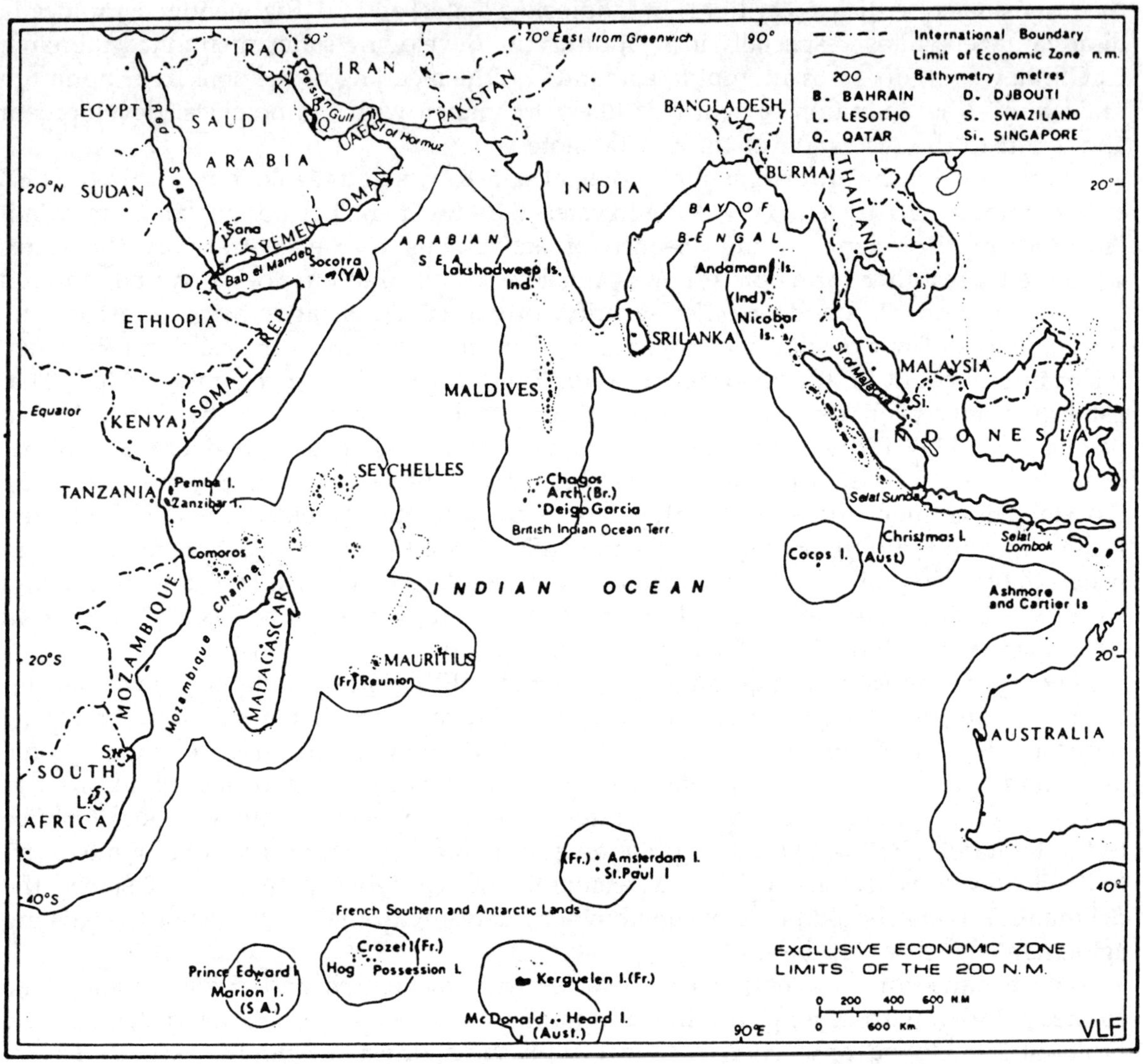

Figure 3.12 Exclusive Economic Zone limits in the Indian Ocean Basin.

or list of geographical coordinates as required by Article 75. On the other hand, a number of states such as Australia and South Africa, have already claimed the width of 200 nm as a Fishing Zone. The Territorial Waters Amendment Act, No. 98 of 1977 of the Republic of South Africa describes this area as ". . . a zone in respect of which the Republic shall in relation to fish and catching of fish have and exercise the same rights and powers as in respect of its territorial waters . . .".

On 16 August 1977 the Australian Minister for Foreign Affairs announced that his government would extend Australian fisheries jurisdiction to 200 nm. Appropriate amendments to the Fisheries Act No. 116 (1952–1967) and related legislation were drafted and on September 26, 1979 the Fisheries Amendment Act established an Australian Fishing Zone (AFZ) to a limit of 200 nm around the mainland and Tasmania and around the distant offshore Australian territories of Cocos (Keeling) Islands, Christmas Island and Heard and McDonald Islands in the Indian Ocean, and Norfolk Island and Macquarie Island in the South West Pacific Ocean.

In accordance with the arrangements agreed to at an Australian Premiers' Conference in 1979, the States and Northern Territory administer fisheries in the relevant sections of the territorial sea, and the Commonwealth Government administers fisheries beyond the three-nautical mile limit regardless of whether the Commonwealth Government increases its territorial sea limit at a later date. Major decisions affecting fishing operations within the zone are made by the Commonwealth Government in consultation with the States (Attorney-General's Dept., Australia, 1979).

Foreign fishing vessels operating within the AFZ are required to possess a fishing licence and to observe the terms and conditions of the contract of access, as determined by Australia. Aliens are not allowed access to fisheries which are fully exploited by Australians or are likely to be so exploited in the near future.

In accordance with international law and under international obligations, Australia will determine the total allowable catch, the amount of that catch to be taken by Australians; and the allocation to foreign fishermen of any available surplus fish, to ensure the proper management, conservation and optimum utilization of the fisheries resources of the AFZ. Failure to comply with the terms and conditions of operation within the AFZ can result in legal action being taken by the relevant Australian authorities. Cases have been recorded where offending boats have been confiscated and skippers penalised (Hudson, 1988). During the period 1991 to October 1994, for example, the total number of Indonesian fishermen arrested for illegally fishing for trochus shells and trepang and charged with offences under the Fisheries Act, the Quarantine Act and the Continental Shelf stood at 1248 (Fisheries Department, Western Australia). The offenders spent up to 134 days in prison, before being returned to Indonesia at the expense of the Australian government.

Generally, foreign fishing operations within the AFZ fall into three categories: commercial joint ventures; fishing under bilateral agreements; and feasibility fishing. In 1991 bilateral agreements existed with the Japanese Government and with Taiwanese and Thai commercial interests. Foreign fishing vessels are allocated areas within the AFZ in which to carry out a specific fishery. Although there could be provision for the landing of a portion of the catch in Australia, normally the catch of such vessels is returned to the country of origin for processing. The benefits to Australia from such agreements, although indirect, are numerous and include the statistical data which each vessel is required to submit. Australia also reserves the right to place observers on board foreign vessels to ensure that terms and conditions of the agreements are being observed, and to assist in gathering information about the fisheries. Different types of agreement exist with Australia's nearest neighbours. The Torres Strait Treaty 1978, between Australia and Papua New Guinea, and the Memorandum of Understanding, 1974 between Australia and Indonesia guarantee the rights of indigenous fishermen to operate in designated waters in the Torres Strait and South of Timor Island within the AFZ. These agreements are good examples of a coastal state's willingness to share its marine resources, in accordance with the spirit of the Law of the Sea.

THE EEZ AND THE CONTINENTAL SHELF REGIMES

Provisions in Articles 56 (1a) and 77 (1) of CLOS expressly stress that a coastal state has sovereign rights to the non-living resources of the seabed and its substratum within the area of both the EEZ and the continental shelf. The outer edge of the EEZ is defined solely in terms of distance from the baseline, regardless of depth of water and whether there is a continental shelf or not (Articles 57 and 76). The continental shelf concept is dependent on the configuration of the seabed and therefore can be theoretically applied only up to a certain depth of the seabed. By definition, a coastal state has to proclaim an EEZ, whereas the continental shelf rights exist for that state independently of any proclamation or occupation (Article 77: 3).

If an EEZ has been established but the continental shelf extends beyond it, two legal regimes will exist with reference to the coastal state's seabed rights. Part of the shelf is then subject to the regime of the EEZ, and is governed by its provisions, which include reference to continental shelf provisions (Article 56: 3). Bernaerts (1988) describes the seabed of the EEZ as the "primary seabed", and the seabed of the continental shelf which extends beyond the EEZ as the "outer shelf". The latter is governed by an independent legal regime (Part VI, Articles 76 to 85).

Notwithstanding the favourable rights given to the coastal states and the freedom for aliens to operate within reason in the EEZ, there is one issue that is irksome to the major maritime powers and the developed nations. Article 82 provides for the yearly payment of fees to the International Seabed Authority for resources exploited from the shelf beyond the 200 nm limit, commencing five years after the start of production and increasing annually to a maximum of seven per cent of the value of production at the site. This is just one of the many reasons offered by nations such as the United Kingdom, the United States of America, France and Germany for their reluctance to ratify the Convention.

Due publicity of the delimitation of the continental shelf must be made by the coastal state after it has consulted with the Commission. It may call upon the expertise and competence of international authorities such as the International Oceanographic Commission of UNESCO and the International Hydrographic Organisation.

DETERMINATION OF CONTINENTAL SHELF BOUNDARIES BETWEEN STATES

A definitive solution to the problem of the determination of seabed boundaries between states with opposite or adjacent coasts is not to be found in CLOS. Article 83, however, states that delimitation of the continental shelf shall be carried out by agreement on the basis of international law in order to achieve an equitable solution. If no agreement is reached within a reasonable period of time, parties to the dispute are directed to procedures which may include compulsory conciliation. Articles 74 and 83 emphasise the need for an agreement which is based on applicable international law.

Johnston (1988: 277) observes that the "most difficult task in developing the theory of ocean boundary-making is to account for the diversity of mental elements involved in the process". He further notes that the task is complicated if the full range of considerations is not known. The scholarly researcher may find it virtually impossible to penetrate the diplomatic and bureaucratic processes of boundary determination, and has to resort to an examination and analysis of the text and map. Even the lengthiest arbitration and judicial decision is unlikely to acknowledge all the considerations addressed by the tribunal or court. Often the tribunal is constrained by the terms of reference which call for compromise or an arbitration agreement. Examples of such decisions are well documented in the literature of maritime boundary determination (Johnston, 1988; Weil, 1989).

The maritime boundary in the Gulf of Maine between Canada and the United States of America was determined by a Chamber of the International Court of Justice in 1984. Unlike the cases that preceded it, this was the first determination of a single maritime boundary that included both continental shelf and fisheries jurisdiction. The Court was directed to decide in accordance with the principles and rules of international law applicable to the terms of reference which defined the contested area. The two states advanced very different claims both in terms of area and methodology. In discussing the Gulf of Maine issue as defined by each of the parties, the Court followed up on the judgement of the Tunisia-Libya Case 1977 by stating that the continental shelf is a single, continuous, uniform and uninterrupted physiographical structure, even if in places it features some secondary characteristics resulting mainly from glacial and fluvial action (Gulf Of Maine Case, 1984: 32–33). The Court, having rejected the claims forwarded by Canada and the United States, prescribed the following method of delimitation. In the innermost part of the Gulf of Maine, the Court noted that the states could be regarded as adjacent and therefore considered delineating a lateral line. Where the shorelines evolved into opposite coasts further seaward, the Court adopted a line that was the mean of the two coastal direction lines extending seawards through the Gulf of Maine. In essence, the

Court rejected the use of natural prolongation as a means of delimitation, but employed a form of lateral equidistance.

According to Johnston (1988), the process of determining ocean boundaries incorporates perceptual, analytical and instrumental stages. The problem, the approach and the geographical area are elements of the first stage. In the analytical stage the various factors include values, interests, attitudes, relationships between the parties to the issue, the physical setting, technology and time. The instrumental stage involves the application of appropriate principles, criteria, methods and techniques.

Although it is not the aim of this study to examine the theory of boundary determination, Johnston's observation nevertheless offers a useful guide to the analysis of the bilateral and trilateral maritime boundary agreements that have been in force in the Indian Ocean Basin since 1958. These agreements and the maps depicting the negotiated boundaries are contained in Appendix A of this study.

It is significant that these agreements have each been negotiated on the basis of mutual friendship between the states who desire to seek cooperation in matters of common interest. Consequently there has been no reason for maritime boundary disputes to be taken to a court or arbitration body.

THE HIGH SEAS AND THE AREA

A declaration in the 1958 Convention on the High Seas defined the High Seas as that part of the sea which was not included in the internal waters or territorial seas of states. Article 86 of CLOS amended the definition to include only that part of the sea which is not included in the internal waters, the territorial sea or the exclusive economic zone of a state or in the archipelagic waters of an archipelagic state.

The high seas are open to all states, whether coastal or landlocked, and should be used only for peaceful purposes. According to Article 87 the five freedoms of the high seas are those of navigation; of overflight; of the laying of submarine cables and pipelines; of construction of artificial islands and other installations; and of fishing and carrying out scientific research. With reference to conducting scientific research, however, this privilege does not include such research on the continental shelf of a coastal state which underlies the high seas (Articles 87 [f] and 257). Nearly two-thirds of the surface of the Indian Ocean will be the regime of the high seas (Figure 3.13). No high seas remain in the Persian Gulf, Andaman Sea, Red Sea, the South China Sea or the Timor Sea, although the waters beyond the territorial seas are, by international customary law, considered as international waters.

Beneath the high seas is the Area, defined by Article 136 of CLOS as comprising "the seabed and ocean floor, the subsoil thereof, beyond the limits of national jurisdiction, (which) as well as the resources of the Area remain the common heritage of mankind". Its legal status is proclaimed in Article 137, under which no state may "claim or exercise sovereignty or sovereign rights over any part of the Area or its resources". If, in due course, the combined surface area of Indian Ocean claimed as EEZ is equivalent to one-third of the total surface area, then the remaining two-thirds will, with those parts of the Area located elsewhere, be "vested in mankind as a whole" and will, in accordance with Article 157, be managed by the International Seabed Authority (ISA). This body will be located in Kingston, Jamaica, with regional offices set up to carry out its functions.

The resources of the Area, which include all solid, liquid or gaseous mineral resources, including polymetallic nodules, are not subject to alienation. However, when minerals are recovered from the Area, they may, in accordance with the procedures of the Authority, be alienated. A royalty will be imposed for the privilege of extracting minerals from the seabed of the Area. Other activities in the Area, which must pay due regard to the protection of human life (Article 146), the protection of the marine environment (Article 145) and the protection and preservation of archaeological and historical objects (Article

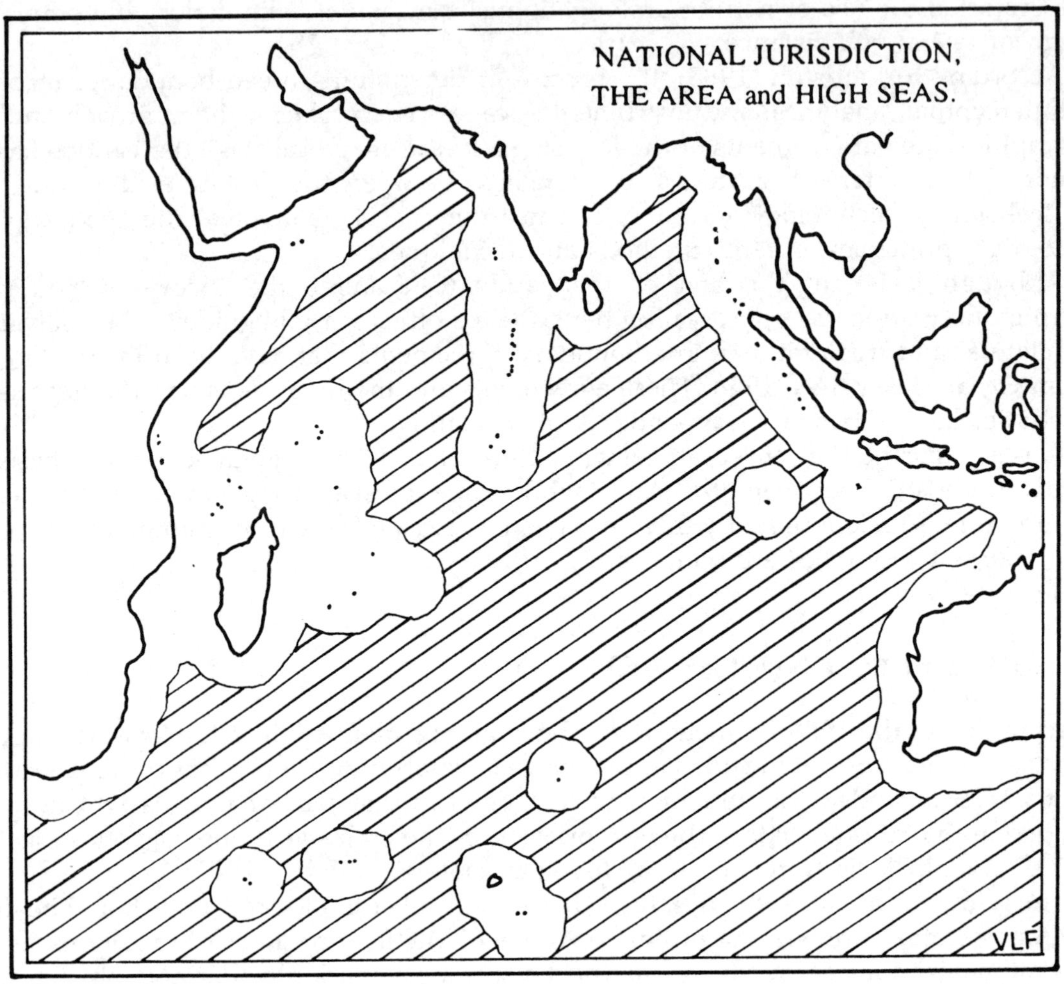

Figure 3.13 The Area and High Seas (shaded).

149) are restricted to marine scientific reasearch, exclusively for peaceful purposes and for the benefit of mankind as a whole.

States are urged to cooperate with the Authority to promote the transfer of technological and scientific knowledge, especially to developing states and to the Enterprise (Article 170) which will be an organ of the Authority. The Enterprise is organised with elements of a private company comprising a Director-General and a 15-member governing board. It is to operate in accordance with sound commercial principles and to carry out or oversee the transporting, processing and marketing of minerals recovered from the area (Annex IV: Statute of the Enterprise, Articles 1–13, CLOS). Amendments to the provisions of Deep Seabed Mining Regime were incorporated in July 1994 after lengthy debates.

CONCLUSION

This chapter has demonstrated the importance of the baseline and its linkage to the establishment of maritime zones for coastal states. The characteristics of the zones have been examined and the inherent rights of the coastal state and of aliens within each zone have been highlighted.

CLOS offers new instruments for promoting and encouraging economic development, ensuring protection of the marine environment, advancing disarmament and creating new forms of scientific and industrial cooperation between the developing and developed nations. It constitutes the most comprehensive and binding political and legal text relating to the law of the sea which has yet been devised. Although the Convention had not achieved legal status by the end of 1991, some nine years after it was generally accepted by the international community, all the states in the region have been prompted into enacting legislation and adopting new or redefining maritime limits in accordance with its articles (Appendix B). CLOS will enter into force on 16 November 1994.

At the international level, organisations and regional associations with competence in maritime affairs, such as the Indian Ocean Marine Affairs Committee and the Committee for the Southeast Asia Policy on Ocean Law and Management were beginning to assess the impact of the Convention on their activities. These organisations were promoting conferences and workshops where discussions and ideas were exchanged in an attempt to speed the implementation processes and the ratification of the Convention (Plates 4, 5).

The following chapter will examine the various claims to maritime jurisdiction made by the states in the Indian Ocean Basin in order to safeguard their security and economic interests.

CHAPTER FOUR

ESTABLISHING MARITIME LIMITS

INTRODUCTION

This chapter outlines the methods adopted by the coastal states of the Indian Ocean Basin in defining their maritime zones. It commences with a review of the territorial sea baseline system adopted by each state where the informations is available, for, although the declared baseline system of a coastal state may be a series of artificial lines, its importance cannot be overstressed. It then analyses the claims to territorial sea widths, highlighting those states that have opted to use other maritime buffer zones, not only to protect themselves from hostile attack, but also to prevent unnecessary or over-zealous exploitation of their resources by those not entitled to. It demonstrates that a lack of such a buffer zone or precisely defined boundary may give rise to occupation or annexation by an other parties.

BASELINE SYSTEMS ADOPTED BY INDIAN OCEAN STATES

The advantage of adopting a LWM as a baseline is that the state obtains the widest possible belt of sea space. As it is possible to make a selection from a range of low-water marks (Figure 4.1) it is understandable that different countries might use different data. In some cases, such as Australia, the relevant authorities have opted to use a lower datum, the ISLW, and even the LAT. In choosing the lowest water level the state secures two possible advantages, in that the area of sea claimed is increased, and the lower data may expose more LTEs from which claims to territorial seas are made in accordance with the provisions of Articles 7:4 and 13 of CLOS. Specifically, LTEs must be within 12 nm of the coast of act as part of the baseline.

There is a disadvantage, however, in determining the lowest low-water mark along the coast. There would be an expense involved in surveying, collecting and processing tidal data in the first instance. Such information would then have to be depicted on amended or new edition large-scale maps and charts produced by or for the country concerned. Along coastlines experiencing a relatively small tidal range (of say, less than half a metre) such additional expenditure would not be warranted. But such additional expenses may be justified for areas along a coastline where the tidal range is appreciable large (say, three to five metres) where a greater portion of the coastline will be exposed when the lowest tide level is attained in the given astronomical and meteorological conditions.

Low-Water Mark Datum as a Baseline

Table 4.1 lists the littoral states according to the datum they employ to measure the widths of their respective maritime zones. It is not surprising to note that nine states specify in their legislation that the width of their territorial sea will be measured from the low-water mark (LWM), or a similar level, along their respective coasts. Three of the states, Jordan

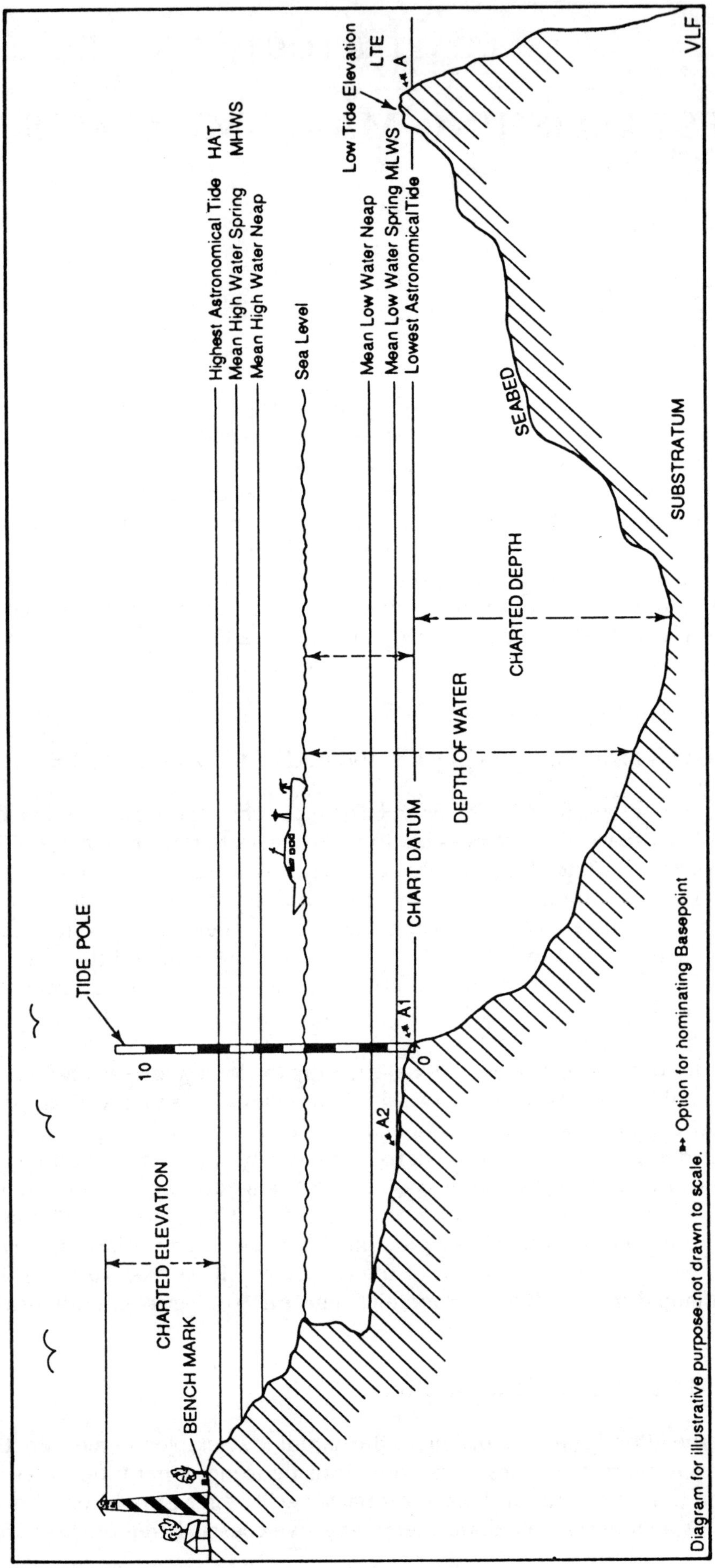

Figure 4.1 Determination of a Territorial Sea basepoint.

(1943), Egypt (1951) and Israel (1956), nominated the datum they would adopt well in advance of the 1958 Geneva Convention. Other countries such as Australia, the Malagasy Republic, Egypt, Saudi Arabia, Sudan, Somalia, Yemen, South Africa, the United Arab Emirates, although noting that they will employ a LWM, have kept their options open to establish straight baseline systems where it is deemed necessary to do so.

Table 4.1 Varied aplication of Indian Ocean littoral states in adopting a territorial sea baseline

GROUP ONE ... LOW-WATER MARK AS A DATUM
AUSTRALIA, EGYPT, ISRAEL, IRAQ, JORDAN, MADAGASCAR, QATAR, SAUDI ARABIA, SOMALIA, SOUTH AFRICA, SUDAN, UNITED ARAB EMIRATES, YEMEN.

GROUP TWO ... COMBINATION OF LWM AND STRAIGHT BASELINE
AUSTRALIA, DJIBOUTI, EGYPT, ETHIOPIA, MADAGASCAR, MAYOTTE (France), MAURITIUS, MOZAMBIQUE, OMAN.

GROUP THREE ... "FLOATING" BASELINE
BANGLADESH

GROUP FOUR ... EXCEPTIONAL STRAIGHT BASELINE SEGMENTS
MALAYSIA, MYANMAR, THAILAND.

GROUP FIVE ... ARCHIPELAGIC BASELINE SYSTEM
AUSTRALIA, COMOROS, INDONESIA, MALDIVES, PAPUA NEW GUINEA.

GROUP SIX ... BAY-CLOSING LINES/HISTORIC BAY CLAIMED
AUSTRALIA, DJIBOUTI, EGYPT, INDIA, KUWAIT, SAINT-PAUL (France), SEYCHELLES.

GROUP SEVEN ... STRAIGHT BASELINES CLAIMED BUT NOT DEFINED
COMOROS, INDIA, IRAN, PAKISTAN, TANZANIA, SAUDI ARABIA, SOMALIA, SUDAN, YEMEN.

Source: Author's research. Compiled from various National Legislation and Proclamations and Smith R. W., *Limits in the Seas* Series No. 36, 1990.

Combination of Low Water Marks and Straight Baselines

A baseline system adopting the LLWM was proclaimed by Egypt in Article 6 of the *Royal Decree* of 15 January 1951, but basepoints were not defined until 9 January 1990. Four months later, Egypt deposited with the United Nations copies of the published charts showing the baselines from which its territorial sea is measured as well as the outer limit of the territorial sea in the Mediterranean Sea and the Red Sea. The baseline system for the Red Sea comprises 56 basepoints. The system commences at the Egyptian/Israeli land boundary in the Gulf of Aqaba and terminates at Point 56 at the Egyptian/Sudanese land boundary post on the Red Sea coastline. Adoption of the system ensures that the Gulf of Suez lies wholly within the internal waters regime.

Baseline data were announced by Ethiopia in *Federal Revenue Proclamation No. 126* of 1952 for the Dahlac archipelago, defining three basepoints and in *Maritime Proclamation No. 137* of 1953 for the territorial waters of the empire. Article 6 (f) noted that the waters "entended from the extremity of seaboard at maximum annual high tide" to an outward distance of 12 nautical miles. This implies that Ethiopia has adopted as its datum the highest annual water level along its coast. In any case, any discrepancy in the vertical level would not appreciably extend the sea space claimed by that state because of its close proximity to its neighbours in the Red Sea. Iran, Saudi Arabia, Somalia, Sudan and the Yemen have proclaimed legislation which would permit the construction of straight baselines without actually defining any points or lines. Sudan had enabling legislation, *Territorial Waters and Continental Shelf Act,* No. 106 of 1970, for straight baselines detailed in Section 6. Likewise, Somalia has enacted legislation, *Law No. 37* of 1972, but has not made public the baseline points, apart from announcing that the "normal baseline ... is the low water line along the coast" (Article 2 para. 1). It further notes that the method of straight baselines joining appropriate points may be employed.

Kenya established a straight baseline in 1972 when it claimed a territorial sea, but did not specify the landmarks. Tanzania had not defined its datum by 1993.

In August 1966 the Portuguese colonial authorities delineated a baseline system for the coastline of Mozambique. It comprises five sectors, and 28 points are specified. The longest segment is approximately 60 nm and the shortest is 2.8 nm (The Geographer, 1970).

The Malagasy Republic proclaimed its baselines by *Decree No. 63-131* in February 1963, employing straight segments to close its internal waters along the north, west and south coasts. In the official *Journal No. 277* of the Repubic dated 9 March 1963 the baseline points and geographical coordinates of those points are listed. There are 37 segments which cover a total length of about 1,578 nautical miles. The longest segment is 123 nm; the shortest a mere 10.7 nm (The Geographer, 1970). The relative lack of embayments along the eastern seaboard for about 450 nm accounts for the employment of the low-water mark as a datum there (Figure 4.2).

Australia's straight baselines have been defined by proclamations published in the *Commonwealth of Australia Gazette S29,* of 9 February 1983 and baseline points for certain historic bays in South Australia in an amendment in 1987. Prescott (1985: 68) concludes in his analysis of Australia's baseline system that it is "above reproach", despite criticism of the declared lines in the vicinity of Flowers Bay, South Australia, and along the coast of Groote Eylandt, Northern Territory (Figures 3.4 and 3.5). India and Pakistan have yet to proclaim systems of straight baselines. Neither country specifies a datum, although mention is made in their respective legislation of a baseline from which the limits of territorial waters will be measured.

Floating Baseline

One of the most controversial baseline systems of the Indian Ocean basin is that proclaimed by Bangladesh. Citing the unique configuration of its coastline associated with peculiar geomorphological and geological conditions that result in a highly fluctuating low-water mark and areas of shallow water so unstable and variable so as not to be amenable to conventional charting, Bangladesh opted for a baseline based on a depth criterion. It chose the 18m (10 fathoms) isobath as the baseline. In correspondence to the Eleventh Session of UNCLOS III, the Bangladeshi representative noted that "these considerations have a manifest impact on the drawing of the baseline in an area where the waters immediately offshore have a closer affinity to the land than to ocean" *(UN A/CONF 62/L.* 140, 1982). Naturally, there was strong opposition to such a proposal from India and Burma. The latter pointed out that the fundamental rule for defining straight baselines may be drawn only from landpoint to landpoint, and not from seapoint to seapoint.

Exceptional Straight Baseline Segments

Myanmar employs straight baselines along some parts of the coast, and uses the low-water line along other parts. Along the Arakan coast there are 10 segments, and a similar number along the Tenasserim coast. A bay-closing line measuring nearly 223 nm has been proclaimed for the Gulf of Martaban. This length is about 10 times in excess of the permitted maximum. The overall length of the 21 segments totals about 827 nm, incorporating all but 30 nm of the coast. None of the basepoints is located on the mainland (The Geographer, 1970). Segments of the territorial sea baselines are depicted on Maps 21 and 22 of Appendix A.

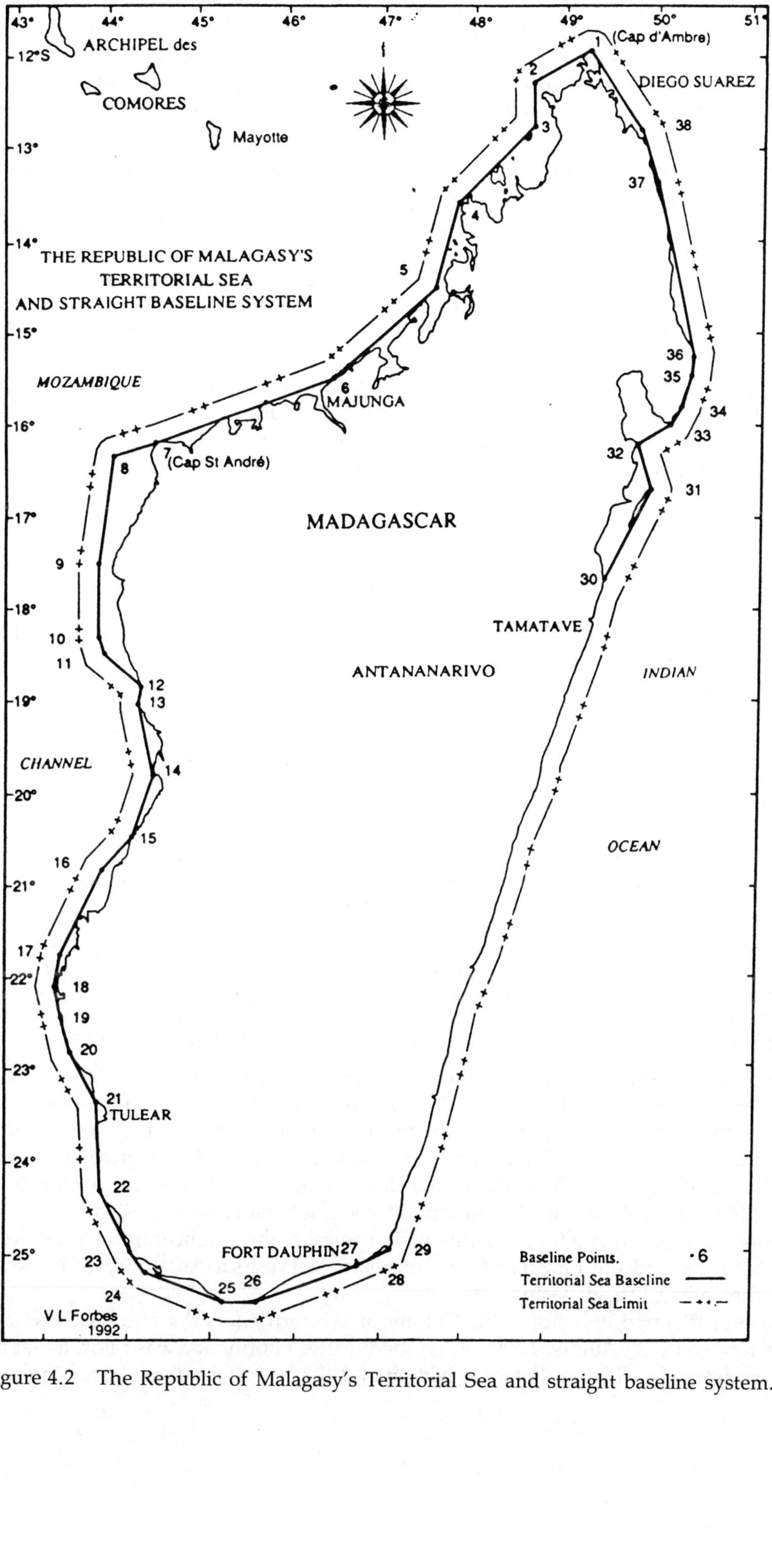

Figure 4.2 The Republic of Malagasy's Territorial Sea and straight baseline system.

Thailand decreed a system of straight baselines on 12 June 1970. The system was divided into three areas. Areas 1 and 2 are designated for baseline systems along the Thai coastline in the northern half of the Gulf of Thailand. These two areas are not taken into consideration here, as the waters are outside the defined limits of this study. The coastline along the Andaman Sea was designated Area 3. It comprises 23 segments which total a mere 156 nm. Point 1 of the system is located at the southernmost tip of Phuket Island and Point 24 is the terminating point of the system at the terminus of the Thai-Malaysia land boundary. Line segments 1 to 8 enclose a large bay-like body of water whose mouth measures in excess of 50 nm. The longest segment measures 16.3 nm; the shortest, a mere 0.7 nm. The system encompasses a large number of scattered islands which are situated relatively close to the mainland. Because of the significant number of excluded islands seaward of the straight baseline system, the straight baselines do not extend the territorial sea appreciably (The Geographer, 1971). The baseline system is depicted on Map 23 in Appendix A.

Straight baselines for the "purpose of boundary determination" were established by decree *Ordinance No. 7* on 2 August 1969 for the coastline of Malaysia. In the vicinity of the Malacca Strait, however, such a system is unnecessary in the light of an established continental shelf boundary and associated agreement with reference to navigation in the strait (Chapter 5).

Archipelagic and Sectorial Baseline Systems

The Indonesian Government established an archipelagic baseline system on 18 February 1960 by *Regulation No. 4* in which the state announced that it would, however, permit innocent passage through internal waters. The system encloses approximately 666,100 sq nm of internal waters and 98,000 sq nm of territorial sea (The Geographer, 1971). It employs 195 basepoints (Figure 4.3). The total length of the 194 segments is about 3,112 nm. Whereas the two longest segments are each 124 nm, the shortest is slightly less than three nm.

The baseline system appears to conform with the provisions of Article 47, unlike the "constitutional rectangle" employed by the Maldives. The concept of a "constitutional rectangle" or a "sector" is not new, for the text of Governor Stirling's *Commission* (2 June 1829) in establishing the Colony of Western Australia, noted

> the boundaries of our Territory called Western Australia extending from Cape Londonderry, in latitude thirteen degrees forty-four minutes south; to West Cape Howe, in latitude thirty-five degrees eight minutes south; and from the Hertogs (sic) Island on the west coast in longitude one hundred and twelve degrees fifty two minutes to one hundred and twenty nine degrees of east longitude reckoning from the meridian of Greenwich.

The Commission also stated that the territory would include "all islands adjacent in the Indian and Southern Oceans within the parallels of latitude aforeside of thirteen degrees forty-four minutes south, and thirty-five degrees eight minutes south and within the longitudes aforesaid . . ." The sector principle is illustrated in Figures 3.7 and 4.4.

Although not specifically stated in the document, it could be implied that the waters surrounding the lands within the prescribed geographical coordinates constituted part of the colony of Western Australia. If this were the case, the publication of the *Commission* would have defined the first maritime boundary of Western Australia, and possibly the first in the Indian Ocean Basin.

These proclaimed limits of "Our Colony of Western Australia and its Dependencies" were in force until 25 August 1890, when the northern boundary was relocated at Lat. 13° 30′ S, as decreed in Letters Patent which stated that the boundaries extended

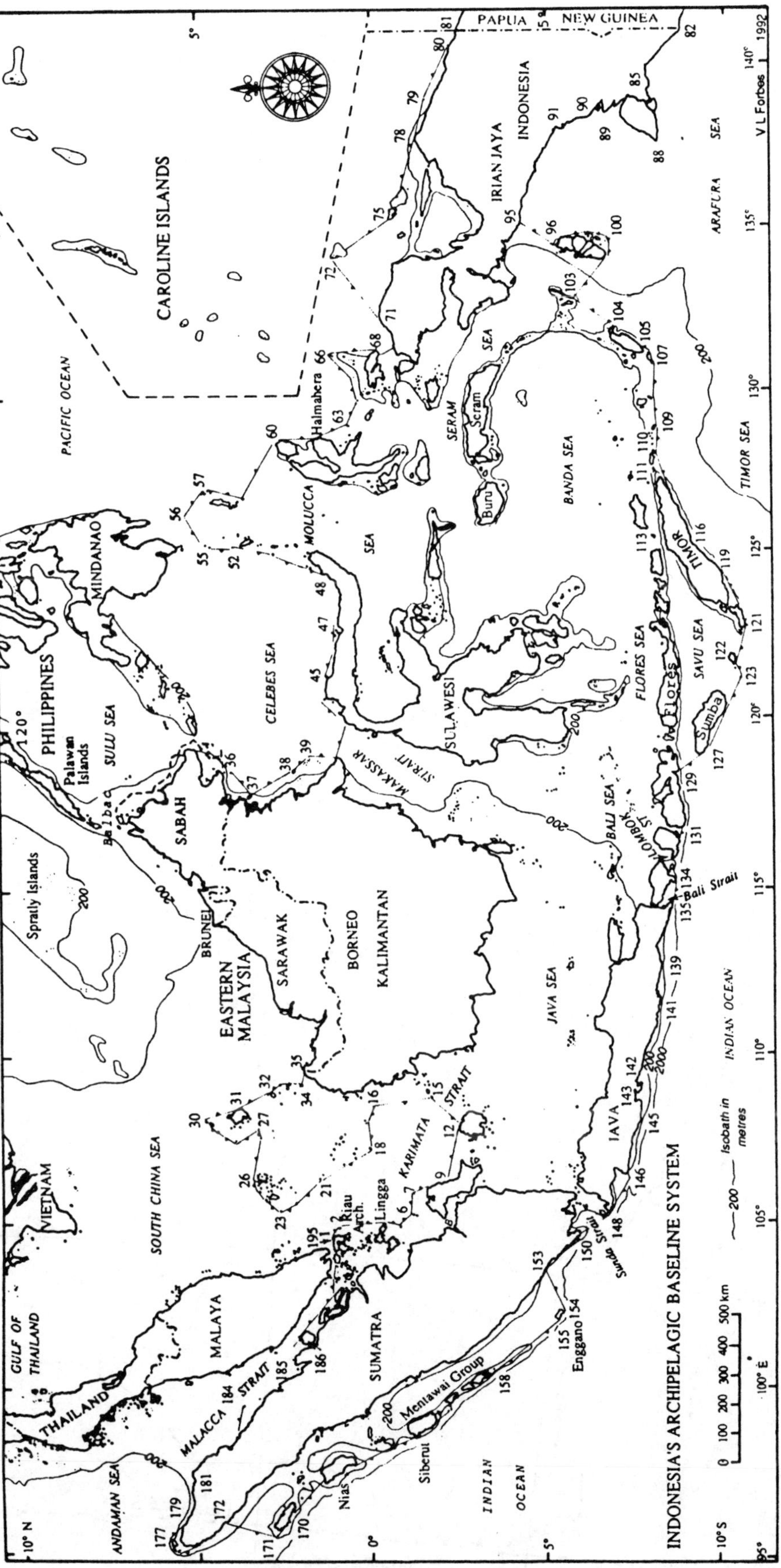

Figure 4.3 Indonesia's archipelagic baseline system.

> ... from the parallel of thirteen degrees thirty minutes south latitude, to West Cape Howe in the parallel of thirty-five degrees eight minutes south latitude ... including all the islands adjacent in the Indian and Southern Oceans within the latitudes aforesaid ...

The northern sections of the eastern and western boundaries would naturally be extended accordingly, as illustrated in Figure 4.4. This extension, in effect encompassed the Scott and Seringapatam Reefs (Lat. 14°00′ S, Long. 121°50′ E), Holothuria Reefs (Lat. 13°35′ S, Long. 126°01′ E) and Browse Island. The Ashmore-Cartier Group lies north of

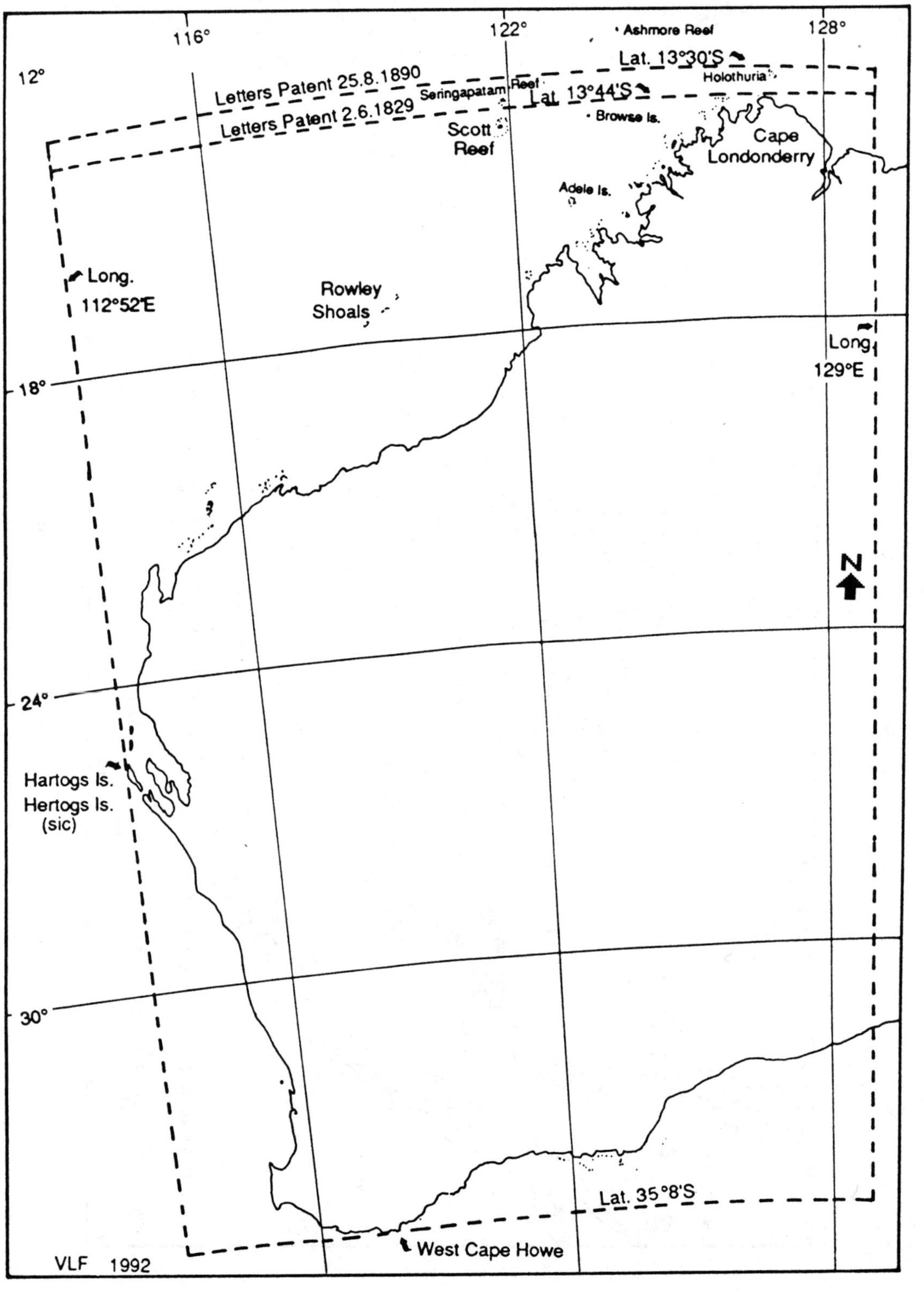

Figure 4.4 The colony of Western Australia and its Dependencies.

the defined line at about Lat. 12°14′ S. The amendments were published in the *Government Gazette, No. 47,* of 23 October 1890.

Although there is no official record of abandonment of the sector principle, if it ever existed, it can be inferred that Western Australia lost its claim to the islands and resources in the offshore waters when it opted to be incorporated into the Australian Federation in 1901. When the Australian colonies federated in that year it was not clear whether the maritime boundaries of the colonies were defined by the low-water mark along the coast or the outer limits of the territorial sea which was then the three nm limit. The *Commonwealth of Australia Constitution Act of 1901* brought together the former colonies, to become the States, but the Constitution did not describe the geographical limits of the Commonwealth. Section 22 of the Constitution enabled the Commonwealth Government to legislate new laws for territories that the former colonies had 'surrendered' with respect to the peace, order and good government of the Commonwealth. Residual power lay with the States of the Federation.

After decades of disputes between the States and the Commonwealth, a number of contentious and complex offshore constitutional issues were finally settled by an agreement signed at the Premiers' Conference on 29 June 1979. The document, *Offshore Constitutional Settlement,* represents a major achievement of the policy of cooperative federalism.

Australia's sovereignty extends, beyond the land and Australia's internal waters to a belt of sea around Australia described as the territorial sea. The width of this zone is 12 nm. The inner limit of this zone is the territorial sea baseline. In pursuance of Section 7 of the *Seas and Submerged Lands Act* 1973 the geographical coordinates of the baseline system were proclaimed on 4 February 1983. Incorporated in the Commonwealth of Australia's *Gazette S29* of 1983 is a list of basepoints which establishes archipelagic baselines for the Houtman Abrolhos Islands (Figure 3.6). The system employed for these islands satisfy the provisions of Article 47 of CLOS.

The islands of Mauritius, Réunion and Seychelles are too widely scattered to produce a ratio of water to land of less than 9:1 so as to claim archipelagic status. The Comoros claim archipelagic status through *Law No. 82-005* of May 1982, but no geographical coordinates are stated.

France has legislated for the establishment of straight baselines and bay-closing lines for its Overseas Dependencies and Territories in the Indian Ocean Basin. Straight baselines for Mayotte Island in the Comores Group were established by *Decree No. 77-1067* of 12 September 1972, and for the islands in the French Southern and Antarctic Lands by *Decree No. 78-112* of 11 January 1978.

Bay-Closing Lines

For the purpose of pollution control legislation, Kuwait established a bay-closing line in 1964 for Kuwait Bay. Kenya's legislation of 1972 claimed Ungwana Bay as an historic bay. In 1967 the Australian Government declared the waters of bays up to 24 nm in width as internal waters of Australia, and delineated straight baselines across entrances to Shark Bay (Figure 4.5), Gulf of Saint Vincent and Spencer Gulf (Forbes, 1991a). Australia's baseline segments 113, 114 and 115 each enclose both the Beagle Gulf and Van Diemen Gulf as internal waters (Figure 3.4). In its 1987 proclamation Australia declared bay-closing lines for Anxious, Encounter, Lacepede and Rivoli Bays in South Australia. Sri Lanka and India entered into an agreement on 8 July 1974 which recognised the historic nature of Palk Bay (The Geographer, 1976; Prescott, 1985). A proclamation made jointly by India and Sri Lanka, on 15 January 1977, claimed that the historic waters of Palk Bay, Palk Strait and the Gulf of Manaar were incorporated as territorial waters of both states [Ref. Map 18].

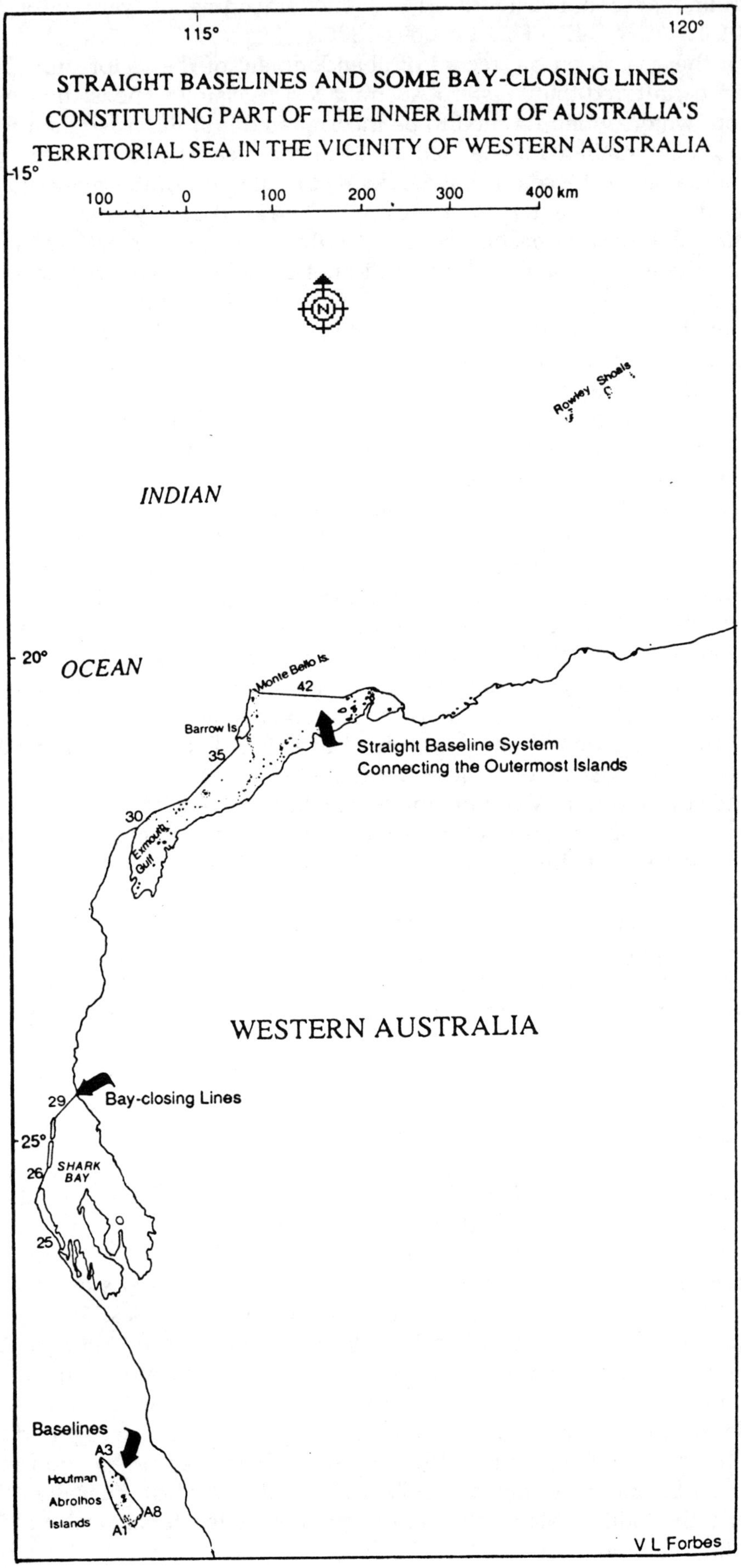

Figure 4.5 Variations of baseline systems along the northwest coast of Australia.

TERRITORIAL SEA AND CONTIGUOUS ZONE CLAIMS

The vexed question of the breadth of the territorial sea has been, for at least three centuries, the most famous and best documented of all the issues in the law of the sea. International practice reveals a significant disparity in territorial sea limits, varying from three nm in the late 17th century and the traditional Northern European limit of four nm, 60 nm, 100 nm (Johnston, 1988: 79) to the rather absurd limit of 200 nm claimed by Somalia in the late 20th century.

Table 4.2 lists the widths of the territorial sea and contiguous zones of the littoral states of the Indian Ocean Basin. Four states — Bahrain, Jordan, Qatar and Singapore and five of the Persian Gulf Emirates — Abu Zabi, Ajman, Dubayy, Ra's al Khaymah and Umm al Qaywayn — retain the three nm limit. Somalia remains steadfast in claiming a territorial sea limit of 200 nm, which is well in excess of what is accepted by international law. The remaining 34 states and emirates in the region have opted for the new international standard of 12 nm although only 13 of these states had ratified the Convention by October 1991 (Appendix B).

Just as states like Australia and Israel have increased their territorial sea limits, there are others who have reduced their claims. Two such states are Malagasy and Tanzania. The former initially increased its limit from 12 to 50 nm on 28 September 1973 by *Ordinance No. 73-060*. The latter adopted the same limits through *Proclamation No. 209*, of 24 August 1973. Both later reverted to the international standard. If Malagasy had insisted on retaining its 1973 limits it would have created the potential for problems in the Mozambique Channel (Forbes, 1991d), as numerous French-held islands are located in that confined water body.

The delineation of territorial sea zones around islands in semi-enclosed waters is best illustrated by the provisions contained in the 1978 *Torres Strait Treaty*. Pressure was exerted on Australia to make concessions to the Government of Papua New Guinea during the negotations between the two countries on the delineation of a seabed boundary in the vicinity of the Torres Strait. The delineated boundary lay south of 15 named islands which were under Australian jurisdiction. In order to establish the seabed boundary, it was necessary to define the limits of the territorial sea surrounding each of the islands, since Australia could justly claim, through the provisions of international law, the seabed and water column below the territorial sea of those islands.

At the time of signing the 1978 Treaty, Australia claimed a territorial sea width of three nautical miles. Provision was incorporated in Article 3 of the Treaty that the territorial seas around the Australian-claimed islands north of Lat. 9°33′ S would not be enlarged or reduced, even if there were to be any change in the configuration of the coastline, a different result from any subsequent topographical survey, or any subsequent increase in the width of Australia's territorial sea. The islands that Australia claimed lie in some instances as close as two nm off the PNG coastline.

The extent of Australia's territorial sea off the islands in the Torres Strait north of the prescribed parallel of latitude was defined in the eight schedules of the *Commonwealth Gazette* of 9 February 1983. The islands of Dauan, Kaumag and Saibai were grouped together: their northern boundary was defined by the geographical coordinates of seven turning points linked by six straight lines. The remaining boundary was described as intersecting arcs with a radius of three nautical miles drawn from 58 points along the southern coasts of the three above named islands (Figure 4.6).

Similarly, the islands of Aubusi, Boigu and Moimi were treated together. To define the northern boundary of their territorial sea, eight turning points were linked by seven straight lines. The southern boundary was formed by the intersecting arcs with a radius of three nm described from 40 specified points on the southern coast of Boigu. The outer limits of the territorial sea surrounding Australia's Torres Strait islands of Anchor and East Cays (Figure 4.7), Black Rocks, Bramble Cay, Deliverance Island, Kerr Islet, Turnagain

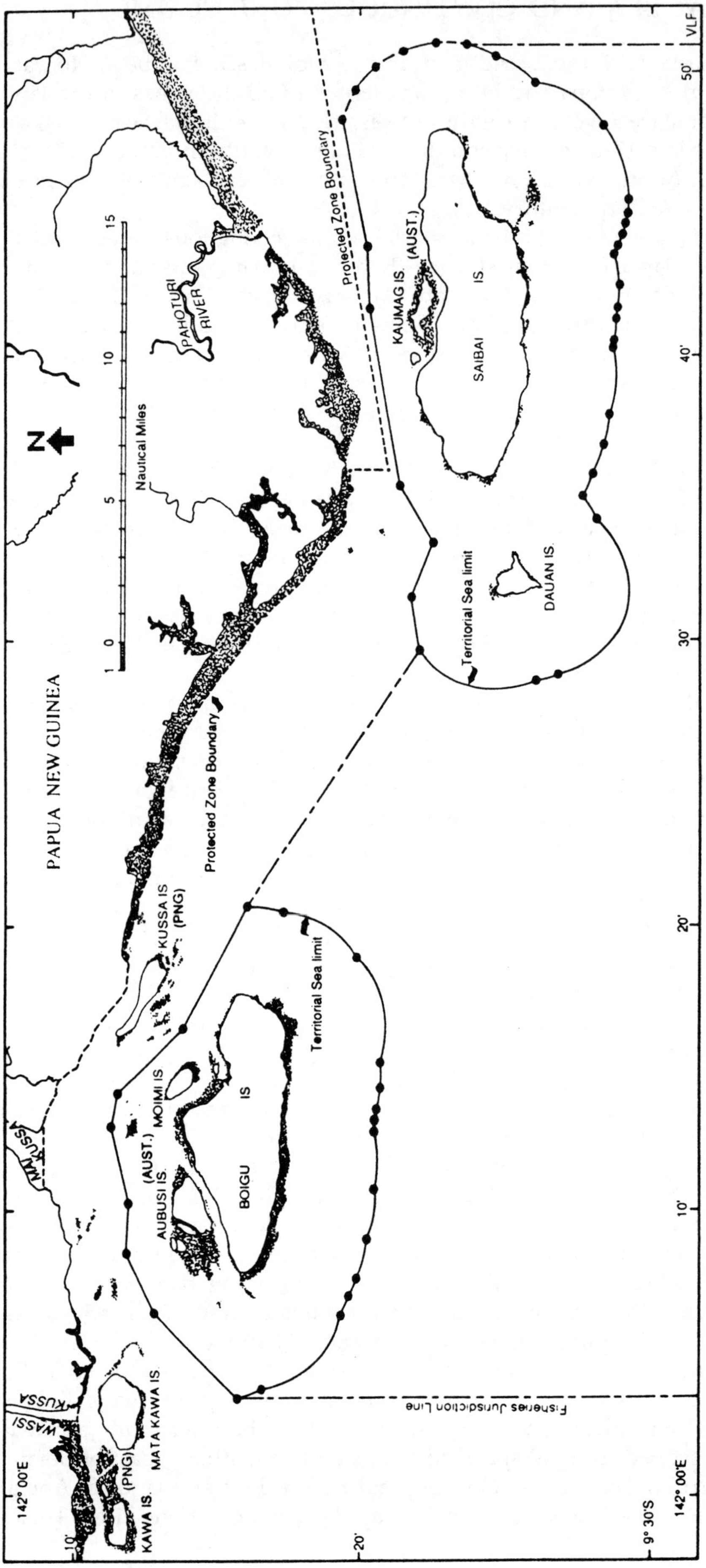

Figure 4.6 The Territorial Sea limits around the Dauan and Boigu Island groups in the Torres Strait.

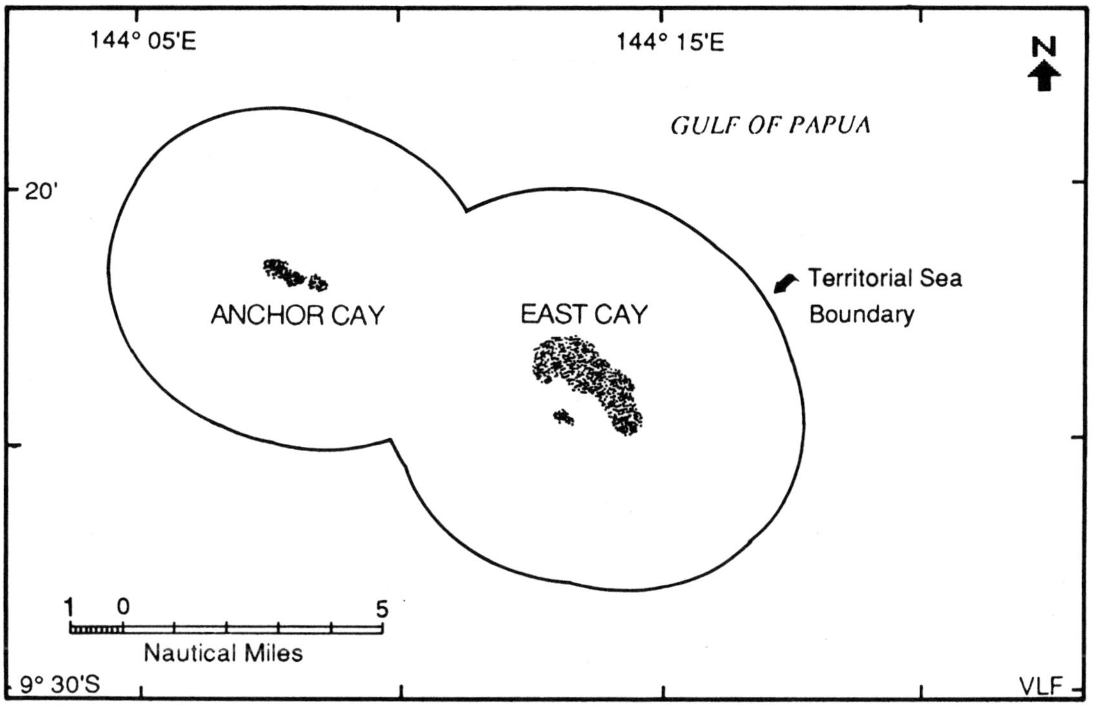

Figure 4.7 Territorial Sea limit around Anchor and East Cays.

Island and Turu Cay (Figure 4.8) are delineated by intersecting arcs with a radius of three nm drawn from specified points along their respective low-water marks.

An unusual case arises with the limit of the territorial sea of Pearce Cay, located in the eastern approaches to Torres Strait. The cay lies about two nm north of the negotiated Seabed and Fisheries Jurisdictional Line (Chapter 5.5). The Line lies along Lat. 9°33′ S in the vicinity of the cay (Figure 4.9). By agreement Australia has limited its territorial sea at three nm north of the Line (Article 3 of the *Torres Strait Treaty).* However, south of the Line the limit is set at 12 nm in keeping with Australia's recent decision to increase its territorial sea width. The resultant boundaries in the vicinity of Pearce Cay are virtually incomprehensible to the mariner.

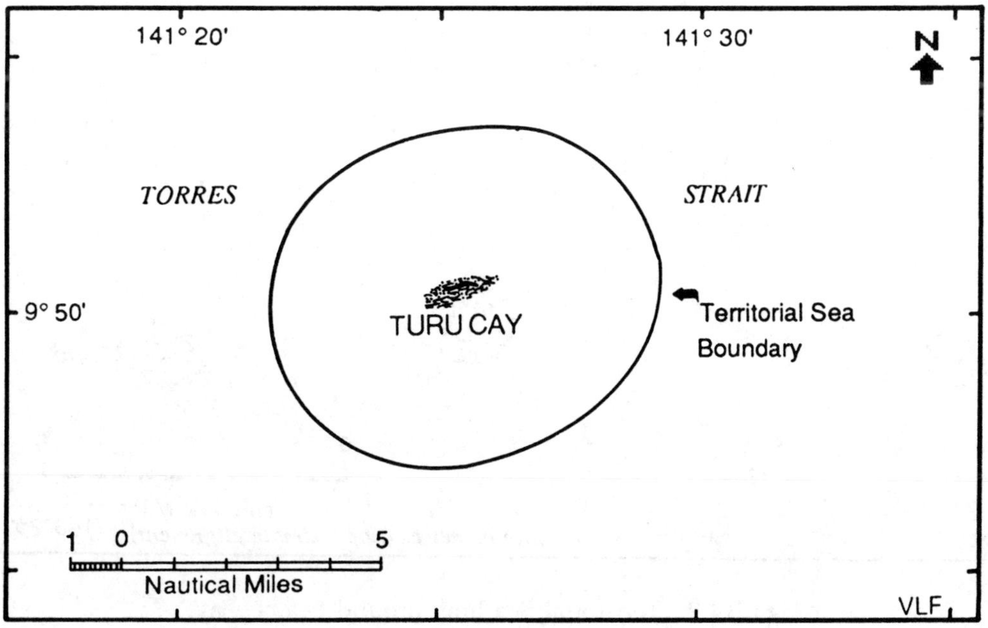

Figure 4.8 Territorial Sea limit around Turu Cay.

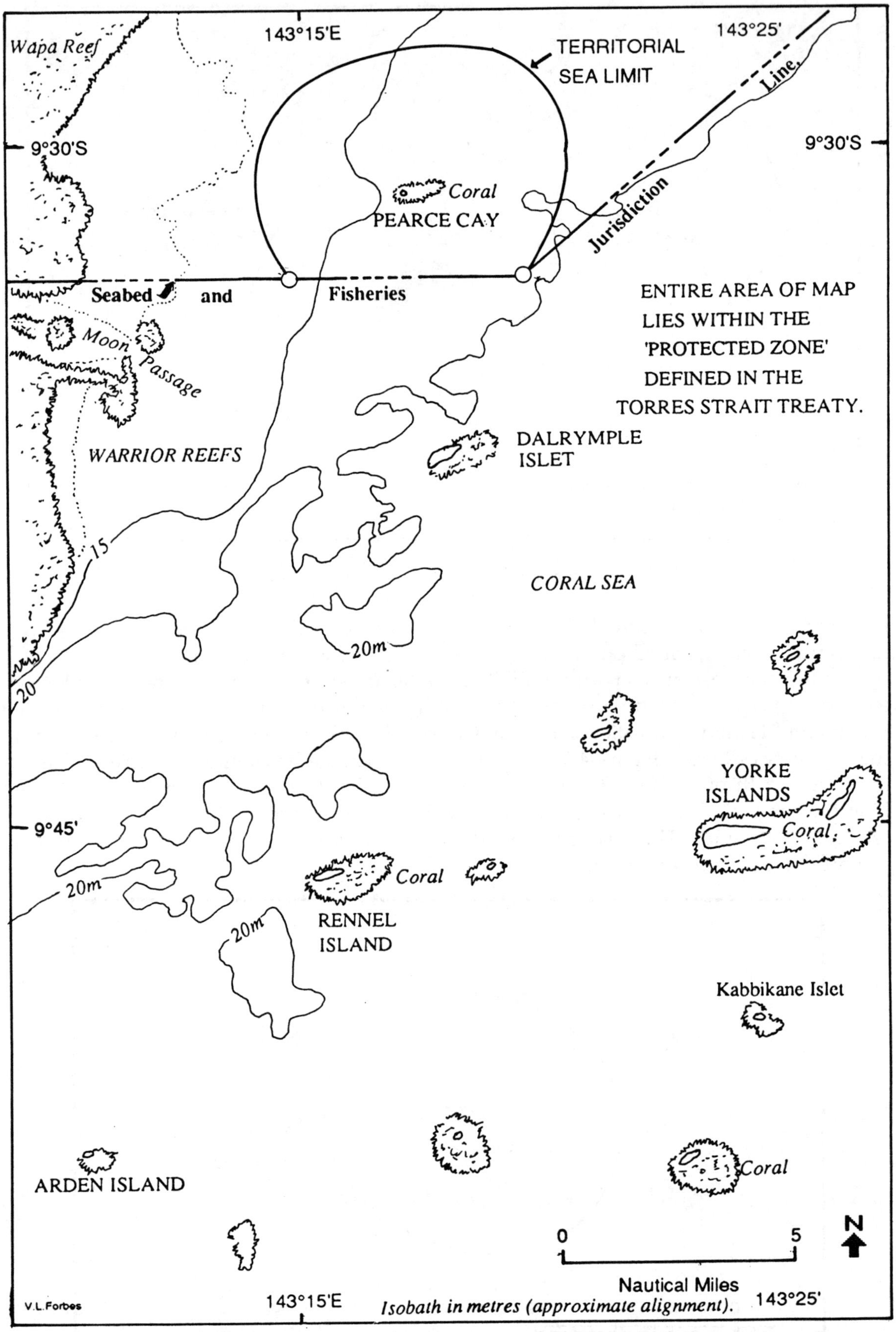

Figure 4.9 Territorial Sea limit around Pearce Cay.

On the much-debated issue of entry of foreign warships into territorial seas, Bangladesh, Egypt, India, Indonesia, Iran, Maldives, Mauritius, Myanmar, Pakistan, Seychelles, Somalia, Sri Lanka, and Sudan indicated that prior permission is required.

Within the Indian Ocean region only Australia, Bangladesh, Yemen, Djibouti, Egypt, India, Madagscar, Myanmar, Oman, Pakistan, Saudi Arabia, Sri Lanka and Sudan had claimed a contiguous zone to the end of 1991 (Smith, 1990; UN Office of the LOS, 1991). All states except Australia, Malagasy and Yemen appeared to claim limits that were in excess of the permitted value as prescribed in Article 33 (Table 4.2).

EXCLUSIVE ECONOMIC ZONE CLAIMS

By the end of 1991 eighteen Indian Ocean states had claimed a 200 nm EEZ. Australia, South Africa and Papua New Guinea preferred to use the term Fishery or Fishing Zone for their claim. Australia subsequently announced in October 1991 that it would enact legislation to formalise its claim to an EEZ (Forbes, 1991). On 1 August 1994 Australia adopted an EEZ. Iran adopted a 50 nm zone, whilst the Maldives claimed a 200 nm extension of the Constitutional Rectangle except in the north and northeast, where seabed boundaries were negotiated with India and Sri Lanka. The Maldives' claim varied from 37 to 310 nautical miles from the nearest Maldivian islands. Table 4.3 indicates the length of the coastline, the approximate area of EEZ, land area and continental shelf area of Indian Ocean states.

Geography dictates that the littoral states of the Malacca Strait, Andaman Sea, Gulf of Oman, Persian Gulf, Red Sea, and Gulf of Aden are unable to claim the full extent of the 200 nm limit. The same situation could arise in the Mozambique Channel, where five states can claim jurisdiction over portions of that water body (see Appendix A, Maps 2, 3 and 6).

Elsewhere in the basin, with some minor exceptions, the majority of the littoral and island states are sufficiently separated from their neighbours to be able to establish an EEZ without great difficulty. When such is not the case, a negotiated settlement will be required. In 1977 Mauritian authorities issued a hydrographic chart which purported to delineate the extent of that country's EEZ, and at the same time defined these limits in *Mauritius Zones Act No. 13* and *Proclamation No. 7.* Turning points were defined by geographical coordinates. The extent of the zone is consistent with the historic Mauritian claim to the Chagos Archipelago, which, as the British Indian Ocean Territory (BIOT), is also claimed by the United Kingdom (Forbes, 1987c). A 200 nm Fisheries Conservation and Management Zone (FCMZ) was proclaimed on 1 October 1991 for BIOT following the *Declaration of Intent* which was issued on 7 August 1991 (Forbes, 1991: 2 and 1992: 17). A sliver of unclaimed sea space no more than four nm wide existed between the claims of the Seychelles and Mauritius to the south of Coetivy Island. This anomaly may be the result of cartographic error, interpretation of the geodetic datum, the particular scale of the chart or just an oversight by the authorities. The anomaly has subsequently been corrected by the authorities in Mauritius and Seychelles (personal correspondence). It is such discrepancies that encourage marine geographers and maritime law experts to become involved in issues of boundary determination.

CONTINENTAL SHELF CLAIMS

By 1991 Australia, Egypt, Kenya, Malaysia, Papua New Guinea, South Africa, Thailand and the United Kingdom (with reference to its Indian Ocean Territory) had claimed rights to the continental shelf to the 200 m depth or the region of exploitability. Bangladesh specified jurisdiction to the edge of the continental margin. India, Mauritius, Myanmar, Pakistan, Seychelles, Sri Lanka and Yemen claimed jurisdiction over the resources of the seabed to a distance of 200 nm or the edge of the continental margin, whichever was the greater. Indonesia's claim covered the region of exploitability. Madagascar claimed a

Table 4.2 The Breadth of the Territorial Sea, Contiguous Zone and EEZ/Fisheries Jurisdictional Claims of Indian Ocean states

COUNTRY CODE	TERR. SEA	CONT. ZONE	EEZ/FZ	
Australia	12	12	200	1
Bahrain*	3	—	—	**
Bangladesh	12	18	200	4
Comoros*	12	—	200	2
Djibouti*	12	24	200	
Egypt*	12	24	200	**
Ethiopia	12	—	—	1
French Terr.	12	12	200	
India	12	24	200	
Indonesia*	12	12	200	2
Iran	12	—	50	1**
Iraq*	12	—	—	
Israel	12	—	12	
Jordan	3	—	3	
Kenya*	12	—	200	1
Kuwait*	12	—	—	
Madagascar	12	12	200	1
Malaysia	12	—	200	1
Maldives	12	—	200	**
Mauritius	12	—	200	**
Mozambique	12	—	200	
Myanmar	12	24	200	1**
Oman*	12	—	200	1
Pakistan	12	24	200	**
Papua New Guinea	12	—	200	2
Qatar	3	—	medianline	
Saudi Arabia	12	18	—	
Seychelles*	12	—	200	
Singapore	3	—	3	
Somalia*	200	—	200	
South Africa	12	—	200	
Sri Lanka	12	24	200	
Sudan*	12	18	—	
Tanzania*	12	—	200	
Thailand	12	—	200	
Abu Zhabi (UAE)	3	—	—	
Ajman (UAE)	3	—	—	
Dubavy (UAE)	3	—	—	
Fujayrah (UAE)	12	—	—	
Ra's al Khaymah (UAE)	3	—	—	
Ash Shariqah (UAE)	3	—	—	
Umm al Qaywayn (UAE)	3	—	—	
Yemen*	12	12	200	
Br. Indian Ocean Terr.	12	—	200	

Code translation

1 = employs straight baseline systems along all or a part of the coast.

2 = claims archipelagic waters

3 = claims waters within the limits defined by geographical coordinates not related to distance from coastline.

4 = claims straight baseline system between points along the 18 metre isobath.

* = indicates a state which has ratified CLOS.

** = indicates a state which reqires prior permission or notification for entry of warships into territorial sea.

Table 4.3 Comparison of Coastal Length, Area of EEZ, Land Area and approximate area of the Continental Shelf (200 m. isobath) as defined in the 1958 Geneva Convention for Indian Ocean littoral states

COUNTRY Area	Coastline (km)	Area of EEZ (sq km)	Land area (sq km)	Shelf (sq km)
Australia*	36,740	7,006,500	7,686,300	2,636,000
Bahrain	140	5,100	600	5,130
Bangladesh	1,320	76,800	144,000	54,720
Comoros	400	228,400	2,200	?
Djibouti	350	6,200	22,000	?
Egypt	1,620	173,500	1,001,400	37,400
Ethiopia	1,000	75,800	1,221,900	47,500
India	9,000	2,014,900	3,280,500	45,500
Indonesia°	60,000	5,408,600	1,904,300	2,768,800
Iran	1,840	155,700	1,648,000	106,700
Iraq	20	700	434,900	680
Israel°	230	23,300	20,700	4,500
Jordan	20	700	97,700	400
Kenya	450	118,000	582,600	14,300
Kuwait	210	12,000	17,800	12,000
Madagscar	4,000	1,292,000	587,000	
Malaysia°	3,430	475,600	329,700	372,438
Maldives	—	959,100	300	10,260
Mauritius	180	1,183,000	1,900	91,300
Mozambique	2,500	562,000	783,000	104,000
Myanmar	2,300	509,500	678,000	229,000
Oman	2,000	561,700	212,500	60,900
Pakistan	1,370	318,500	803,900	58,140
Papua N. Guinea°	5,000	—	461,700	—
Qatar	400	24,000	11,000	24,000
Saudi Arabia	2,400	186,000	2,149,700	78,000
Seychelles	—	729,700	400	?
Singapore	300	300	600	340
Somalia	3,200	782,800	637,700	60,500
South Africa°	3,000	1,016,700	1,222,200	143,000
Sri Lanka	1,700	517,400	65,600	27,000
Sudan	950	91,600	2,505,800	22,230
Tanzania	725	223,200	945,100	41,000
Thailand	2,960	324,700	514,000	256,100
United Arab Em.	2,420	59,300	83,600	59,000
Yemen	170	584,200	482,700	76,000

° Indicates states have coastlines abutting waters other than the Indian Ocean
Coastline distances measured on maps at a scale of 1: 1 000 000
EEZ areas are approximate
Land area taken from National sources.
Shelf area indicates the seabed upto the 200 m isobath.

breadth of 200 nm or 100 nm from the 2,500 m isobath, thus amending its original claim noted in *Article 2 of Ordinance No. 73-060* of 1973. That article stated that the "continental shelf of the Malagasy Republic (exclusive economic zone) shall extend to a limit fixed at 100 nm beyond its territorial sea". But the width of the territorial sea zone as established by Article in 1973 was 50 nm. Qatar and the United Arab Emirates claimed jurisdiction to the median line between them.

From the above classification it becomes apparent that Article 6 of the 1958 Convention and Article 76 of CLOS have not given clear messages to the states. Indeed, whereas the former was brief and vague, the latter is very complex and requires careful interpretation. Indeed, one of its provisions is to establish a Commission on the Limits of the Continental Shelf which will "make recommendations to coastal states on matters related to the establishment of the outer limits of their continental shelf". It is on the basis of these recommendations that the coastal state should establish the outer limits of its continental shelf. Until the Commission is fully functional, apprehension and uncertainty will continue over the interpretation and application of Article 76.

MARITIME BOUNDARY DELINEATION BY AGREEMENT IN THE INDIAN OCEAN BASIN

By July 1991 there were 35 maritime boundary agreements on bilateral or trilateral basis in the Indian Ocean Basin (Appendix F) compared to 140 in the global context.

The first bilateral agreement was between Bahrain and Saudi Arabia in 1958 in the Persian Gulf (Map 11, Appendix A). An analysis of this agreement is detailed in Chapter Five. By July 1991 there were eight sets of bilateral maritime boundary agreements among Persian Gulf states: between Bahrain and Saudi Arabia (1958); Abu Dhabi and Dubai (1968); Iran and Saudi Arabia (1968); Abu Dhabi and Qatar (1969); Iran and Qatar (1969); Bahrain and Iran (1971); Iran and Oman (1974); and Iran and the United Arab Emirates (1974). The areas in this water body that need most attention are at the head of the Persian Gulf, where there is scope for five bilateral agreements, and at the southern end of its waters, where disputes continue between Iran and the UAE over ownership of a number of islands. The primary concern for delimitation of maritime boundaries in this semi-enclosed sea is to provide a sound legal environment in which exploration and exploitation of offshore hydrocarbon deposits could take place.

In the Red Sea the seabed agreement between Saudi Arabia and Sudan is the only one in existence. It is analysed in Chapter Five. There are 12 sets of boundaries that could be subject to negotiations in the Red Sea, the Gulf of Aden and the vicinity of the Horn of Africa.

Along the eastern seaboard of Africa and in the vicinity of the Mascarene basin there are three sets of maritime boundary agreements: between Kenya and Tanzania (1976); between Mozambique and Tanzania (1989 but not yet in force); and between France (Réunion) and Mauritius (1980). No less than eight potential boundaries require determination in these regional seas, the most complex of which are within the Mozambique Channel (Forbes, 1991).

The possibility of determination, in the immediate future, of maritime boundaries between India and Pakistan, and Iran and Pakistan in the northern waters of the Arabian Sea is remote. Each of the nations has land-based issues to contend with before turning its attention to ocean boundary delineation. For instance, India and Pakistan both believe that the settlement of the Kashmir and Jammu territorial issue has to be realised before thought can be given to the determination of a maritime boundary. This may seem an surprising policy, because both states complain about encroachment into their territorial waters by fishing boats from the other state, and the likely presence of hydrocarbons in the continental shelf off the Indus Delta attracts exploration.

Seabed boundaries in the Laccadive Sea, Gulf of Manaar and Palk Bay have been determined through bilateral or trilateral agreements. The first of these agreements was negotiated in June 1974 between India and Sri Lanka, with reference to Palk Bay, which is an inlet of the Bay of Bengal (Figure 4.10). Its surface area is about 5,624 sq nm, and it measures approximately 74 nm along its longitudinal axis. Its historicity was established in Article 4 of the 1974 agreement, which declared that each state possessed sovereignty and exclusive jurisdiction and control over the waters, the islands, the continental shelf and the substratum falling on its own side of the delineated boundary. This article was based on a decision handed down in the *Annakumaru Pillai v. Muthupayal* Case heard in the Appellate Criminal Division of the Indian High Court in Madras, 1903–1904. The case

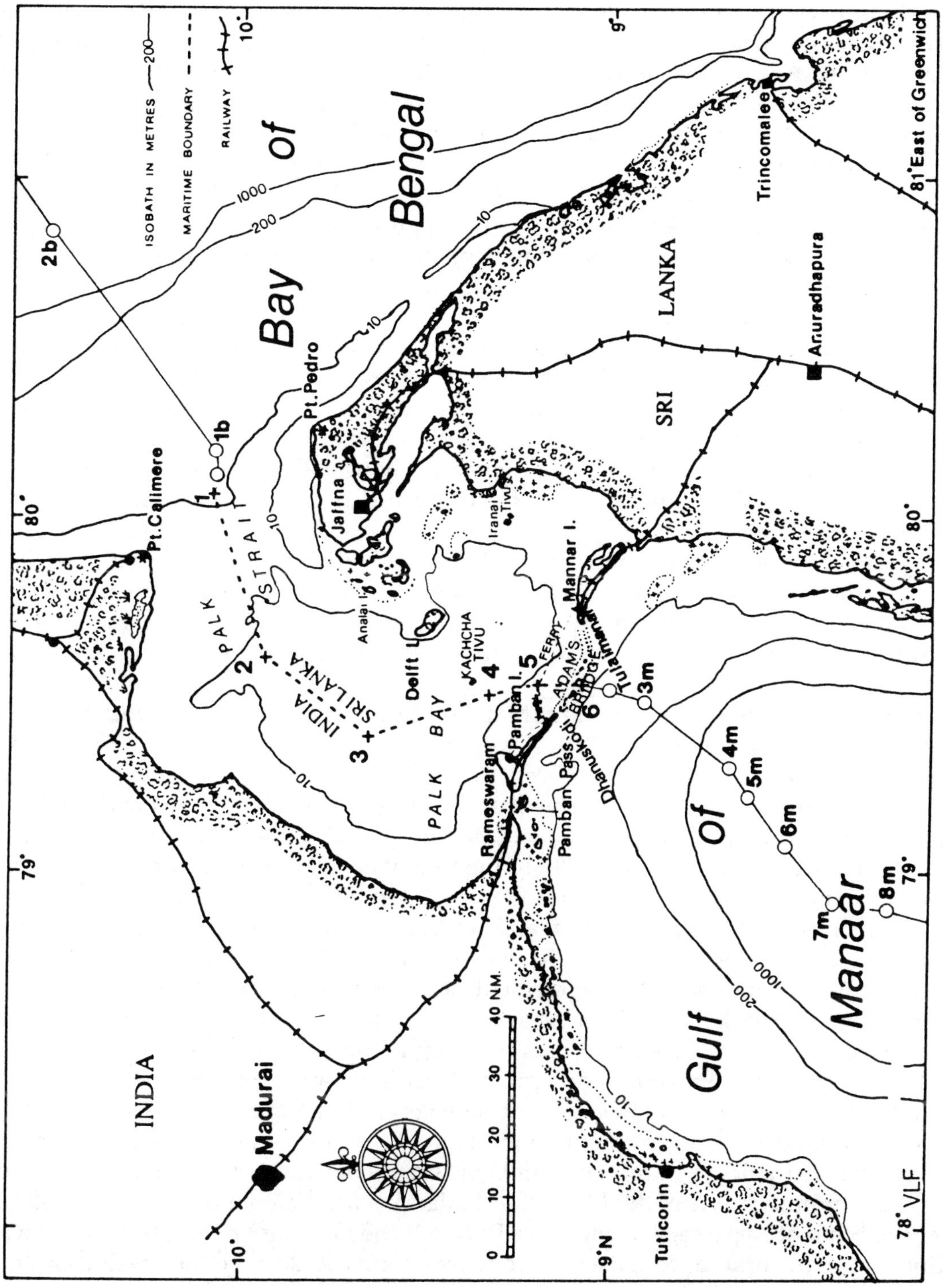

Figure 4.10 Delineation of a Seabed boundary in Palk Strait, Palk Bay, Gulf of Manaar and Bay of Bengal in the vicinity of northern Sri Lanka and Peninsular India.

involved rights to chank (conch shells used for bangle making) beds and pearl beds in Palk Bay and the adjacent Gulf of Manaar. Recognising that the bay was virtually landlocked and effectively occupied "for centuries by the inhabitants of the adjacent districts of Ceylon and India", the Court was not of the opinion that the bay "can be regarded as being in any sense the open sea and therefore outside the territorial jurisdiction of His Majesty". The agreement defines two terminal points and four turning points through the historic waters of the bay. The overall length of the boundary is 85.4 nm. Water depths along the designated line are less than 16 m. Although the agreement does not specify it, a bay-closing line may be inferred from the geographical coordinates of turning point 1 and the adjacent coastal features of India and Sri Lanka, namely Point Calimere and Palmyrah Point. The total length of the closing line is 35.1 nm (The Geographer, 1975: 4). Under the agreement both states also recognised the historical significance of Palk Bay, and undertook to respect the traditional fishing rights of the indigenous peoples. In addition, Indian fishermen and pilgrims have rights to visit Kachchativu (Article 5). Ships of both states will continue to enjoy in each other's waters such rights as they have traditionally been accustomed to (Article 6). Finally, any trans-boundary resources on and below the seabed will be explored and exploited by mutual understanding and cooperation (Article 7).

Two years later, in another agreement, India and Sri Lanka delineated a seabed boundary in the Gulf of Manaar, which extended through Palk Strait into the Bay of Bengal (The Geographer, 1987; Forbes, 1988). Also during 1976, a trilateral agreement established a maritime boundary between India, the Maldives and Sri Lanka in the Laccadive Sea.

During 1969 and 1970 Indonesia and Malaysia negotiated a seabed boundary in the Strait of Malacca. This agreement is analysed in Chapter Five. Maritime jurisdictional claims in the Andaman Sea have also been established and are now recognised by the littoral states and the international community (Figure 4.11). Between 1969 and 1987, 10 sets of seabed boundaries were negotiated there. The first agreement was between Indonesia and Malaysia in 1969 and 1970. In the following year three separate agreements were entered into, to come into force three years later. The first, a trilateral declaration signed by Indonesia, Malaysia and Thailand, established a Common Point (CP) of the three maritime boundaries. The geographical coordinate of the CP is located at Lat. 5°57′ N Long. 98°1.5′ E (Figure 5.6). This agreement permitted the delineation of a northward extension of the 1969 Indonesian-Malaysian boundary from Point 1 to the CP, measuring a distance of 35.9 nm. An agreement was also signed by Indonesia and Thailand for a partial determination of their common maritime boundary, incorporating the CP and two turning points. In 1975, a second agreement between Indonesia and Thailand permitted an extension of their common maritime boundary in the Andaman Sea. The agreement entered into force in 1978. A third agreement was signed between Malaysia and Thailand, defining three turning points of the Malaysia-Thailand maritime boundary in the northern sector of the Strait of Malacca. As with the CP, which the Geographer (1978: 1) notes was not delineated on the basis of equidistance, the three points lie closer to the baseline system of Thailand than to the Malaysian system. As there is no consistent ratio of the distance between the turning points and the nearest points on the respective baselines it can be assumed that boundaries were negotiated on the basis of equity. Malaysia and Thailand signed a maritime boundary agreement in 1979, which entered into force in 1982.

In 1974 India and Indonesia negotiated a boundary in the vicinity of the Great Channel which separates Nicobar Islands and Sumatra Island. The boundary, which is 48 nm long, is defined by four turning points. Article III of the agreement provides for the parties of seek to reach accord as to the manner in which any trans-boundary resource will be most effectively exploited, and any profits from the exploitation equally shared. The agreement entered into force in 1984.

An extension to the boundary was negotiated in 1977. Further negotiations led to bilateral agreement between India and Indonesia, and a trilateral agreement between

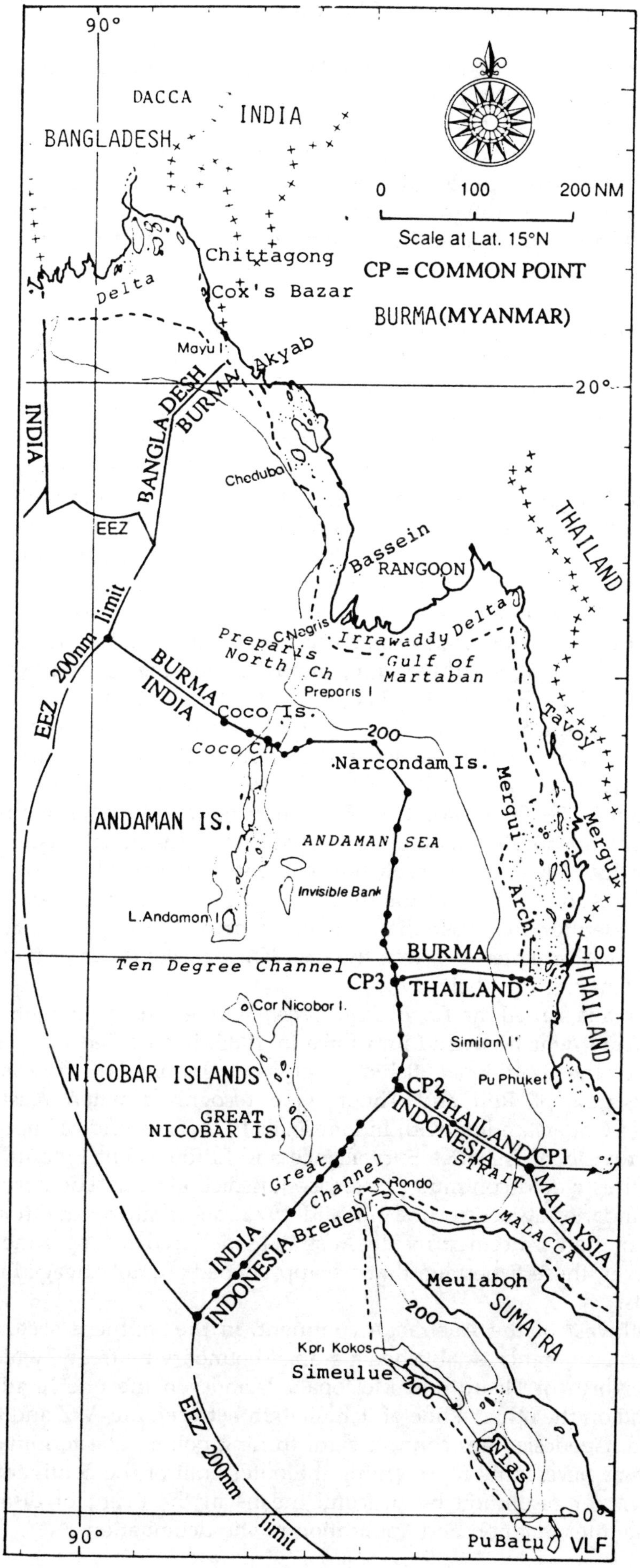

Figure 4.11 Political divisions of the Andaman Sea.

India, Indonesia and Thailand in 1978. The former entered into force the same year, and the latter in 1979.

The 140 nm common maritime boundary between Burma and Thailand in the Andaman Sea was defined in 1980 and entered into force in 1982. As a result of this agreement the waters of the Andaman Sea south of Lat. 10° N were accounted for with respect to maritime jurisdictional claims. North of this parallel, however, conflict over the sovereign status of Narcondam Island was not resolved until 1986. In that year, Burma and India reconciled their differences over the ownership of Narcondam Island and determined a 620-nm boundary at the northern end of the Andaman Sea extending to a terminating point in the Bay of Bengal (Forbes, 1988). The agreement entered into force the following year.

In 1974 Indonesia and Singapore signed an agreement to delineate the territorial sea limits of each state in the Straits of Singapore. East of the eastern terminating point of the boundary line, provision is made for its extension pending negotiations between Singapore and Malaysia. An agreement will only occur once the two states can settle the issue of ownership of the island Pedra Branca, upon which Horsburgh Lighthouse is sited. The maintenance of the lighthouse is undertaken by the Port of Singapore Authority. Malaysia disputes Singapore's claim (Forbes, 1989). Authorities from both states refuse to comment on the issue, making researchers reluctant to broach the topic of the rightful ownership of Pedra Branca with them. In order to resolve the dispute the issue has been referred to International Court of Justice (personal correspondence).

To the south of the equator, within this subregion, exists the island of Timor whose sovereign status has been debated extensively. Between 1971 and 1973 Australian and Indonesian delegations signed three agreements establishing seabed boundaries in the Arafura and Timor Seas (Figure 4.12). Each consists of a series of geodesic lines. One has its origin in the Arafura Sea about 100 nm southwest of the southern end of the Irian Jaya/Papua New Guinea land boundary, and consists of 15 lines terminating of Point A16 located at Lat. 9°28′ S, Long. 127°56′ E. The other, which consists of eight lines, runs from Lat. 10°28′ S Long. 126°00′ E (Point A 17) connecting nine turning points. It terminates at Point A 25 which is located about 35 nm northeast of Australia's Ashmore Reef in the Timor Sea. The 130 nm span between the boundaries came to be known as the Timor Gap. The Gap lines to the south of the former Portuguese colony of East Timor. It would have been in order for the Australian Government of the day to negotiate a seabed boundary with the Portuguese to close the gap. The consequences of its failure to do so are outlined in Chapter Five below.

In 1978 Australia signed the *Torres Strait Treaty* with its nearest neighbour Papua New Guinea. The Treaty, which entered into force in 1985, is analysed in Chapter Five.

Concern for the traditional fishing rights of Indonesian fishermen from the neighbouring islands of Roti and Timor were recognised when Australia signed a Memorandum of Understanding with Indonesia in 1974. A second Memorandum in 1981 established a Provisional Fisheries Surveillance and Enforcement Line. It also confirmed that both countries would continue to exercise jurisdiction over sedentary fish species to the seabed boundaries agreed to in 1971 and 1972, and that the traditional subsistence fishing by Indonesian fishermen inside Australia's declared fishing zone would not be affected. However, those fishermen that are apprehened are not engaged in "traditional" fishing methods.

To the southwest of the Australian continent, in the southern sector of the Indian Ocean, Australia and France established a seabed boundary by treaty, which entered into force in 1983. North of Heard and McDonald Islands on the one hand, and south of Kerguelen Island on the other, a line of delimitation between the AFZ and the French EEZ was established. Geodesic lines connect eight turning points. The terminating points are not to be taken as necessarily representing the outer limit of the continental shelf. There is also provision for resolution by peaceful means in the event of disagreement with reference to the interpretation and application of the delimitation.

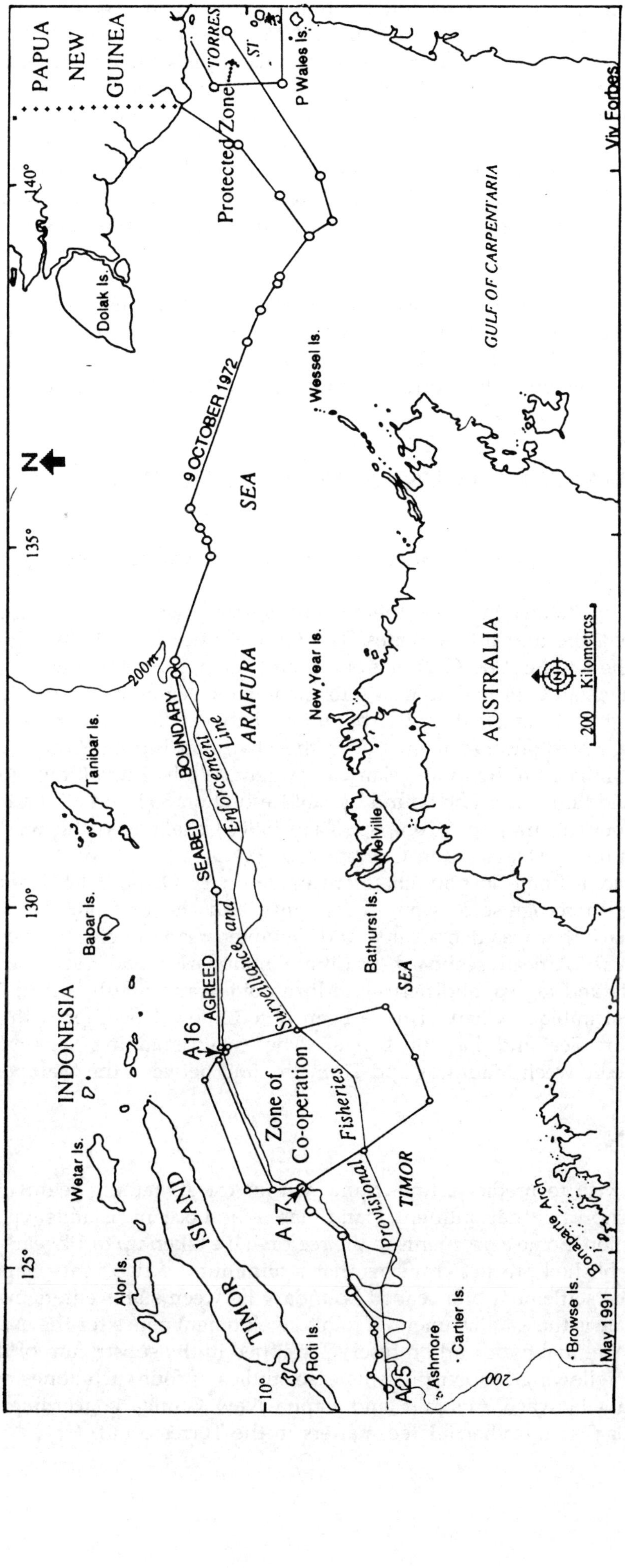

Figure 4.12 Maritime Jurisdiction in the Timor and Arafura Seas and Torres Strait.

France's second negotiated maritime boundary in the basin was the determination of a seabed line between Mauritius and Réunion (Map 27, Appendix A). The agreement entered into force in 1980. The delimitation formula applies the equidistance or median line method, which is referred to in the preamble to the agreement as "an equitable system of delimitation on the boundary of the two islands". The maritime boundary line, which is about 365 nm long, connects seven turning points. Point 4 is located equidistant from both islands, a distance of 47 nm. Point 1 is an equidistant common point which is approximately 153 nm from each of the islands of Tromelin, Réunion and Mauritius. Point 7 is located on the intersection of the 200 nm arcs drawn from the southerly seaward end of Mauritius and Réunion (Forbes, 1990: 9). This boundary line crosses water depths ranging from 3,000 to 5,000 metres.

Boundary negotiations in this region are incomplete. Mauritius is of the opinion that an earlier agreement between France and Britain in 1954 did not transfer sovereignty of Ile de Tromelin to the former from the latter. Thus, by inference, in a map published by the Mauritian government delineating that country's EEZ, Ile de Tromelin is encompassed within this limit (Forbes 1987: 8).

POTENTIAL MARITIME BOUNDARIES IN THE INDIAN OCEAN BASIN

The potential exists for at least 26 additional maritime boundaries to be negotiated within the Indian Ocean Basin.

In the Gulf of Aqaba in 1994 there were possibly six sets of boundaries to be established among the four littoral states. The Gulf of Suez lies wholly within Egyptian jurisdiction. In the Red Sea and Gulf of Aden there were ten potential boundaries (Forbes 1991: 14). The Persian Gulf had at least four incomplete segments of the Gulf, although work on defining and demarcating the boundary between Iraq and Kuwait was being supervised by a UN sponsored team under the chairmanship of Professor Mochtar, a former Foreign Minister in the Indonesian Goverment. Whilst Kuwait announced in May 1993 that it would honour and be bound by UN Resolution 833 and all other Resolutions (UN Security Council), Iraq on 6 June 1993 (S/25905) challenged the work of the UN Iraq–Kuwait Boundary Demarcation Commission (IKBDC).

However, a joint Iraqi–Russian statement made on 14 October 1994 noted that Iraq was now ready to recognise Kuwaiti sovereignty and the common land border and maritime boundary that was demarcated and delimited respectively, by the IKBDC.

Along the East African seaboard, maritime boundaries had yet to be negotiated between Somalia and Kenya, and between Mozambique and South Africa. The complex issues in the Mozambique Channel have been noted above, together with those in the northern Arabian Sea and Bay of Bengal. The two remaining segments requiring negotiation were between Mauritius and Tromelin, and between the Maldives and BIOT.

CONCLUSION

It would be unwise to predict a time frame within the remaining segments of seabed adjacent to the shores of the continental land masses and oceanic islands will come under national jurisdiction. Some agreements in the region have taken up to 14 years to negotiate. In addition, established practice confirms that a minimum of two years elapse before an agreement on the settlement of a seabed boundary between states enters into force.

A related issue is the establishment of joint development zones for the exploration and exploitation of potential hydrocarbon reserves trapped in the substratum of the continental shelves. The following chapter presents case studies of four such zones and examines the unique treaty between Australia and Papua New Guinea concerning sovereignty, maritime boundaries and other related matters in the Torres Strait.

CHAPTER FIVE

COOPERATIVE APPROACHES TO OCEAN BOUNDARY DEMARCATION

INTRODUCTION

The previous chapter examined the varied practices by states in defining and claiming maritime limits. This chapter analyses the treaties that states have entered into for the joint development of the resources of the ocean and its seabed, in regions where it was not possible to determine a maritime boundary. Such solutions arise where there is the possibility of resources such as hydrocarbon fields beneath the seabed, or where established fisheries extend across perceived borders or frontiers.

CLOS brought to the fore the potential importance of ocean space and its resources in national economic and social development. This potential lies in such areas as fisheries, minerals and hydrocarbons, transport, energy and tourism. Whilst clearly enunciating national and international jurisdiction, CLOS also envisaged and encouraged cooperation on a regional basis.

The settlement of boundary disputes involving resources has traditionally centred on the demarcation of specific lines dividing the disputed resource area between the states involved. Modern practice has developed a number of possible alternatives, ranging from the limited case of unification of trans-boundary deposits such as the Frigg Oilfield in the North Sea, to an agreed draft covering the resources of an entire continent, as is the case with Antarctica. Articles 74 and 83 of CLOS requires that, pending agreement on boundary delineation of the EEZ and continental shelf, the states concerned shall make every effort to enter into provisional arrangements and, in the meantime, not jeopardise or hamper the reaching of the final determination.

Coastal state jurisdiction over the resources of the continental shelf has its origins in the Truman Proclamation of 1945 and the Geneva Convention on the Continental Shelf, 1958 which entered into force in 1964. By then it was generally accepted that, as a matter of customary international law, a coastal state could exercise sovereign rights over the natural resources of its continental shelf out to a maximum water depth of 200 metres and beyond that, as far as available technology permitted exploitation. Confirmation of the coastal state's rights to explore and exploit the natural resources of the sea, seabed and substratum adjacent to its coast with the assertion that this was the natural prolongation of its land territory was propounded in the 1969 North Sea Continental Shelf Cases.

Figure 5.1 demonstrates graphically three options for states with opposing coastlines to take, in determining a maritime boundary between them. Consider, then State X, an island state and State Y, on a continental landmass; their facing coastlines are less than 400 nm apart. The natural prolongation of State X extends into a trough, whose bathymetric axis is nearer to State Y. The physical-geographical reality (Figure 5.1a) to boundary determination and in keeping with customary international law would suggest that rights to the seabed regime would extend from the coastlines of the respective states throughout the natural prolongation of their continental shelves. Based on the interpretation of Article 76 of CLOS the edge of the shelf ends at the bathymetric axis of the trough. The trough, a trench in the seafloor, has a long axis, about 100 nm, running parallel to the coastline

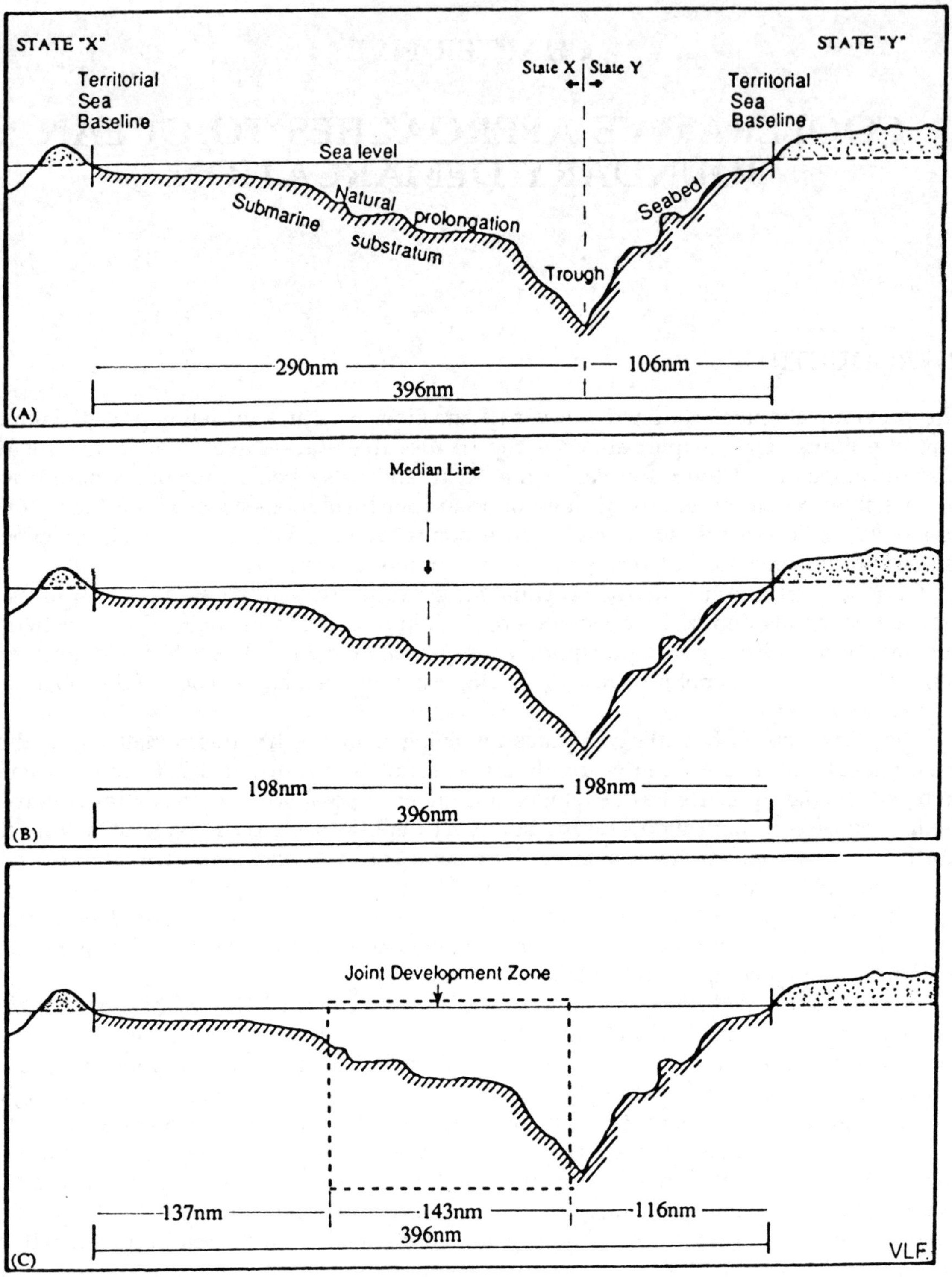

Figure 5.1 Some variations in determining a maritime boundary along the natural prolongation of a landmass: (a) the physical-geographical reality (CLOS, Art. 76); (b) the legislative approach; and (c) the cooperative approach (eg; the Timor Gap Treaty Zone of Cooperation).

of State Y. Its distance from the coastline of that state varies from about 45 to 70 nm. Water depths in the vicinity of the trough are in excess of 2,500 m.

State Y may argue that there is one shared continental shelf between the two countries, and hold the view that a legalistic approach be adopted. The determination of a median line would be the preferred option (Figure 5.1b). It might further argue that the concept of the EEZ with seabed rights out to 200 nm supports the median line. Indeed, the ICJ judgement in the 1985 Libya-Malta Continental Shelf Case substantiates this approach.

The recommendations of CLOS, however, do not provide any definitive solution to the problem. Article 83 suggests that delimitation of the continental shelf shall be carried out by agreement on the basis of international law in order to achieve an equitable solution. A cooperative approach such as the establishment of a joint development zone (Figure 5.1c), to share the disputed area would be a solution and would avoid potential conflict between the states.

Such an approach would be determined by bilateral agreement including clauses indicating the treaty's temporary or permanent status, its continuity and lifespan. Articles in the treaty would also include the nature of the joint development zone, the kind of natural resources concerned, the rules for sharing of the resources, taxation, pollution control legislation and customs, excise, health and work practice regulations (Lagoni, 1984).

There has been disagreement (e.g. Miyoshi, 1988: 9) as to whether customary international law specifically provides for positive cooperation for joint development. The lack of certainty on custom and the growing number of agreements suggest that the focus is best placed on negotiated treaties as indications of the various possible solutions available in the absence of conventional boundary determination.

Thus states may opt to take the cooperative approach to jointly explore, exploit and manage the area of dispute. Alternately, agreements may be drawn between states where one party is seen as benevolent, undertaking to finance the project and yet willing to share the work in and profits from the development with the other party. Finally, when bilateral or even trilateral meetings fail to achieve a solution an arbitrator may be requested to intervene, as demonstrated in the North Sea Continental Shelf Cases of 1969.

Within the Indian Ocean Basin there are three joint development zones (JDZ) for the exploration and exploitation of the mineral resources in the substratum of the continental shelf. Two of the JDZ agreements belong to the first classification, with Saudi Arabia as the benevolent partner. They are the Bahrain/Saudi Arabia Agreement in the Persian Gulf, the Saudi Arabia/Sudan Agreement in the Red Sea. The Australia/Indonesia Treaty for the establishment of a JDZ in the Timor Sea is a most detailed regime for the development of continental shelf petroleum resources. It must be viewed within the overall framework of Australia/Indonesia relations. Each of the above agreements is examined and analysed below.

THE BAHRAIN–SAUDI ARABIA AGREEMENT

The first of the joint development zones established in the Indian Ocean Basin was initiated by Bahrain and Saudi Arabia in a spirit of affection and mutual friendship. Indeed, the preamble of the agreement noted that the King of Saudi Arabia wished to extend every possible assistance to the Government of Bahrain. Thus, on 22 February 1958 a simple and concise agreement concerning the delimitation of the continental shelf between Saudi Arabia and Bahrain and of the joint development zone entered into force.

The zone, which lies wholly within the territory of Saudi Arabia, is bounded by six geodesic lines connecting the six turning points whose geographical coordinates are defined (Figure 5.2). Its surface area is about 1,244 sq km. Approximately 80 percent of the Abu Saafah Oilfield lies within it about 50 km northeast of the refinery port Ras Tanura on the Saudi Arabian coastline.

The Agreement notes that the exploitation of the oil resources in this zone will be carried out in the way chosen by Saudi Arabia on the condition that the Government of Bahrain is granted one-half of the net revenue accruing to the Government of Saudi Arabia and arising from this exploitation, and on the understanding that this does not

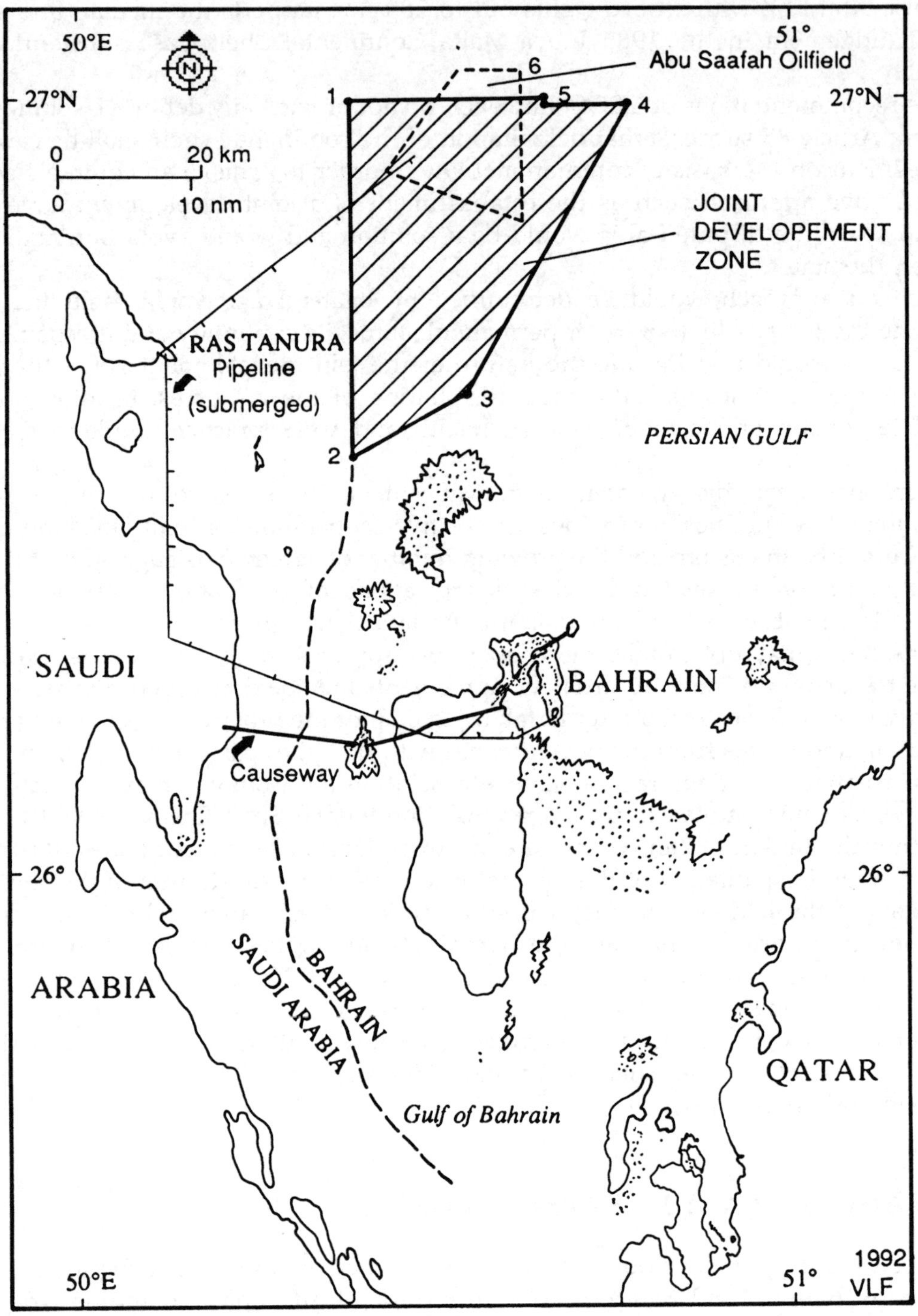

Figure 5.2 The Bathrain–Saudi Arabia Joint Development Zone in the Persian Gulf.

infringe the right of sovereignty of the Government of Saudi Arabia nor the right of administration over the defined zone.

THE SAUDI ARABIA–SUDAN AGREEMENT

An agreement was signed in 1974 between Saudi Arabia and Sudan relating to the joint exploration and exploitation of the hydrocarbon and other mineral resources of the seabed and substratum in the Red Sea Deeps in waters adjacent to their respective continental shelves. Saudi Arabia, the benefactor, undertook to provide financial support for any such project.

Detailed exploration of the Red Sea Deeps by the West German Company Preussag began in the 1960s, although a Swedish expedition in 1948 had earlier become aware of the peculiarities of this semi-enclosed sea. There are 17 deeps in a rift valley running longitudinally down the middle of the sea (Figure 5.3). The deepest is the Suakin Deep (about 2850 m); the richest is the Atlantis II which lies due west from Jeddah. Within it, mineral-rich sediments occur at about 2180 m, covering a surface area of about 60 sq km. These metalliferous sediments are known to contain millions of tonnes of zinc and copper ore, and thousands of tonnes of silver. Other minerals that may be extracted when economically feasible are cadmium, cobalt, lead and gold.

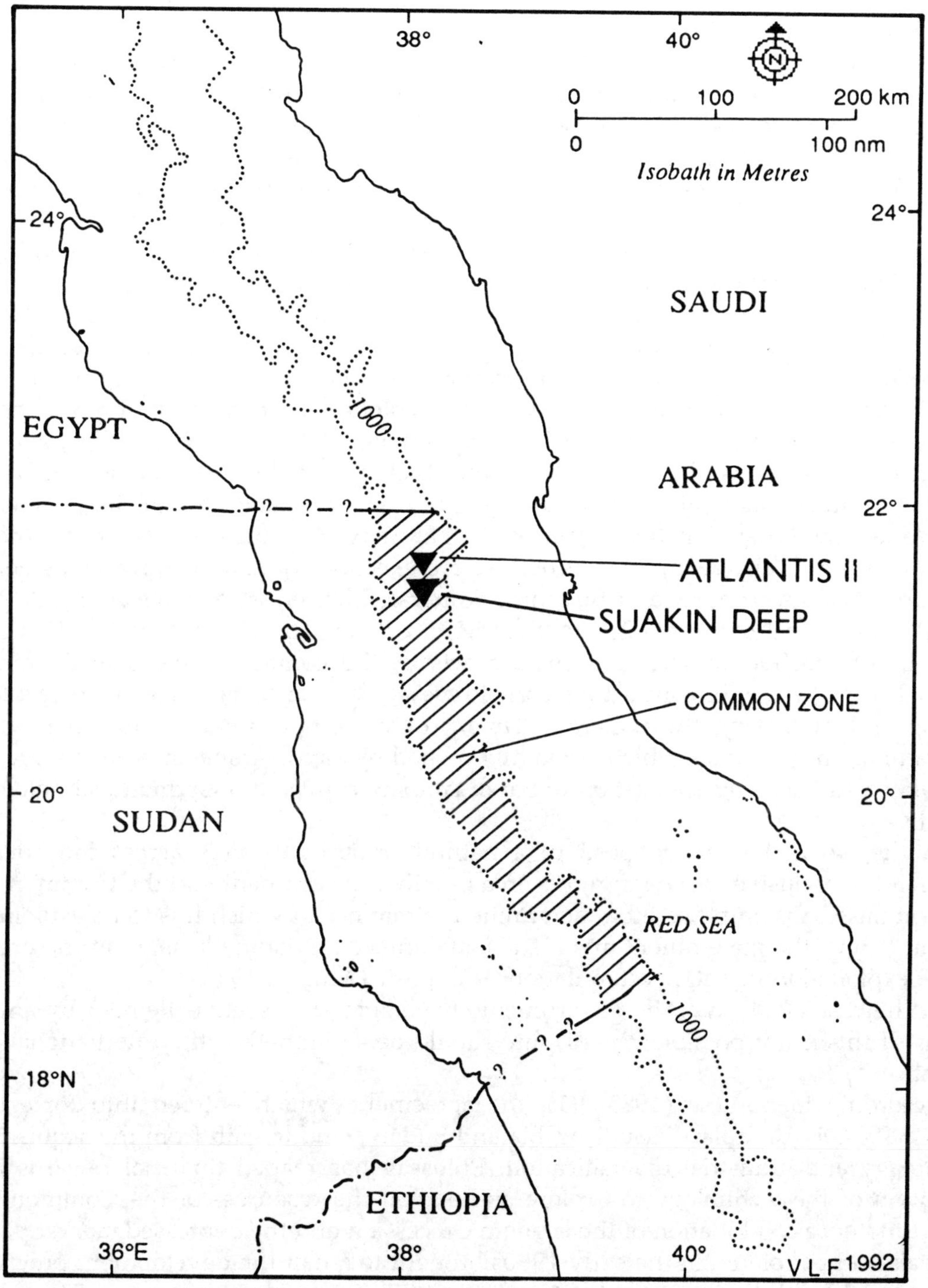

Figure 5.3 The Saudi Arabia–Sudan Common Zone of Exploitation in the Red Sea.

This Saudi Arabia/Sudan agreement is simple in its text and approaches the determination of a JDZ in a constructive and cooperative way. Like the above agreement, it is not a temporary conflict resolution. Both parties recognize that each has exclusive sovereign rights in the area of the seabed adjacent to its respective coasts and extending seawards to a line where the depth of the superjacent waters is uninterruptedly 1,000 m (Articles III and IV). The length of the defined area is about 400 km, with an average width of 45 km.

Article V of the agreement establishes a Common Zone comprising the 18,000 sq km of the seabed encompassed by the 1,000 m isobath. The two governments have equal sovereign rights to all the natural resources of the Common Zone, which rights are exclusive to them. No part of the territorial sea of either government is included in the Common Zone. The two governments undertake to protect their sovereign rights and defend them against third parties.

To ensure the prompt and efficient exploitation of the natural resources of the Common Zone, a Joint Commission, financed in the first instance by Saudi Arabia, was established. It possesses in the Kingdom of Saudi Arabia and the Democratic Republic of the Sudan such legal capacity as may be necessary for the exercise of all the functions assigned to it. It is composed of an equal number of representatives from both countries, headed in each case by the competent Minister (Article IX). Its functions are: to survey, delimit and demarcate the Zone's boundaries; to undertake studies concerning the exploration and exploitation of its natural resources; to encourage the specialized bodies to undertake operations for the exploration of such resources; and to consider and decide, in accordance with the conditions it prescribes, on the applications for licences and concessions concerning exploration and exploitation. Furthermore, the Joint Commission would take the steps necessary to expedite the exploitation of the natural resources of its seabed; to organise the supervision of the exploitation at the production stage; and make such regulations as may be necessary for the discharge of the functions assigned to it.

The Commission is also required to prepare the estimates for all its expenses; to undertake any other functions or duties that may be entrusted to it by the two governments. It is also required to supervise pre-existing exploration agreements between the Sudanese Government and Sudanese Minerals Limited, and between Saudi Arabia and Preussag, without prejudice to the rights of the Government of the Democratic Republic of the Sudan. The Commission acts as the common enterprise to mine the Deeps within the zone, contracting with Preussag for the technical work of exploring, mining and processing the minerals. Thus, in this unique international joint venture programme, the resources which are jointly owned by Saudi Arabia and Sudan, are being exploitated through the application of Saudi Arabian capital and German technology and expertise.

In the event that any deposit of a natural resource extends across the boundary between the exclusive sovereign rights area of either government and the Common Zone, the Commission is empowered to determine the manner in which it is to be exploited. At the same time, the government involved is guaranteed an equitable share in the proceeds of the exploitation of such accumulation or deposit (Article XIV).

In the case of dispute, the governments have agreed to seek settlement by amicable means. If this is not possible, the dispute should be submitted to the International Court of Justice.

According to Borgese (1985: 91), the agreement, which entered into force on 26 August 1974, is exemplary. Saudi Arabia and Sudan stand to gain from the acquisition of technology and industrial diversification. Preussag has reaped financial rewards in the utilisation of the technology to explore and exploit the resources of the Common Zone. Unfortunately a combination of the economic recession and the depressed market price for minerals and petroleum in the early 1990s brought to a halt the development programme (Oceans of Wealth Series — Salt of the Earth, SBS, Television Programme, Thursday 13 February 1992).

THE AUSTRALIA-INDONESIA TIMOR GAP AGREEMENT

The Timor Gap is in an area of seabed adjacent to and south of the former Portuguese territory of East Timor, which was annexed by Indonesia during the 1975 revolution in Portugal. Although the United Nations General Assembly does not recognise this action and calls for self-determination by the East Timorese, the Australian Government has recognised East Timor as part of Indonesia since 1978. Suter (1989) argues that this act of recognition arose specifically out of Australia's desire to resolve the Timor Gap problem, for the area is of considerable interest to petroleum exploration geologists. It contains a geological feature known as the Kelp Structure which has substantial hydrocarbons potential.

Negotiations with Indonesia on the seabed boundary in the Timor Gap began in February 1979. Initial discussions did not produce a satisfactory result because Australia and Indonesia hold differing views as to the principles of international law which govern the concept of the continental shelf and the natural prolongation of the land mass (see pp. 111–113). Australia argues that, under customary international law, Australia's and Indonesia's rights to the seabed regime extend from their coastlines throughout the natural prolongation of their continental shelves. Article 76 of CLOS would suggest that the edge of the shelves is the bathymetric axis of the Timor Trough, which is a trench in the seafloor with a long axis running parallel with and southeast of Timor Island. Its distance from the southeastern coastline of Timor varies from about 30 to 60 nm. Water depths in the vicinity of the trough are in excess of 3000 metres. Indonesia's viewpoint is that there is one shared continental shelf between the two countries and therefore a median line would be acceptable. Additionally, Indonesia argues that the concept of the EEZ with seabed rights out to 200 nautical miles supports the median line.

The wording of CLOS does not provide any definitive solution to the problem. Article 83 states that delimitation of the continental shelf shall be carried out by agreement on the basis of international law in order to achieve an equitable solution. Indonesia could gain some encouragement from the introduction of the 200 nm concept into the continental shelf. However, Australia would rely on the specific reference to natural prolongation. Indonesia would also refer to the use of the 200 nm concept in post-1982 continental shelf delimitations, in particular the case of Libya v Malta Continental Shelf Arbitration. In that particular judgement, the ICJ took the relevant length of the coastline of Libya and compared it with that of Malta. Employing a proportionality method it determined that the adjusted median line lay 18 nm northward of the original median line. It has been pointed out that, in the Australia/Indonesia case, a tribunal would not base a decision on any single factor, but rather arrive at an equitable solution, taking into account all factors used in the cases. Although it is predictable that such a judgement would settle a boundary north of the median line and south of the bathymetric axis, the various factors held to be relevant are so numerous and so difficult to weigh, that one cannot predict the specific boundary which might be adopted.

In reconciling the two countries' competing claims, their negotiating teams began exploring the possibility of a provisional joint development regime to operate pending final delimitation of the seabed. Detailed discussions were held at ministerial level in 1985. Finally, on 5 September 1988 the Governments of both countries announced that an agreement had been reached in which a three-area Zone of Cooperation was being proposed for the Timor Gap. Endorsement in principle was announced the following month. A year later, officials from both countries initialled the text of the Treaty and its four Annexes. The Treaty entered into force on 9 February 1991 (Forbes and Auburn, 1991). Prima facie, it deals only with the exploration and exploitation of petroleum and natural gas resources (Moloney, 1990: 129).

The Zone of Cooperation in the disputed seabed boundary area between East Timor and Australia covers 60,000 sq km (Figure 5.4). In Area B, which is that part of the Zone closest to Australia, Australia will pay to Indonesia 10 percent of the gross Resource Rent

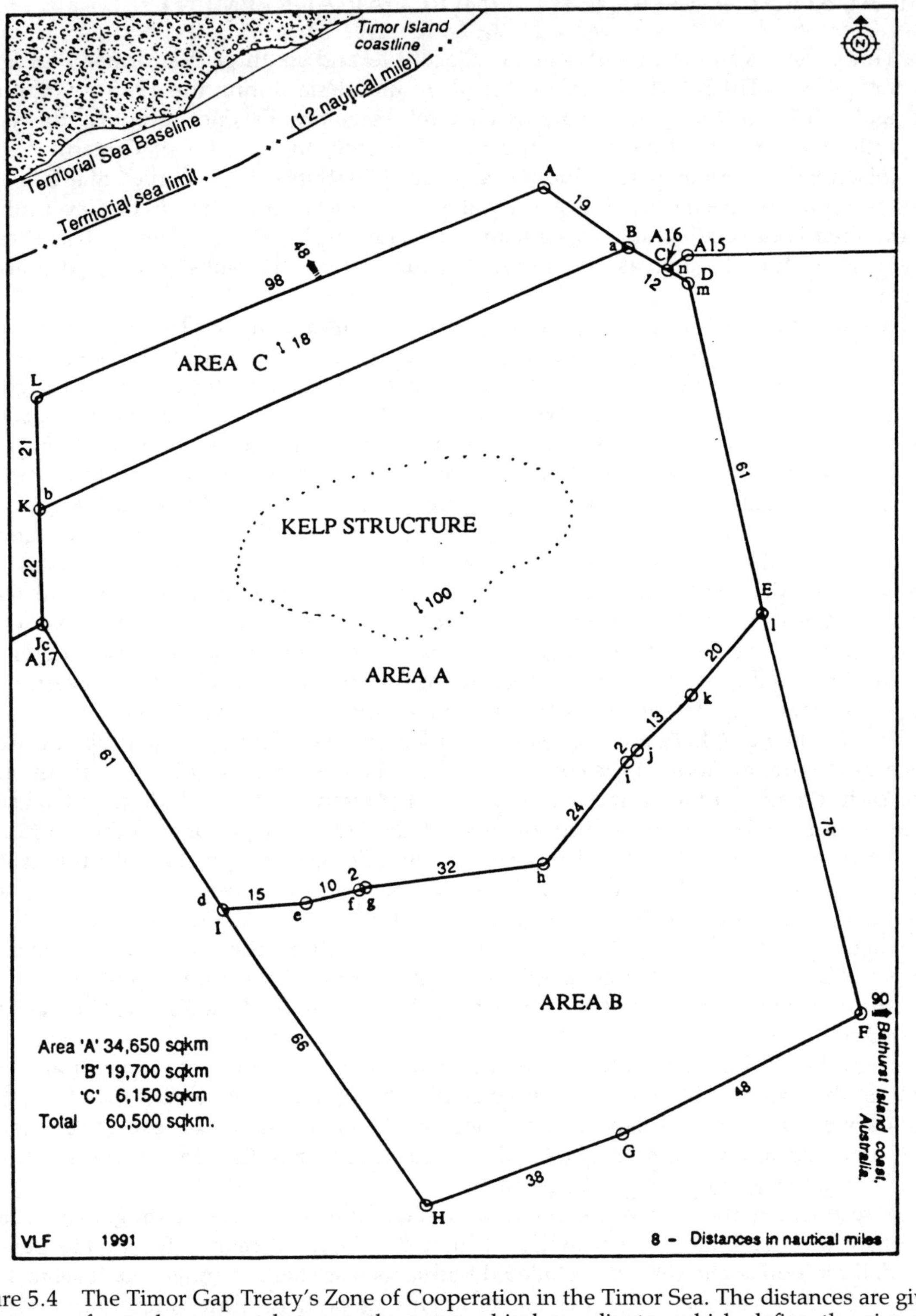

Figure 5.4 The Timor Gap Treaty's Zone of Cooperation in the Timor Sea. The distances are given for each segment between the geographical coordinates which define the size and shape of this irregular-shaped zone.

Tax collected from petroleum production (Articles 2: 2b and 4: 1b). Indonesia makes analogous payments of 10 percent of Contractors' Income Tax collected in Area C, which is that part of the Zone closest to Indonesia (Articles 2: 2c and 4: 1c). Area A, which is the largest and central portion with a surface area of about 35,000 sq km, is subject to a detailed joint development regime. It is in Area A that the Kelp Structure is located.

A Ministerial Council, consisting of an equal number of ministers designated by each Contracting State and operating by consensus, has overall responsibility for Area A. The

Council meets annually. A Joint Authority, with managerial functions, is responsible to the Ministerial Council. It manages petroleum exploration and exploitation activities and is responsible for environmental management according to the provisions of the Treaty and the regulations issued by the Ministerial Council. It began operating in July 1991. One of its initial functions, in December 1991, was to allocate permits for the exploration programme within Area A.

Specific provision is also made for cooperation in Area A, in such matters as search and rescue, air traffic services and protection of the marine environment (Articles 14 to 17). The parties are required to negotiate agreement on the exploitation of petroleum accumulations extending across the boundary of Area A (Article 20). The Zone of Cooperation shall be in force for 40 years and it may be renewed for successive terms of 20 years if no permanent continental shelf delimitation has been reached. There is thus no incentive to attempt a permanent settlement, especially if it leads to the breakdown of an interim agreement which is satisfactory to both parties.

The two-tier management structure of the Timor Gap Treaty has been described as unusual (Onorato and Valencia, 1990: 6). The close cooperation between the two countries required for consensus decision-making at each level demands a high level of integration and constitutes a problematical procedure. In case of disagreements the entire Treaty would be at risk. However, the decision to jointly manage Zone A, without any resolution of sovereign rights, explains the two tiers and the insistence upon close cooperation at both levels. It remains to be seen whether the arrangement will prove satisfactory in practice.

The Timor Gap Treaty adopts the clean-slate approach by not giving recognition to pre-existing rights (Livesley, 1990: 19). Prior to the negotiations Australia had issued licences in Area A. Their abrogation raised the possibility of compensation claims against the Australian Commonwealth Government under Section 51(31) of the Constitution. The Australian Government has publicly rejected the possibility that such claims could succeed. Nevertheless, in unpublished side-letters to the Treaty, Australia and Indonesia have allegedly agreed that the Ministerial Council would give favourable consideration to applications by existing Australian permit-holders (Poll, 1990: 57). Since the possible losses could amount to hundreds of millions of dollars for the companies concerned, they have a strong incentive to sue the Commonwealth for compensation should a satisfactory solution not be reached. In fact, however, Indonesia has publicly insisted on the clean-slate approach as reflecting the withdrawal of Australia's sovereign rights from Areas A and C (Smart 1990, Part 2: 387). Preference to existing Australian permit holders, especially in the highly prospective Kelp Structure would naturally contradict this stance. It is scarcely surprising, therefore, that one such company, the Western Mining Corporation, commenced proceedings against the Commonwealth Government in June 1991 (Pheasant, 1991).

It remains to be seen, however, whether and to what extent permit holders will be compensated by receiving priority in areas equivalent to their original holdings. If a total joint development regime is to be adopted without sovereignty complications, then the clean-slate approach is logical. On the other hand, no government will be ready to face large compensation claims. If there is an unpublished compromise in the Timor Gap Treaty, it may help solve the Australian Goverment's problems with licenses, but at the cost of compromising the sovereignty issue.

Finally, although Australia is a party to the Statute of the International Court of Justice, Indonesia is not, making it risky and impracticable to refer the matter to the Court, or a Chamber of the Court. Furthermore, the location of the Kelp Structure in the disputed area and the uncertainty as to the specific location of hydrocarbons raises the risks for both countries. The obvious solution was, therefore, to share the disputed area to avoid serious conflict. It is not suprising that this was done, and the time taken to reach agreement in principle may be ascribed to other political differences between the two countries.

An additional complication has resulted from the action of Portugal, which on 22 February 1991 commenced proceedings in the International Court of Justice to challenge the Timor Gap Treaty. Portugal requested the ICJ to declare that Australia must recognise the rights of the East Timorese to self-determination and to sovereignty rights over their wealth and natural resources. Furthermore, the ICJ was asked to recognise the fact that Portugal was not party to the negotiations. The note of protest implied that Australia failed in its duty to negotiate the respective rights; incurred international responsibility and caused damage; and must accept that it owes reparation to the people of East Timor (Auburn and Forbes, 1991: 15). Portugal maintains that Indonesia has no legitimate claim to the wealth and resources of East Timor. The case is still awaiting its hearing at the ICJ in October 1994.

The agreements analysed above were negotiated with a focus on the joint exploration and exploitation of the minerals, including hydrocarbons, in the seas between the countries party to the agreements. Similar agreements can also be applied to the joint development of other marine resources in an area of sea space pending the settlement of the maritime boundary between the disputing states.

THE AUSTRALIA–PAPUA NEW GUINEA AGREEMENT

Negotations leading to the signing of the Torres Strait Treaty followed Prime Minister Whitlam's letter in December 1972 to the Premier of Queensland, suggesting that discussions between officials of the Australian, Papua New Guinea and Queensland Governments be held on the settlement of the jurisdiction of the Torres Strait islands. The treaty, which was signed in 1978, came into force in 1985.

It set in place several delimitation lines running through the Torres Strait area (Figure 5.5). These include: the Seabed Resources Line; the Swimming Fisheries Resources Line; the Protected Zone Delineation Line; lines delimiting the territorial sea between Papua New Guinea and Boigu; and between Papua New Guinea and Dauan/Saibai, and a straight line linking these two lines.

The Seabed Resources Line has the potential to become a major dividing line between the two nations. If such is the case, the Torres Strait Islanders face division of their land and people, and restriction on their traditional activities and movements. Further, a major dividing line would create an enclave of the inhabited islands of Boigu, Saibai and Dauan (Figure 4.6). This may in the long term lead to a Papua New Guinean claim to the three islands, especially should illegal migration and occupation by Papua New Guineans continue. The Treaty provides an opportunity for the indigenous culture of the Torres Strait Islanders to be preserved.

The question of ownership of the islands Kawa, Mata Kawa and Kussa (Figure 4.6) has virtually become a non-issue (Article 2: 3). From the evidence put forward it has been conceded that Papua New Guinea does have rightful claim to sovereignty over these islands. Indeed, the Torres Strait Islanders have always considered the three islands as traditionally belonging to Papua New Guinea. Obviously, little credence is given to the 1879 Queensland proclamation that Kawa, Mata Kawa and Kussa were part of the group known as the Talbot Islands, and therefore included within the boundaries of Queensland by the Queensland Coast Islands Act 1879.

The Torres Strait Treaty recognises that the territorial seas of the Australian islands lying north of the Seabed Resources Line have a maximum breadth of three nm. The Papua New Guinean Territorial Sea along its southern coastline between meridians 142°03′ 30″ E and 142°51′ 00″E has a maximum breadth of three nm. The limit does not extend south of the territorial sea lines surrounding Boigu, Dauan and Sabai, nor south of the straight line linking these two areas. It does not extend into the area south of the seabed line, nor into agreed Australian Territorial Sea north of the seabed line, nor encroach upon the agreed area of Australian fisheries jurisdiction north of the seabed line. Neither nation will in future extend its territorial seas across the seabed delimitation line.

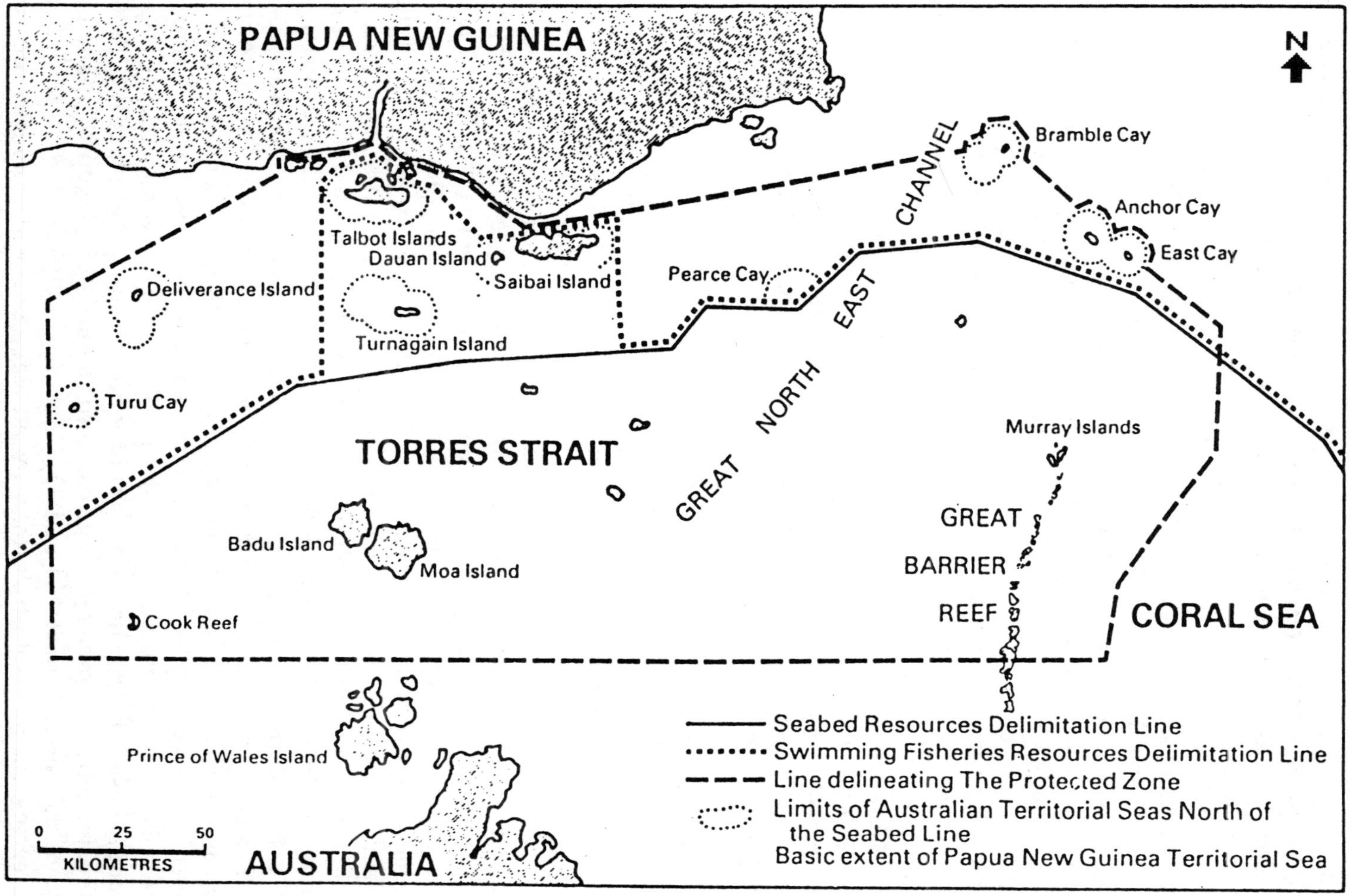

Figure 5.5 The suite of maritime jurisdictional zones in the Torres Strait as defined in the Torres Strait Treaty which also establishd a Protected Zone for the Torres Strait. Source: *The Torres Strait Treaty*, 1985.

On the issue of exploration of seabed resources, the Treaty contains a provision (Article 6) that if any single accumulation of liquid hydrocarbons or natural gas, or any other mineral deposit beneath the seabed, extends across a boundary line, the two governments will seek to reach agreement on the most effective way to exploit it, and on the sharing of subsequent benefits.

The concept and implementation of the Protected Zone, which encompasses all the reserve land of the Torres Strait, provides an opportunity for the indigenous culture of the Torres Strait Islanders to be preserved. The Protected Zone was also established to regulate the exploration and exploitation of the mineral resources and the conservation and management of the biotic resources of the Torres Strait. The preservation of the traditional fishing rights and the freedom of movement within the Zone is guaranteed. An embargo was placed on mining and oil drilling of the seabed within the Protected Zone until 1995, which is 10 years after the Treaty came into force. The provisions of the Treaty allow for the embargo to be extended beyond the 10-year period, by agreement between Papua New Guinea and Australia and after consultation with the Torres Strait Islanders.

Australia was also concerned to regulate movement in the area. Once a natural barrier to the spread of exotic diseases into Australia, the Torres Strait can no longer be regarded as such, due to the importation of animals to the islands in the late 19th century and the increased movement of the traditional population and other persons in and through the area. Illegal entry of Papua New Guineans to Australian territory is known to occur despite some official restrictions on movement in the Strait. The removal of all restrictions would only cause the existing position to worsen.

Provisions regarding the Protected Zone fisheries state that traditional fishing will have precedence over commercial fishing. Both countries are to consult and cooperate in the issue of migration, customs, health and quarantine arrangements. In addition, each country retains the right to implement national controls to prevent abuses or other possible adverse effects of the Protected Zone provisions. The promotion of economic development and employment opportunities in the Torres Strait and adjacent coastal area of Papua New Guinea is to be taken into regard by the relevant authorities of both countries in the administrative process of issuing fishing licences. There is to be periodic consultation with the people of the area on the licensing arrangements. The responsible authorities of each country will issue licences to their own nationals and, when necessary, endorse the licences of nationals of the other country. Unless agreed otherwise by Papua New Guinea and Australia, only these two countries will commercially fish the Protected Zone. In the process of allocating licences, and in deciding upon management and access arrangements of the two countries in respect of the commercial Protected Zone fisheries, regard is held to the levels of catch by each country prior to 1985. Provided such levels remain within the optimum sustainable yield of the fishery concerned, they were not to be reduced before 1990. After that date, the levels of catch by Australia and Papua New Guinea are being adjusted progressively so that Papua New Guinea will have a 25 percent share of the catch of the commercial Protected Zone fisheries in waters under Australian jurisdiction, and Australia will have a similar share in Papua New Guinean waters. There are a number of minor exemptions to this sharing arrangement including, for example, the provision for Papua New Guinea to have the total catch of the commercial barramundi fishery near its coasts. Finally, should one country not take up its full share of a Protected Zone fishery, the other has preference against third countries to take up all or any part of the surplus of that share (Articles 24 and 25).

The foregoing examples illustrate that, by mutual agreement, countries are able to reconcile their differences when there are benefits to be gained in determining the most appropriate means of sharing the resources of the seabed adjacent to their respective coastlines. Similarly, in confined waterways shared by coastal states, mutual arrangements can be made whereby the states adjacent to and those beyond such waters may establish rules and regulations to ensure the safe passage of ships and pollution control measures. This is best illustrated with reference to the Malacca Strait.

THE MALACCA STRAIT

The Malacca Strait provides the most efficient sea route from European and Middle East ports to commercial trading ports of Southeast Asian countries, Japan, China, Eastern Australia and New Zealand. It is approximately 500 nm in length, and varies in width from about 150 nm at the latitude of Penang Island, to about 8 nm where it joins the Straits of Singapore, north of Karimun Islands (Figure 5.6). About 50,000 ships use this 500 nm seaway annually, including small local craft as well as large tankers and cargo carriers (PSA, 1989). Only the Strait of Dover carries more traffic (Couper, 1987). The Strait is a comparatively shallow seaway and is reported to be silting up, notwithstanding the continuous dredging that is being undertaken. The dune-like characteristics of the seabed topography are influenced by ocean currents, which create areas of shallow seas and shoal waters. Furthermore, tidal range varies from 3.8 metres at the northwestern entrance of the strait to 1.4 metres at its southeastern section, where it joins the Straits of Singapore.

The legal status of the Malacca Strait is a subject of great concern, not only to the bordering countries of Indonesia, Malaysia, Singapore and Thailand, but also to the international maritime community.

The 1969 Agreement Between the Government of the Republic of Indonesia and the Government of Malaysia relating to the delimitation of the Continental Shelves between the two Countries established the geographical coordinates of ten turning points which define the boundary of the Indonesian and Malysian continental shelf in the Malacca Strait (Figure 5.6). The overall length of the nine lines joining the turning points is about 400 nm. (The Geographer, 1970). The northern terminus of the boundary is located 39 nm between the declared baselines of the two states. Perak Island (Pulau Perak), which is claimed by Malaysia, influences the location of this turning point. At the southern terminus, the boundary lies midway between P. Kulup (Kobob) Island, on the Malaysian side, and Greater Karimun (The Brothers) Island on the Indonesian side, a distance of about six nm. About 55 percent of the shelf boundary lies in water depths of less than 50 m, the remainder in depths between 50 and 100 m. The shelf boundary equally divides the seabed between the Indonesian and Malaysian baselines.

Article 1:3 of the agreement made provision for the extension of the Indonesian-Malaysian continental shelf boundary from Point 1, established in 1969, to the CP of the future Malaysia-Thailand-Indonesia Agreement, once that point was established.

Because of increasing concern over navigational safety, serious pollution problems and security, specifically piracy in the region, the Malacca Strait Council (MSC) was formed in 1971. Earlier, in July 1967, Japan had submitted to the Inter-Governmental Maritime Consultative Organisation's (IMCO) Sub-Committee on Safety of Navigation a proposal to establish sea lanes in the Malacca Strait and Straits of Singapore on the grounds that a large number of its big tankers used these waters (Koh, 1982: 57). It offered financial support and expertise to ensure maintenance of the navigational channels for the safety of all shipping in the region. In November 1971, a joint Statement on the Malacca Straits was issued by the Governments of Indonesia, Malaysia and Singapore.

The three governments agreed that, although the safety of navigation in the Malacca Strait and Straits of Singapore was the responsibility of the coastal state concerned, there was, nevertheless, a need for tripartite cooperation on the issue. They therefore planned to establish a body for the coordination of efforts for the safety of navigation in the two straits. Furthermore, they regarded the safety problem and the question of internationalisation of the straits as two separate issues, while agreeing that the Malacca Strait and Straits of Singapore are not international straits. The MSC has been responsible for numerous hydrographic surveys resulting in the detection and charting of a number of shallows of less than 23 metres in the shipping lanes.

The grounding of the 237,698 dwt Japanese supertanker Showa Maru during the pre-dawn hours of 6 January 1975, west of Buffalo Rocks in the Straits of Singapore in

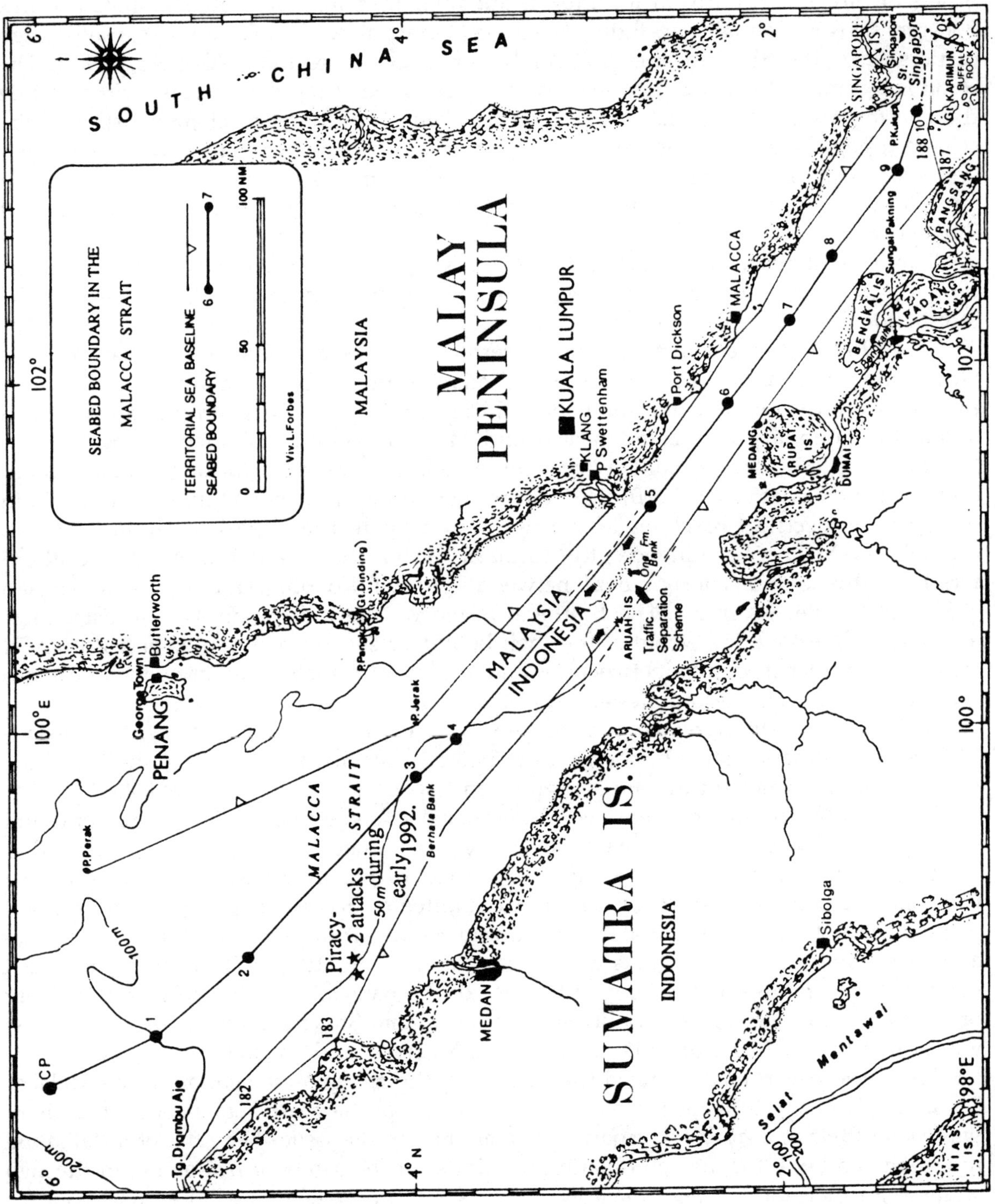

Figure 5.6 Continental Shelf Boundary in the Malacca strait.

Indonesian waters, and the subsequent spillage of approximately 4500 tonnes of crude oil in the confined waters heightened concern, brought about urgent discussions and gave rise to drastic measures to prevent further environmental problems and disasters of similar magnitude. Following the mishap, a Joint Statement was issued by the governments of the three straits states. It reported that, in order to protect the coastal states from damages resulting from oil pollution, there was unanimous agreement on the need to maximise the safety of navigation in the Straits of Malacca and Singapore. It recommended the establishment of traffic separation schemes in the appropriate sections of the the two straits in accordance with international regulations (Figure 5.7). Due to the shallowness and narrowness of the straits, the density of traffic and the limited manoeuvrability of the very large crude carriers (VLCCs) limitations would be placed on the passage of VLCCs, according to the recommendations of an appropriate group of experts. Expert advice would also be sought on measures to enhance the safety of navigation, the introduction of advanced navigation aids and other means of improving navigation.

Following the inter-government discussions a Tripartite Agreement was signed on 24 February 1977, requiring ships to maintain a single under-keel clearance (UKC) of at least 3.5 m at all times during the entire passage through the Malacca Strait and Straits of Singapore and to take all necessary safety precautions, especially when navigating in the One Fathom Bank area, the Main Straits and Philip Channel, and off Horsborg Lighthouse (Appendix A, Map 25). In terms of the proposed traffic separation schemes, it also required vessels having draughts of 15 metres and above, to keep to the designated Deep Water Route (DWR) in the Straits of Singapore up to Buffalo Rock, and recommended that they navigate in the specified route from Buffalo Rock up to the Batu Berhenti area. Speeds were to be restricted to a maximum of 12 knots and overtaking was not to be permitted in the DWR. Other vessels were advised not to enter the DWR except in an emergency. It called for improvement in ships' navigational aids, the maintenance of existing voluntary reporting procedures and the use of pilots through critical areas in the Straits of Singapore. The Traffic Separation Scheme came into force on 1 May 1981.

The Council also formulated a joint policy to deal with marine pollution. Experts from the three countries set to work on measures to achieve close consultation, coordination and cooperation on an anti-pollution policy. They were also required to formulate a system of compensation and restitution for damage caused by oil pollution. In addition, tankers and large vessels navigating through the Malacca Strait and Straits of Singapore were required to carry insurance and compensation coverage.

Bilateral and trilateral agreements to maritime boundary determination are thus a means, not only of establishing the limits of jurisdictional control of coastal states through cooperative approaches, but also of creating mutual arrangements to explore and exploit the marine and mineral resources within the limits of national jurisdiction, and to provide for safe passage through geographically restricted waters.

CLAIMS TO SEABED RESOURCES BEYOND NATIONAL JURISDICTION

The revision of the continental shelf regime has brought into focus the issue of the legal status of the deep seabed. If there is an outer limit to continental shelf claims, then it is logical to question the extent to which the regime beyond the shelf differs from that of the shelf areas (Vasciannie, 1990: 141). General guidance on this issue was provided to UNCLOS from the deliberations within the International Law Commission and at the 1958 UN Conference on the Law of the Sea. Significantly, no state contended that the deep seabed areas could be appropriated, and although Monaco argued for the internationalisation of the area this proposal was not universally accepted (UNCLOS I, Official Records, Vol. VI, p. 18). Indeed, none of the 1958 Geneva Conventions contained detailed rules on the legal regime of the seabed beyond national jurisdiction.

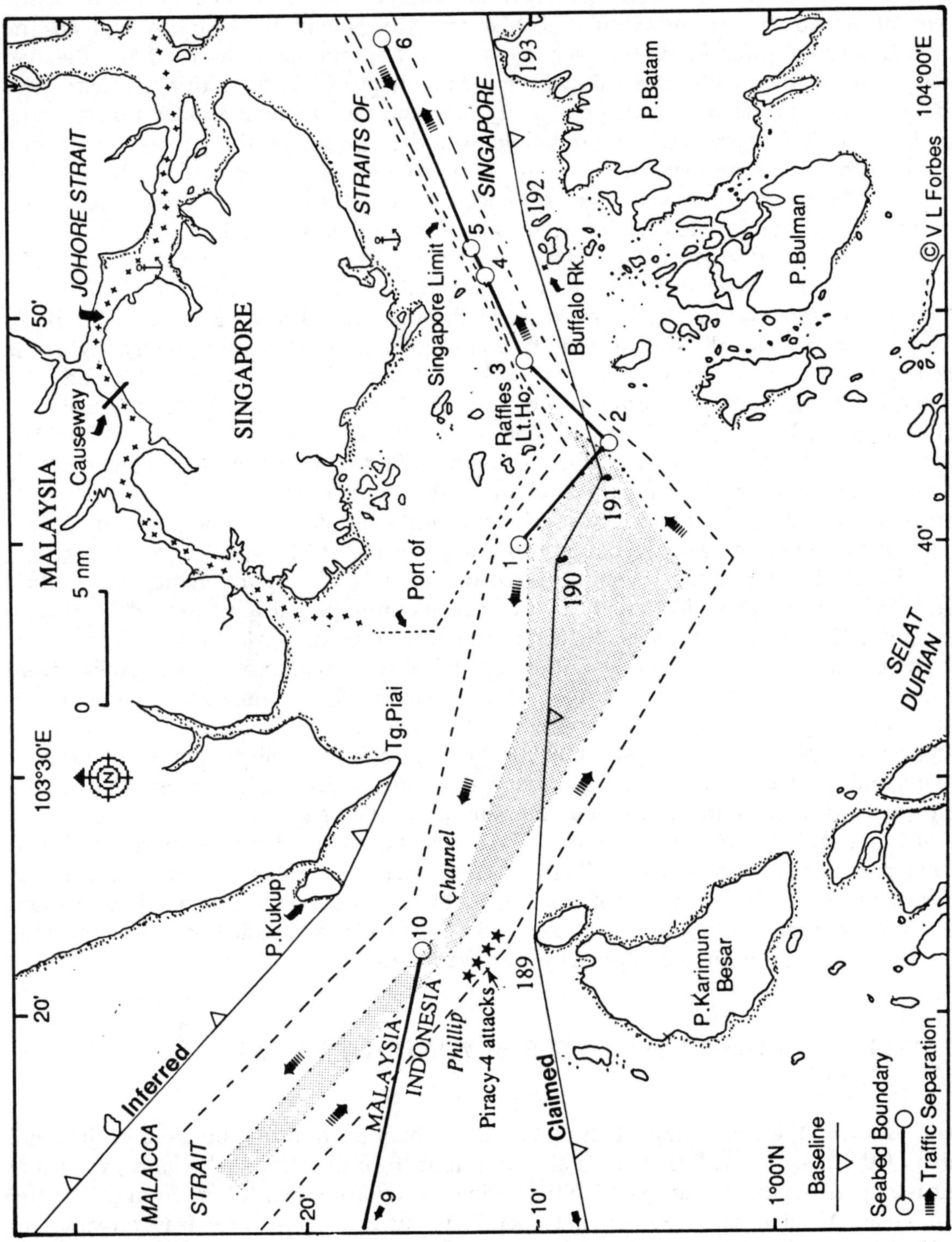

Figure 5.7 Maritime Jurisdiction in the Straits of Singapore. The stipled area separates the flow of traffic, namely, deep-draught ships. Shallow-draught ships must as far as practicable traverse the zone at right angles to the general flow of traffic.

In 1966 the Economic and Social Council requested the Secretary-General of the United Nations to undertake a survey of the state of knowledge of the resources of the sea — mineral and food, but excluding fish — beyond the continental shelf (ECOSOC Resolution No 1112, March 1966). In that same year, President Johnson of the United States warned that the mineral resources of the deep seabed should not become open to colonial competition among maritime nations (US House of Representatives, 88th Congress, 1967: 7). Such studies and pronouncements not only had legal significance, but also paved the way for Dr. A. Pardo's unprecedented declaration at the 22nd Session of the General Assembly, that the resources of the seabed were "a common heritage of mankind" (UN Doc. A/6695, Aug. 1967). The address, whose timing and manner of presentation were perfect, had an effective impact within the UN, whose immediate decision was to establish an ad hoc Committee on Peaceful Uses of the Seabed and the Ocean Floor Beyond the Limits of National Jurisdiction (the Seabed Committee).

In 1971, the General Assembly declared the seabed and ocean floor and its subsoil to be beyond national jurisdiction and, together with their resources, to be the common heritage of mankind. Thus a new concept was established.

The Seabed Committee was instructed to make preparations for UNCLOS III and draft treaty articles embodying the international regime of the Deep Sea Area. The principles governing the Area are contained in Part XI of CLOS, Articles 133 to 149. The activities and the development of the resources in the Area are organised, carried out and controlled by the International Seabed Authority (ISA). All states and other bodies which are entitled to ratify or accede to the CLOS (Article 305) are members of the ISA. The duties entrusted to the ISA go beyond simple administration. It has an international legal personality and such legal capacity as may be necessary for the exercise of its functions (Article 176). The ISA will take any measures to promote the growth, efficiency and stability of markets of commodities produced from minerals derived from the Area. The ISA is based on the principle of the sovereign equality of all its members and is the organisation through which the states organise and control activites in the Area relating to the exploitation of its resources (Article 157). The ISA is required to avoid discrimination in the exercise of its power and functions and monopolisation of activities in the Area (Articles 151 and 152).

CLOS established four organisational arms to enable the ISA to fulfil its tasks, three of which are the Assembly, the Council and the Secretariat (Article 158: 1). The fourth arm is the Enterprise, which is a unique organisation. Although it must act in accordance with the general policy of the Assembly and by the directives of the Council (CLOS Annex IV), it also enjoys autonomy in the conduct of its operations. It is through this arm that the ISA will formally plan activites in the Area and control the transporting, processing and marketing of minerals recovered from the seafloor (Articles 153, 158 and 170). The Enterprise is organised to operate according to sound commercial principles and must sell its products on a non-discriminatory basis according to commercial considerations only (CLOS, Annex IV, Articles 4 to 7). It may carry out activities under joint arrangements, require transfer of technology, choose reserved areas and apply to conduct activities in other parts of the Area (CLOS, Annex III). One of the main tasks of the Enterprise is to act as an agent to ensure the effective participation of developing states. The Enterprise is expected to become self-supporting. It will be exempt from payments of contributions to the ISA for the first 10 years of operation. Additionally, funds are to be raised inter alia by a system of interest-free loans and debt guarantees of signatory states.

A regime for pioneer activites in the Area was established, to ensure immediate commencement of deep seabed mining operations upon entry into force of CLOS. In accordance with UN Resolution II of CLOS (UN Doc. A/CONF. 62/121) any state which has signed the Convention may apply to the ISA to register as a pioneer investor. The concept of pioneer investor emerged from the request of industrialised states for a safeguard for the considerable investments in deep seabed mining which had been made by some companies and consortia, with the intention of giving these pioneers priority for the recovery of investments as soon as possible after the conclusion of UNCLOS III.

The pioneer regime will remain in effect until the Convention enters into force. Nevertheless, the events of this interim period will continue to have an influence long after that date (Article 308: 5). Resolution II provides that any company, consortium or state enterprises which had invested at least US$30 million before 1983 or, in certain cases, before 1985 may under certain conditions apply to the Preparatory Commission (PREPCOM) — the caretaker body of the ISA — for registration as a pioneer investor of a pioneer area which may not exceed 150,000 sq km. The sponsoring state must certify the level of the investment expenditure, and the prospective area applied for must not overlap other areas already allocated or applied for.

Prior to the entry into force of CLOS the pioneer investor may: undertake only pioneer activities as defined by Resolution II, which do not include commercial operations; pay a registration fee of US$ 250,000; agree to periodic expenditure; carry out exploration in the reserved area at the request of the Enterprise; provide training and offer transfer of technology. When the Convention has entered into force, application may be made for approval of a plan of work and for production authorisation. An annual fee of US$ 1,000,000 is required.

By the end of 1991, four states and four multinational consortia had declared an interest in mining the Area. India was the only one to be granted an application to operate in the Indian Ocean Basin.

INDIA'S PIONEER INVESTOR STATUS

India contends that it has a new role to play and a responsibility to meet, in both the exploration and exploitation of the Indian Ocean Basin. Its interest in the exploration of polymetallic nodules began in 1977 when the National Institute of Oceanography, established at Goa, initiated a project to explore the mineral resources of the deep seabed. Within four years, the research vessel Gaveshani was operational and in early 1981 it collected several samples of nodules from the Arabian Sea. As a first step towards its objective, India created a new Department of Ocean Development on 24 July 1981, under the direction of Prime Minister Indira Gandhi. Since that date, the department has played a key role in effectively projecting India's participation in all international meetings, in seabed research, in the organisation of successful expeditions to Antarctica and in the survey of polymetallic nodules.

Polymetallic nodules are known to be of economic importance because, besides manganese and iron, they contain nickel, copper, cobalt, lead, molybdenum, cadmium, vanadium, titanium, silver, gold and other metals. They vary in colour, shape, size and weight. They are usually porous, have a specific gravity in the range of 2 to 3, and their cross-section reveals concentric rings. The nodules usually have one or two nuclei of palagonite, pumice or other volcanic material, and are found in high concentrations in regions of submarine volcanic activity. The concentration of nodules at the surface of the sediment may be due to burrowing organisms, upward diffusion of manganese, or seismic activity. Their normal growth rate is a few atomic layers per day, which constitutes an average annual rate of 10 million tonnes. Polymetallic nodules are therefore considered a renewable resource. Although there are several methods using dredging techniques to mine the nodules from the deep sea, there are a number of problems associated with such ventures, including the possible destruction of the benthic organisms present on the ocean floor. Any disturbance by mining is also likely to impair the growth of the nodules (Borgese, 1985: 74).

The Department of Ocean Development, as a state enterprise of India, has identified two mining sites in the Indian Ocean Basin. The highest concentrations of nodules have been found at depths ranging from 3,500 m to 6,000 m and covering an area of about

15,000,000 sq km. On 12 January 1984, India first applied for registration as a pioneer investor. A revised application was submitted on 20 July 1987, together with the appropriate registration fee and an undertaking to comply with the requirements of CLOS. The technical data and report accompanying India's application were subject to close scrutiny by the Group of Experts, comprising 14 members from the international scientific community.

India was registered as a pioneer investor on 17 August 1987. Its Certificate of Registration (Figure 5.8) defines the boundary of its pioneer area, which is divided into Areas A and B, each covering 150,000 sq km (Figure 5.9). An area of 52,300 sq km was also delineated and identified as Area S for incorporation in the pioneer area to be allocated to the applicant in accordance with the provisions of CLOS (LOS/PCN/L.41/Rev. 1, 1986). The geographical coordinates for area S have not been made public. Areas A and B are approximate, within less than one percent margin of error (LOS Bulletin, Special Issue III, 1991: 23). In the Group's assessment, Areas A and B were determined to be of equal estimated commercial value at the prospecting or exploration stage. The most important factors taken into consideration were metal content, nodule abundance and bathymetry.

After careful examination of the alternatives for adjusting Areas A and B and taking into consideration all relevant technical factors, the Group unanimously agreed to recommend that Area A, as adjusted, should be designated as the pioneer area for allocation to the applicant and that Area B, as adjusted, should be designated as the reserved area for the ISA. The precise geographical coordinates of the adjusted Areas A and B, having been determined by the Group of Technical Experts, were listed (Table 5.1) and deposited with the Secretary-General of the United Nations.

CONCLUSION

This chapter has examined three joint development zones for the exploration and exploitation of mineral resources of the seabed in areas where a single maritime boundary has not been delineated between coastal states. One zone is productive, another has potential but is currently uneconomical, and the third has the potential to bring wealth to Australia and Indonesia and to the operators working the oilfields within the Timor Sea Zone of Cooperation. An analysis of the unique Torres Strait Treaty has also been undertaken. This chapter has shown that cooperation between states in the management and conservation of the marine living resources can be effected by treaty. The agreement can be used as a model by other states who may wish to cooperate with their coastal neighbours where there is failure to determine maritime jurisdiction, especially in narrow waters. The Malacca Strait Council, the authority whose task is to ensure the safe passage of ships through the Malacca Strait and the Straits of Singapore, has demonstrated its efficiency in all aspects of navigation, communication and maintenance of the relatively narrow international waterway that has been vital to seaborne trade for many centuries and to many of the littoral states of the Indian Ocean basin. The issue of piracy in territorial and international waters, however, is a problem that no single state can tackle. Within the Southeast Asian region coastal states have decided to impose a levy on ships operating in the region to raise money to combat piracy and clean up marine pollution (The West Australian, 8 May 1992: 16). The imposition of a levy on users of the straits is not the solution. There is a need for joint patrols between the littoral states. There is an obvious need to settle maritime jurisdictional issues which has been working in favour of the pirates for many centuries. The mineral resources, specifically the polymetallic nodules lying on the floor of the Central Indian Ocean, basin, may in the very near future be mined, processed and sold by India and the Enterprise for the common benefit of mankind. By mutual agreement it is possible that exploration and exploitation, conservation and management of the marine mineral and biotic resources of the whole Indian Ocean Basin can be equitably shared.

Certificate of Registration

This is to certify that

Pursuant to

The United Nations Convention on the Law of the Sea,
Resolution II of the Third United Nations Conference on the Law of the Sea governing preparatory investment in pioneer activities relating to polymetallic nodules,
The statement on the implementation of resolution II of 5 September 1986 and
The statement of understanding on the implementation of resolution II of 10 April 1987 of the Preparatory Commission for the International Sea-Bed Authority and for the International Tribunal for the Law of the Sea, and

Pursuant to

The decision of the Preparatory Commission for the International Sea-Bed Authority and for the International Tribunal for the Law of the Sea to register the Government of India as a pioneer investor adopted by its General Committee on 17 August 1987 in accordance with the Rules of Procedure of the Preparatory Commission,

the Government of India,

Having signed the United Nations Convention on the Law of the Sea on 10 December 1982,
Having submitted an application for registration as a pioneer investor on 12 January 1984,
Having submitted a revised application on 20 July 1987,
Having made payment to the Preparatory Commission of the fee for registration as pioneer investor,
Having undertaken to comply with its obligations under the said resolution II and the aforementioned statements, and

Having, as a certifying State, undertaken to ensure that the pioneer activities are conducted in a manner compatible with the United Nations Convention on the Law of the Sea,

is registered as a Pioneer Investor

and has been allocated the pioneer area,
defined in the Schedule hereto,
in accordance with the said resolution II
and with the aforementioned statements; and
By virtue of the aforementioned decision and registration
the Government of India as a pioneer investor
shall have the exclusive right to carry out pioneer activities
in the pioneer area in accordance with the said resolution II.

GIVEN UNDER MY HAND and the official seal of the United Nations for and on behalf of the Preparatory Commission for the International Sea-Bed Authority and for the International Tribunal for the Law of the Sea at United Nations Headquarters,
This 18th *day of* December *1987.*

Javier Pérez de Cuéllar
Secretary-General of the United Nations

Figure 5.8 Certificate of Registration of Pioneer Status bestowed on India.

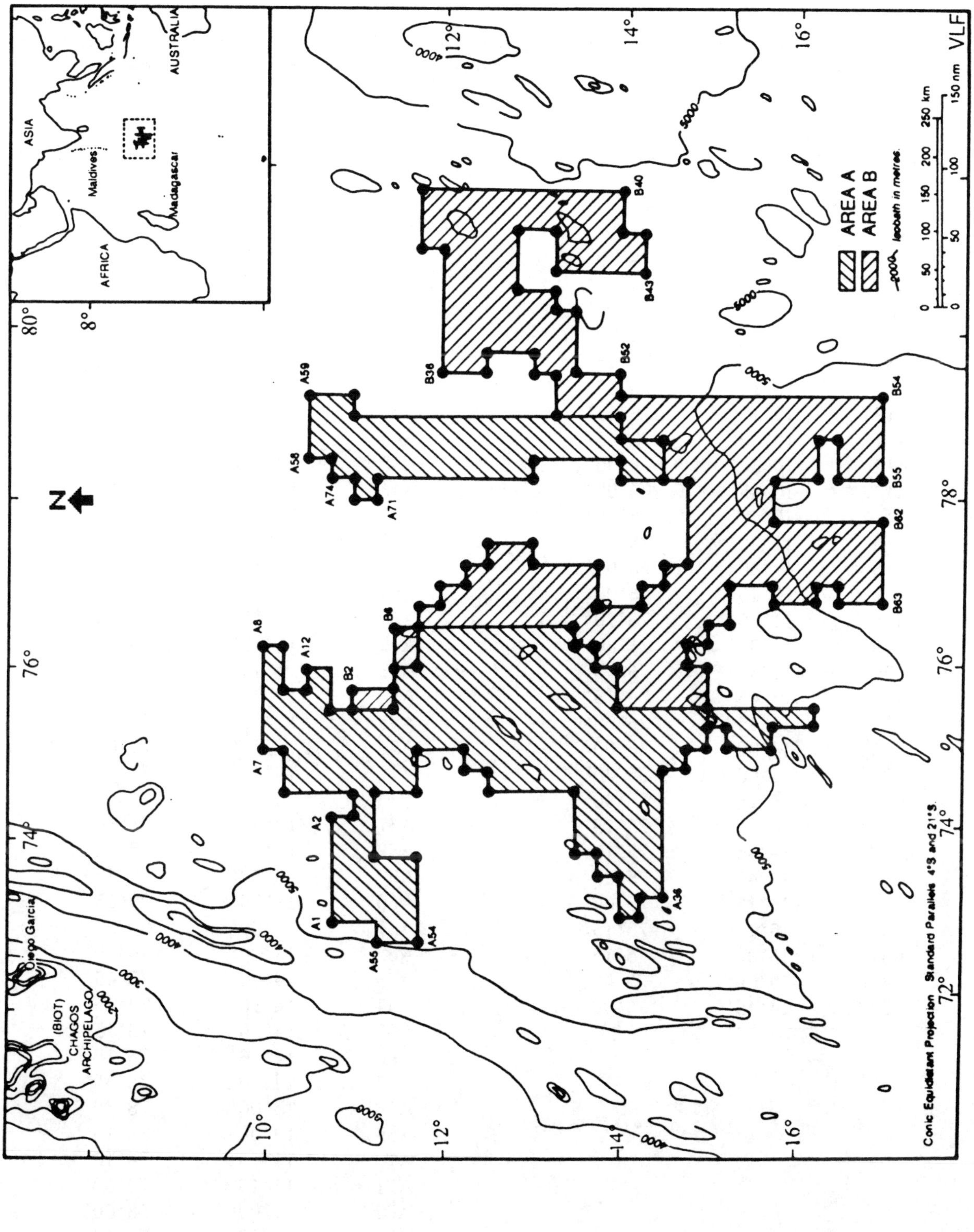

Figure 5.9 Areas A and B in the Central Indian Ocean Basin designated as Pioneer Areas for the exploitation of nodules.

Table 5.1 List of Geographical Coordinates defining Areas A and B in the Central Indian Ocean Basin.

CO-ORDINATES OF THE TURNING POINTS OF AREAS A AND B AS REFERRED TO IN PARAGRAPH 6 (a), (b) AND (c)

These co-ordinates previously formed annex 2 of the report of the Group of Technical Experts (LOS/PCN/BUR/R.1, para. 32).

I. Area A, allocated as a pioneer area to the Applicant, the Government of India, is bounded by lines joining the following turning points, the co-ordinates of which are listed below:

TURNING POINTS	LATITUDE (S)	LONGITUDE (E)
A1	10°45′	73°00′
A2	10°45′	74°15′
A3	10°30′	74°15′
A4	10°30′	74°30′
A5	10°15′	74°30′
A6	10°15′	75°00′
A7	10°00′	75°00′
A8	10°00′	76°15′
A9	10°15′	76°15′
A10	10°15′	75°45′
A11	10°30′	75°45′
A12	10°30′	76°00′
A13	10°45′	76°00′
A14	10°45′	75°30′
A15	11°30′	75°30′
A16	11°30′	76°00′
A17	10°45′	76°00′
A18	11°45′	76°30′
A19	13°30′	76°30′
A20	13°30′	76°15′
A21	13°45′	76°15′
A22	13°45′	76°00′
A23	14°00′	76°00′
A24	14°00′	75°30′
A25	16°15′	75°30′
A26	16°15′	75°15′
A27	15°45′	75°15′
A28	15°45′	75°00′
A29	15°15′	75°00′
A30	15°15′	75°15′
A31	15°00′	75°15′
A32	15°00′	75°00′
A33	14°45′	75°00′

TURNING POINTS	LATITUDE (S)	LONGITUDE (E)
A34	14°45′	74°45′
A35	14°30′	74°45′
A36	14°30′	73°15′
A37	14°15′	73°15′
A38	14°15′	73°00′
A39	14°00′	73°00′
A40	14°00′	73°30′
A41	13°45′	73°30′
A42	13°45′	73°45′
A43	13°30′	73°45′
A44	13°30′	74°30′
A45	12°30′	74°30′
A46	12°30′	74°45′
A47	12°15′	74°45′
A48	12°15′	75°00′
A49	11°45′	75°00′
A50	11°45′	74°30′
A51	11°15′	74°30′
A52	11°15′	73°45′
A53	11°45′	73°45′
A54	11°45′	72°45′
A55	11°15′	72°45′
A56	11°15′	73°00′
A1	10°45′	73°00′
A57	10°45′	78°30′
A58	10°30′	78°30′
A59	10°30′	79°15′
A60	11°00′	79°15′
A61	11°00′	79°00′
A62	14°00′	79°00′
A63	14°00′	78°45′
A64	14°30′	78°45′
A65	14°30′	78°15′
A66	14°00′	78°15′
A67	14°00′	78°30′
A68	13°00′	78°30′
A69	13°00′	78°15′
A70	11°15′	78°15′
A71	11°15′	78°00′
A72	11°00′	78°00′
A73	11°00′	78°15′
A74	10°45′	78°15′
A57	10°45′	78°30′

II. Area B, designated as the reserved area for conduct of activities by the Authority in the Area through the Enterprise or in association with developing States, is bounded by lines joining the following turning points, the co-ordinates of which are listed below:

TURNING POINTS	LATITUDE (S)	LONGITUDE (E)
B1	11°00′	75°30′
B2	11°00′	74°45′
B3	11°30′	75°45′
B4	11°30′	75°30′
B1	11°00′	75°45′
B5	11°30′	76°00′
B6	11°30′	76°30′
B7	11°45′	76°30′
B8	11°45′	76°00′
B5	11°30′	76°00′
B7	11°45′	76°30′
B9	11°45′	76°45′
B10	12°00′	76°45′
B11	12°00′	77°00′
B12	12°15′	77°00′
B13	12°15′	77°15′
B14	12°30′	77°15′
B15	12°30′	77°30′
B16	13°00′	77°30′
B17	13°00′	77°15′
B18	13°45′	77°15′
B19	13°45′	76°45′
B20	14°15′	76°45′
B21	14°15′	77°00′
B22	14°30′	77°00′
B23	14°30′	77°15′
B24	14°45′	77°15′
B25	14°45′	78°15′
B26	14°30′	78°15′
B27	14°30′	78°45′
B28	14°00′	78°45′
B29	14°00′	79°00′
B30	13°15′	79°00′
B31	13°15′	79°30′
B32	13°00′	79°30′
B33	13°00′	79°45′
B34	12°30′	79°45′
B35	12°30′	79°30′
B36	12°00′	79°30′
B37	12°00′	81°00′

TURNING POINTS	LATITUDE (S)	LONGITUDE (E)
B38	11°45′	81°00′
B39	11°45′	81°45′
B40	14°00′	81°45′
B41	14°00′	81°15′
B42	14°15′	81°15′
B43	14°15′	80°45′
B44	13°15′	80°45′
B45	13°15′	81°15′
B46	12°45′	81°15′
B47	12°45′	80°30′
B48	13°15′	80°30′
B40	13°15′	80°15′
B50	13°30′	80°15′
B51	13°30′	79°30′
B52	14°00′	79°30′
B53	14°00′	79°15′
B54	17°00′	79°15′
B55	17°00′	78°15′
B56	16°30′	78°15′
B57	16°30′	78°45′
B58	16°15′	78°45′
B59	16°15′	78°15′
B60	15°45′	78°15′
B61	15°45′	77°45′
B62	17°00′	77°45′
B63	17°00′	76°45′
B64	16°30′	76°45′
B65	16°30′	77°00′
B66	16°15′	77°00′
B67	16°15′	76°45′
B68	15°45′	76°45′
B69	15°45′	77°00′
B70	15°15′	77°00′
B71	15°15′	76°30′
B72	15°00′	76°30′
B73	15°00′	76°15′
B74	14°45′	76°15′
B75	14°15′	76°00′
B76	15°00′	76°00′
B77	15°00′	75°30′
B78	14°00′	75°30′
B79	14°00′	76°00′
B80	13°45′	76°00′
B81	13°45′	76°15′
B82	13°30′	76°15′
B83	13°30′	76°30′
B7	11°45′	76°30′

CHAPTER SIX

CONCLUSION

This study has adopted a geographical approach, concentrating on the spatial distribution of maritime jurisdiction, with an emphasis on the use of maps, and relating the maritime zones to the geographical, geophysical and geopolitical issues of the littoral states.

Previous Indian Ocean boundary studies have taken a legalistic approach and have concentrated upon specific case studies or subregional themes. By contrast, this study has adopted an integrated approach to the whole ocean basin, with specific reference to its rim countries and island states. It is in this context that the following conclusions are made.

The Indian Ocean basin is now partially divided by political boundaries determined, to some extent, by the need of states to claim sovereignty over the resources of the ocean. It is possible that, by the turn of this century, maritime jurisdictional lines will have been established over a greater part of the ocean, by which time CLOS will have entered into force. Where negotiations have failed to determine a single maritime boundary between states, it has been shown that a number of practices have been developed offering possible alternatives, such as the establishment of a joint development zone. Three such zones for the exploration and exploitation of hydrocarbons and/or other minerals have been examined. Other similar zones exist in Southeast and East Asian waters.

The Bahrain/Saudi Arabia Agreement has been an outstanding success to date, both states benefiting financially from the hydrocarbon flow of the oilfield located within the defined zone. Mutual agreements also exist between Kuwait and Saudi Arabia whereby any trans-boundary hydrocarbon deposits within their common maritime jurisdiction will be exploited jointly. In the Red Sea, the agreement between Saudi Arabia and Sudan has achieved acclaim for the manner in which the exploration programmes have been undertaken. All that remains is for the exploitation and processing of the minerals from the Red Sea Deeps, when it becomes economically feasible to do so, employing German technology and expertise.

Two joint development zones for the exploration and exploitation of hydrocarbons were ratified and entered into force within as many months in the Southeast Asian region. One was the object of an agreement between Malaysia and Thailand in the Gulf of Thailand, the other was negotiated between Australia and Indonesia in the Timor Sea.

The former agreement (which established a joint development zone that is located beyond the geographical limits of this study) is exceedingly brief, does not provide for such basic issues as the application of industrial law and offers no specific agreement to continue attempts to delineate the boundary (Auburn, Forbes and Scott, 1991: 19). The latter agreement was arrived at between two neighbouring countries with very different cultural and political systems. It is the most comprehensive oil and gas agreement to date, and could be used as a model for other potential joint development projects envisaged in the Indian Ocean basin. The Treaty has been enhanced by the very detailed Regulations issued by the two governments in February 1991. The crucial test of the treaty was successfully concluded when licenses were issued to prospective explorers in December 1991, six months after the establishment of the Joint Authority. The Treaty will be in force until 2031, with a provision for successive 20-year renewals if agreement has not been reached on a permanent boundary (Article 33: 2).

The application of an agreement to jointly manage the marine resources of the Torres Strait has also been analysed. The success of the agreement has demonstrated that near neighbours can work together to exploit the resources of the ocean by respecting each other's historic rights and cultures. The give-and-take principle is the underlying factor behind the uniqueness and success of the treaty. Similarly, neighbouring states have proved that in a cooperative approach a narrow international waterway can be effectively managed by a nominated body as exemplified in the Malacca Strait Council, whose sole task is to ensure the safe and efficient movement of ships through those waters.

The abundant resources of the Indian Ocean Basin, ranging from the high density brines in the Red Sea, the polymetallic nodules in the Central Indian Ocean Basin and other placer minerals, to the rich fishing grounds of the Bay of Bengal, Andaman Sea and Mascarene Basin, have continued to attract the attention of both littoral and extra-regional states. China, the European Community, the Commonwealth of Independent States, Japan, South Korea and Taiwan continue to harvest millions of tonnes of fish annually. In some instances, such fishing ventures are undertaken jointly with littoral states when the fishery involved is within national jurisdiction.

Beyond national jurisdictions the living resources of the ocean are free to be exploited by any state on the proviso that careful conservation and management policies must prevail for the sustainable development of those resources. Such is not the case, however, with the mineral resources of the ocean. Exploitation of the minerals on the deep seabed will be managed by the ISA through its commercial operating arm, the Enterprise. States must make application to the ISA to explore and exploit the minerals of the deep seabed. By 1991, only India, had shown any interest in mining the manganese nodules known to be strewn on the seafloor of the Central Indian Ocean basin. In attaining pioneer status, India stood alongside France, Japan and the USSR which had applied to mine parts of the Area in the Pacific Ocean.

Indian Ocean states participated vigorously in UNCLOS III. They strongly supported, for example, the concept of the EEZ and the archipelagic state principle in boundary determination. On the other hand, there was a sharp difference of opinion among Indian Ocean states over the desirable extent of continental shelf rights. Overall the Conference opened windows of opportunity for nations, at the individual, regional and collective levels, to take advantage of the possibilities for economic development utilising the resources of the ocean. It took into account the demands of the developing countries and the rights and interests of geographically advantaged and disadvantaged states and of coastal and landlocked countries. CLOS is the outcome of a new international political order, and has enunciated a clear legal regime for the various uses of the seas.

If the resources of the ocean within and beyond national jurisdiction are to be explored, exploited, managed and conserved in an orderly manner, it is essential that maritime boundaries between coastal states be determined, delineated on large-scale maps and made available for public inspection. Before UNCLOS III there were 15 segments of negotiated seabed boundaries in the Indian Ocean basin. Since 1982 a further nine seabed boundaries have been negotiated including two joint development zones. The potential exists for satisfactory agreements in other parts of the basin. However, until there is political and economical stability in many of the states of the region, maritime boundary determination will take a low priority.

Some maritime boundaries separate states such as Bahrain and Saudi Arabia, which are so harmoniously related that conflict between them is unthinkable. Indeed, a causeway carrying traffic both ways links the two countries. Others, such as the one which marks the division between Australia and Papua New Guinea, are in some respects at least, more akin to internal boundaries than to international frontiers. Ideally, states in the region should define and proclaim their maritime limits, negotiate any outstanding boundaries no matter what their differences with their neighbours, and work together towards the optimum utilisation of the ocean's resources. Failure to agree on a common boundary may result in a decision by an arbitrator or the establishment of a joint development zone.

By October 1991, of the 51 states that had ratified CLOS, only 13 were from the Indian Ocean Basin. In chronological order of ratification they were Egypt, Sudan, Bahrain, Iraq, Tanzania, Indonesia, Kuwait, Yemen, Kenya, Somalia, Oman, Seychelles and Djibouti. It is interesting to note, however, that all coastal states in the region and indeed in many other parts of the world, while reluctant to ratify the Convention, have been swift to claim spatial extension into previously unclaimed ocean territory, thus implementing those provisions of CLOS that are advantageous to their needs and purposes.

Once the Convention comes into force, 12 months after the date of the 60th ratification, it will attain the status of a treaty. In the meantime, however, several states have already enacted national legislation based on CLOS. Under such national legislation, states have asserted and protected their sovereignty in the maritime zones, regulated activities in the zones of national jurisdiction, and created institutions to administer the various laws and regulations on safety, environment and marine scientific research. National legislation has brought significant benefits to states that have claimed an EEZ, notably island states such as Mauritius and Seychelles. In some cases states have acquired more than 30,000 sq nm (one million sq km) of maritime space while their land areas are comparatively small. Some countries, Singapore and Thailand notably, have had less spectacular acquisitions of the EEZ.

Indian Ocean states, including the hinterland states, can, at a regional level, optimise the benefits provided by CLOS by cooperating in various fields of marine scientific research and maritime affairs. The states can also explore the possibilities of bilateral, multilateral and regional cooperative arrangements in the fishery sector; of sharing and strengthening existing agreements on offshore oil and gas development; and of exchange of information and data and transfer of technology. Regional cooperation can also be extended to the fields of communications, marine transport, sea lanes and traffic separation schemes, and marine pollution control and compensation (Plate 6).

UNCLOS III was held under the auspices of the United Nations whose principal aim is to maintain peace and security, take effective collective measures for the prevention and removal of threats to peace, and strengthen universal peace. Thus, the Convention imposes a duty on all states, international organisations, national companies, and individuals to use the oceans and seas for peaceful purposes. To this end, the states of the Indian Ocean and those other nations which are major users of its shipping lanes and consumers of its resources have an obligation to transform into reality the UN Resolution on the Indian Ocean Zone of Peace.

GLOSSARY

Note: Words which are the subject of a separate entry in this glossary are shown in CAPITAL letters.

ABYSSAL FLOOR or ABYSSAL PLAIN. The flat, relatively featureless deep seabed between depths of 2000 and 5000 metres. It is a term used generally to refer to the seabed which lies seaward of the continental rise.

AFZ = Australian Fishing Zone.

ARCHIPELAGO. A group of islands. An archipelago may consist of mountain tops whose lower slopes and valleys have been submerged or of isolated volcanic SEAMOUNTS.

ARCHIPELAGIC BASELINES. A series of straight lines delineated on a map or chart by archipelagic states to connect the outermost points of their outermost islands (Article 47).

ARCHIPELAGIC STATE. State composed entirely of one or more archipelagoes (Article 46). The Maldives and Indonesia are examples of archipelagic states.

ARCHIPELAGIC WATERS. The waters which lie inside of the baselines which surround the archipelagic state.

AREA. In a specialised sense a concept proposed by UNCLOS III in the context of the seabed and its substratum beyond the limits of national jurisdiction (Article 133).

ARTIFICIAL ISLANDS. Islands which are not formed by nature. Offshore installations and structures such as oil-drilling and production platforms are considered artificial islands.

ASSEMBLY. In a specialised sense a branch of the International Seabed Authority (ISA).

ATOLL. A coral island or a small group of islands consisting of a circular or nearly circular reef enclosing a lagoon.

AUSTRALIAN FISHING ZONE (AFZ). A fishing zone 200 nautical miles wide established by Australia on 1 November 1979.

AUSTRALIAN PLATE. A large tectonic PLATE underlying the eastern portion of the Indian Ocean, Australia and New Zealand.

AUTHORITY (ISA). In this context The International Seabed Authority, through which states that are signatories to CLOS will organise and control activities in the AREA (Article 156–158).

AZIMUTH. An angular bearing measured clockwise from true North; thus the azimuth of South is 180°.

BACKSHORE. The most landward part of a shoreline. It is on the land side of the mean spring high water mark and is inundated only during storms and storm-generated high tides.

BARRIER BEACH. A feature consisting of sandy bars which are aligned on a similar azimuth to the coast, which stand above high tide and are separated from the coast by a LAGOON.

BARRIER REEF. A partially submerged coral outcrop on the seaward side of a LAGOON or COASTAL WATERS. Such a reef lies parallel or nearly parallel to the coastline, that is, in the general direction of the coast.

BATHYAL ZONE. The region of the ocean from the edge of the continental shelf to that depth where the water is at a constant temperature of 4° C, usually at about − 4000 metres. The zone is referred to as the continental SLOPE.

BATHYMETRY. The surveying, recording and charting the depth of the ocean floor below sea level (see ISOBATH).

BAY. A well-marked but less than semi-circular indentation of a shoreline, especially between two headlands, e.g. Geographe Bay, or peninsulas, e.g. Bay of Bengal. Generally, a bay is more open than a GULF and larger than a COVE (see also BIGHT).

BEACH. A gently sloping stretch of loose materials (sand, rocks, and accumulation of shingles and pebbles) along the shore extending from the highest high-tide mark to the lowest low-tide mark. The seaward limit of a beach — unless otherwise specified — is the MEAN LOW-WATER LINE. The structure of a beach is subject to considerable variation, depending on tide, storms, season, and long-term geological processes.

BEACH EROSION. The carrying away of beach materials by wave action, tidal streams, littoral currents, or wind.

BEACH WIDTH. The horizontal dimension of the BEACH measured normally to the shoreline.

BEARING. The horizontal direction of one terrestrial point or feature from another, expressed as an angular distance from a referenced point, usually from True or Magnetic North.

BENCH MARK. A permanently fixed point of known elevation and geographical coordinates. A primary bench mark is one close to a tide station to which the tide staff and tidal DATUM are originally referenced.

BIGHT. A large slightly curved indentation in a coastline forming an open bay. Examples are the Bight of Thailand and the Great Australian Bight (see also BAY).

BRITISH INDIAN OCEAN TERRITORY (BIOT). British sovereign territory in the Indian Ocean comprising the Chagos Archipelago.

BLUFF. A high, very steep bank or CLIFF.

BOLD COAST. A prominent land mass that rises steeply from the sea.

BOTTOM. In this context the ground or bed under any body of water; the bottom of the sea.

CANAL. An artificial watercourse cut through a land area for such uses as navigation and irrigation. A good example is the Suez Canal.

CANYON. A relatively elongated, narrow, deep depression with steep slopes, the bottom of which grades continuously downward. It may be underwater (submarine) or on land (subaerial).

CAPE. A relatively extensive land area projecting seaward from a continent or large island which marks a change in, or interrupts notably, the coastal trend, that is, the direction of the coast; a prominent feature. An excellent example is Cape Guardafui of Somalia.

CARTOGRAPHY. The art and science of portraying graphically, by maps or CHARTS, the known features of the earth (or of any celestial body).

CAUSEWAY. A raised road, across damp or marshy ground, or across water linking a string of islands or an island to the mainland, e.g. the transport link between Singapore and MALAY peninsula.

CAY. A low flat island of coral and sand fragments, awash or drying at low water. Also KEY.

CHANNEL. That part of a body of water (sometimes dredged) deep enough for navigation through an area otherwise not suitable. The deepest part of a stream, bay or strait through which the main tidal stream or current flows. A large strait, such as the Mozambique Channel.

CHART. A special purpose map generally designed for air or marine navigation, such as aeronautical charts and nautical (hydrographic) charts.

CHART, BATHYMETRIC. A topographic map (chart) of the bed of a body of water, or a part of it. Generally bathymetric charts show depths by contour lines (ISOBATHS) and gradient tinting.

CLIFF. A high, steep face of rocks.

CLOS = Convention on the Law of the Sea, 1982.

COAST. A strip of land of indefinite width that extends inland from the shoreline to the point of the first major change in terrain features. The coast is an area of change.

COASTAL AREA. The land and sea area bordering the shoreline.

COASTAL STATE. A political entity, a state, which possesses a coastline.

COASTAL WATERS. The zone of sea lying adjacent to the coast generally out to the 20 m isobath. Sometimes referred to as close inshore waters.

COASTLINE. The line where the water and shore meet, that is the boundary line. Although the terminology of SHORE and COAST is rather confusing, shoreline and coastline are generally used as synonymous. It is the line on maps and charts which separates the land and sea.

CONCORDANT COAST. A coastline which is parallel to the general morphological trend-lines of the hinterland.

CONTIGUOUS ZONE. A maritime zone, lying seaward of the territorial sea, which a coastal state may claim. The width of the zone is measured from the territorial sea baselines of the coastal state.

CONTINENT. One of the earth's major continuous land masses, rising from the ocean floor. Structurally it includes the shallow submerged adjacent areas, that is, the CONTINENTAL SHELF. The continents occupy about thirty per cent of the earth's surface.

CONTINENTAL BORDERLAND. The region adjacent to a continent, normally occupied by or bordering on a continental shelf.

CONTINENTAL DRIFT. The concept that there was originally only one continent (PANGAEA) which broke up, resulting in the newly formed continents drifting to their present positions. The land masses of present day Africa, Australia and peninsular India, together with South America and Antarctica formed one unit, referred to as GONDWANA (see PLATE TECTONIC).

CONTINENTAL ISLAND. An island which lies (close to, and is structurally related to, a continent) on the continental shelf. As an example: the island of Sri Lanka (Ceylon).

CONTINENTAL MARGIN. The underwater extension of the continents comprising the continental shelf, slope and rise (q.v.).

CONTINENTAL PLATFORM. A term for the continent and its surrounding shelf as far as the continental slope. The structural continent, that is, the surface granitic rocks of the continental crust.

CONTINENTAL RISE. The term used to define the slope of the seabed in a seaward direction from the edge of the continental slope to the plain of the ocean floor.

CONTINENTAL SHELF. In a morphological sense this term refers to the zone bordering a continent and extending from the low water line to a depth (usually about 200 metres) where there is a marked or steeper descent toward a greater depth. The continental shelves are very important biologically, ecologically and geologically. In many locations they may be of economic benefit to the adjacent coastal state or states. In a legal sense, and in particular in the Law of the Sea literature, the term (CS) is used more extensively and refers to the continental margin, consisting of the continental shelf, slope and rise. Off the north and northwest coast of Australia the continental shelf is broad, whereas off the eastern coast of Africa the shelf is relatively narrow.

CONTINENTAL SLOPE. The marked gradient from the edge of the continental shelf to the deep-sea or abyssal plain.

CONVENTION ON THE LAW OF THE SEA (CLOS). The Convention resulting from the Third Law of the Sea Conference and series of negotiations between 1973 and 1982 (see Chapter 3.2).

CORAL. A hard calcareous formation composed of living or dead skeletons of many species of marine polyps.

CORAL REEF. Rock masses composed of colonies of living coral. Such reefs normally lie in warm (28 °C), well-oxygenated water between latitudes 30° north and south.

COUNCIL. (In a specialised sense) The administrative branch of the AUTHORITY which will consist of 36 elected members.

COVE. A small sheltered BAY with a narrow mouth, often inside a larger embayment.

CP. Common Point negotiated by two or more states to determine the start point for the delineation and demarcation of a boundary.

CURRENT. Horizontally well defined movement of water, as a result of one or more causes, such as difference in temperature, difference in salinity or the influence of prevailing winds. Some ocean currents may be temporary or seasonal, others permanent. (see DRIFT).

DALHOUSIE OCEAN STUDIES PROGRAMME, CANADA (DOSP). See Chapter 1.7.

DATUM. The base value, known or assumed, from which any quantity is measured for direction, distance or position in a horizontal or vertical plane.

DATUM, CHART. The plane or level to which soundings (or elevations) or tide heights are referenced. To provide a safety factor for marine navigation, some level lower than MEAN SEA LEVEL is generally selected for the hydrographic charts, such as MEAN LOW WATER, or INDIAN SPRINGS LOW WATER. More recently the LOWEST ASTRONOMICAL TIDE datum has been adopted by a few states.

DEI = Dutch East Indies (Indonesia after 1945).

DELIMITATION. Determination of territorial limits.

DELINEATION. In a cartographic sense, the portrayal on a map or chart of a geographical feature by means of lines; a line marking a territorial boundary or the extent of maritime jurisdiction of a coastal state.

DELTA. Generally, a fan-shaped plain at the mouth of a river, created by the deposition of sediment carried by the river from higher ground. An example is the Ganges Delta at the head of the Bay of Bengal.

DEMARCATION, DEMARKATION. The precise definition or marking out of a boundary, by erecting border posts, fences, etc. or, in the marine environment, by the placement of buoys and other navigational markers. Such markers may prove adequate for indicating the limits or extent for example, of a port authority, but would not be practicable in defining the outer limit of the territorial sea of a coastal state.

DEPTH, CHARTED. The vertical distance from the chart datum to the seabed as shown on a hydrographic chart.

DIURNAL TIDE. A tide with one low water and one high water in a tidal day.

DOSP = Dalhousie Ocean Studies Programme, Canada.

DRIFT, CURRENT. The horizontal movement in the upper layers of the ocean caused by the wind, e.g. West Wind Drift experienced in the southern Indian Ocean.

DRYING BANKS or ROCKS. Natural features which are periodically covered by the rise or fall of the TIDE.

DUMPING GROUND. An offshore area set aside by the relevant authority of a coastal state, where dredged material is deposited. The area is also referred to as SPOIL GROUND and is marked accordingly on the chart to warn chart users of its existence.

EBB TIDE. The period of tide between high water and the succeeding low water; a falling or outgoing tide. The direction and strength of an ebb stream may be indicated on a chart with an appropriate symbol or annotation.

EC = European Community.

ECOSOC = Economic and Social Committee of the United Nations.

EDDY. A circular movement of water formed on the side of a main current, and caused by the obstacles in the path of the main stream or where two adjacent currents flow counter to each other.

EEZ. see EXCLUSIVE ECONOMIC ZONE.

EMBAYMENT. An indentation in the shoreline forming an open bay.

ENCLOSED or SEMI-ENCLOSED SEA. A water body such as a GULF, BASIN or SEA which is connected to the open sea by a narrow outlet and is surrounded by two or more coastal states. The Red Sea the Persian (Arabian) Gulf, and the Gulf of Thailand are examples of such features.

ENTERPRISE, THE. (In a specialised sense) an administrative branch of the AUTHORITY responsible for mining and associated activities on the deep seabed on behalf of the Authority (Article 170).

ENTRANCE. The avenue of access or opening to a navigable channel.

ENTREPOT. A centre through which regional and inter-regional trade is channelled. The port of Singapore provides a good example.

EQUIDISTANT LINE. A line which is or is deemed to be at equal distances from the coastlines of adjacent or opposite states.

ESTUARY. The mouth of a river (that is affected by tides) where the fresh water of the river mixes with the salt water of the sea.

EUSTASY. Pertaining to absolute changes in sea-level (see ISOSTASY).

EXCLUSIVE ECONOMIC ZONE (EEZ). An area of ocean space lying seawards of and adjacent to the territorial waters of a coastal state. It is generally of a maximum permissible width of 200 nautical miles measured from that state's territorial sea baselines. It is an area within which the claimant state has exclusive authority over the resources of the sea and the seabed (Article 55).

FAIRWAY. A marine thoroughfare; the parts of a waterway that are open and kept unobstructed for navigation.

FAO = Food and Agricultural Organisation, UN.

FAST ICE. Sea ice which remains attached to the landmass.

FATHOM. A British unit of measurement used for soundings and water depths. It is equal to six feet (1.83 metres). Such units of measurements may still be seen on some hydrographic charts.

FATHOM LINE. A depth line showing equal depths on a chart or map with depths expressed in fathoms (see Isobath).

FIORD (Norw. FJORD) A narrow, deep, steep-walled inlet of the sea, usually formed by partial submergence of a deep glacial valley, as on the coasts of Norway and New Zealand.

FISHING ZONE (FZ). An area in which fishing is frequently carried on.

FLAG STATE. Any state which registers foreign owned ships and permits those ships to fly its flag. The states of Liberia and Panama were renowned for this practice. In 1988, the United States accepted the registration of Kuwaiti ships, thus permitting these ships to fly the American flag.

FLOE. A comparatively thin piece of sea-ice which has become detached from a larger mass of sea-ice.

FLOOD TIDE. The vertical tidal movement; the period of tide between low water and the succeeding high water, a rising tide.

FOUL GROUND (SPOIL GROUND). An area of the seabed where the holding qualities for an anchor are poor.

FRINGING REEF. A coral reef attached directly to an insular or continental shore; it might be separated from the coast by a lagoon.

FZ = FISHING ZONE.

GDS = Geographically Disadvantaged State.

GEBCO General Bathymetric Chart of the Oceans. A series of charts of the bathymetry of the oceans prepared by Canadian Hydrographic Service under the authority of the International Hydrographic Organisation, Monaco and the Intergovernmental Oceanographic Commission, to conform to international standards.

GEODESIC LINE (GEODETIC). The shortest line between two points on a mathematically derived surface.

GEOGRAPHICAL COORDINATES. The system of spherical coordinates for defining the position on the earth's surface.

GEOGRAPHICALLY DISADVANTAGED STATE. In a legal sene a state which either has a very short coastline compared to its total land area, such as Sudan, or which possesses a coastal configuration which restricts its claim to the continental shelf and exclusive economic zone to very small areas; this latter situation is experienced by Iraq and Singapore.

GEODESY. The art and science which treats the determination of the size and shape of the Earth (GEOID) by surveying techniques.

GROYNE. A solid structure constructed seawards, generally at right angles to the coast, to retard erosion (of the coast) or to trap littoral drift.

GULF. A portion of the sea, proportionally narrower at the mouth than a bay, and surrounded by the coast. An example is the Gulf of Aden and Exmouth Gulf, Australia.

GUT. A narrow passage of water such as a strait or inlet.

GUYOT. A flat-topped SEAMOUNT rising from the sea floor.

HALF TIDE LEVEL. The water level midway between Mean High Water and Mean Low Water. It may differ from Mean Sea Level.

HARBOUR. A protected body of water, natural or artificial, affording a place of safety for vessels.

HAT = Highest Astronomical Tide.

HEADLAND. A relatively high, steep-faced promontory extending into the sea.

HIGH TIDE, HIGH WATER. The highest level reached at a place by the water surface in one tidal oscillation.

HIGH WATER LINE. The intersection of the plane of mean high water with the shore. Specifically, the highest elevation on the shore reached during a rising tide or storm.

HIGHEST ASTRONOMICAL TIDE (HAT). The highest level of the tide which can be predicted to occur under average meteorological conditions and under any combination of astronomical conditions. This level will not be reached every year.

HIGHLY MIGRATORY SPECIES. Species of fish which travels across wide areas of ocean space and might pass through the EXCLUSIVE ECONOMIC or FISHING ZONE of several coastal states. Such species include frigate mackerel, sailfish, swordfish and tuna.

HIGH SEAS. An area of the ocean that lies beyond any kind of national maritime jurisdiction which, since UNCLOS III, encompasses the EXCLUSIVE ECONOMIC and FISHING ZONES.

HINTERLAND. The stretch of land beyond (i.e. landwards from) the coastal strip (of undefined width).

HISTORIC BAY. A body of water claimed as the exclusive property of the adjacent state based on historical title, continuous jurisdiction and use. For example, Encounter Bay, in South Australia. A historic bay based on a historical title forms part of the internal waters, even if part of the bay is not on the landward side of the baseline drawn according to the principles of the Convention.

HOOK. A SPIT or narrow cape of sand and gravel which turns landward at the outer end.

HOT PURSUIT. The authorisation of an official vessel to extend the sovereignty of the coastal state beyond the seaward limit of the territorial sea by maintaining an uninterrupted chase of a fleeing merchant vessel from another state.

HYDROGRAPHY. The study of lakes, rivers, seas and other waters. A configuration of the underwater surface including the relief, bottom materials and coastal structures.

ICE BARRIER. A term used in association with the edge of the ice sheets in Antarctica.

IHB = International Hydrographic Bureau.

IHO = International Hydrographic Organisation.

IIOE = International Indian Ocean Expedition.

INDIAN OCEAN COMMISSION (IOC 1)

IMCO = Intergovernmental Maritime Consultative Organisation.

IMO = International Maritime Organisation.

INDIAN SPRINGS LOW WATER. (ISLW) The arbitrary level of the mean of lower low waters at spring tides. A chart datum used principally in the Indian Ocean and along the east coast of Asia and the north and west coasts of Australia. Also called INDIAN TIDE PLANE.

INLET. A narrow opening by which the water penetrates into the land. An arm of the sea or other body of water, that is long compared to its width. It may extend a considerable distance inland.

INNOCENT PASSAGE. A transitory navigation through the territorial sea-passage of a coastal state. It must not be prejudicial to the peace, good order and security of the coastal state (Article 17).

INTERNAL WATERS. Waters which lie on the landward side of the coastal state's territorial sea baseline and recognised HISTORIC BAYS (Articles 5–14).

INTERNATIONAL HYDROGRAPHIC BUREAU (IHB).

INTERNATIONAL HYDROGRAPHIC ORGANISATION (IHO). An international organisation, the seat of which is in the Principality of Monaco.

INTERNATIONAL INDIAN OCEAN EXPEDITION (IIOE).

INTERNATIONAL MARITIME ORGANISATION (IMO).

INSULAR SHELF. The zone surrounding an island extending from the low water line to a depth where there is a slope to greater depths.

IOC = 1 Indian Ocean Commission, 2 Intergovernmental Oceanographic Commission,

IOMAC = Indian Ocean Maritime Affairs Committee.

IOZP = Indian Ocean Zone of Peace.

ISA = International Seabed Authority.

ISLAND. A relatively small tract of land surrounded by water. Islands may be either continental or oceanic in origin. As an example, Madagascar is of the former classification and Réunion of the latter.

ISOBATH. A line on a map, chart or diagram joining points of equal depth.

ISOSTASY. The change of level of the land due to tectonic or other movements; it is independent of changes in sea level (EUSTASY).

ISTHMUS. A narrow strip of land, bordered on both sides by water and connecting two larger land masses; a neck of land, such as the Kra Isthmus between the Gulf of Thailand and the Andaman Sea.

JDZ = Joint Development Zone.

JETTY. A solid artifcial partly open structure designed as a berthing place for vessels (cf. MOLE).

KELP. (Botanical) One of an order (laminariales and fucales) of usually large blade-shaped or vine-like brown algae.

KELP STRUCTURE. A name given to a geological formation in the Timor Sea thought to contain potential hydrocarbon reserves.

KEY. A low or flat island or reef, usually a coral and sand islet. Same as CAY.

LAGOON. An enclosed area of shallow water separated from the open sea by SANDBARS, BARRIER ISLANDS and CORAL REEFS.

LANDLOCKED STATE. A state which does not possess a coastline, for example, Nepal and Afghanistan.

LAT = Lowest Astronomical Tide.

LATITUDE (Lat.). The angular distance (measured in degrees, minutes and seconds of arc) of a point on the Earth's surface north or south (and parallel to) of the Equator. One degree (1°) of latitude = 111.1 km or 60 nautical miles; 1 nautical mile = 6080 feet or 1852 metres.

LEAGUE. A varying obsolete measure of distance, usually about three miles.
LIGHTHOUSE. A structure on land that is a mariner's aid to navigation, producing a light as a danger signal or navigation aid.
LITTORAL. A coastal region (cf. COAST, SHORE).
LLS = Land-locked State.
LONGITUDE (Long.). Angular distance to the Equator (measured in degrees, minutes, and seconds) of a point on the earth's surface, from an adopted reference line, for example the Greenwich Meridian or Prime Meridian (Long. 0°).
LOW TIDE. The minimum elevation reached by each falling tide.
LOW-TIDE ELEVATION (LTE). Land which is surrounded by and above the water at low tide but is submerged at high tide. It is a legal term for what are generally described as DRYING BANKS or ROCKS.
LOW WATER LINE. The intersection of any standard low tide datum plane with the shore.
LTE = Low Tide Elevation.

MANGANESE NODULES. Nodules, generally greater than three centimetres in diameter, found on the ocean floor. They contain about 27 elements, manganese being the dominant one. These nodules represent a potentially significant source of minerals.
MEAN HIGHER HIGH WATER (MHHW). The average level of the two daily high waters over a 19-year period.
MEAN HIGH WATER SPRINGS (MHWS). The average level of the heights of two successive high waters taken at a time during a 24-hour period when the range of the tide at that locality is greatest.
MEAN LOW WATER LINE (MLWL). The intersection of the plane of the mean low level with the shore.
MEAN LOW WATER SPRINGS (MLWS). The average level of the heights of two successive low waters taken at a time during a 24-hour period when the range of the tide at that locality is greatest.
MEAN LOWER LOW WATER (MLLW). The average level of the two daily low waters over a 19-year period.
MEAN SEA LEVEL (MSL). The average height of the surface of the sea for all stages of the tide over a 19-year period, usually determined from hourly readings. It may approximate MEAN TIDE LEVEL.
MEAN TIDE LEVEL. A tidal plane midway between Mean High Water and Mean Low Water in a given period of time.
MEDIAN LINE. A line, or series of short lines, which at every point is equidistant from the shores between which it is being drawn. A median line may delineate the shared boundary of two states.
MERIDIAN. A semi-circle of Longitude, such as 90°east. All meridians extend from Pole to Pole.
MID-OCEAN RIDGE. A series of continuous undersea mountain ranges, such as the Carlsberg Ridge or the Ninety East Ridge.
MLLW = Mean Lower Low-Water.
MLWN = Mean Low-Water Neap.
MLWS = Mean Low-Water Spring.
MOLE. A massive structure of large stones or masonry which serves as a pier or breakwater (cf. JETTY).
MOUTH. The entrance to a BAY or GULF from the ocean or the final place of discharge of a stream (into the ocean or another stream).
MSC = Malacca Strait Council.

NAUTICAL MILE. A unit of measurement of distance used in marine navigation. A nautical mile is equal to one minute of arc of latitude at Lat. 45°, which is standardised at 6080 feet or 1852 metres.

NEAP TIDE. A tide occurring at or near the time of the first and last quarter phases of the moon.

NECK. Geographically, narrow strip of land connecting two larger masses of land, such as an ISTHMUS.

NEI = Netherlands East Indies (= Indonesia after 1945).

NOTICE TO MARINERS (NTM). A periodical or casual notification promulgated by hydrographic offices or other competent authorities regarding changes in aids to navigation, dangers to navigation and, in general, all such information as affects charts and other nautical publications. A comparative publication, Notice to Airmen (NOTAM) is essential to persons concerned with flight operations.

OCEAN. The body of water representing nearly 70 per cent of the Earth's surface. Geographers divide this body usually into three: the Atlantic, Indian and Pacific Oceans (cf. Chapter 2.4).

OCEANIC ISLANDS. Islands rising from the sea floor rather than from continental shelves. These islands are likely to be volcanic in origin, e.g. Mauritius, Réunion.

OCEANOGRAPHY. The science of the marine environment.

OCEANOLOGY. The study of the oceans and related sciences (same as OCEANOGRAPHY. A term used more frequently in Eastern Europe).

PARALLEL. A circle on the surface of the Earth, parallel to the Equator and connecting points of equal LATITUDE.

PENINSULA. An elongated portion of land projecting into the sea. The term can refer to small local peninsulas such as Jaffna in Sri Lanka or large regional peninsulas such as Malaya.

PLATE TECTONICS. The geological term given to the process of the movement of huge blocks or plates of the Earth's crust and the subsequent renewal of the seabed (see CONTINENTAL DRIFT).

PNG = Papua New Guinea.

POLLUTION. The term given to the contamination of the environment (air, land or water) by waste material or any other product as a result of direct or indirect human activity.

PREPCOM = Preparatory Commission on Deep Seabed Mining.

PROJECTION. The representation of a figure on a surface, either plane or curved, according to a mathematical formula. In cartography, any systematic arrangement of meridians of longitude and parallels of latitude portraying the curved surface of a sphere or spheroid upon a plane.

QUAY. A solid artificial landing place parallel to the navigable waterway for use in loading and unloading vessels (see MOLE).

REEF. A mass or ridge of rock in either a freshwater or marine environment.

RHUMB LINE. A line on the surface of the Earth making the same angle with all meridians. A rhumb line appears straight on Mercator's Projection.

RISE. A long, broad elevation that rises gently and generally smoothly from the sea floor.

ROADSTEAD. An ocean area near the shore where vessels can anchor in safety. Also called road or roads, for example, Gage Roads, off Fremantle.

ROUTING. A series of measures concerning routes followed by ships which aim at reducing the risk of collision and casualties.

SANDBAR. A submerged or emerged embankment of sand.

SCALE. The ratio between the actual dimensions of the surface portrayed and its linear dimensions on a chart or map. A small-scale chart portrays a relatively large area of the land or sea. A large-scale chart portrays a relatively small area of the land or sea.

SEA. A large marginal part of a particular ocean, e.g. Red Sea and Timor Sea of the Indian Ocean.

SEA LANE. A designated corridor through an area of claimed waters, for example TRAFFIC SEPARATION SCHEME, Deep-Draught Routes and other designated routes for ships.

SEAMOUNT. An isolated peak rising from the seabed to within 1000 metres of the surface (see also GUYOT).

SEAPOL = Southeast Asian Programme on Ocean Law and Management.

SEDENTARY SPECIES. With reference to marine organisms, these species which are either immobile on or under the seabed, or able to move only in contact with the seabed when they are in an adult stage.

SEMIDIURNAL TIDE. A tide with two high and two low waters in a tidal day.

SHELF EDGE. The line along which there is a marked increase of slope at the outer margin of a continental or island shelf (q.v. CONTINENTAL SLOPE).

SHOAL. A shallow underwater BANK formed of mud, sand or shingle.

SPECIAL GEOGRAPHICAL CHARACTERISTICS, STATES WITH — A term commonly used by negotiators during UNCLOS to refer to coastal states which are unable to optimise the potential resources of the adjacent seas because of their geographical configuration, such as Iraq, Singapore and Thailand.

SPIT. A small point of land or narrow shoal projecting from the shore.into a body of water (cf. HOOK).

SPRING TIDE. A tide that occurs at or near the time of new or full moon and results in higher high tides and lower low tides than normal.

STORM SURGE. A rise in the normal water level above predicted tide levels caused by wind and low pressure, and augmented by high tides.

STRAIT. A relatively narrow body of water connecting two larger bodies of water such as the Torres Strait which connects the Arafura Sea with the waters of the south Pacific Ocean.

STREAM. Body of water flowing in bed, brook or river or, if well defined, in the ocean (e.g. Gulf Stream).

SUBCONTINENT. A land-mass that is large, but generally smaller than those called continents, e.g. Indian subcontinent.

SUBMARINE CANYON. A valley or system of valleys etched into the ocean floor.

TERRITORIAL SEA. A zone of the sea, of specified width, adjacent to and seaward of the baseline. The maximum permitted width of this zone is 12 nautical miles measured from the baseline. (Article 3).

THALWEG. A German term, literally 'down stream' with reference to river navigation. The deep channel in a river, generally the most suitable channel for navigation at the normal lowest water level. The THALWEG is a functional boundary, based on the same principle as a MEDIAN LINE, e.g. inter-state boundary of Malaysia and Singapore in the Johore Strait.

TIDAL FLAT. A marsh or sandy or muddy coastal flatland which is covered and uncovered by the rise and fall of the TIDE.

TIDE. The periodical rise (FLOOD-TIDE) and fall (EBB-TIDE) of the sea due to the combined gravitational attraction of the moon and sun.

TOMBOLO. A sand bar or spit that connects an island to another island or to the mainland.

TRAFFIC SEPARATION SCHEME. A scheme which aims at reducing the risk of collision in congested and/or converging areas by separating traffic moving in opposite or nearly opposite directions.

TRANSIT PASSAGE. The right of uninterrupted passage of a vessel through international straits. It does not apply to warships.

TRANSIT STATE. A term referring to a state through which the trade of a landlocked state passes, whether or not the transit state has a coastline. The commerce and trade of land-locked Zimbabwe passes through the transit state of Mozambique.

TRENCH. A long, narrow and deep depression of the sea floor with relatively steep sides, for example the Java Trench, southwest of Java.

TSS = Traffic Separation Scheme.

TSUNAMI (TUNAMI). A long-period wave caused by an underwater disturbance such as an earthquake or a volcanic eruption. Incorrectly called a tidal wave.

UKC = Under Keel Clearance.

UN = United Nations.

UNCLOS III = Third United Nations Conference on the Law of the Sea.

UNEP = United Nations Environment Programme.

UNESCO = United Nations Educational Scientific and Cultural Organisation.

UPWELLING. The rise of subsurface cold, dense water. It is most noticeable in tropical latitudes off the western coasts of continents.

VOC = Vereenigde Oostindische Compagnie (United Dutch East India Company)

ZOC = Zone of Cooperation.

ZOPAN = Zone of Peace and Neutrality.

APPENDIX A

ATLAS OF MARITIME BOUNDARIES OF THE INDIAN OCEAN REGION

Appendix A consists of two sections. The first section contains a map depicting agreed and potential maritime boundaries of the Indian Ocean Basin and nine maps which portray regional overviews of spatial claim with accompanying commentaries. Eight maps were compiled at a natural scale of 1:10 000 000 on specified latitudes employing the Mercator's Projection. It was found to be the most convenient map projection for the purpose of plotting geographical coordinates and geodesic lines connecting those coordinates. For the convenience of presentation, however, the original fair drawings have been photographically reduced to suit the format of the thesis.

The maps portray the Territorial Sea Baseline system where these have been defined and published, the 12-nautical mile arc to indicate the extent of the Territorial Sea and the 200-nm arc to delineate the limits of the EEZ. In instances where coastal states are not able to claim the maximum permissible width of sea because of their geographical proximity to their coastal neighbours a hypothetical median-line has been delineated.

The second part contains a brief analysis of maritime boundary determination between coastal states of the Indian Ocean Region. Generally medium- and large-scale maps and charts were used to plot the geographical coordinates which define the maritime boundary between the states as declared in the text of the Agreements. These agreements are the primary source of this study.

Geodesic distances were calculated on a NC-77 *Tamaya* Navigation computer and the results were compared with the plotted values. The resultant distances, in nautical miles, are given to the nearest whole number. Such accuracy was considered sufficient for the purpose of the exercise in the brief analyses.

Dates noted are those of ratification of the agreement or the date of entry into force.

The following sources, in addition to texts of the agreements, the primary source, were used in the compilation of the data.

Agreements between the negotiating states.
The *Limits in the Sea* Series, (Limits) Bureau of Intelligence and Research, Department of State, Washington, DC.
United Nations Treaty Series (UNTS).
National Legislation and Treaties Relating to the Law of the Sea. (ST/LEG/SER. B/16, 1974; SER. B/18, 1976; SER. B/19, 1980).
International Legal Materials (ILM).
International Boundary Studies (IBS).

AN ATLAS OF MARITIME BOUNDARIES

This section contains a regional map, an index map and nine subregional maps depicting the extent, real and potential, of maritime claims in the Indian Ocean Basin.

This section contains maps of special case studies of Seabed boundary determination.

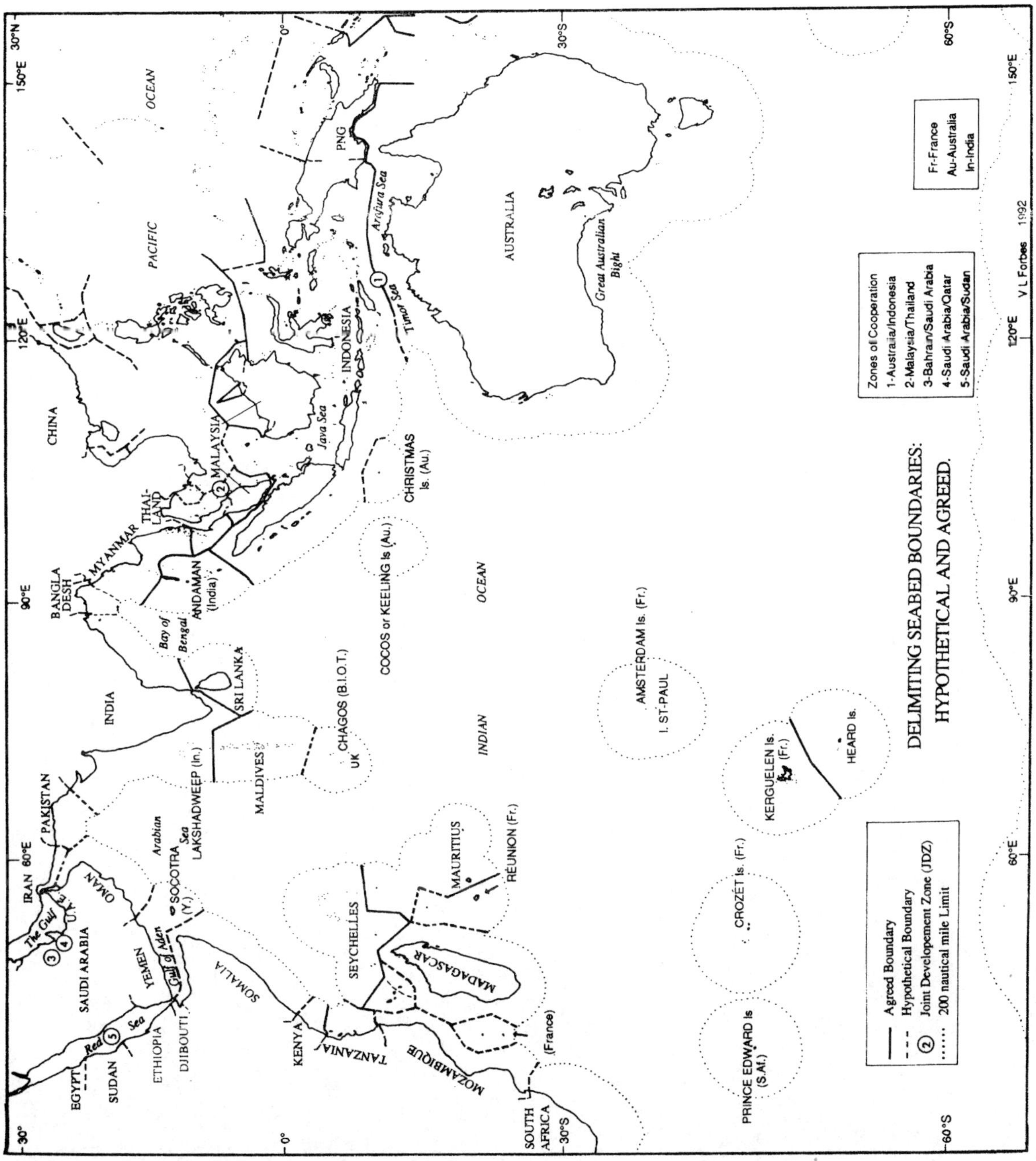
DELIMITING SEABED BOUNDARIES:
HYPOTHETICAL AND AGREED.
Agreed Boundary
Hypothetical Boundary
Joint Developement Zone (JDZ)
200 nautical mile Limit
Zones of Cooperation
1-Australia/Indonesia
2-Malaysia/Thailand
3-Bahrain/Saudi Arabia
4-Saudi Arabia/Qatar
5-Saudi Arabia/Sudan
Fr-France
Au-Australia
In-India
V L Forbes 1992

Map 0

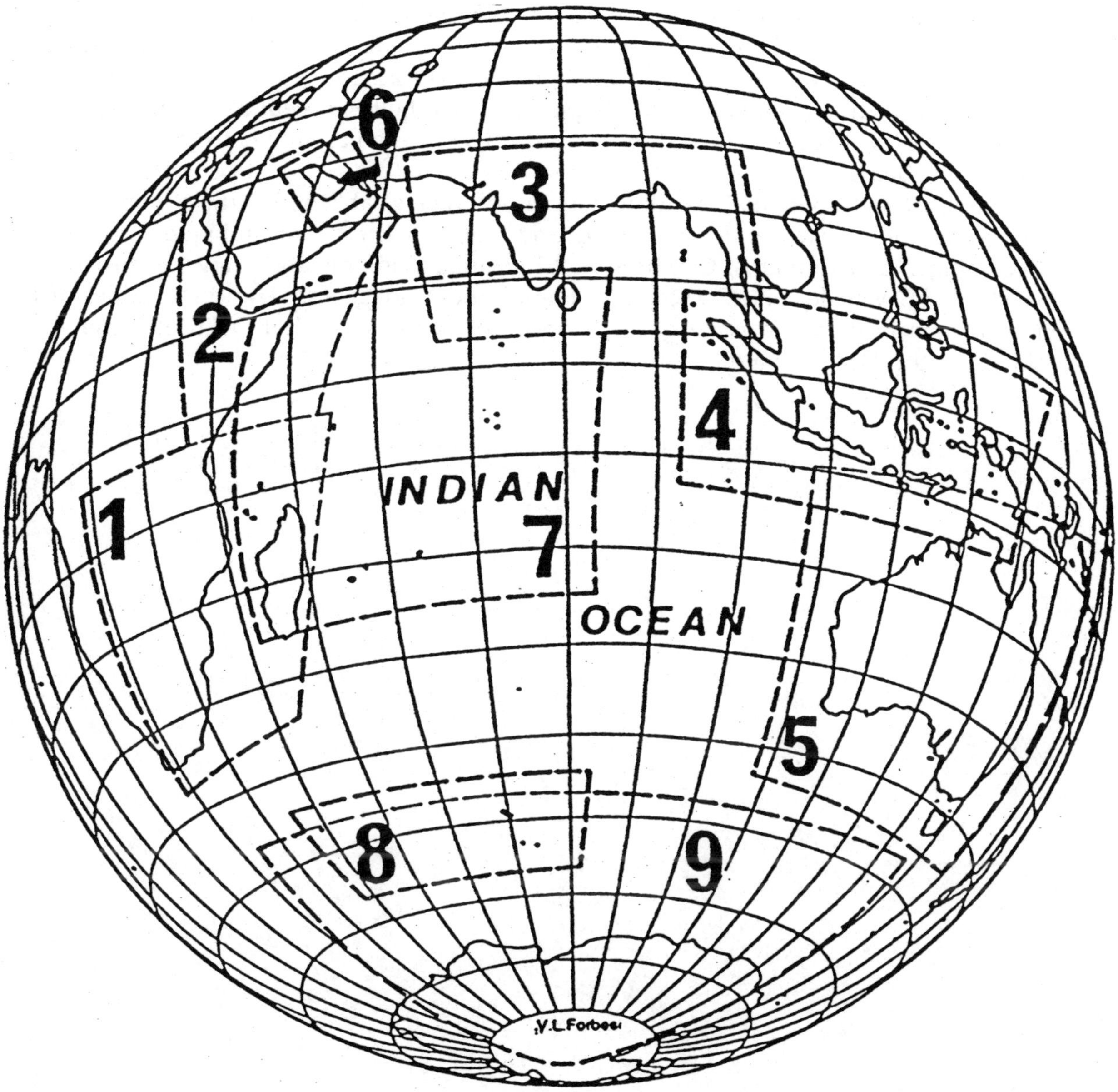

Map 00

MAP 1
MARITIME JURISDICTIONS IN THE VICINITY OF THE SOUTHEAST OF THE AFRICAN CONTINENT

Two continental shelf boundaries have been established in the western margin of the Indian Ocean Basin by agreement. The boundary between Kenya and Tanzania has entered into force: The boundary between Mozambique and Tanzania has been negotiated but is pending ratification.

The Seychelles Government has defined geographical coordinates to delineate the extent of its Exclusive Economic Zone. The proclamation was based on a unilateral decision. Apparently no discussion took place with its neighbours prior to the announcement being made. For the most part the boundary is formed by the locus of a point 200 nm from the nearest landmass of the Republic of Seychelles, except between Points 13 to 18 and 19 to 29 where the boundary is formed by the median line between the Republic and its neigbours.

There are eight potential maritime boundaries to be established in the region. They are the boundaries between: Mozambique and South Africa; Mozambique and France, Mozambique and Comoros; Comoros and Tanzania; Comoros and France; Comoros and Seychelles; Seychelles and France; and, France and Madagascar. The complexities of the negotiations rest on the issue of sovereignty of some small but politically significant islands in the Mozambique Channel.

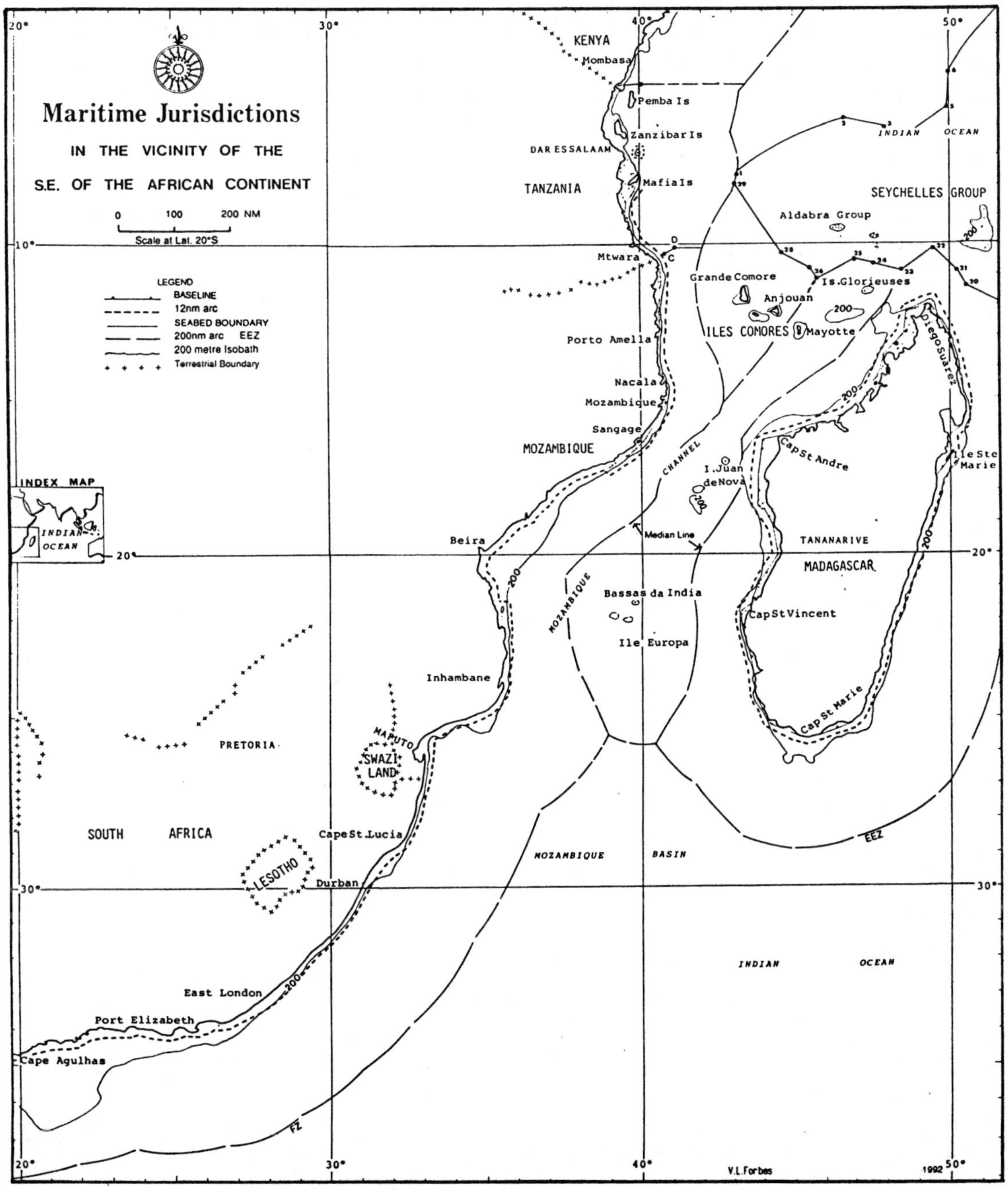
Maritime Jurisdictions
IN THE VICINITY OF THE
S.E. OF THE AFRICAN CONTINENT
0 100 200 NM
Scale at Lat. 20°S
LEGEND
BASELINE
12nm arc
SEABED BOUNDARY
200nm arc EEZ
200 metre Isobath
Terrestrial Boundary
INDEX MAP
INDIAN OCEAN
KENYA
Mombasa
Pemba Is
Zanzibar Is
DAR ES SALAAM
TANZANIA
Mafia Is
Mtwara
Porto Amella
Nacala
Mozambique
Sangage
MOZAMBIQUE
CHANNEL
Beira
Inhambane
MAPUTO
SWAZI LAND
PRETORIA
SOUTH AFRICA
LESOTHO
Cape St Lucia
Durban
East London
Port Elizabeth
Cape Agulhas
SEYCHELLES GROUP
Aldabra Group
Grande Comore
Anjouan
Is.Glorieuses
ILES COMORES
Mayotte
Diego Suarez
Cap St Andre
I.Juan de Nova
Median Line
Ile Ste Marie
TANANARIVE
MADAGASCAR
Bassas da India
Ile Europa
Cap St Vincent
Cap St Marie
MOZAMBIQUE
MOZAMBIQUE BASIN
EEZ
INDIAN OCEAN
FZ
V.L.Forbes
1992

Map 1

MAP 2
MARITIME JURISDICTIONS IN THE VICINITY OF THE ARABIAN PENINSULA AND THE HORN OF AFRICA

In the southern portion of the map only one negotiated maritime boundary exists. It is the boundary between Kenya and Tanzania. Further east from this boundary the Seychelles government has defined its EEZ.

The only negotiated boundary in the Red Sea is the Common Zone of Exploitation established by Saudi Arabia and Sudan. The boundary of the Common Zone is the 1000 m isobath. The negotiated continental shelf boundaries in the Persian Gulf are analysed in Map 6 and Maps 10 to 17 below. Excluding the undefined boundaries in the Persian Gulf there are 14 potential boundaries to be negotiated in the region. They are the boundaries between: Kenya and Somalia; Somalia and Djibouti; Somalia and Yemen; Yemen and Oman; Djibouti and Yemen; Djibouti and Ethiopia; Ehtiopia and Sudan; Ehtiopia and Saudi Arabia; Saudi Arabia and Yeman; Egypt and Saudi Arabia; Egypt and Israel; Egypt and Jordan; Jordan and Israel; and, Jordan and Saudi Arabia.

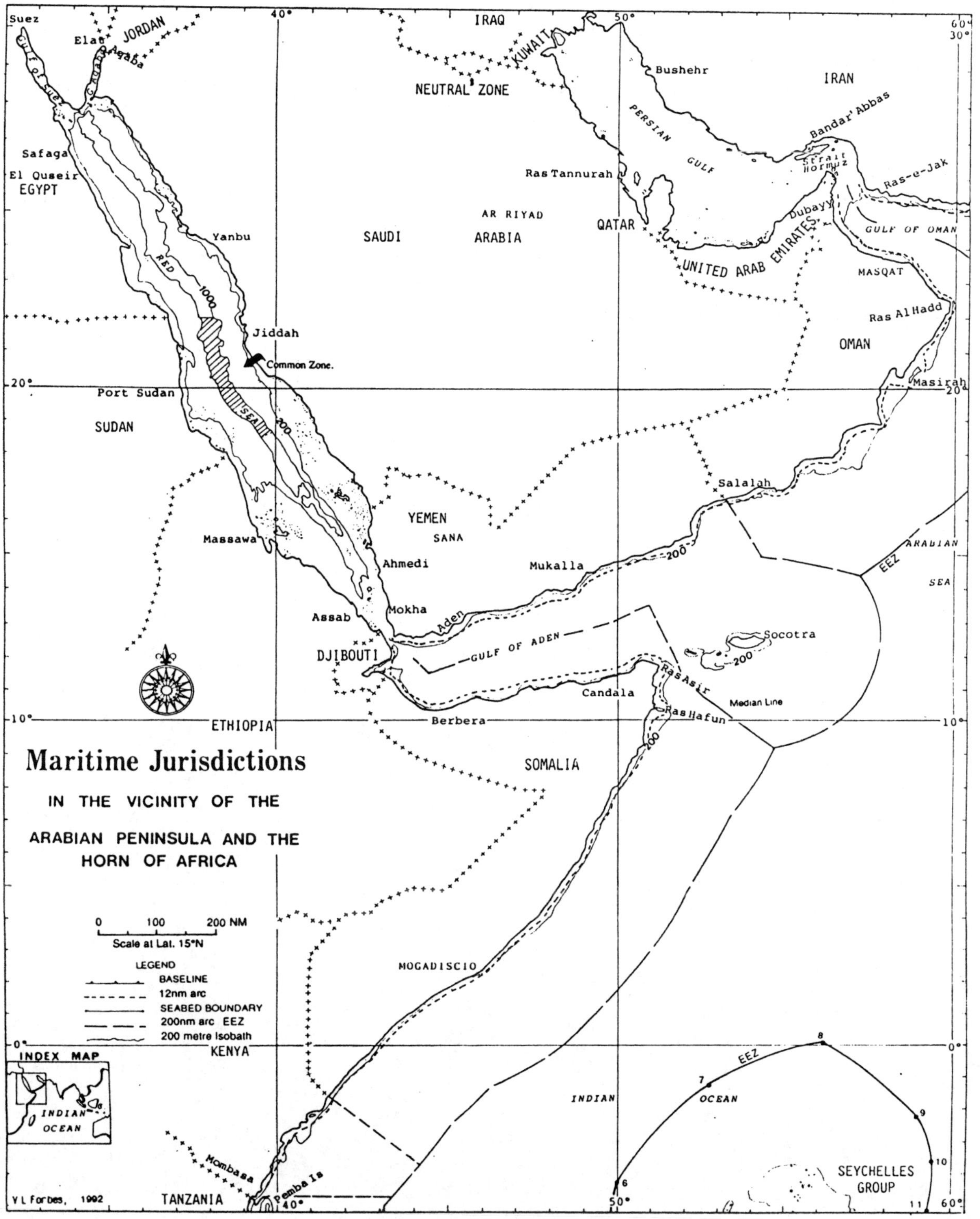
Maritime Jurisdictions
IN THE VICINITY OF THE
ARABIAN PENINSULA AND THE
HORN OF AFRICA
0 100 200 NM
Scale at Lat. 15°N
LEGEND
BASELINE
12nm arc
SEABED BOUNDARY
200nm arc EEZ
200 metre Isobath
INDEX MAP
INDIAN OCEAN
Y L Forbes, 1992
Suez
Elat
Aqaba
JORDAN
IRAQ
KUWAIT
NEUTRAL ZONE
Bushehr
IRAN
PERSIAN GULF
Bandar'Abbas
Strait Hormuz
Ras-e-Jak
Ras Tannurah
QATAR
Dubayy
UNITED ARAB EMIRATES
GULF OF OMAN
MASQAT
Ras Al Hadd
OMAN
Masirah
SAUDI ARABIA
AR RIYAD
Safaga
El Quseir
EGYPT
Yanbu
RED SEA
Jiddah
Common Zone.
Port Sudan
SUDAN
Massawa
YEMEN
SANA
Ahmedi
Mukalla
Salalah
Mokha
Assab
Aden
GULF OF ADEN
Socotra
DJIBOUTI
Candala
Ras Asir
Median Line
Ras Hafun
Berbera
ETHIOPIA
SOMALIA
ARABIAN SEA
EEZ
MOGADISCIO
KENYA
INDIAN OCEAN
Mombasa
Pemba Is
TANZANIA
SEYCHELLES GROUP

Map 2

MAP 3
MARITIME JURISDICTIONS IN THE VICINITY OF THE INDIAN SUBCONTINENT

Continental shelf boundaries have been determined by bilateral and trilateral agreements in the Andaman Sea, southwest corner of the Bay of Bengal, Palk Bay, Gulf of Mannar and the Laccadive Sea.

Only two states in this regional context have not precisely defined their Territorial Sea Baseline system. They are India and Pakistan. Bangladesh has defined its system which is most unusual in that the basepoints are not located on land. Instead, the points lie along the 18 metre isobath. From this baseline system (ref. Map 20) Bangladesh has delineated the boundaries of its claimed economic zone. Although this irregularly shaped zone has its merits, it remains to be seen whether the two adjacent states will recognise the claim.Failure to do so will mean that there remain three potential continental shelf boundaries to be negotiated. These are the boundaries between: Pakistan and India; India and Bangladesh; and Bangladesh and Myanmar.

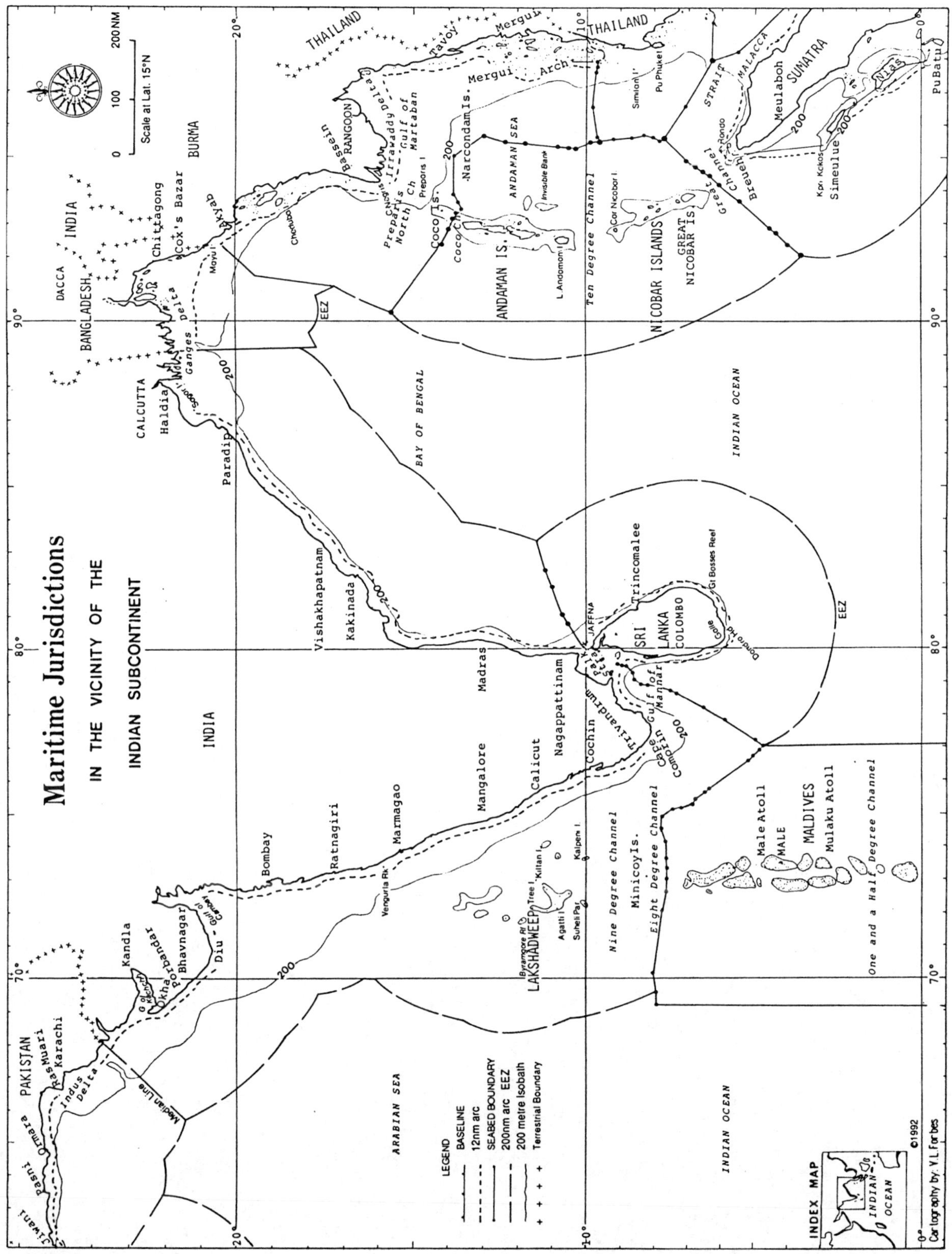
Maritime Jurisdictions
IN THE VICINITY OF THE
INDIAN SUBCONTINENT
LEGEND
BASELINE
12nm arc
SEABED BOUNDARY
200nm arc EEZ
200 metre Isobath
Terrestrial Boundary
Scale at Lat. 15°N
INDEX MAP
©1992
Cartography by: Y.L.Forbes
INDIA
PAKISTAN
BANGLADESH
BURMA
THAILAND
SRI LANKA
MALDIVES
SUMATRA
ARABIAN SEA
BAY OF BENGAL
ANDAMAN SEA
INDIAN OCEAN

Map 3

MAP 4
MARITIME JURISDICTIONS IN THE VICINITY OF THE INDONESIAN ARCHIPELAGO AND ADJACENT REGIONS

Only a portion of the Indonesian archipelago is depicted on this map. By virtue of its declaration of archipelagic status and the adoption of a straight baseline system connecting the outermost islands of the archipelago Indonesia has gained vast areas of sea space which now fall within its internal waters regime.

It is apparent from the geographical extent of the archipelago that Indonesia has been keen and indeed taken the initiative in many instances to bring about negotiations on determining continental shelf boundaries with its neighbours in the adjacent seas. Successful negotiations have brought to fruition the signing of agreements with Australia, India, Malaysia, Singapore, Thailand and Papua New Guinea.

With reference to the map and within the context of the defined limits of this study there remain only two boundaries to be negotiated. These are in the vicinity of Christmas and Java Islands and a westward extension of Point A 25 of a previously agreed seabed boundary in the Timor Sea.

Two features which are prominent on the map are the Joint Development Area in the Gulf of Thailand and the Zone of Cooperation in the Timor Sea.

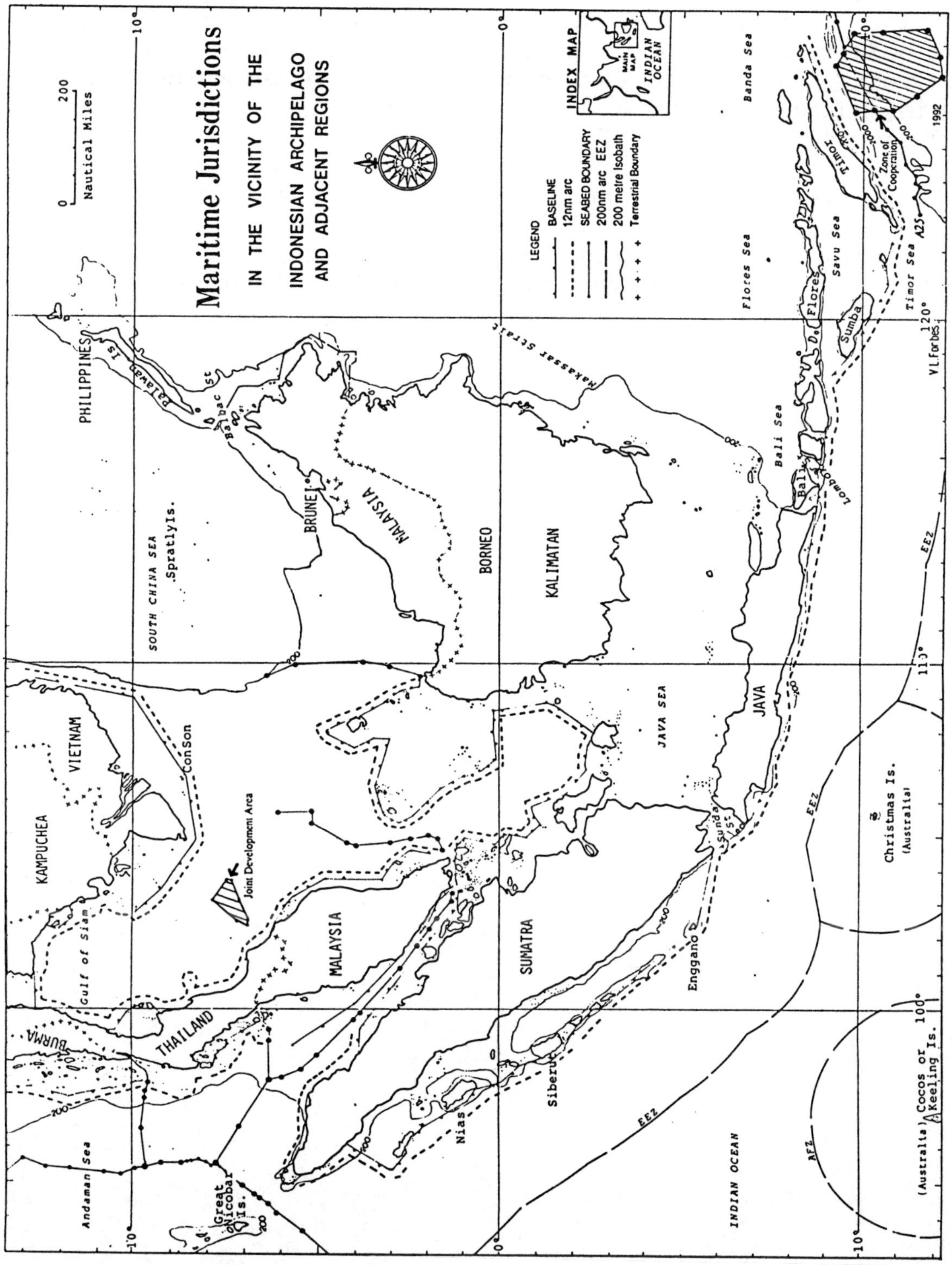
Maritime Jurisdictions
IN THE VICINITY OF THE
INDONESIAN ARCHIPELAGO
AND ADJACENT REGIONS
LEGEND
BASELINE
12nm arc
SEABED BOUNDARY
200nm arc EEZ
200 metre Isobath
Terrestrial Boundary
INDEX MAP
INDIAN OCEAN
Nautical Miles
0
200
PHILIPPINES
Palawan Is.
Balabac St.
SOUTH CHINA SEA
Spratly Is.
BRUNEI
MALAYSIA
BORNEO
KALIMATAN
Makassar Strait
KAMPUCHEA
VIETNAM
Con Son
Gulf of Siam
Joint Development Area
BURMA
THAILAND
MALAYSIA
SUMATRA
JAVA SEA
JAVA
Sunda St.
Andaman Sea
Great Nicobar Is.
Nias
Siberut
Enggano
INDIAN OCEAN
Christmas Is.
(Australia)
(Australia) Cocos or Keeling Is.
EEZ
Bali Sea
Bali
Lombok
Flores Sea
Flores
Sumba
Savu Sea
Timor
Timor Sea
Banda Sea
Zone of Cooperation
1992
V.L.Forbes

Map 4

MAP 5
MARITIME JURISDICTIONS IN THE VICINITY OF THE AUSTRALIAN MAINLAND AND TASMANIA

Continental shelf boundaries between Australia and its northern neighbours, Indonesia and Papua New Guinea, have been determined. Interrupted only by the creation of a Zone of Cooperation (ZOC), the agreed seabed boundary extends from the western margin of the Timor Sea through the Arafura Sea, Torres Strait and into the Coral Sea. Its total length is about 2000 nm.

The map depicts the extent of the Australian Fishing Zone (AFZ) and an interpretation of the limits of the continental shelf as defined in Article 76 of the Convention on the Law of the Sea. This limit contrasts with the 1958 *Geneva Convention on the Continental Shelf's* definition of the edge of the continental shelf — the 200 metre isobath.

The approximate boundaries of the Zone of Cooperation and the Torres Strait Protected Zone have been delineated. These zones are depicted in maps and analysed in detail in Chapter Five.

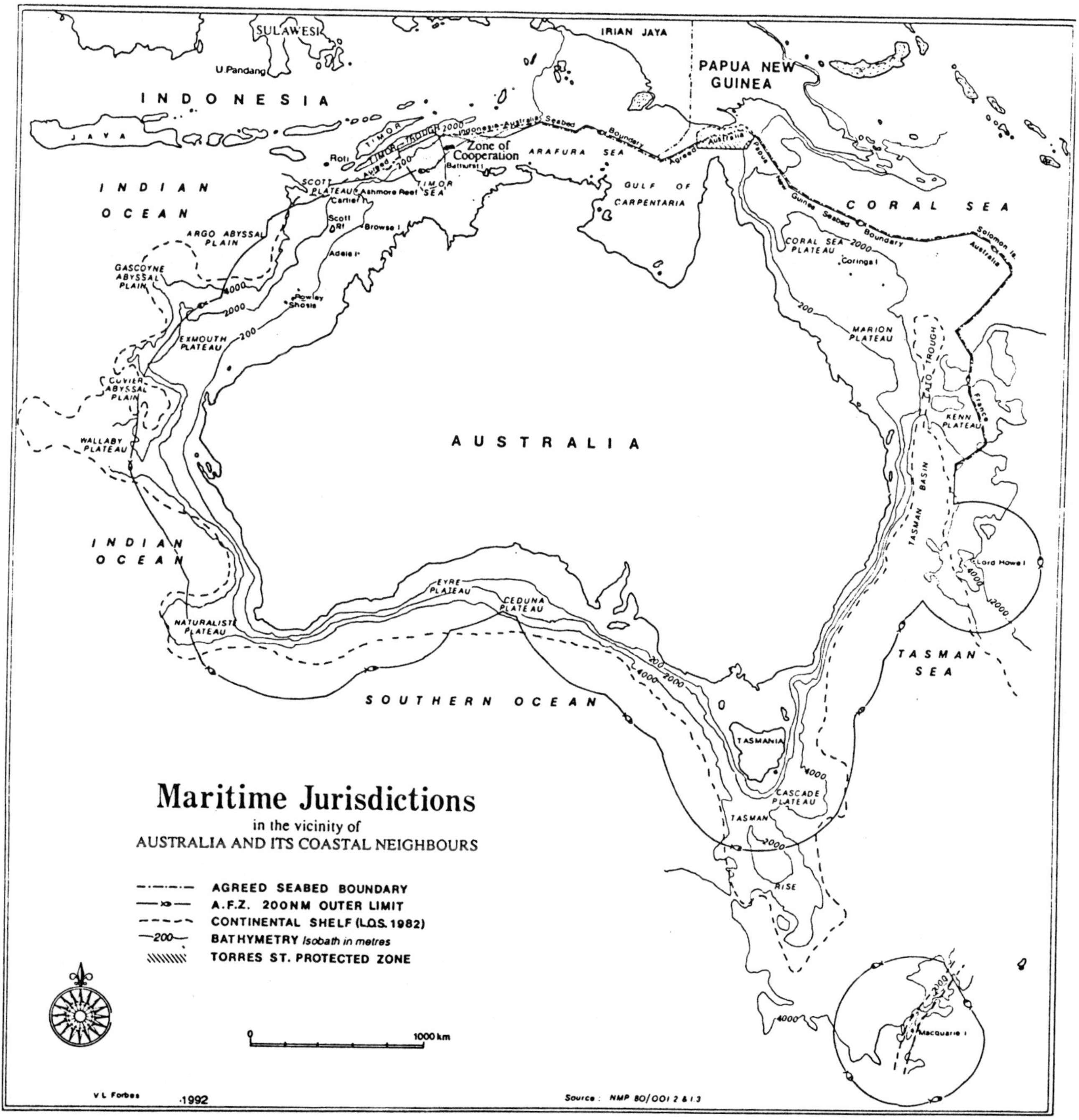
Maritime Jurisdictions
in the vicinity of
AUSTRALIA AND ITS COASTAL NEIGHBOURS
AGREED SEABED BOUNDARY
A.F.Z. 200NM OUTER LIMIT
CONTINENTAL SHELF (LOS 1982)
BATHYMETRY Isobath in metres
TORRES ST. PROTECTED ZONE
1000 km
V L Forbes
1992
Source: NMP 80/001 2 & 13
SULAWESI
U.Pandang
INDONESIA
JAVA
IRIAN JAYA
PAPUA NEW GUINEA
Zone of Cooperation
ARAFURA SEA
TIMOR SEA
Roti
Ashmore Reef
Cartier I
Scott Rf
Browse I
Adele I
Rowley Shoals
SCOTT PLATEAU
INDIAN OCEAN
ARGO ABYSSAL PLAIN
GASCOYNE ABYSSAL PLAIN
EXMOUTH PLATEAU
CUVIER ABYSSAL PLAIN
WALLABY PLATEAU
GULF OF CARPENTARIA
CORAL SEA
CORAL SEA PLATEAU
Coringa I
MARION PLATEAU
KENN PLATEAU
TASMAN BASIN
Lord Howe I
AUSTRALIA
EYRE PLATEAU
CEDUNA PLATEAU
NATURALISTE PLATEAU
SOUTHERN OCEAN
TASMAN SEA
TASMANIA
CASCADE PLATEAU
TASMAN
RISE
Macquarie I

Map 5

MAP 6
MARITIME BOUNDARIES IN THE PERSIAN GULF

Continental shelf boundaries have been determined for the central portion of the Persian Gulf and in the Strait of Hormuz and the northern waters of the Gulf of Oman. Maps 11 to 17 below delineate the boundaries.

Boundaries in the process of being negotiated or to be determined are those between Kuwait and Iraq, Iraq and Iran, and Iran and Kuwait at the Head of the Gulf. In the southeastern sector of the Gulf, Iran and individual Emirates of the United Arab Emirates have yet to determine their common continental shelf boundary. Delays in negotiations are centred on the issue of sovereignty of some small islands; in particular Abu Musa, that lie between the coastlines of the two states. The insular geography of the region favours Iran in boundary determination if all the islands it claims were to be considered as points of measurements.

The map also shows the approximate location of offshore hydrocarbon reserves, pipelines to the producing oil and gas fields, tanker loading facilities and traffic separation schemes. The 12-nm arc, the maximum permissable territorial sea width, is depicted by a pecked line.

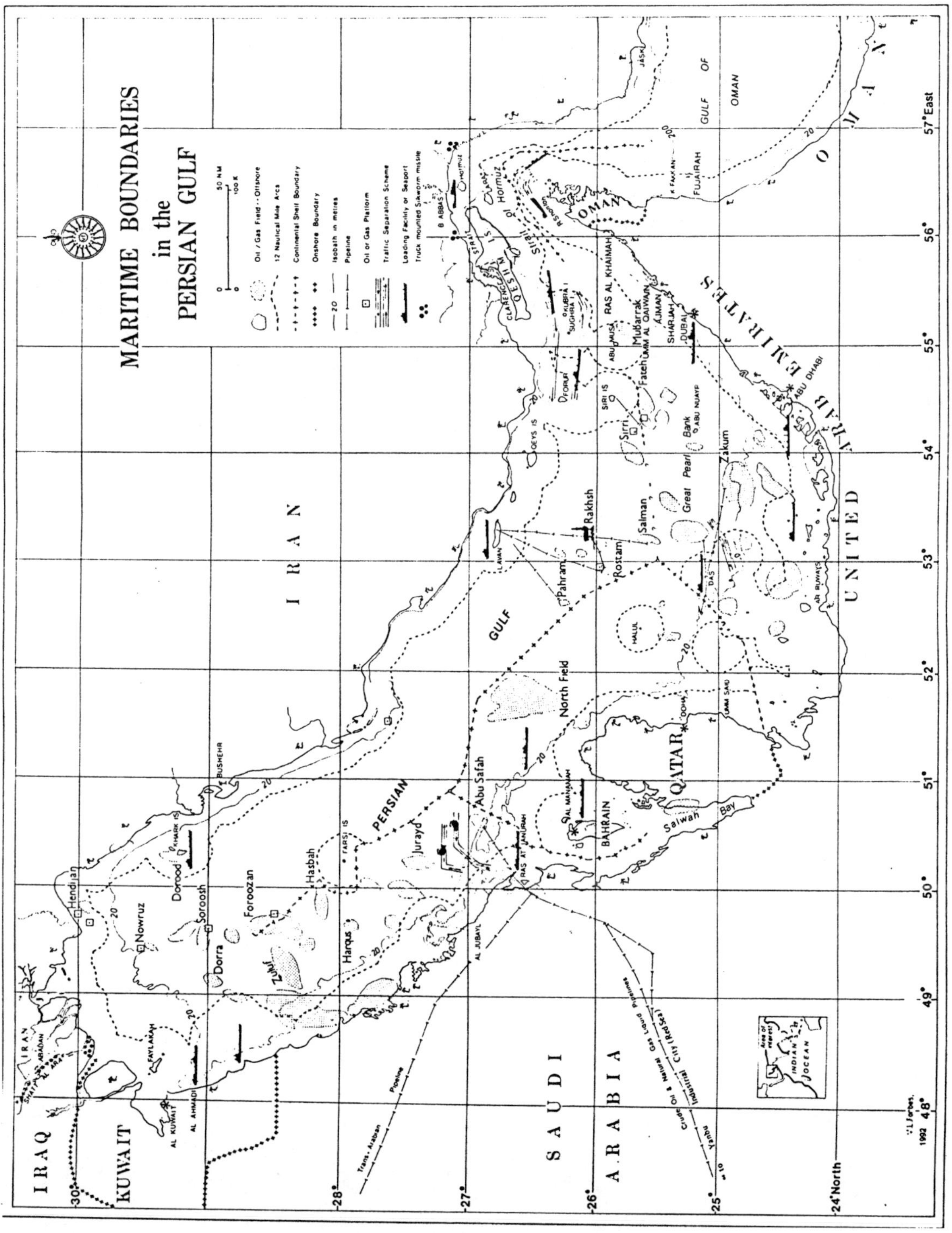
MARITIME BOUNDARIES
in the
PERSIAN GULF
IRAQ
KUWAIT
IRAN
SAUDI
ARABIA
QATAR
BAHRAIN
UNITED
ARAB
EMIRATES
OMAN
PERSIAN
GULF
GULF OF OMAN
Strait of Hormuz
North Field
Abu Safah
Rakhsh
Rostam
Salman
Great Pearl Bank
Zakum
Mubarrak
Fateh
Sirri
Pahram
Hasbah
Jurayd
Harqus
Zuluf
Dorra
Nowruz
Dorood
Soroosh
Foroozan
Hendijan
Salwah Bay
24°North
57°East

Map 6

MAP 7
EXCLUSIVE ECONOMIC ZONES OF THE SOUTHWEST INDIAN OCEAN BASIN

Vast areas of the sea and its substratum, as depicted on this map, now fall under the regime of the Exclusive Economic Zone of a few maritime states.

Maldives, Mauritius and Seychelles have each defined, by geographical coordinates, the geographical limits to their claims for the exclusive rights to explore and exploit the resources of the sea. The claim by Mauritius is intriguing. It comprises two parts. The west part, consisting of 40 turning points, encompasss Tromelin Isle. The delineated zone incorporates the common agreed boundary with France (Réunion Island). The eastern part of the claim, defined by 21 turning points labelled A to U, encompasses the islands of the Chagos Archipelago. Part of the claim overlaps the Maldives' declared Territorial Sea and Fishing Zone Rectangle. The map depicts the negotiated boundaries between India and Maldives and India and Sri Lanka.

The complexity of the issue over sovereignty of the Chagos Archipelago is highlighted by the recent decision of the Administration of the British Indian Ocean Territory (BIOT) to declare a Fishing and Conservation Management Zone (FCMZ) of 200-nm radius around the Chagos Archipelago (Forbes, 1992: 12–14). This zone overlays the earlier Mauritian claim. Maritime boundaries have as yet to be determined between Madagascar and the neighbouring states of Seychelles, Mauritius, Comoros and France.

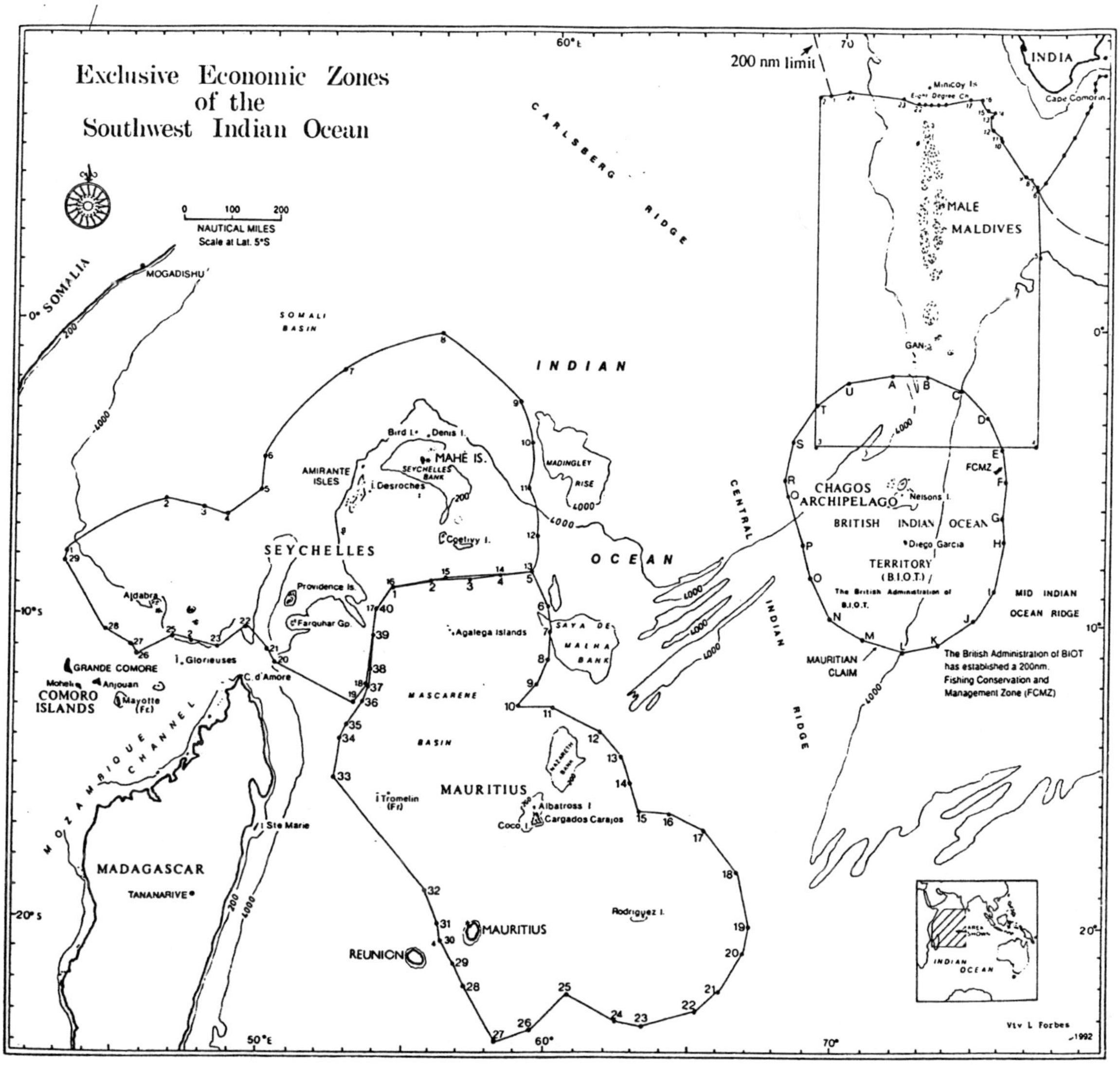
Exclusive Economic Zones
of the
Southwest Indian Ocean
NAUTICAL MILES
Scale at Lat. 5°S
200 nm limit
INDIA
MALE
MALDIVES
INDIAN
OCEAN
CARLSBERG RIDGE
SOMALIA
MOGADISHU
SOMALI BASIN
MAHÉ IS.
AMIRANTE ISLES
SEYCHELLES
CHAGOS ARCHIPELAGO
BRITISH INDIAN OCEAN TERRITORY (B.I.O.T.)
Diego Garcia
CENTRAL INDIAN RIDGE
MID INDIAN OCEAN RIDGE
MAURITIAN CLAIM
The British Administration of BIOT has established a 200nm. Fishing Conservation and Management Zone (FCMZ)
COMORO ISLANDS
GRANDE COMORE
MOZAMBIQUE CHANNEL
MADAGASCAR
TANANARIVE
MASCARENE BASIN
MAURITIUS
REUNION
Rodriguez I.
Agalega Islands
Tromelin (Fr)
Cargados Carajos
Viv L Forbes 1992

Map 7

MAP 8
THE APPROXIMATE EXTENT OF THE EXCLUSIVE ECONOMIC ZONES OF SOME ISLANDS IN THE SOUTHERN INDIAN OCEAN

A continental shelf boundary between Kerguelen and Heard and McDonald Islands has been determined. It consists of eight turning points.

Elsewhere on the map the extent of the 200-nm EEZ around the groups of islands has been delineated. Small islands, when sufficiently separated geographically and politically from other islands, can generate vast areas of space under the regime of the EEZ.

France and South Africa both benefit from the extended maritime jurisdictional zones in this southern region of the basin, gained by claiming exclusive 200 nm zones around the islands of Amsterdam-Saint Paul, Iles Crozet and the Prince Edward Group.

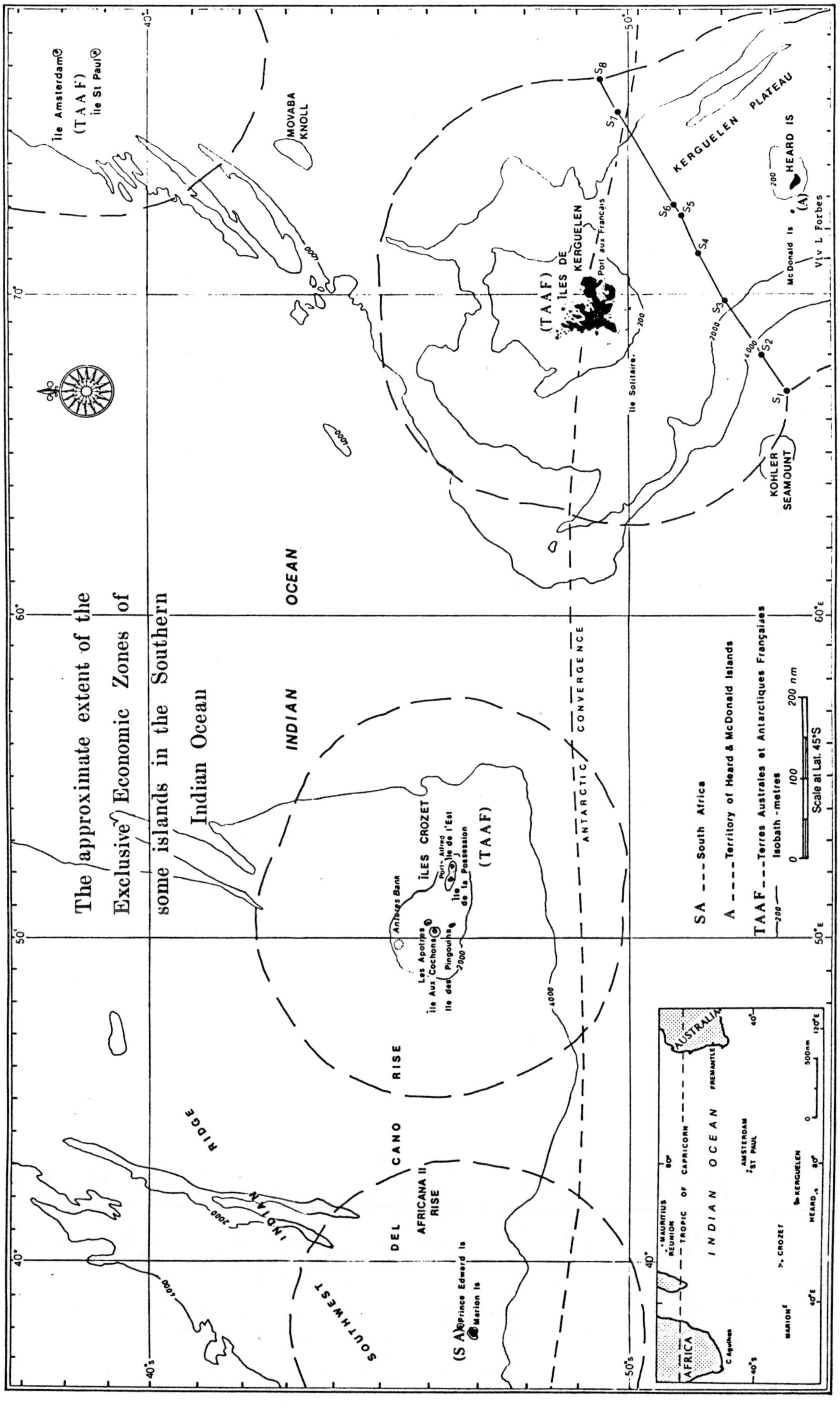
The approximate extent of the Exclusive Economic Zones of some islands in the Southern Indian Ocean
Île Amsterdam
(T A A F)
Île St Paul
MOVABA KNOLL
INDIAN OCEAN
ÎLES DE KERGUELEN
(T A A F)
Port aux Français
Île Solitaire
KERGUELEN PLATEAU
HEARD IS
(A)
McDonald Is
KOHLER SEAMOUNT
Viv L Forbes
ANTARCTIC CONVERGENCE
ÎLES CROZET
(TAAF)
Port Alfred
Île de l'Est
Île de la Possession
Les Apotres
Île Aux Cochons
Île des Pingouins
Antares Bank
DEL CANO RISE
AFRICANA II RISE
SOUTHWEST INDIAN RIDGE
(S A) Prince Edward Is
Marion Is
SA ---- South Africa
A ---- Territory of Heard & McDonald Islands
TAAF ---- Terres Australes et Antarctiques Françaises
—200— Isobath - metres
0 100 200 nm
Scale at Lat. 45°S
AFRICA
AUSTRALIA
INDIAN OCEAN
TROPIC OF CAPRICORN
MAURITIUS
REUNION
CROZET
KERGUELEN
HEARD
AMSTERDAM
ST PAUL
FREMANTLE
MARION
C Agulhas

Map 8

MAP 9
ANTARCTICA'S INDIAN OCEAN SECTOR: CLAIMS, BASES AND MARITIME JURISDICTIONS

This simplified map shows the extent of the 200-nm zone off the islands of Prince Edward, Crozet, Kerguelen, Heard and McDonalds and Macquarie and the Antarctic iceshelf bordering the southern limits of the Indian Ocean. Other maritime limits in these waters include The Living Resources Convention Boundary and the Antarctic Treaty and Seals Conservation Convention Boundary.

Scientific research bases on the continent are depicted by numerals. The national occupants are recorded in the legend. It should be noted that any claim to an EEZ or Fishing Zone in Antarctic waters south of Lat. 60° S is against the spirit of Article II of the *Antarctic Treaty*. The Treaty prohibits sovereignty claims to the continent. International agreement during 1991 has also restricted any exploitation of the mineral wealth beneath the ice continent.

Australia, France and Norway are three states that claim between them the sector of the continent bordering the Indian Ocean. Norway's claim (Queen Maud Land) extends from Long. 20° W to 45° E; Australia (Enderby Land, Wilkes Land, George V Coast, part of Oates Coast) from 45° to 136° E and from 142° to 160° E; France (Adélie Coast) from 136° to 142° E.

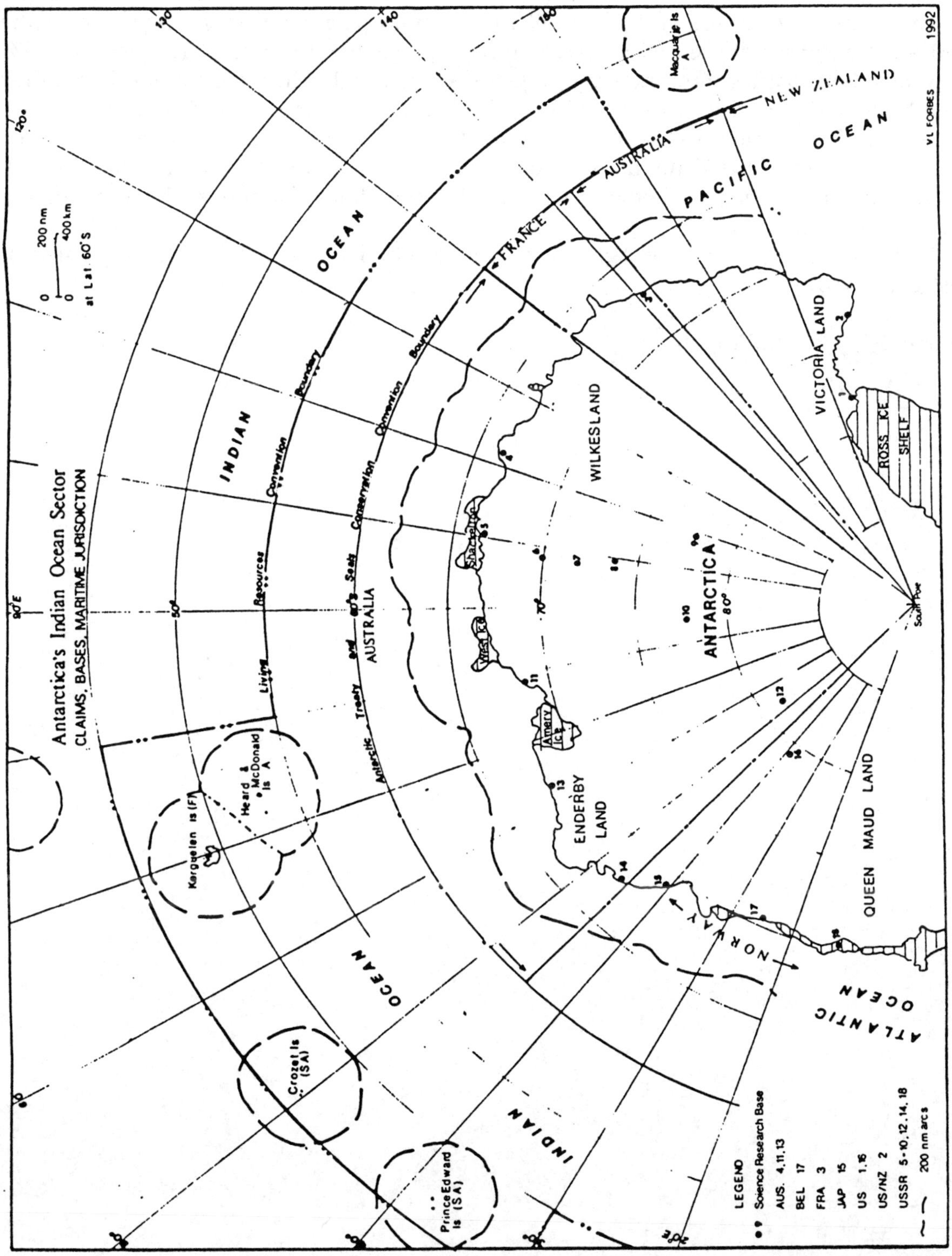
Antarctica's Indian Ocean Sector
CLAIMS, BASES, MARITIME JURISDICTION
0 200 nm
0 400 km
at Lat. 60°S
INDIAN OCEAN
PACIFIC OCEAN
ATLANTIC OCEAN
Antarctic Treaty and 60°S Seals Conservation Convention Boundary
Living Resources Convention Boundary
AUSTRALIA
FRANCE
NEW ZEALAND
NORWAY
Kerguelen Is (F)
Heard & McDonald Is A
Crozet Is (SA)
Prince Edward Is (SA)
Macquarie Is A
ANTARCTICA
WILKESLAND
ENDERBY LAND
QUEEN MAUD LAND
VICTORIA LAND
ROSS ICE SHELF
Amery Ice
South Pole
LEGEND
Science Research Base
AUS. 4,11,13
BEL 17
FRA 3
JAP 15
US 1,16
US/NZ 2
USSR 5-10,12,14,18
200 nm arcs
V L FORBES
1992

Map 9

MAP 10
THE COMMON ZONE OF EXPLOITATION: SUDAN/SAUDI ARABIA

An agreement was signed in Khartoum, Sudan, on May 16, 1974 by representatives of the Governments of Sudan and Saudi Arabia, to explore and exploit the natural resources of the seabed and substratum of the Red Sea in a Common Zone which was bounded by the 1,000-metre isobath of the Red Sea. The Agreement came into force on August 26, 1974.

Whilst both parties confirmed their equal sovereign rights in the Common Zone, they would undertake to protect these rights and defend them against third parties.

A Joint Commission was set up to ensure the prompt and efficient exploitation of the natural resources of the Zone. Its functions were many and varied and included the task of encouraging specialized bodies to undertake operations for the exploitation of the natural resources there.

Both parties noted that the Agreement would not affect the status of the high seas or obstruct navigation.

Source: ST/LEG/SER.B/18: 452.

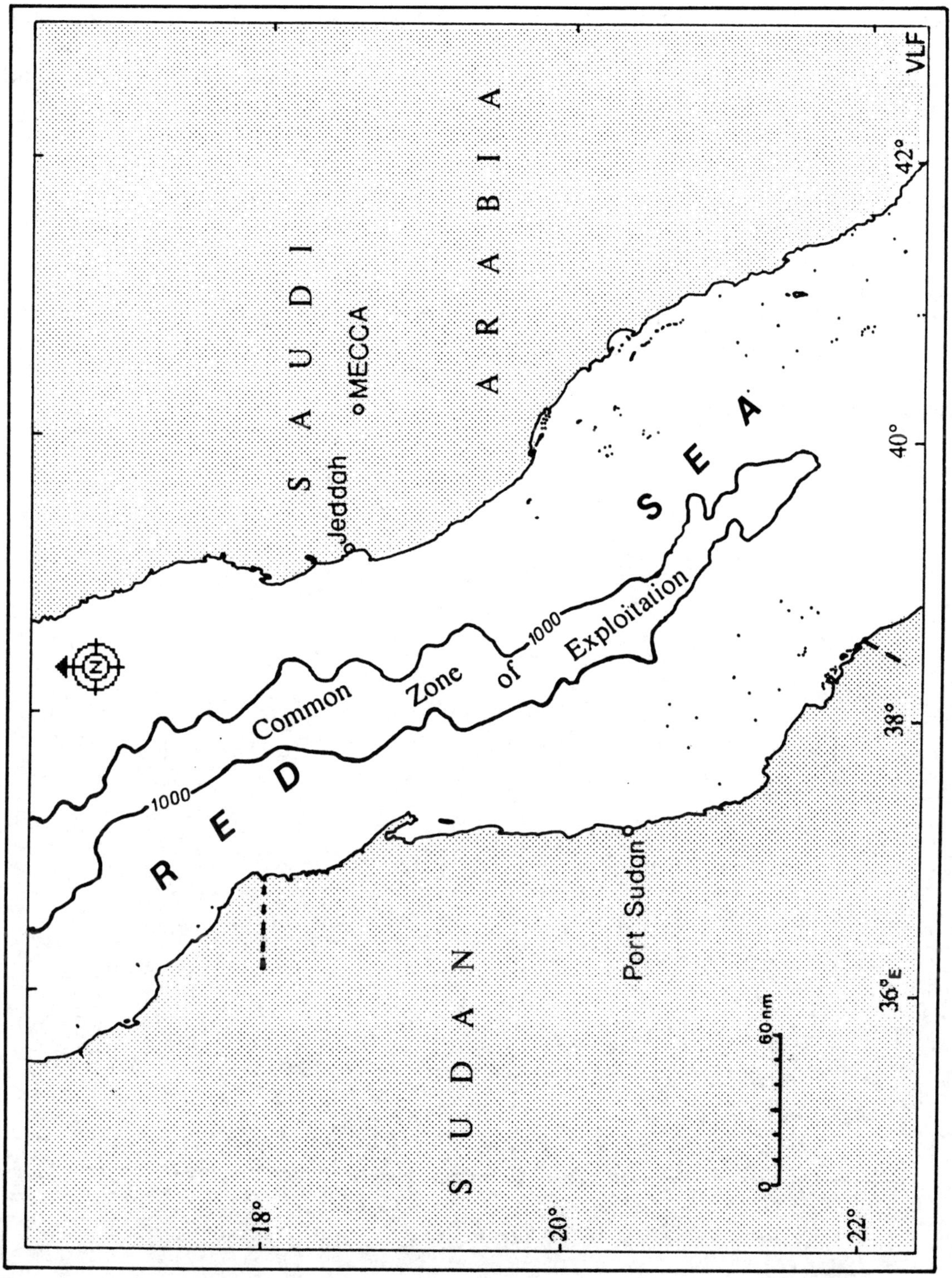
SAUDI ARABIA
Jeddah
MECCA
RED SEA
Common Zone of Exploitation
1000
1000
SUDAN
Port Sudan
60 nm
0
18°
20°
22°
36°E
38°
40°
42°
VLF

Map 10

MAP 11
SEABED BOUNDARY AND ZONE OF EXPLOITATION: BAHRAIN/SAUDI ARABIA

An agreement between these two coastal states on 22 February 1958 determined a continental shelf boundary and established a special zone wherein exploration and exploitation of hydrocarbons would be undertaken. The operations of such works would be funded by the Saudi Arabian government, but the profits gained from the zone would be shared equally by the two states.

The single maritime boundary has been determined on the principle of equidistance. Seven points were chosen on the Bahrainian coast and eight points along the Saudi Arabian coast. The geographical coordinates of 11 mid-points of the lines connecting the specified coastal features on the respective coastlines are determined. Geodesic lines link these 11 turning points. The combined length of the 11 lines is 55 nm. From turning point 11 the boundary trends in a northeasterly direction to turning point 14. Geodesic lines 12 to 13 and 13 to 14 form the eastern boundary of the common zone of exploitation. The length of the boundary from point 11 to 14 is 35 nm.

Source: St/LEG/SER.B/16,409.

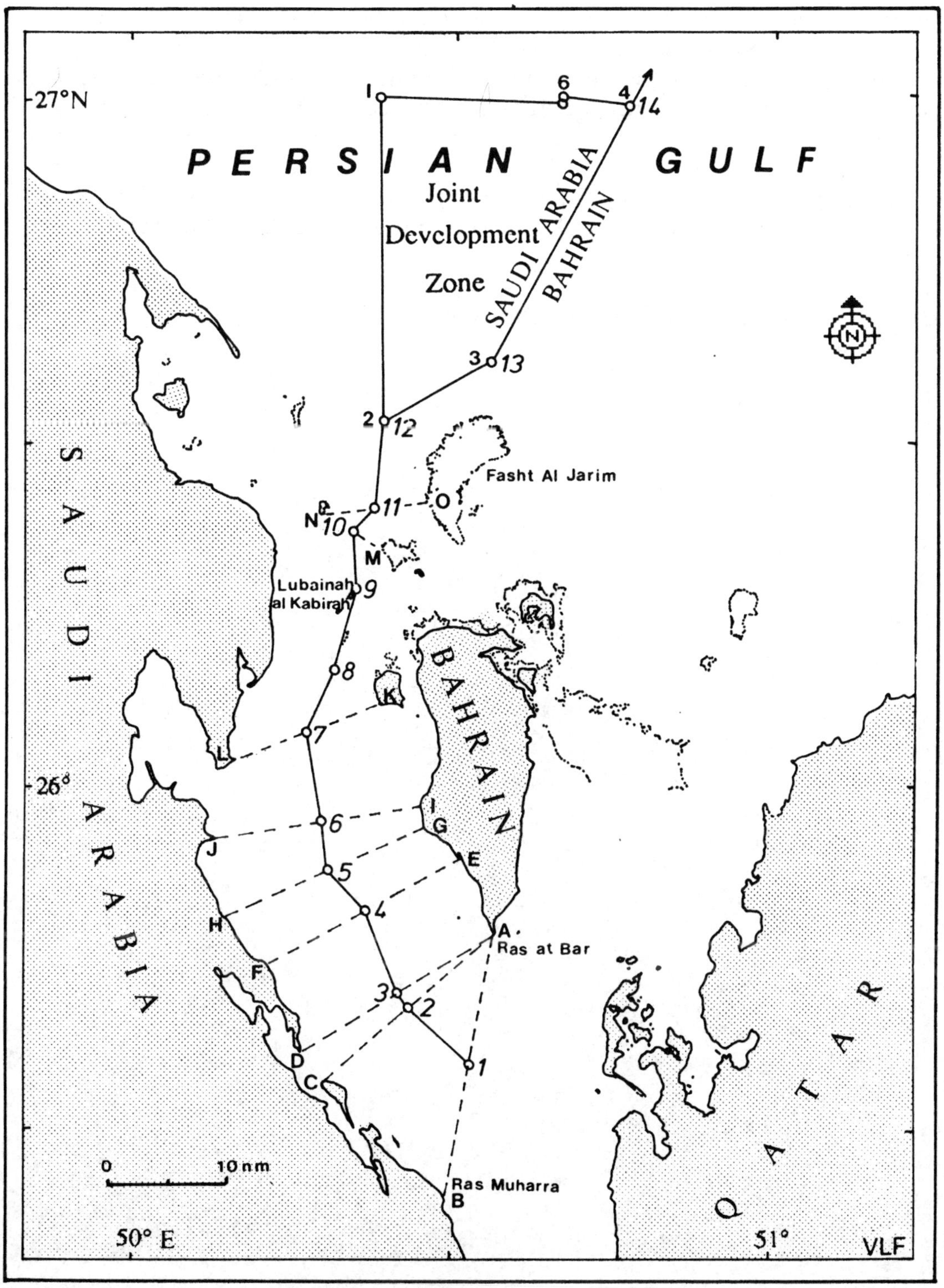

27°N
PERSIAN GULF
Joint Development Zone
SAUDI ARABIA
BAHRAIN
Fasht Al Jarim
Lubainah al Kabirah
BAHRAIN
SAUDI ARABIA
Ras at Bar
Ras Muharra
QATAR
26°
0 10 nm
50° E
51°
VLF

Map 11

MAP 12
CONTINENTAL SHELF BOUNDARY: IRAN/QATAR

The negotiated continental shelf boundary has been determined on the basis of the equidistance principle. The presence of islands between the two states in the Persian Gulf, however, was disregarded for the purpose of delineation of the boundary. The agreement entered into force on 10 May 1970.

At the time of negotiations the location of Point 1 was indefinite. Its location would be dependent on the potential boundary between Bahrain and Qatar. Thus the geographical coordinates of turning points 2 to 6 are given in the text of the agreement. Geodesic lines connect these points. The overall length of the boundary is 131 nm. Point 2 is located about 31 nm from the Bahrain/Saudi Arabia continental shelf boundary. Point 6 coincides with Point A which marks the seaward extent of the Abu Dhabi/Qatar shelf boundary.

Source: 787 UNTS 165; ST/LEG/SER.B/16, 416; Limits No. 25, 1970.

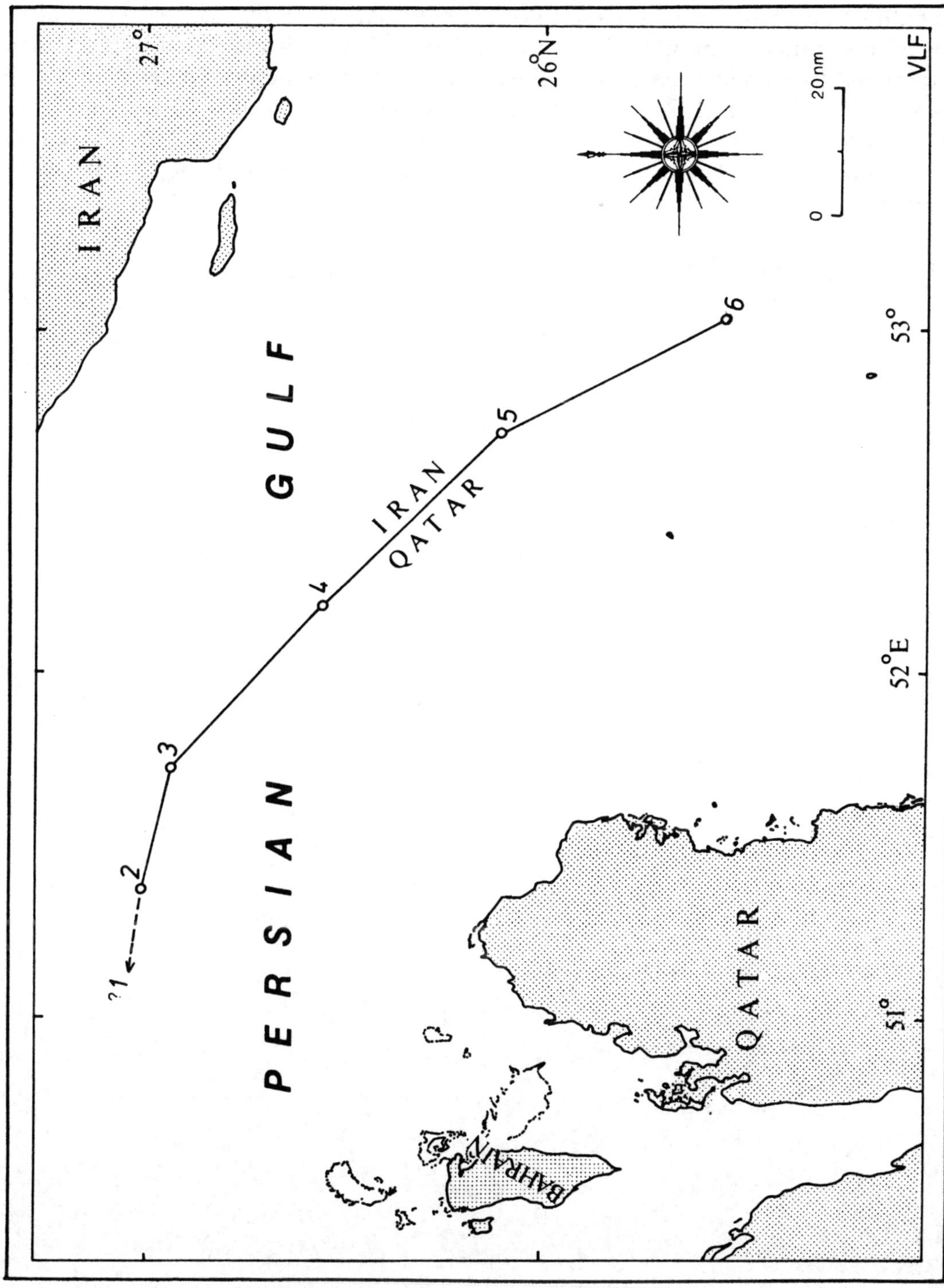
IRAN
PERSIAN GULF
IRAN
QATAR
QATAR
BAHRAIN
1
2
3
4
5
6
27°
26°N
53°
52°E
51°
0
20nm
VLF

Map 12

MAP 13
CONTINENTAL SHELF BOUNDARY: BAHRAIN/IRAN

The agreement defining the continental shelf boundary between Bahrain and Iran entered into force on 14 May 1972.

Four turning points connected by geodesic lines define the continental shelf boundary between Bahrain and Iran. The total length of the boundary is 28 nm. Water depths along the series of lines range from 60 to 80 metres. Whereas Points 1 and 4 of this agreement were determined by existing continental shelf boundary agreements, Points 2 and 3 are equidistant points. Point 1 of the boundary is coextensive with Point 2 of the Iran-Qatar continental shelf boundary. It is located about 10 nm nearer Iran than Bahrain. On an average the turning points are 50 nm from Iranian territory and 54 nm from the Bahrainian soil.

Source: UNTS, Limits No. 58.

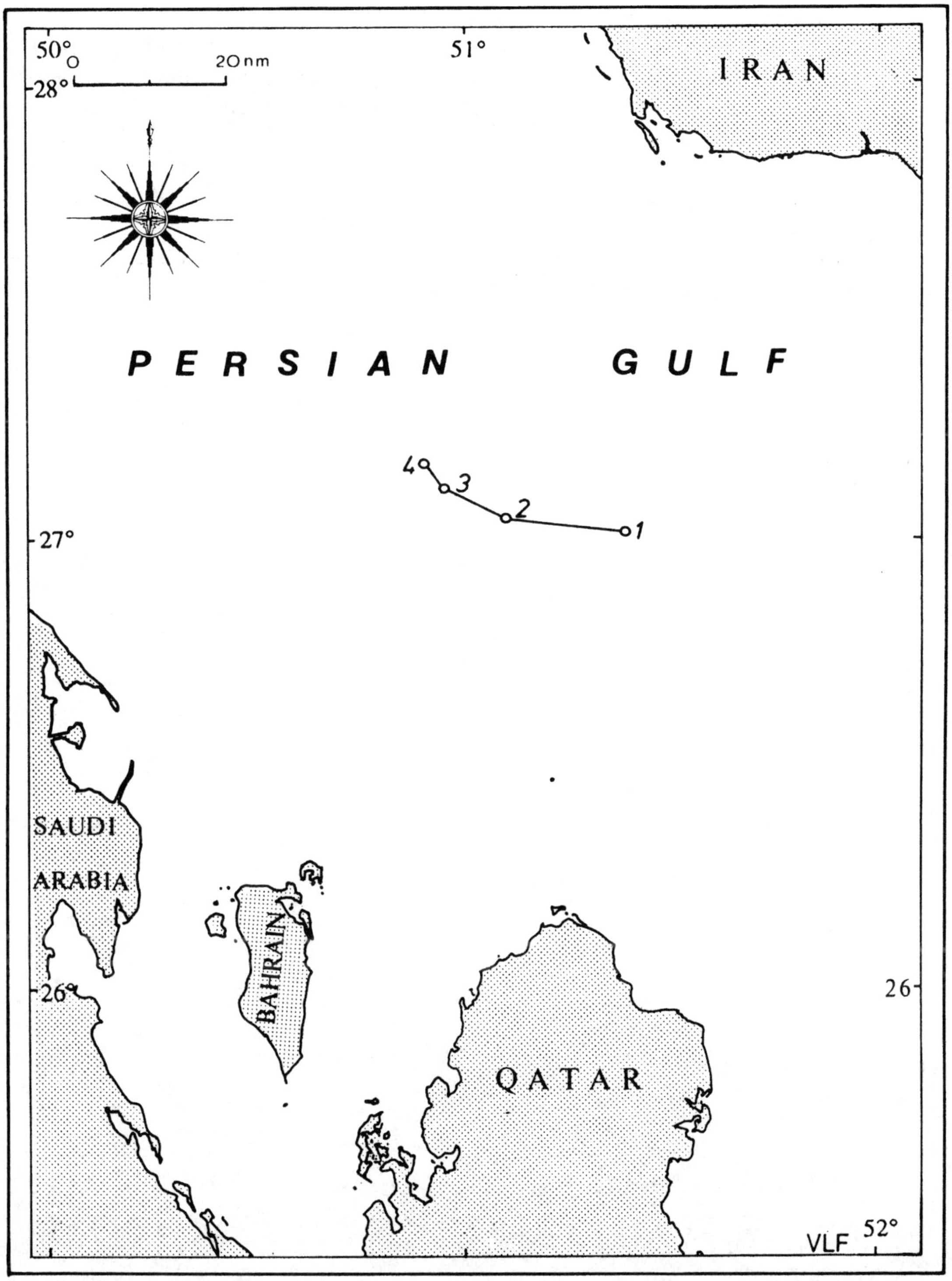
50°
0
20nm
28°
51°
IRAN
PERSIAN GULF
4
3
2
1
27°
SAUDI
ARABIA
BAHRAIN
26°
26
QATAR
VLF
52°

Map 13

MAP 14
CONTINENTAL SHELF BOUNDARY: IRAN/UNITED ARAB EMIRATES (DUBAI)

The agreement establishing a continental shelf boundary between Iran and Dubai of the United Arab Emirates entered into force on 15 March 1975.

Five turning points, connected by geodesic lines for a total distance of 39 nm, define the continental shelf boundary between these states. Water depths along this series of lines are less than 55 metres. The boundary is not determined on the equidistance principle evident from the fact that four of the five turning points are nearer to Sirri Island than to any UAE territory. Indeed, the agreement appears to ignore the presence of the islands. However, between Points 3 and 4 the line follows an arc of 12 nm which coincides with the southern territorial sea limit of Iran's Sirri Island.

The continental shelf boundary has been determined without reference to the Iranian islands of Qeys, Forur as well as the disputed island of Abu Musa

Source: UNTS, Limits No. 63.

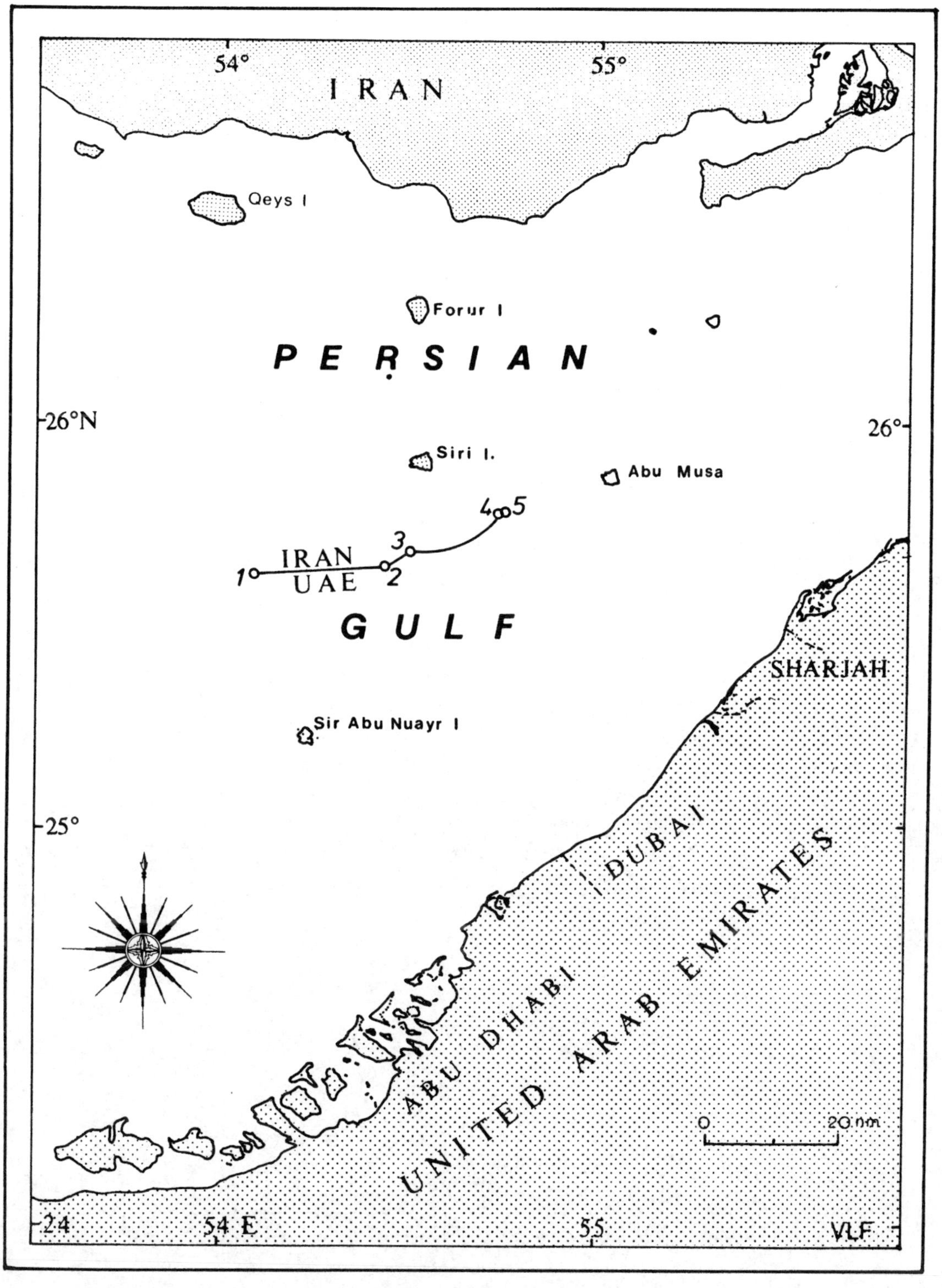
54°
55°
I R A N
Qeys I
Forur I
P E R S I A N
26°N
26°
Siri I.
Abu Musa
4
5
3
IRAN
UAE
1
2
G U L F
SHARJAH
Sir Abu Nuayr I
25°
DUBAI
ABU DHABI
UNITED ARAB EMIRATES
0
20nm
24
54 E
55
VLF

Map 14

MAP 15
CONTINENTAL SHELF BOUNDARY: IRAN/OMAN

The agreement which established the continental shelf boundary between Iran and Oman entered into force on 28 May 1975

Turning Point 1 of the continental shelf boundary between these two states is located in the eastern margin of the Persian Gulf. The delineated boundary extends through the Strait of Hormuz and into the Gulf of Oman. Geographical coordinates for points 1 to 21 inclusive are listed in the text of the agreement. Geodesic lines connect these points. The overall length of the boundary is 125 nm. Point 22 is defined as being located 'on an azimuth of 190° from Point 21 to the intersection of the Oman-Sharjah lateral offshore boundary'. This latter boundary has not been established. Point 22, in the Gulf of Oman, remains an undefined mark.

Source: UNTS, LIMITS No. 67; 14 ILM (1975): 1478.

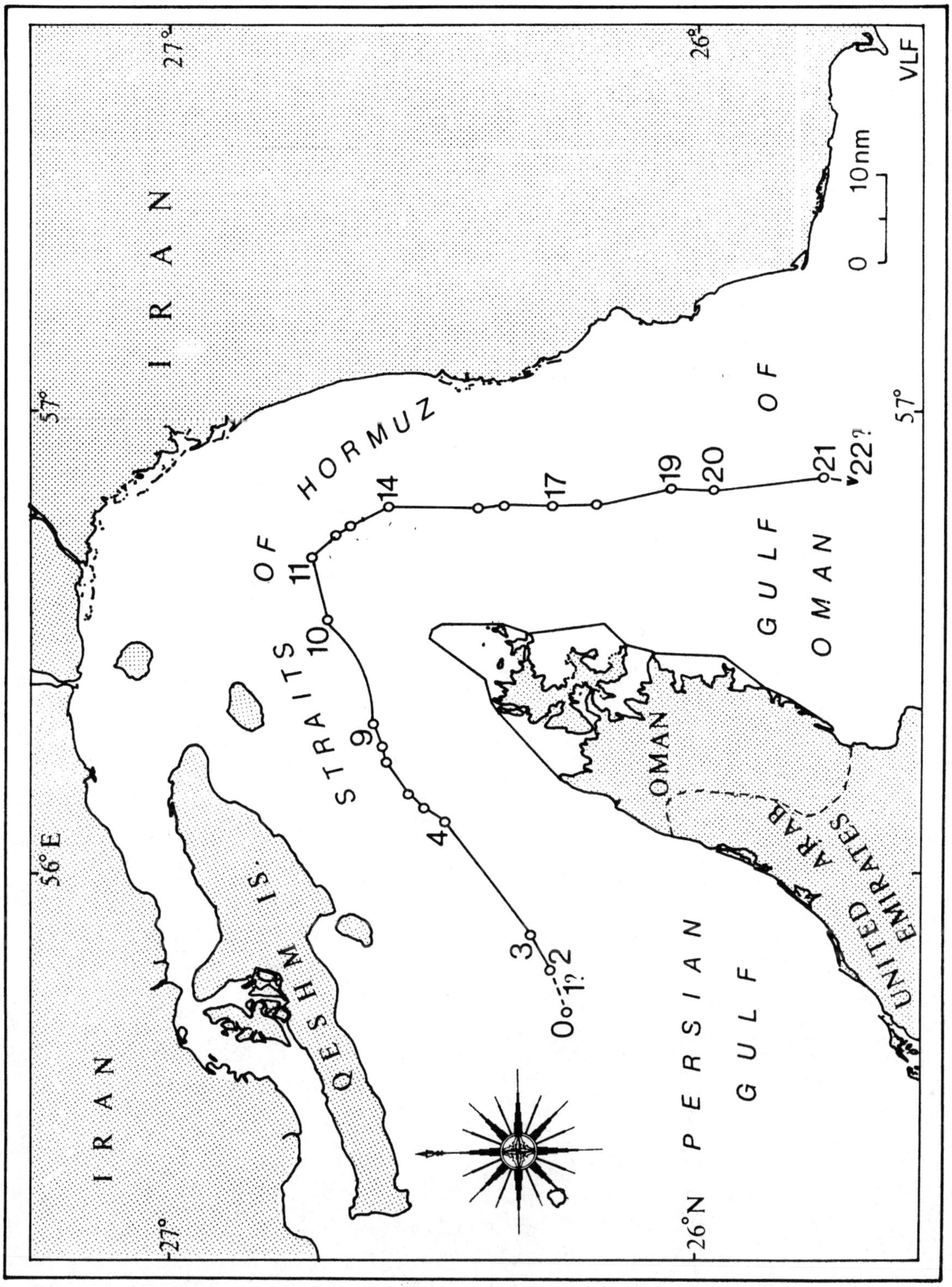
IRAN
IRAN
QESHM IS.
STRAITS OF HORMUZ
PERSIAN GULF
GULF OF OMAN
OMAN
UNITED ARAB EMIRATES
56°E
57°
57°
27°
27°
26°N
26°
0
10nm
VLF
0
1?
2
3
4
9
10
11
14
17
19
20
21
22?

Map 15

MAP 16
CONTINENTAL SHELF BOUNDARY: ABU DHABI/QATAR

A strict application of the equidistance principle was not evident in the determination of the CSB between Abu Dhabi and Qatar. The overall length of the boundary is 115 nm. It comprises four turning points and lies in water depths ranging from 10 to 40 metres. With the exception of a 15 nm arc around Dayyinah Island (as a result of a three-nm territorial sea radius) favouring Abu Dhabi, the CSB consists of three geodesic lines.

Point A was determined as being apparently the common point of the maritime boundary of three states, being equidistant from the mainlands of Abu Dhabi, Iran and Qatar. The line linking point A to point B is 35 nm long. Point B was located at the position of an oil well named al-Bunduq. Point D, which is the landward teminus of the boundary, is defined as the intersection of the three-nm arcs which represent the limits of the territorial sea of each of the states. The line linking Point D to Point C was delineated so as to be equidistant along selected sectors between the shoals which are part of the respective Abu Dhabi and Qatar sovereignties.

Source: ST/LEG/SER.B/16: 403; Limits, 18.

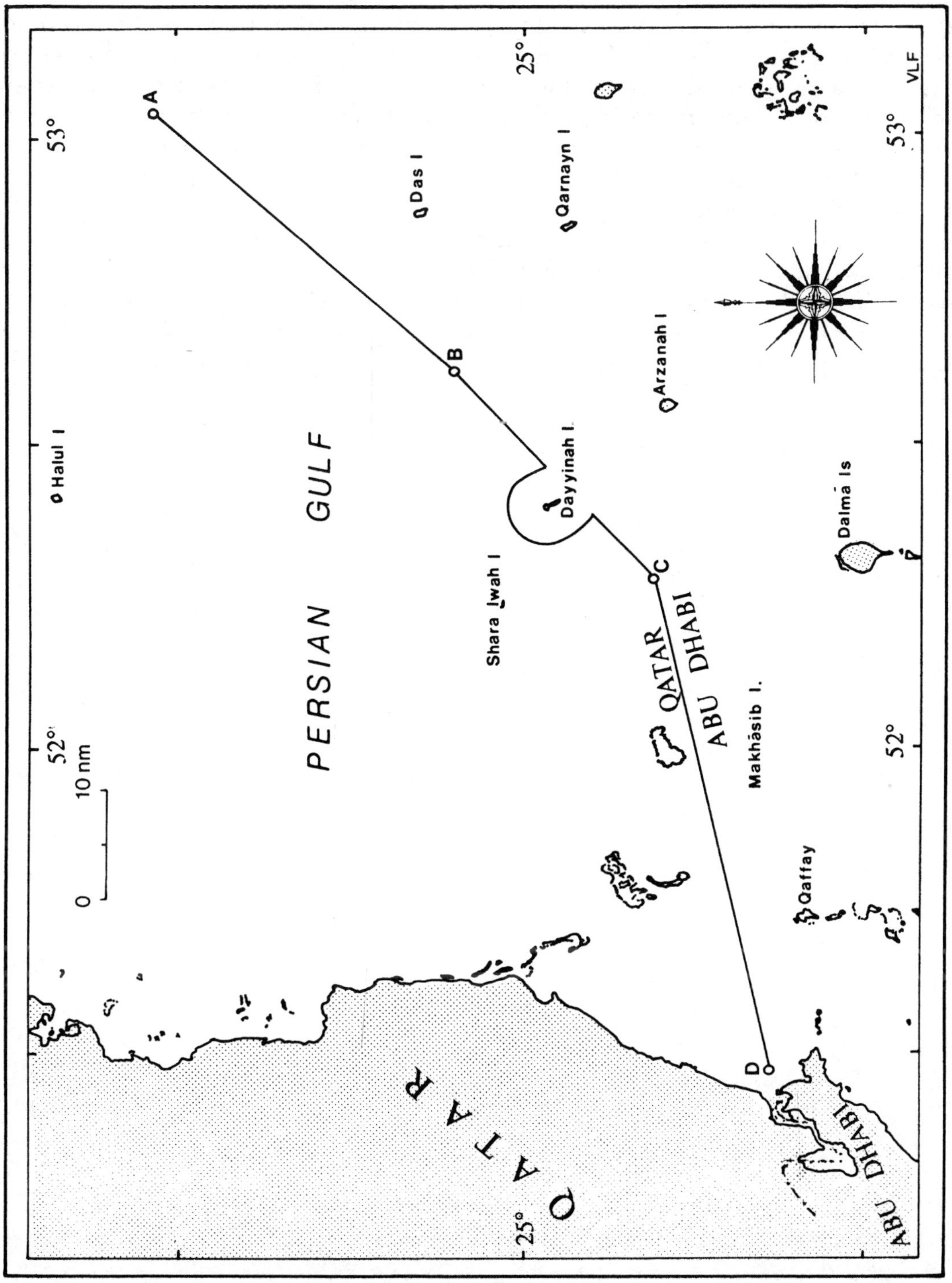
PERSIAN GULF
QATAR
ABU DHABI
QATAR
ABU DHABI
Halul I
Das I
Qarnayn I
Arzanah I
Dayyinah I.
Dalma Is
Shara Iwah I
Makhasib I.
Qaffay
A
B
C
D
53°
52°
25°
10 nm
0
VLF

Map 16

MAP 17
CONTINENTAL SHELF BOUNDARY: IRAN/SAUDI ARABIA

On October 24, 1968 representatives of the Governments of Iran and Saudi Arabia signed an Agreement, at Tehran, Iran, in which the parties mutually recognised the sovereignty of Saudi Arabia over the island of Al'Arabiyah (Arabi Is.) and of Iran over the island of Farsi. Each island possesses a belt of territorial sea, twelve nautical miles in width, which is measured from the line of the lowest low water on each of the islands. In the area where these belts overlap a boundary line separating the territorial sea of the two islands would be drawn so as to be equidistant throughout its length from the above-mentioned datum.

The delimitation of the boundary line separating the submarine areas are the points given as geographical coordinates, and joined by straight lines, except in the vicinity of the territorial sea around Farsi Island and Al-'Arabiyah Island. The 1968 boundary agreement between the two states is a modified version of a median line negotiation initiated in 1965 but never ratified. The overall length of the continental shelf boundary, comprising 16 turning points, is 139 nm. It lies in water depths ranging from 40 to 80 metres. Although the boundary is not precisely a median line in its entirety, an effort was made to achieve this objective where feasible.

Source: 696 UNTS, 189; ST/LEG/SER./B/18: 403.

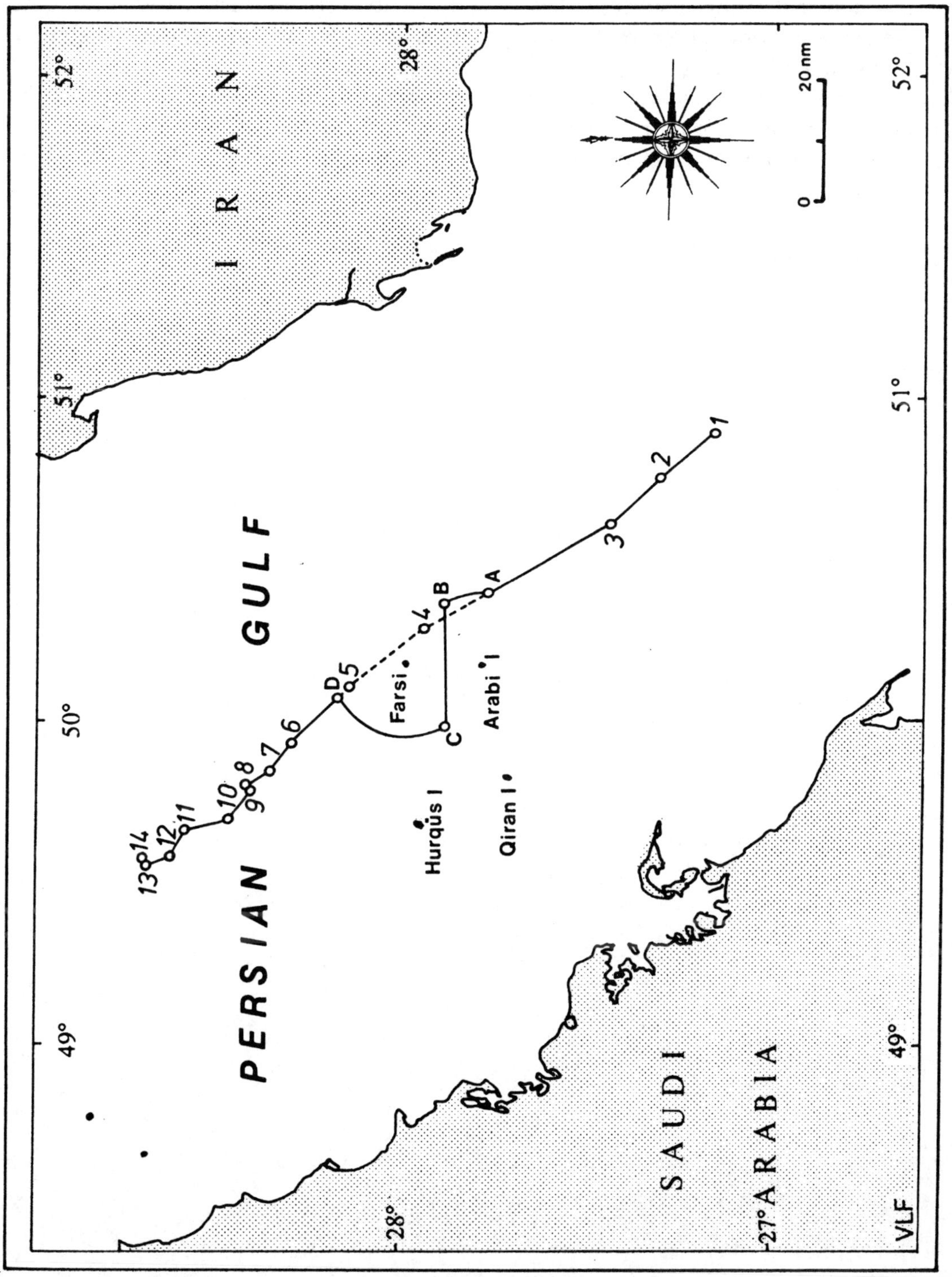
IRAN
PERSIAN GULF
SAUDI ARABIA
Farsi
Arabi I
Hurqūs I
Qiran I
0
20 nm
52°
51°
50°
49°
28°
27°
VLF

Map 17

MAP 18
CONTINENTAL SHELF BOUNDARY: INDIA/SRI LANKA

The delineated boundary in Palk Bay and Palk Strait is defined by six turning points whose geographical coordinates are listed in the text of the agreement which entered into force on 8 July 1974. The equidistance principle, applied in a modified form, determines the political division of the historic waters and the seabed in the bay. The overall length of the geodesic lines connecting the turning points is about 85 nm. Water depths along the boundary average 13 metres.

Geographical coordinates were later defined for extensions to the boundary in Palk Bay. From Point 1 eastwards into the Bay of Bengal and from Point 6 southwesterly into the Gulf of Manaar terminating at the common point of the India/Maldives/Sri Lanka maritime boundary.

Source: UNTS, Limits No. 66; 13 ILM (1974): 1442.

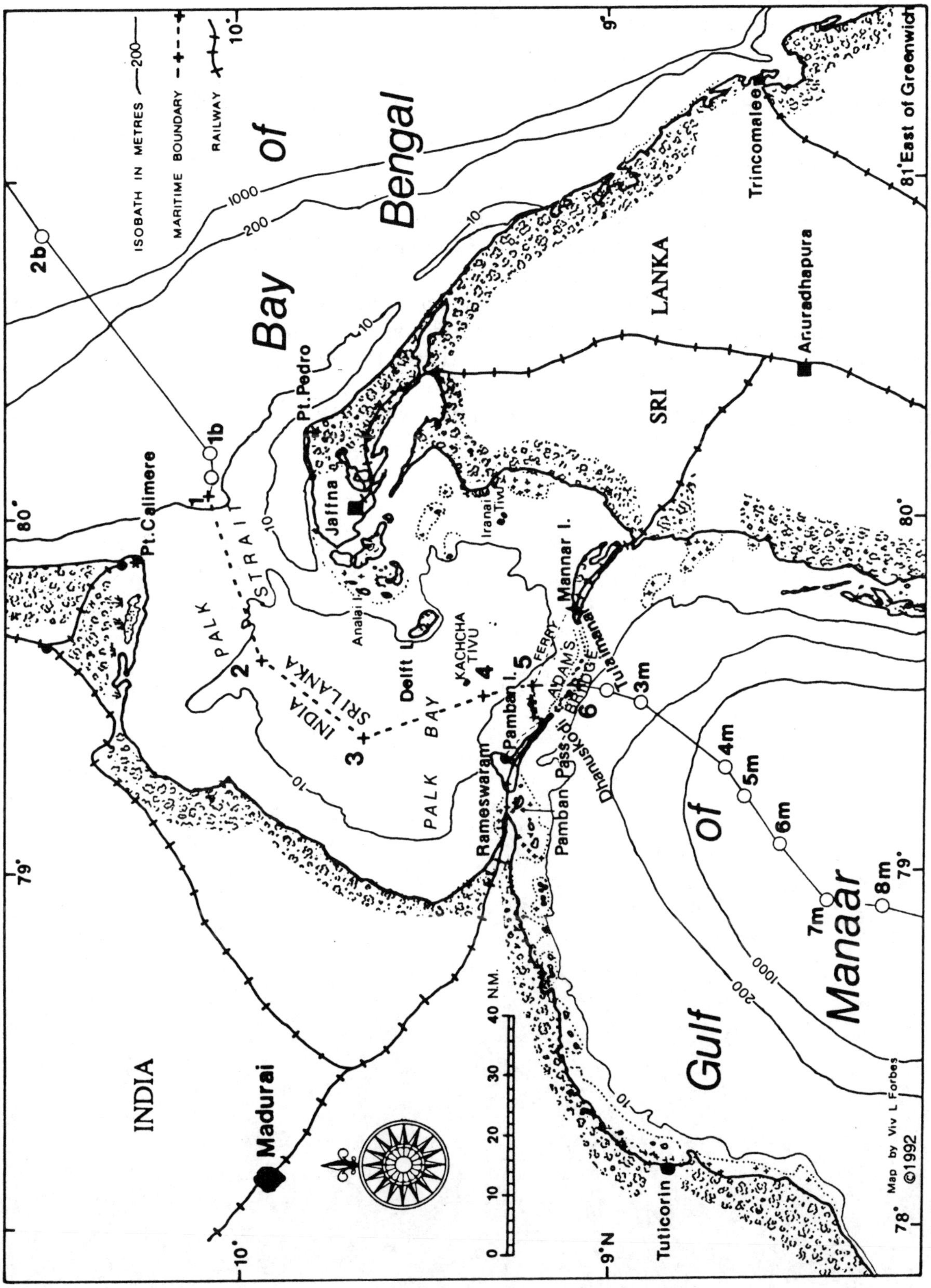

ISOBATH IN METRES
MARITIME BOUNDARY
RAILWAY
INDIA
Madurai
Bay of Bengal
SRI LANKA
Gulf of Manaar
PALK STRAIT
PALK BAY
INDIA SRI LANKA
Pt. Calimere
Pt. Pedro
Jaffna
Trincomalee
Anuradhapura
Tuticorin
Rameswaram
Pamban I.
Pamban Pass
Dhanuskodi
Talaimannar
Mannar I.
ADAMS BRIDGE
FERRY
Delft I.
KACHCHA TIVU
Analai I.
Iranai Tivu
81° East of Greenwich
40 N.M.
Map by Viv L Forbes ©1992

Map 18

MAP 19
CONTINENTAL SHELF BOUNDARY: INDONESIA/MALAYSIA

The geographical coordinates of 25 turning points define the continental shelf boundary between Indonesia and Malaysia in the Malacca Strait and in the South China Sea. The delineated boundary represents an attempt at dividing the shelf equally between the territorial sea baselines of the two states. It consists of three separate segments. The overall length of the boundary is 974 nm and lies in depths of less than 200 metres.

The first segment, represented by turning points 1 to 10, is located in the Malacca Strait. Its length is 400 nm. The average distance of the mid points from the Indonesian and Malaysian baselines is 18 nm along this segment.

The other two segments lie in the South China Sea. Points 11 to 20 comprise the second segment. Geodesic lines connect these points. Point 11 is located in the eastern margin of the Straits of Singapore, Point 20 is in the South China Sea. The total length of the geodesics is 310 nm. The third segment, consisting of Points 21 to 25, measures 264 nm. Point 25 is located on the land border of Indonesia and Malaysia on the northwestern coast of Borneo Island. The agreement entered into force on 7 November 1964.

Source: UNTS, ST/LEG/SER. B/16: 417; Limits No. 1, 1970.

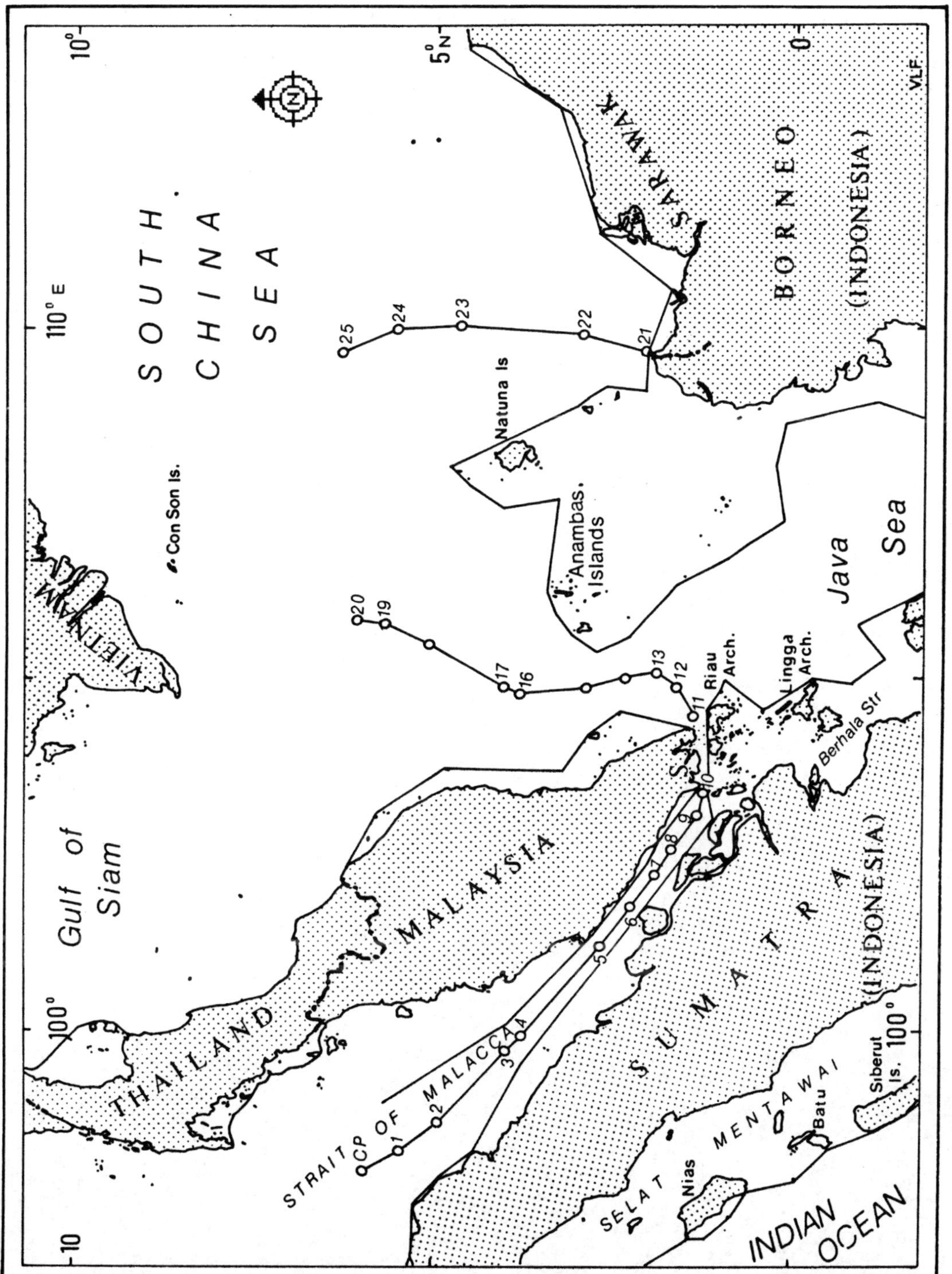
SOUTH CHINA SEA
Gulf of Siam
VIETNAM
Con Son Is.
THAILAND
MALAYSIA
SARAWAK
BORNEO
(INDONESIA)
Natuna Is
Anambas Islands
Riau Arch.
Lingga Arch.
Berhala Str
Java Sea
STRAIT OF MALACCA
SUMATRA
(INDONESIA)
SELAT MENTAWAI
Nias
Batu
Siberut Is.
INDIAN OCEAN
VLF

Map 19

MAP 20
CONTINENTAL SHELF BOUNDARY: INDIA/INDONESIA

An agreement signed between India and Indonesia to establish a continental shelf boundary entered into force on 17 December 1974.

This continental shelf boundary, determined on the equidistance principle, is in the Great Channel between Great Nicobar Island (India) and Sumatra Island (Indonesia). It lies in about 1800 metres of water. Geographical coordinates of four turning points define the boundary. Geodesic lines which connect these points, have an overall length of 48 nm. The western extension of the line terminates at the intersection of the 200 nm arcs from the westerly point on the coast of each state.

Source: 62 IBS; Limits No. 62, 1975.

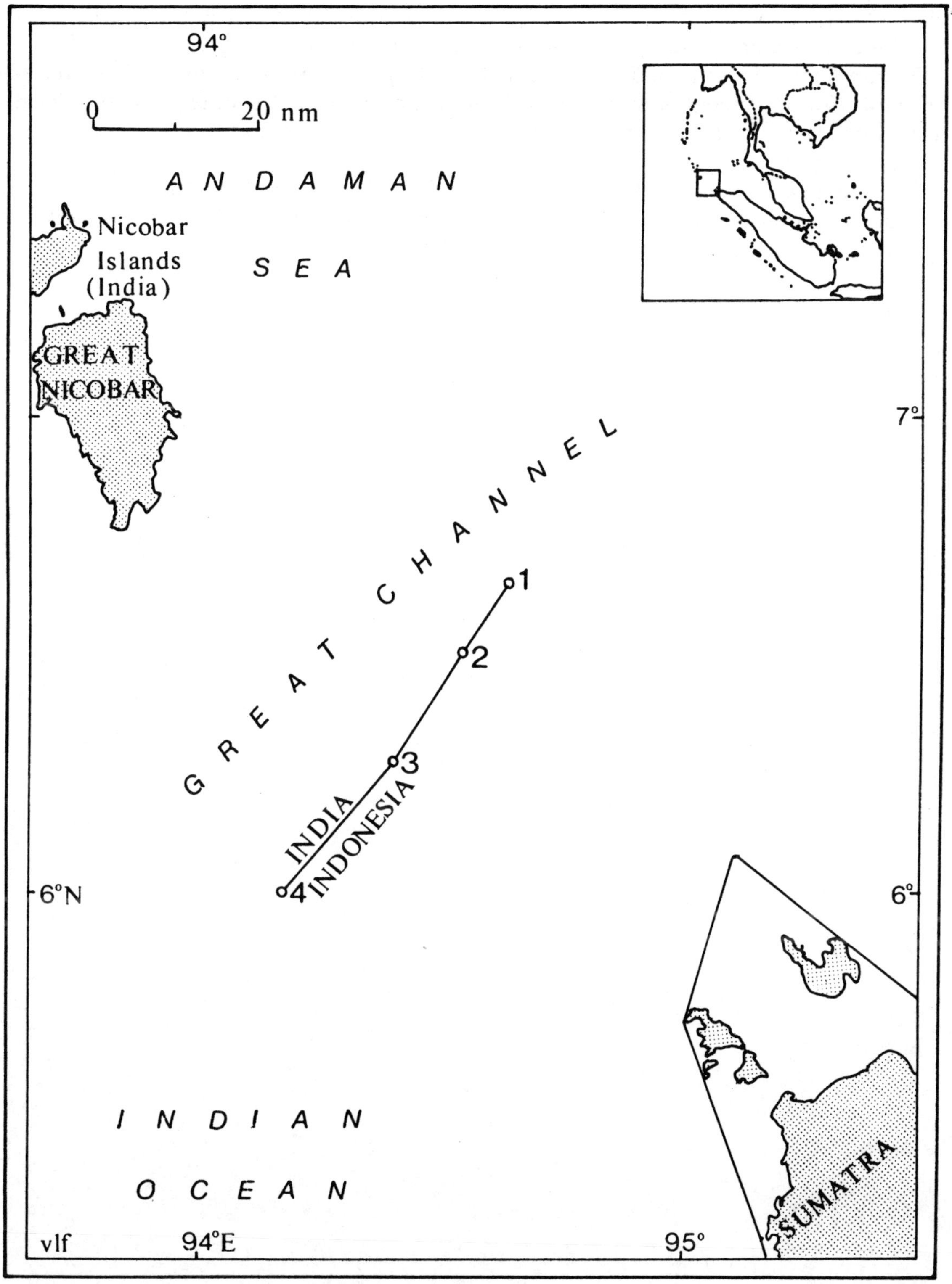
94°
0 20 nm
ANDAMAN
SEA
Nicobar
Islands
(India)
GREAT
NICOBAR
7°
GREAT CHANNEL
1
2
3
4
INDIA
INDONESIA
6°N
6°
INDIAN
OCEAN
SUMATRA
vlf
94°E
95°

Map 20

MAP 21
CONTINENTAL SHELF BOUNDARY: BURMA/INDIA

Burma and India settled their differences over sovereignty of Narcondam Island when they negotiated a single continental shelf boundary in December 1986. This boundary is defined by 16 turning points whose geographical coordinates are listed in the text of the agreement. It has an overall length of about 540 nm.

Turning point 1 of the boundary coincides with the Common Point (CP3 on Map 24) of the trilateral agreement between Burma, India and Thailand. Turning point 16 is located on the intersection of the 200 nm arcs from the nearest Indian and Burmese territories in the Bay of Bengal.

The line segment connecting points 9 and 10 lies 20 nm north of Narcomdam Island and point 12 is located in the Coco Channel equidistant from each state's territory. Line segments 1 to 9 and 15 to 16 are shown on Map 24.

Source: Forbes, 1989 (a): 12–13.

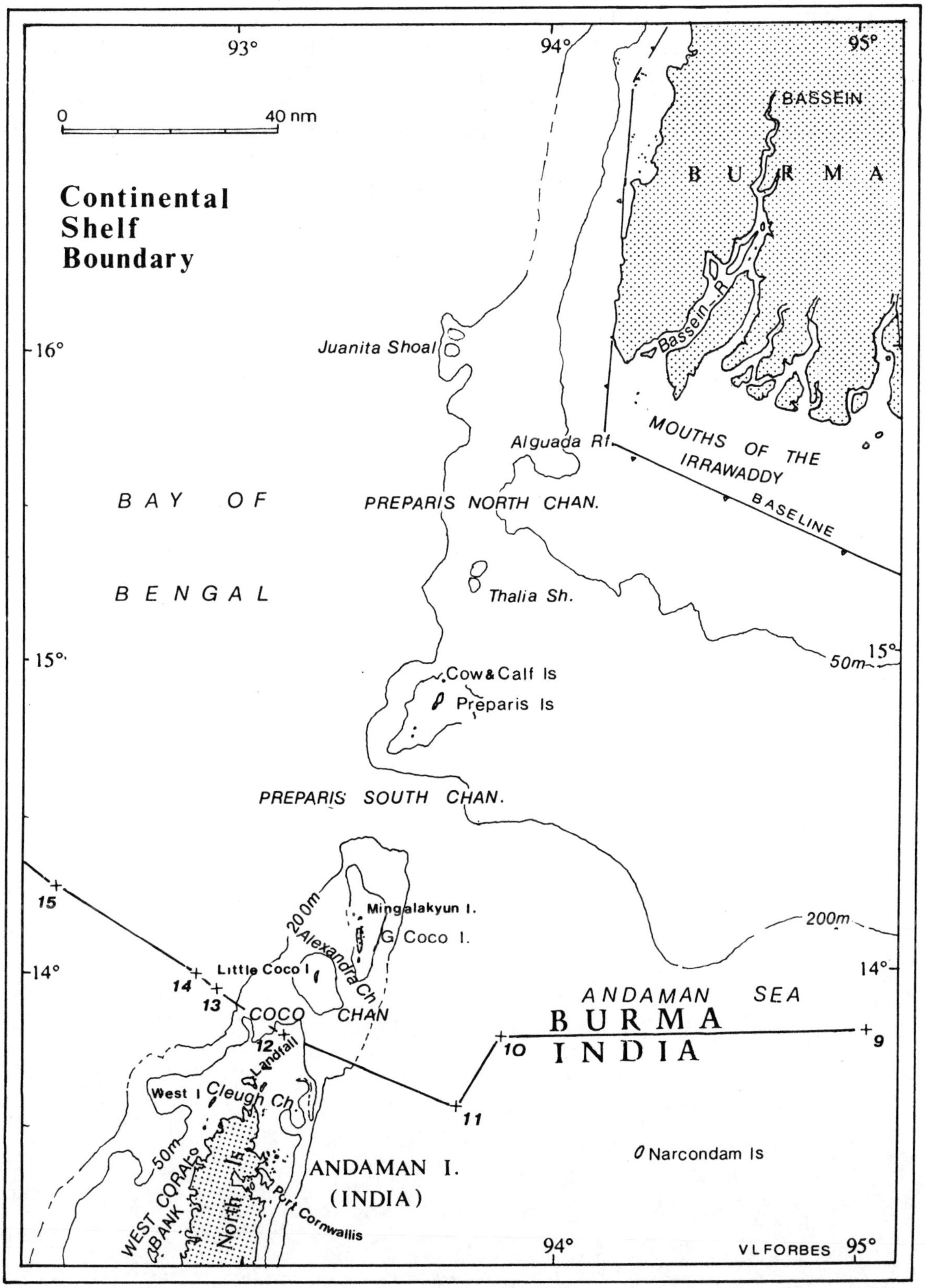
Continental
Shelf
Boundary
0
40 nm
93°
94°
95°
16°
15°
14°
BASSEIN
B U R M A
Bassein R.
Juanita Shoal
Alguada Rf.
MOUTHS OF THE IRRAWADDY
BASELINE
BAY OF
BENGAL
PREPARIS NORTH CHAN.
Thalia Sh.
50m
Cow & Calf Is
Preparis Is
PREPARIS SOUTH CHAN.
15
14
13
12
11
10
9
Mingalakyun I.
Coco I.
Little Coco I
200m
Alexandra Ch
COCO CHAN
ANDAMAN SEA
BURMA
INDIA
Landfall
West I
Cleugh Ch.
50m
WEST CORAL BANK
North I.
Port Cornwallis
ANDAMAN I.
(INDIA)
Narcondam Is
VLFORBES

Map 21

MAP 22
CONTINENTAL SHELF BOUNDARY: BURMA/THAILAND

The continental shelf boundary between these two states begins at Point 1 which is located eqidistance from the Burmese territory of Murray Island and Thailand's Stork Island. The eastward extension of the marine boundary follows a predetermined mutually agreed alignment which leads to the river boundary further east.

The geographical coordinates of the seven turning points define a segment of the continental shelf boundary. The length of the series of geodesic lines measures 30 nm. A westward extension of boundary was to be negotiated when a common point in the Andaman Sea of the maritime boundaries of the two states and that of India was eventually established.

Source: *Limits* 102.

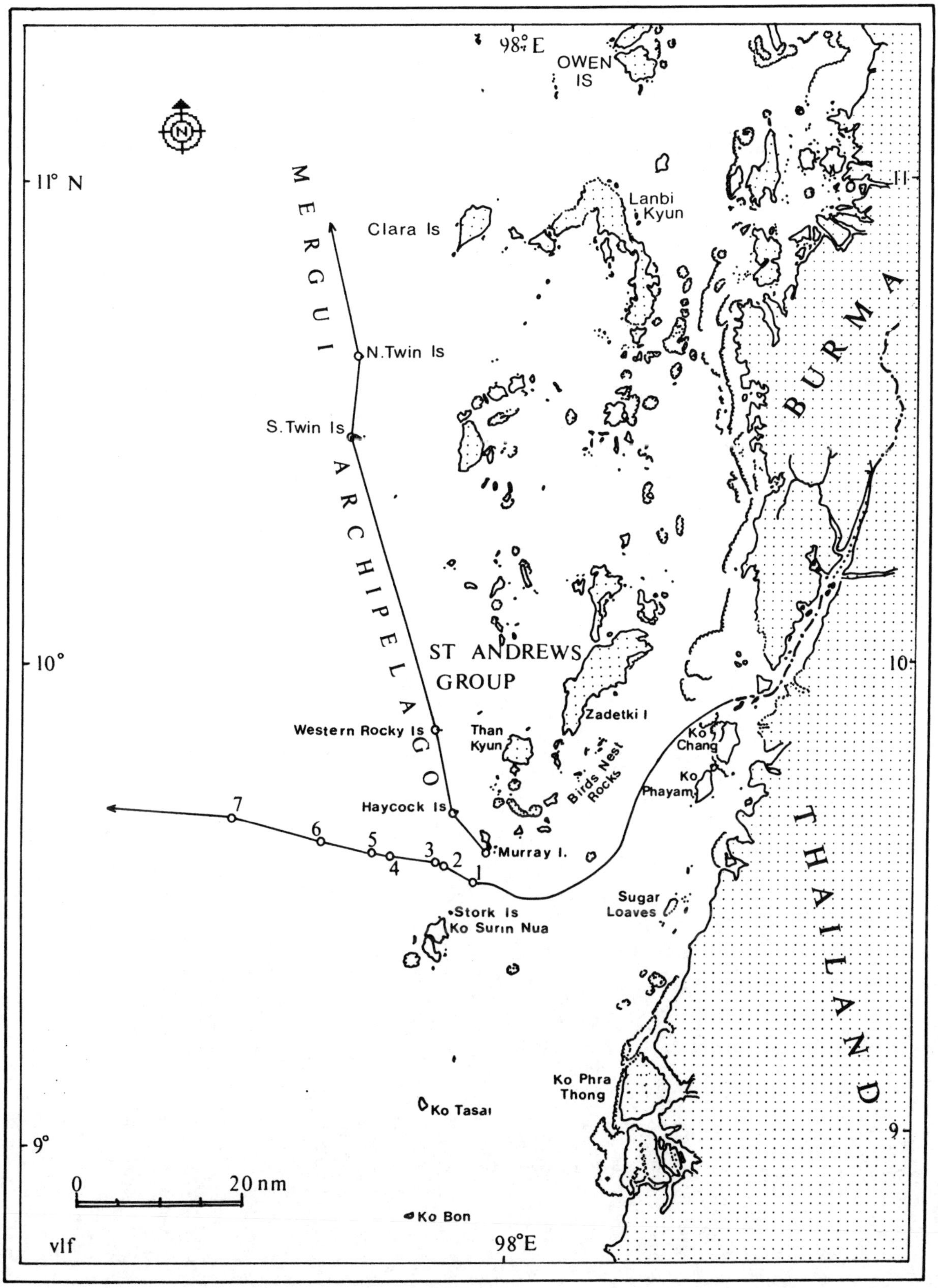
98° E
OWEN IS
11° N
MERGUI ARCHIPELAGO
Clara Is
Lanbi Kyun
N.Twin Is
S.Twin Is
BURMA
ST ANDREWS GROUP
10°
Zadetki I
Western Rocky Is
Than Kyun
Birds Nest Rocks
Ko Chang
Ko Phayam
Haycock Is
Murray I.
7
6
5
4
3
2
1
Stork Is
Ko Surin Nua
Sugar Loaves
THAILAND
Ko Phra Thong
Ko Tasai
9°
0
20 nm
Ko Bon
vlf
98°E

Map 22

MAP 23
ESTABLISHMENT OF A COMMON POINT; AND CONTINENTAL SHELF BOUNDARY INDONESIA/MALAYSIA/THAILAND

Agreements signed between 17 and 21 December 1971 established a Common Point (CP) for the respective maritime boundaries of the three states. The agreements entered into force on 16 July 1973. The negotiated CP is located at Lat. 5°57′ N, Long. 98°1.5′ E. It lies 52 nm from Sumatra Island (Indonesia), 99 nm from Pulau Langkawi (Malaysia) from 76 nm from Kho Butang (Thailand). The establishment of the CP enabled the three states to link this point to their pre-existing agreed maritime boundaries. A geodesic line linking the CP to Point 1 of the Indonesia-Malaysia continental shelf boundary in the northern sector of the Malacca Strait measures 36 nm. Water depths along this line vary from 80 to 120 metres.

Indonesia and Thailand incorporated the CP and two additional turning points to define the remaining segment of their continental shelf boundary in the Andaman Sea. The geodesic lines linking these points, extends in a northwesterly direction for about 148 nm. One segment measures 59 nm the other 89 nm. An existing maritime boundary between Malaysia and Thailand in the northern waters of the Malacca Strait was linked the CP by geodesic lines connecting four turning points whose geographical coordinates were defined in the agreement. The three segments measures 68, 13 and 8 nm. The negotiated boundary lies at all four turning points closer to the Thai Baseline system than to the Malaysia Baselines.

Source: UNTS., Limits No. 81.

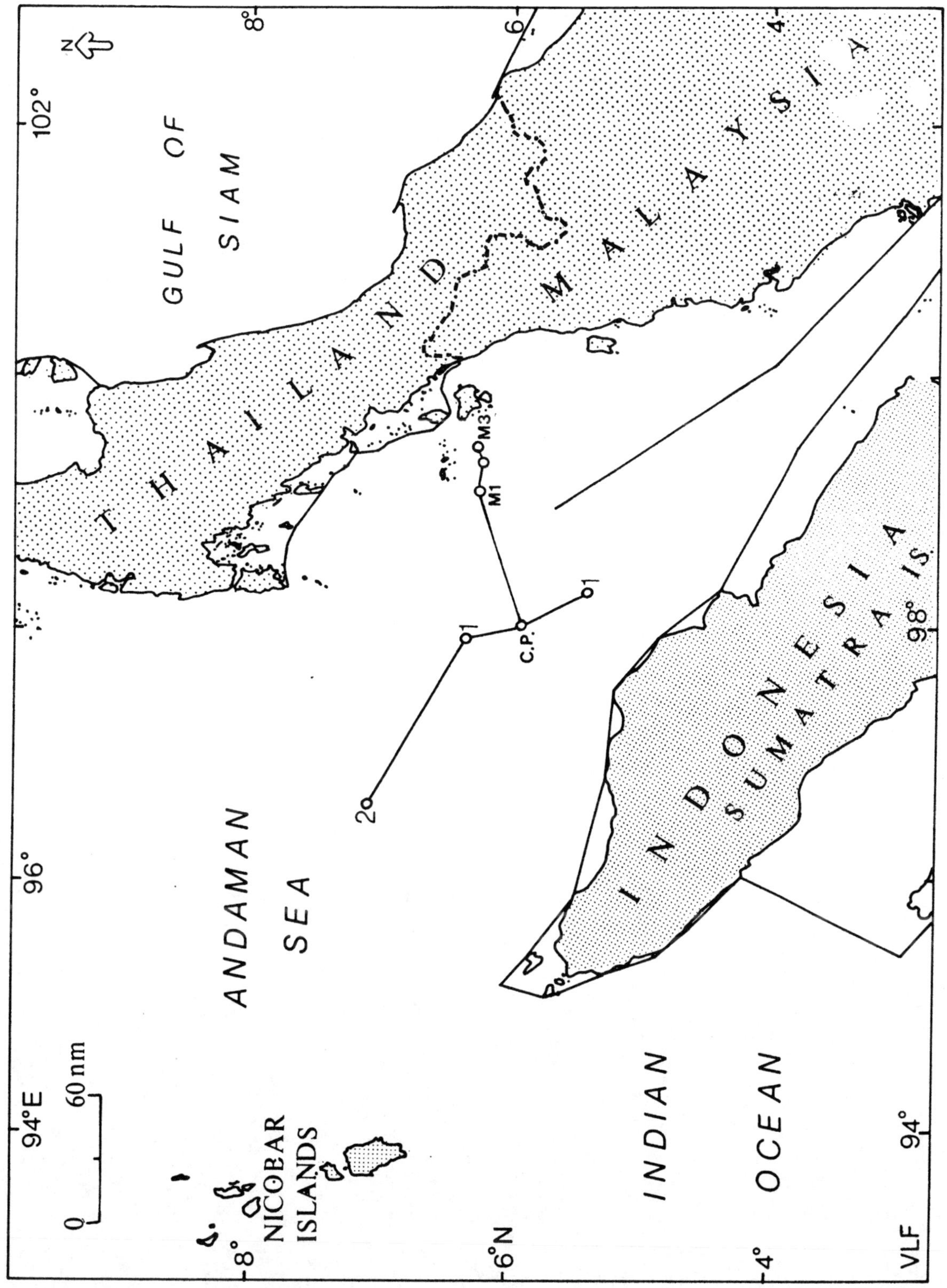
GULF OF SIAM
THAILAND
MALAYSIA
ANDAMAN SEA
INDIAN OCEAN
INDONESIA
SUMATRA IS.
NICOBAR ISLANDS
0
60 nm
N
94°E
96°
102°
8°
6°N
4°
94°
98°
VLF
C.P.
M1
M3
1
2

Map 23

MAP 24
CONTINENTAL SHELF BOUNDARIES IN THE ANDAMAN SEA: INDIA/BURMA; BURMA/THAILAND; INDIA/INDONESIA; INDONESIA/THAILAND AND THAILAND/MALAYSIA

The Common Point of the maritime boundaries of India, Indonesia and Thailand (CP 2) is located at Lat. 7°47′ N, Long. 95°31.8′ E. Although essentially equidistant (104 nm) from India's and Indonesia's territory in the Andaman Sea, it is about 133 nm from Thailand.

The continental shelf boundary between India and Thailand links CP2 and CP3, utilising seven sets of geodesic lines. The overall length of this boundary is 125 nm. CP3 was established by trilateral negotiation.

A westward extension from Turning Point 7 of a pre-existing negotiated boundary between Burma and Thailand is linked to CP3 by a series of geodesic lines. The geographical coordinates of the turning points define the continental shelf boundary which measured from Point 7 to CP3, is 135 nm.

The maritime boundary between Burma and India has an overall length of 540 nm.

Source: ST/LEG/SER.B/18:437; Limits, 62, 81, 87; Forbes 1989 (a): 12–13.

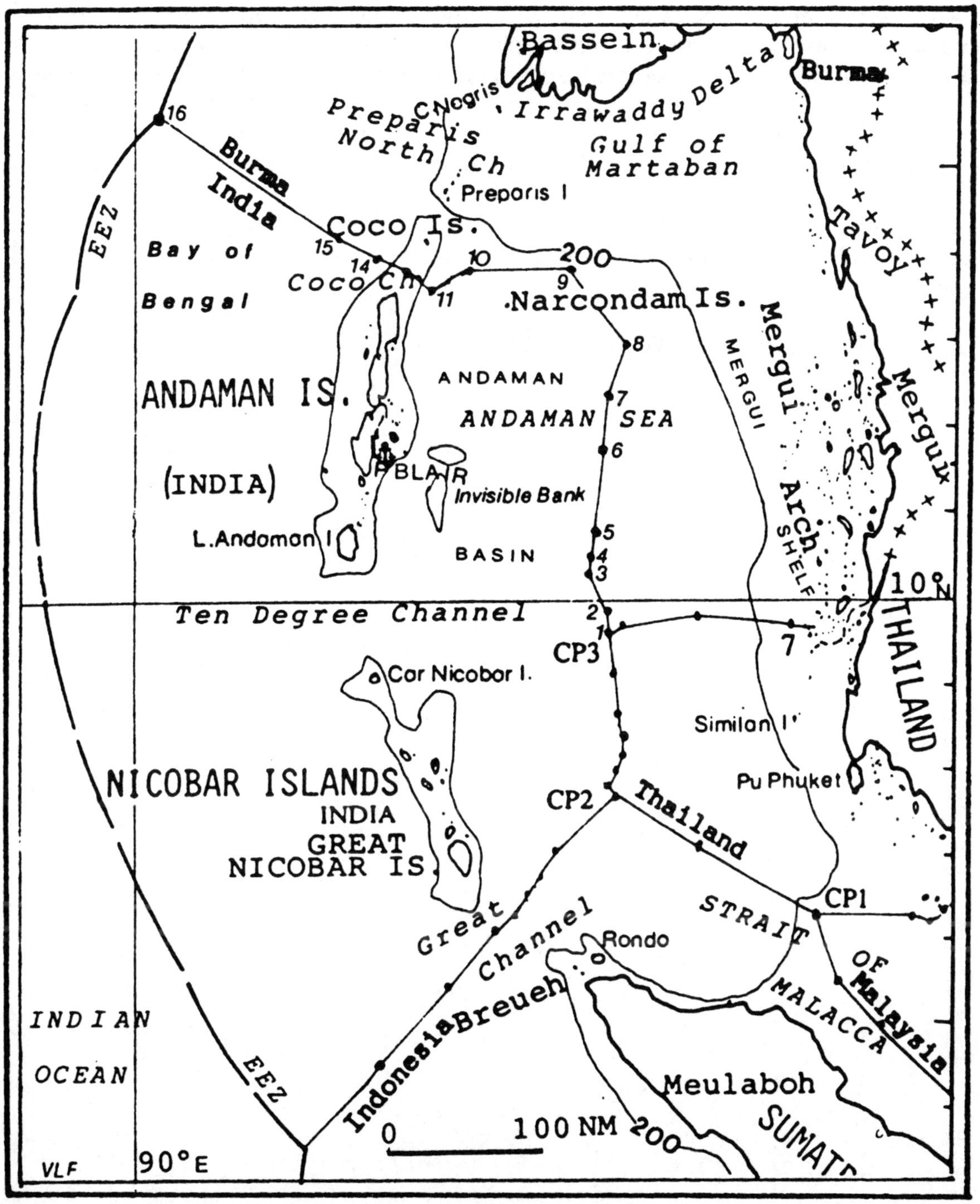
Bassein
Burma
Irrawaddy Delta
C Negris
Preparis North Ch
Gulf of Martaban
Preparis I
Burma India
Coco Is.
Bay of Bengal
Coco Ch
Narcondam Is.
Tavoy
Merguí Arch
MERGUI
ANDAMAN
ANDAMAN IS.
ANDAMAN SEA
(INDIA)
P BLAIR
Invisible Bank
L.Andoman I
BASIN
10°N
Ten Degree Channel
CP3
Cor Nicobor I.
THAILAND
Similon I
NICOBAR ISLANDS
INDIA
GREAT NICOBAR IS
CP2
Thailand
Pu Phuket
CP1
STRAIT OF MALACCA
Great Channel
Rondo
Breueh
Malaysia
INDIAN OCEAN
EEZ
Indonesia
Meulaboh
0
100 NM
200
VLF
90°E

Map 24

MAP 25
TERRITORIAL SEA BOUNDARY: SINGAPORE/MALAYSIA (1928) AND INDONESIA/SINGAPORE (1974)

The territorial sea boundary between Singapore and Malaysia in the vicinity of the Malay peninsula is the thalweg of the Johore Strait.

The territorial sea boundary between Indonesia and Singapore employs the equidistance principle for three turning points and negotiated positions for three other points. Five of the six turning points lie on the Indonesian side of an Indonesia-Singapore median line. Point 2 is located inside the Indonesian straight baseline system and is therefore in Indonesian internal waters. The total length of the five geodesic lines connecting the six point is 25 nm. Water depths along the boundary vary from 35 to 50 metres.

Extensions to the west of Point 1 and to the east of Point 6 of the Indonesia/Singapore boundary will be determined when negotiations are held by the littoral states in the region.

Source: Limits No. 60, 1974; Forbes, 1989d: 14–18.

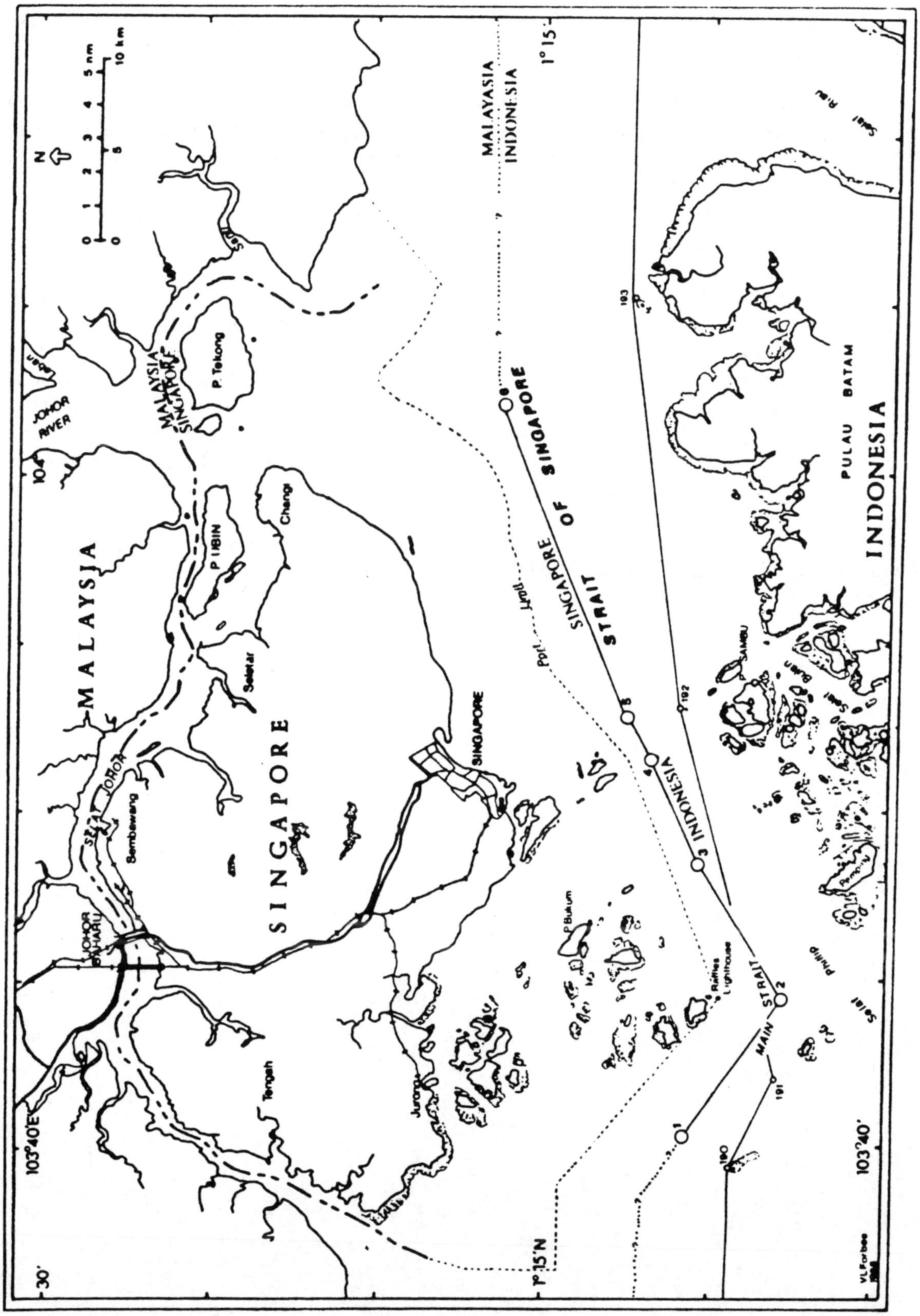
MALAYSIA
SINGAPORE
INDONESIA
JOHOR RIVER
SELAT JOHOR
MALAYSIA
SINGAPORE
P. Tekong
P. UBIN
Changi
Seletar
Sembawang
JOHOR BAHARU
Tengah
Jurong
SINGAPORE
P. Bukum
Raffles Lighthouse
Port Limit
SINGAPORE STRAIT
STRAIT OF SINGAPORE
MAIN STRAIT
MALAYASIA
INDONESIA
PULAU BATAM
103°40'E
104°
1°15'N
1°15'
103°40'
30'
5 nm
10 km
N

Map 25

MAP 26
CONTINENTAL SHELF BOUNDARY AUSTRALIA/INDONESIA

During the early 1970s Australia and Indonesia reached agreements on the determination of two sections of seabed boundaries: one section in the Arafura Sea; the other, in a part of the Timor Sea.

The first agreement defined the continental shelf boundary through the Arafura Sea for about 530 nm. The boundary is delineated by geodesics linking Turning points A1 to A12 whose geographical coordinates are listed in the Agreement. The boundary lies in water depths less than 200 m.

In a second agreement, geographical coordinates for Turning points A13 to A16 and A17 to A25 were defined. Geodesics linked to these points to establish a boundary and at the same time created a 'Gap' between A16 and A17.

Negotiations to close the 'gap' culminated when an agreement was reached to establish a Zone of Cooperation in the Timor Sea. The northern boundary of the Zone is the bathymetric axis of the Timor Trough, about 3,500 m depth. The southern boundary of the Zone is an arc of 200-nm radius from Indonesia's archipelagic baseline system. The Zone is divided into three Areas — A, B and C. The northern boundary of Area A is the simplified 1,500 m isobath. The southern boundary of Area A is coincident with the Provisional Fisheries Surveillance and Enforcement Line adopted by the two countries in a Memorandum of Understanding signed on 29 October 1981.

Source: *Australian Treaty Series,* No. 31 and 32, 1973; Memoranda of Understanding, 7 November, 1974 and 29 October 1981; Forbes, 1991(b).

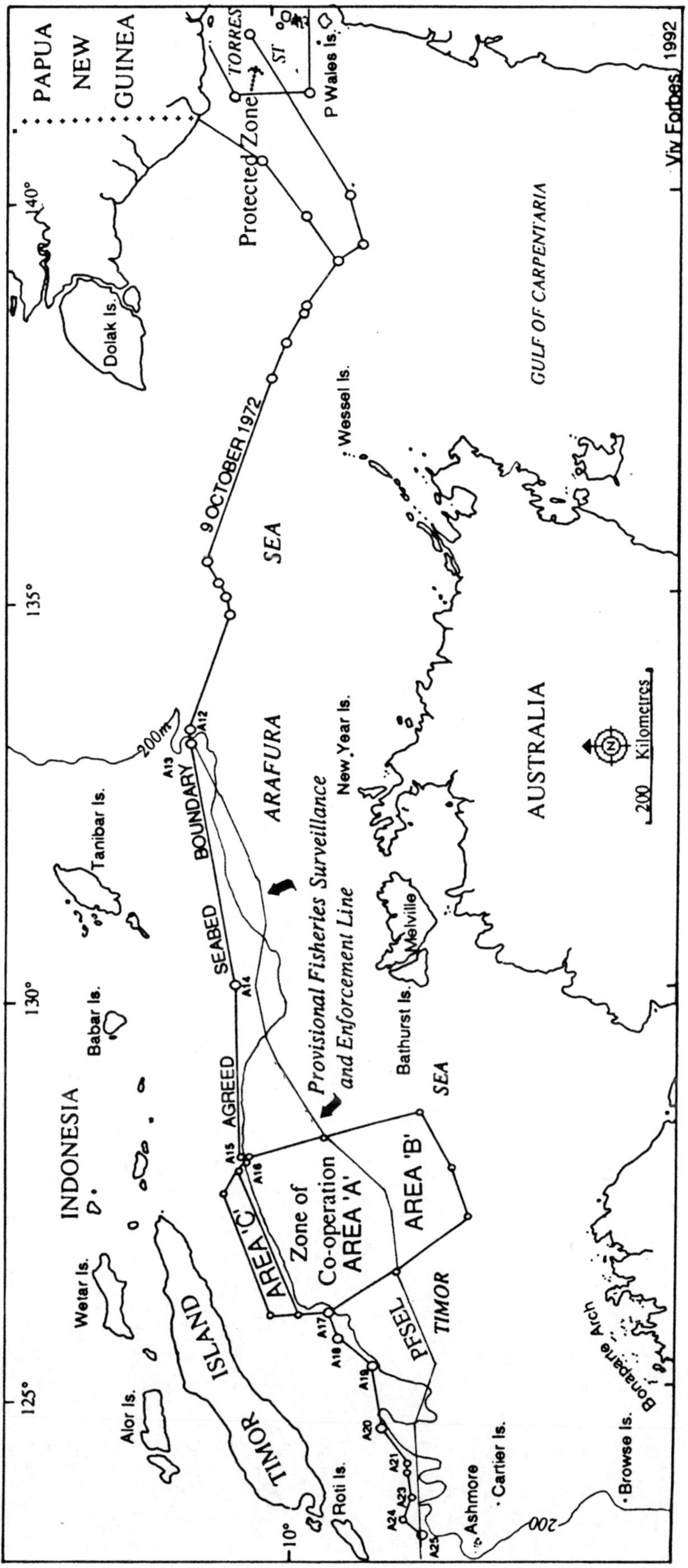
PAPUA
NEW
GUINEA
INDONESIA
AUSTRALIA
ARAFURA
SEA
TIMOR
SEA
GULF OF CARPENTARIA
TIMOR
ISLAND
Dolak Is.
Tanibar Is.
Babar Is.
Wetar Is.
Alor Is.
Roti Is.
Ashmore
Cartier Is.
Browse Is.
Bonaparte Arch
Bathurst Is.
Melville
New Year Is.
Wessel Is.
P Wales Is.
TORRES
ST
Protected Zone
9 OCTOBER 1972
AGREED
SEABED
BOUNDARY
Provisional Fisheries Surveillance
and Enforcement Line
Zone of
Co-operation
AREA 'A'
AREA 'B'
AREA 'C'
PFSEL
A12
A13
A14
A15
A16
A17
A18
A19
A20
A21
A23
A24
A25
200m
200
125°
130°
135°
140°
10°
200 Kilometres
Viv Forbes 1992

Map 26

MAP 27
CONTINENTAL SHELF BOUNDARY: FRANCE (RÉUNION)/MAURITIUS

The seabed boundary consists of seven turning points. It is 365 nm in length and has a northwest/southeast alignment. Point 4, the mid-point of the boundary, lies about 95 nm from each of the islands.

Point 1 is located equidistant, about 135 nm from Mauritius, Réunion and Tromelin. Point 7 has been defined as the intersection of the 200 nm arcs from the southern coastlines of Mauritius and Réunion.

Source: Limits No. 95; Forbes, 1990 c: 8–9.

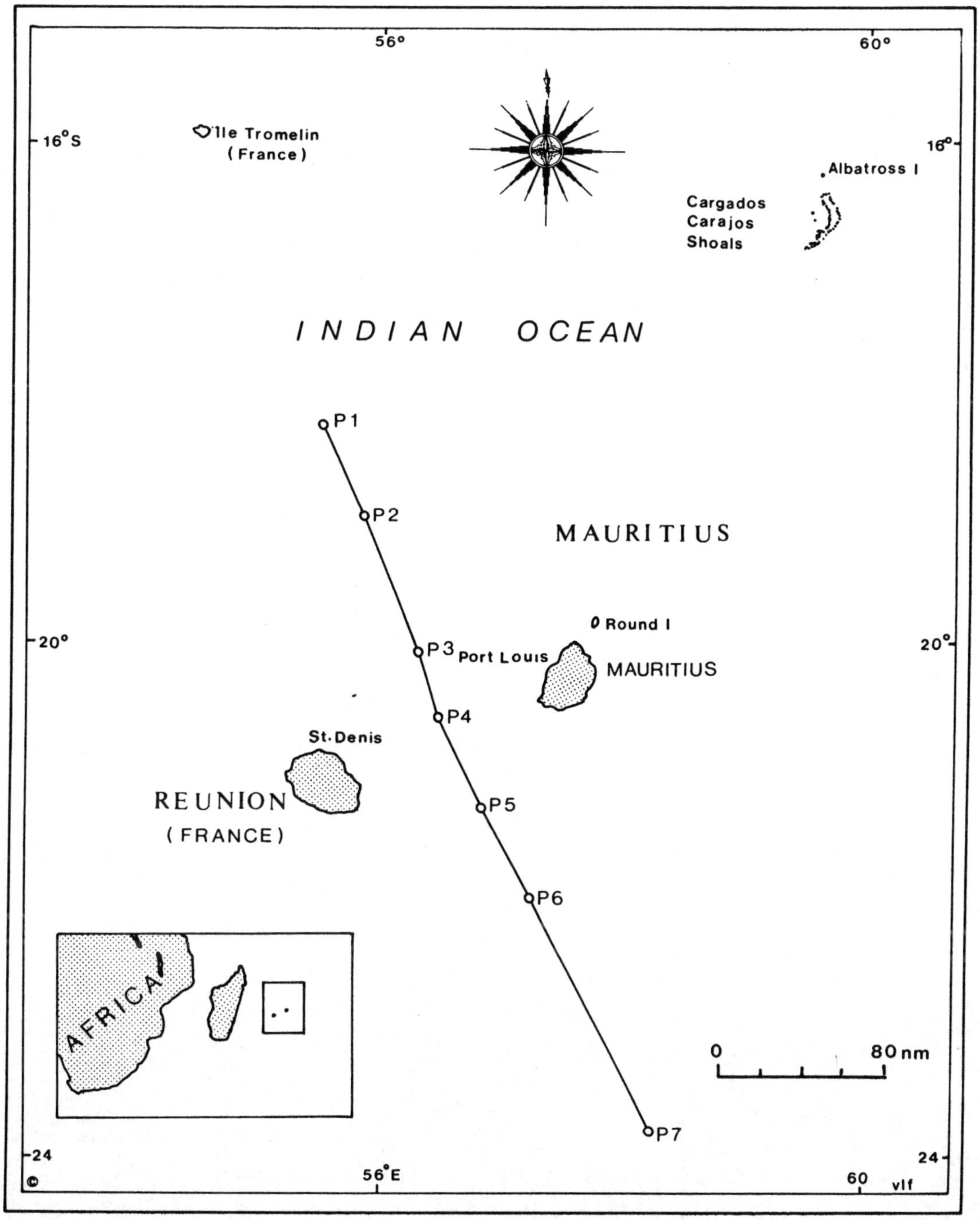
56°
60°
16°S
16°
Ile Tromelin
(France)
Albatross I
Cargados
Carajos
Shoals
INDIAN OCEAN
P1
P2
MAURITIUS
Round I
20°
20°
P3
Port Louis
MAURITIUS
P4
St. Denis
REUNION
(FRANCE)
P5
P6
AFRICA
0
80 nm
P7
24
24
56°E
60
vlf

Map 27

MAP 28
SEABED BOUNDARY; KENYA/TANZANIA

The determination of the maritime boundary between Kenya and Tanzania was achieved by agreement between the two countries. The principle of equidistance is applied in establishing the location of the turning points. The boundary consists of three turning points marked A, B and C and an undefined seaward terminus along the latitude of Point C. They are located in the Pemba Channel and are within 12 nm of the coast. At the time the agreement was negotiated Kenya claimed a 12 nm territorial sea width whereas Tanzania adopted a 50 nm territorial sea zone.

The maritime boundary commences at Ras Jimbo beacon on the land boundary terminus. This first segment is 12 nm long and is equidistant between the declared baselines. Turning points B and C have been established at the intersection of 12 nm arcs. Point X was created to determined the arc AB of radius six nm. Points B and C are connected by a straight line. The overall length of the boundary is about 35 nm.

Seaward of Point C the boundary extends to a point where it intersects the outermost limits of the areas of national jurisdiction of the two states. Without overlapping any claims to the east both countries are able to extend their single maritime boundary eastward to a full 200 nm.

Source: *Limits* No. 92, 1981.

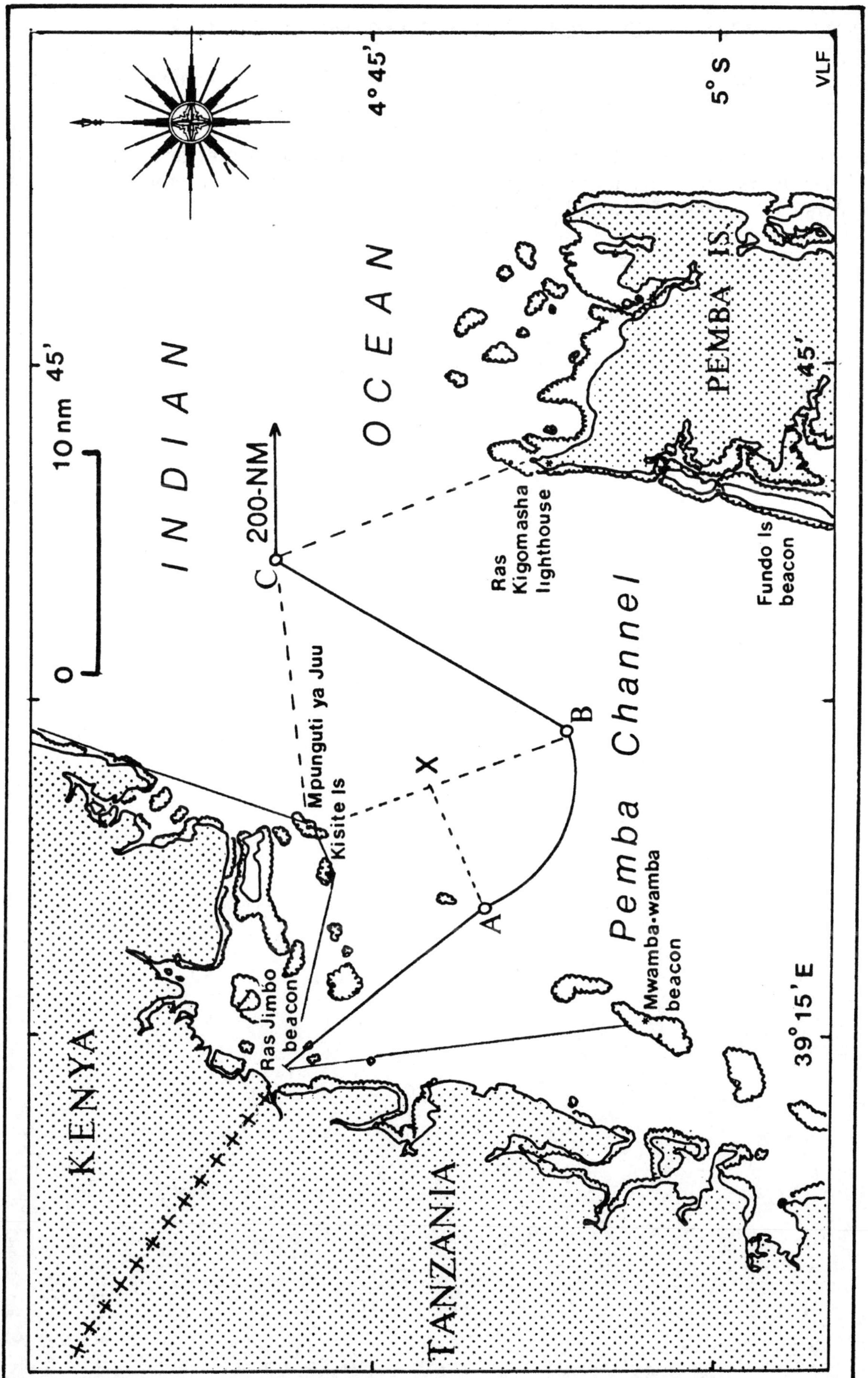
KENYA
TANZANIA
INDIAN
OCEAN
Pemba Channel
PEMBA IS.
0
10 nm
45'
4°45'
5°S
VLF
200-NM
A
B
C
X
Mpunguti ya Juu
Kisite Is
Ras Jimbo beacon
Mwamba-wamba beacon
Ras Kigomasha lighthouse
Fundo Is beacon
39°15'E
45'

Map 28

MAP 29
CONTINENTAL SHELF BOUNDARY: MOZAMBIQUE/TANZANIA

Although initally signed by both parties in December 1988 this agreement establishing a maritime boundary between Mozambique and Tanzania has not been ratified.

The agreement defines the basepoints at the mouth of Rio Ruvuma which establishes Point A. Point B is located equidistant from nominated land features forming the mouth of Baia do Ruvuma. The lines joining B to the coasts forms the outer limit of the internal waters of the states. The length of AB is 4.8 nm.

The agreement defines the geographical coordinates of the four turning points. Point C was determined on the basis of equidistance. Line segment BC is 12 nm. The overall length of the defined boundary is about 20 nm. Water depths along the boundary range from 20 to over 1000 metres.

Source: *Agreement Between the Government of the United Republic of Tanzania and the Government of the People's Republic of Mozambique regarding the Tanzania/Mozambique Boundary.*

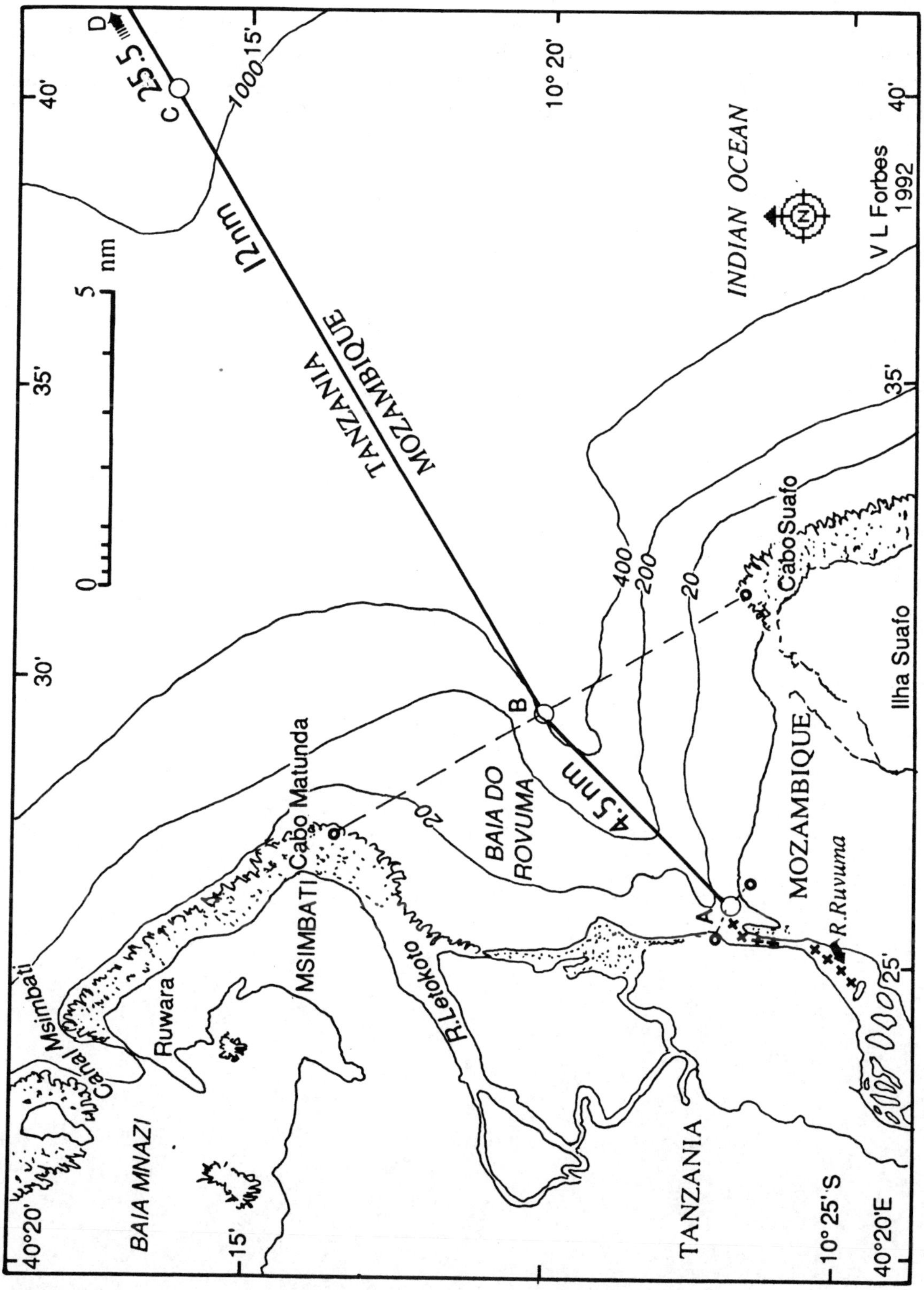

TANZANIA
MOZAMBIQUE
12nm
4.5nm
25.5
A
B
C
D
0
5
nm
INDIAN OCEAN
V L Forbes
1992
BAIA MNAZI
Canal Msimbati
Ruwara
MSIMBATI
Cabo Matunda
BAIA DO ROVUMA
R.Letokoto
TANZANIA
MOZAMBIQUE
R.Ruvuma
Ilha Suafo
Cabo Suafo
20
200
400
1000
40°20'
40°20'E
30'
35'
40'
15'
10° 20'
10° 25' S
25'

Map 29

MAP 30
CONTINENTAL SHELF BOUNDARY: AUSTRALIA (HEARD AND MCDONALD ISLANDS)/FRANCE (KERGUELEN ISLAND)

A continental shelf boundary was established in an agreement which entered into force on 10 January 1983. The boundary is defined by geodesics linking the geographical coordinates of eight Turning points which lie along the Kerguelen submarine plateau.

The boundary is based on the equidistant principle. The agreement specifically states that Points S1 and S8 are not to be taken as necessarily representing the outer limits of the continental shelf. Each state claims a 200-nm EEZ/AFZ.

Source: *Australian Treaty Series,* No. 3, 1983.

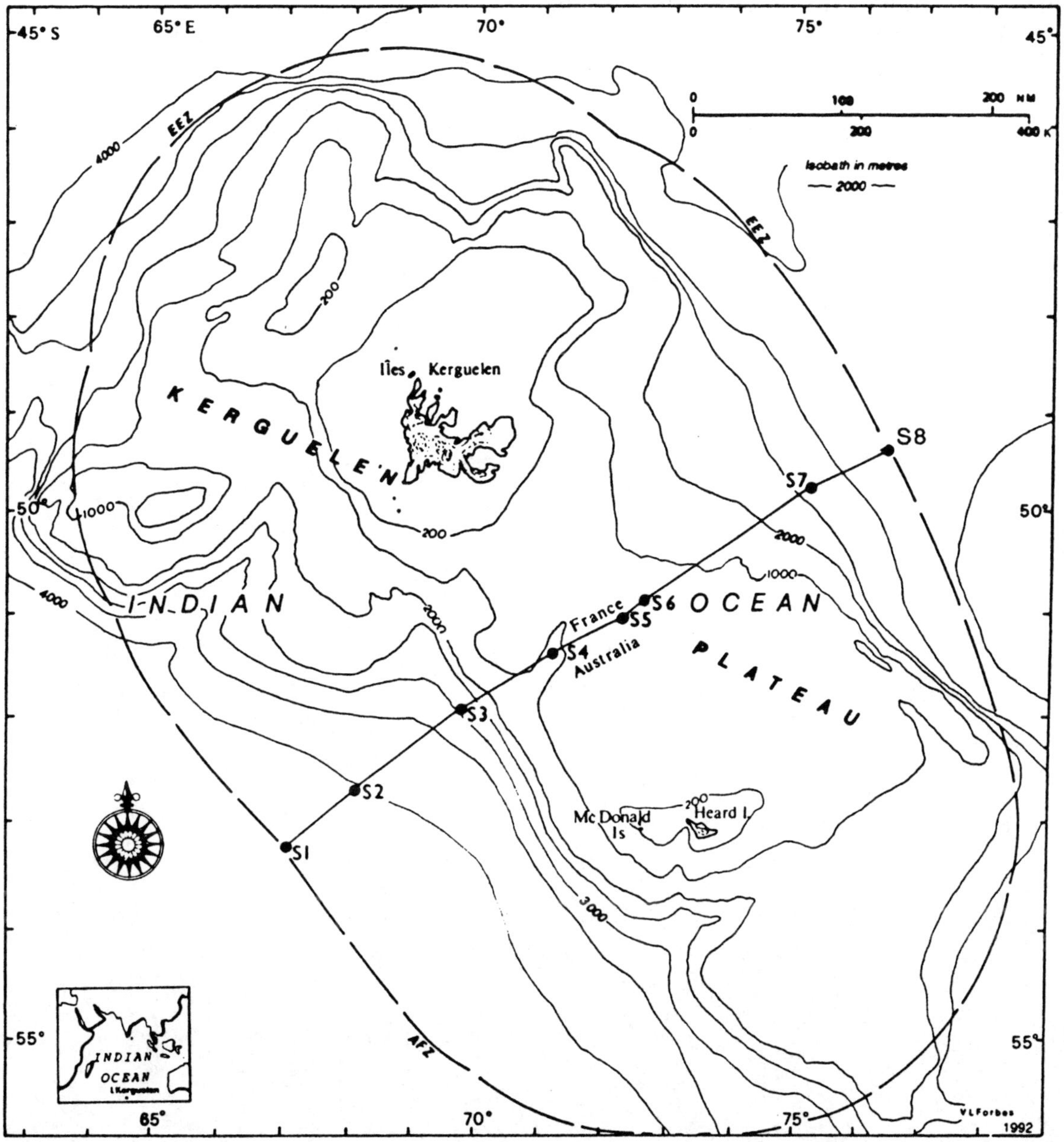
Îles Kerguelen
KERGUELEN
INDIAN OCEAN PLATEAU
France
Australia
Mc Donald Is
Heard I.
S1
S2
S3
S4
S5
S6
S7
S8
EEZ
AFZ
Isobath in metres
2000
INDIAN OCEAN
V.L.Forbes 1992

Map 30

MAP 31
AUSTRALIAN FISHING ZONE: CHRISTMAS AND COCOS (KEELING) ISLANDS

An Australian Fishing Zone (AFZ) with a width of 200 nm was established on 1 November 1979. The AFZ included the ocean space around all Australian external territories.

The map depicts the 200 nm limit around Cocos (Keeling) Islands and the extent of the AFZ to the south of Christmas Island.

To the north of Christmas Island, a potential boundary — a median line — is shown between the Indonesian island of Java and Christmas Island.

Source: *The Australian Fishing Zone,* Australian Goverment Publishing Service, Canberra, 1980.

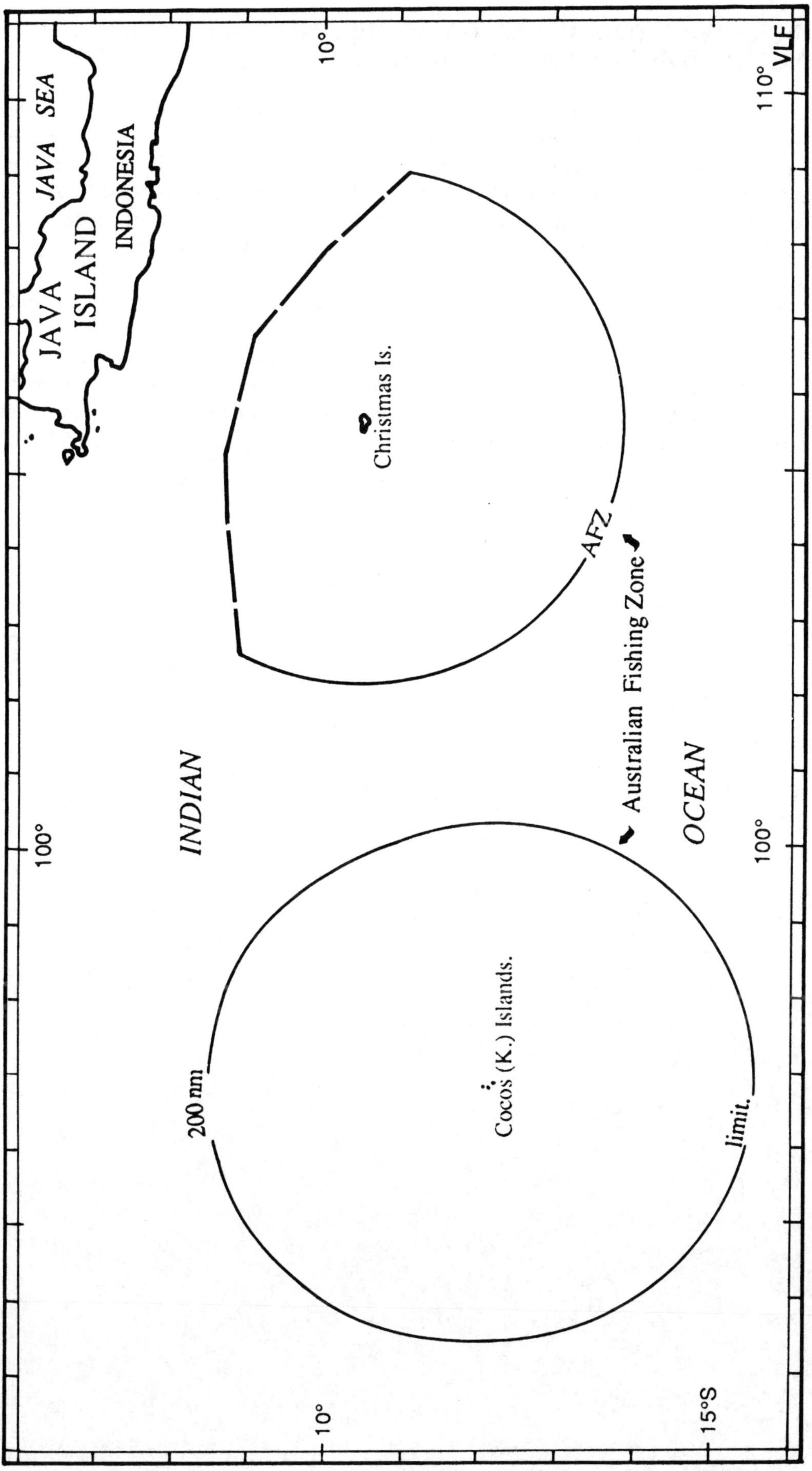
JAVA SEA
JAVA ISLAND
INDONESIA
Christmas Is.
AFZ
Australian Fishing Zone
INDIAN
OCEAN
Cocos (K.) Islands.
200 nm
limit.
10°
110°
100°
100°
10°
15°S
VLF

Map 31

MAP 32
CLAIMED TERRITORIAL SEA BASELINE AND EXCLUSIVE ECONOMIC ZONE OF BANGLADESH

Bangladesh claims a territorial sea zone of 12 nm width measured from the declared territorial sea baselines. There is nothing unusual about this claim. However, the basepoints, whose geographical coordinates were defined, which are connected by baselines are not located on land but rather on the 18 m (10 fathom) isobath. The nearest approach of the baseline system to the landmass is at Elephant Point, about 5 nm. In essence the system is a floating baseline. The overall length of the series of lines is over 220 nm.

Bangladesh's unilateral decision in adopting this baseline system has met with opposition from its near-neighbours Indian and Myanmar.

The map shows the approximate extent of the claimed exclusive economic zone of this coastal nation which perceives itself as a geographically disadvantaged state in the context of CLOS. This unusually shaped zone when viewed within the framework of maritime jurisdictional claims in the Bay of Bengal would appear to be in order (Appendix A, Map 3).

Source: Forbes, 1988b: 12–13.

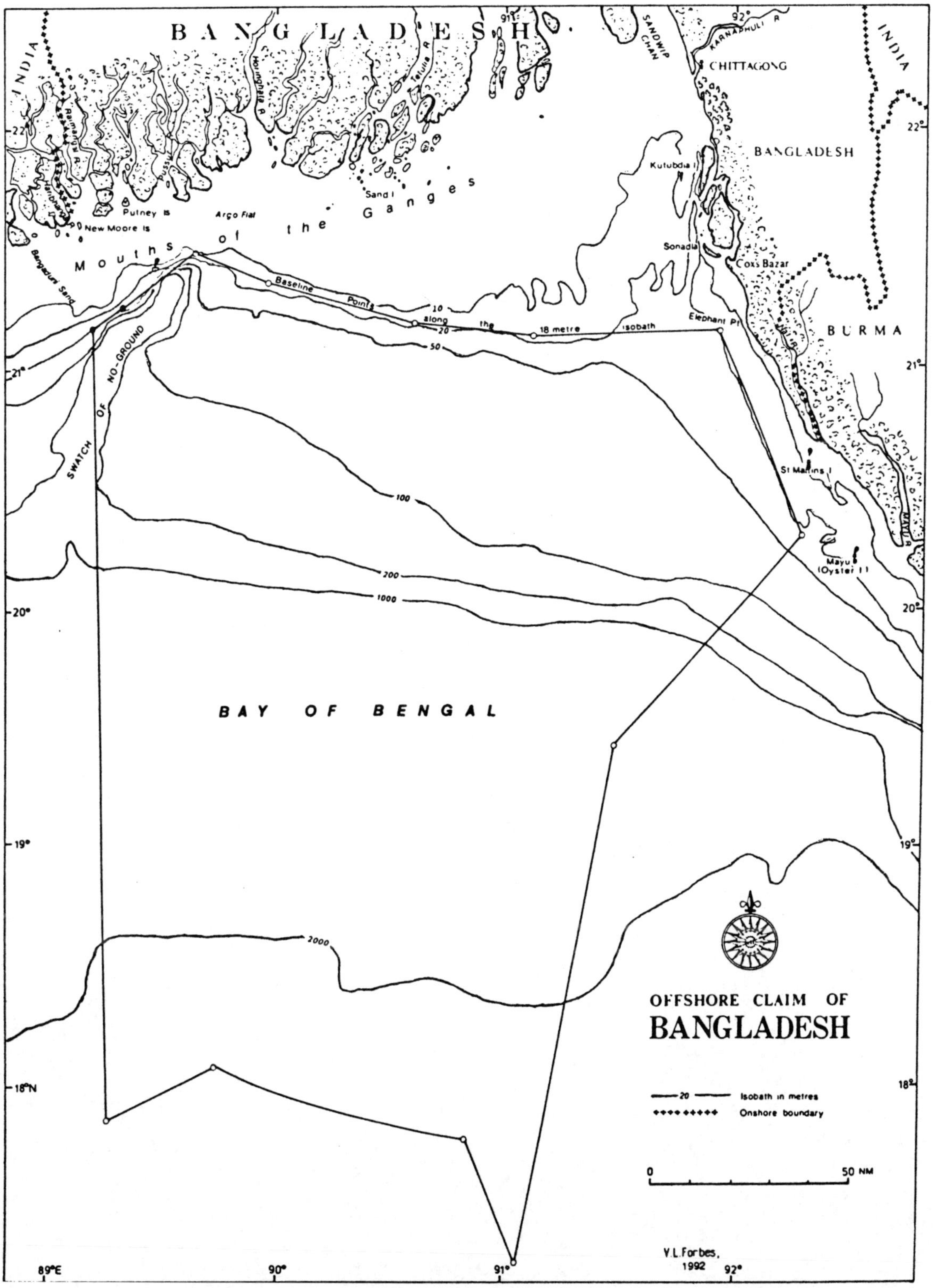
BANGLADESH
INDIA
CHITTAGONG
BANGLADESH
Kutubdia I
Sonadia
Coxs Bazar
Elephant Pt
BURMA
St Martins I
Mayu (Oyster I)
Sand I
Putney Is
New Moore Is
Arço Flat
Mouths of the Ganges
Baseline Points along the 18 metre isobath
SWATCH OF NO-GROUND
BAY OF BENGAL
OFFSHORE CLAIM OF
BANGLADESH
Isobath in metres
Onshore boundary
0
50 NM
V.L.Forbes, 1992
89°E
90°
91°
92°
22°
21°
20°
19°
18°N

Map 32

APPENDIX B

THE THIRD UNITED NATIONS CONVENTION ON THE LAW OF THE SEA

List of Ratifications in Chronological Order

1	10 December 1982	Fiji
2	7 March 1983	Zambia
3	18 March 1983	Mexico
4	21 March 1983	Jamaica
5	18 April 1983	Namibia
6	7 June 1983	Ghana
7	29 July 1983	Bahamas
8	13 August 1983	Belize
9	26 August 1983	Egypt*
10	26 March 1984	Cote d'Ivoire
11	8 May 1984	Philippines
12	22 May 1984	Gambia
13	15 August 1984	Cuba
14	25 October 1984	Senegal
15	23 January 1985	Sudan*
16	27 March 1985	Saint Lucia
17	16 April 1985	Togo
18	24 April 1985	Tunisia
19	30 May 1985	Bahrain*
20	21 June 1985	Iceland
21	16 July 1985	Mali
22	30 July 1985	Iraq*
23	6 September 1985	Guinea
24	30 September 1985	United Republic of Tanzania*
25	19 November 1985	Cameroon
26	3 February 1986	Indonesia*
27	25 April 1986	Trinidad & Tobago
28	2 May 1986	Kuwait*
29	5 May 1986	Yugoslavia
30	14 August 1986	Nigeria
31	25 August 1986	Guinea-Bissau
32	26 September 1986	Paraguay
33	21 July 1987	Yemen*
34	10 August 1987	Cape Verde
35	3 November 1987	Sao Tome & Principe
36	12 December 988	Cyprus
37	22 December 1988	Brazil

38	2 February 1989	Antigua & Barbuda
39	17 February 1989	Zaire
40	2 March 1989	Kenya*
41	24 July 1989	Somalia*
42	17 August 1989	Oman*
43	2 May 1990	Botswana
44	9 November 1990	Uganda
45	5 December 1990	Angola
46	25 April 1991	Grenada
47	29 April 1991[1]	Micronesia (Federated States of)
48	9 August 1991[1]	Marshall Islands
49	16 September 1991	Seychelles*
50	8 October 1991	Djibouti*
51	24 October 1991	Dominica
52	21 September 1992	Costa Rica
53	10 Decemberember	Uruguay
54	7 January 1993	St. Kitts and Nevis
55	24 February 1993	Zimbabwe
56	20 May 1993	Malta
57	1 October 1993	St. Vincent and the Grenadines
58	5 October 1993	Honduras
59	12 October 1993	Barbados
60	16 November 1993	Guyana
61	12 January 1994[2]	Bosnia & Herzegovina
62	21 June 1994	Comoros*

62 ratifications/accessions/succession deposited with the Secretary-General.
* Indian Ocean Regional States
[1]Accession to the Convention.
[2]Succession to the Convention.
Source: *Law of the Sea Bulletin* No. 25, June 1994, pp. 8–10.

APPENDIX C

STATUS OF THE 1958 GENEVA CONVENTIONS ON THE LAW OF THE SEA

Indian Ocean Littoral and Island States

The following Conventions are included in this Table:

1. The Geneva Convention on the Territorial Sea and the Contiguous Zone, 1958.
2. The Geneva Convention on the High Seas, 1958.
3. The Geneva Convention on Fishing and Conservation of the Living Resources of the High Seas, 1958.
4. The Geneva Convention on the Continental Shelf, 1958.
5. Optional Protocol of Signature Concerning the Compulsory Settlement of Disputes, 1958.

	Terr. Sea	High Seas	Fishing	Cont. Shelf	Protocol
Date of Signature	29.4.58	29.4.58	29.4.58	29.4.58	29.4.58
Entry into Force	10.9.64	30.9.62	20.3.66	10.6.64	30.9.62
Australia	14.5.63	14.5.63	14.5.63	14.5.63	14.5.63
France	—	—	18.9.70	14.6.65	30.10.58
Indonesia	—	10.6.61	—	—	—
Israel	6.9.61	6.9.61	—	6.9.61	—
Kenya	20.6.69	20.6.69	20.6.69	20.6.69	—
Madagascar	31.7.62	31.7.62	31.7.62	31.7.62	10.8.62
Malaysia	21.12.60	21.12.60	21.12.60	21.12.60	1.5.61
Mauritius	5.10.70	5.10.70	5.10.70	5.10.70	5.10.70
Pakistan	—	—	—	—	6.11.58
S. Africa	9.4.63	9.4.63	9.4.63	9.4.63	—
Sri Lanka	—	—	—	—	30.10.58
Thailand	2.7.68	2.7.68	2.7.68	2.7.68	—
United Kingdom	14.3.60	14.3.60	14.3.60	11.5.64	9.9.58

The dates tabulated refer to the date of ratification, accession or other form of acceptance by the state concerned. In some instances Parties are bound by the Convention concerned subject to reservations. No indication of such reservation has been included in this Table.

APPENDIX D

STATUS OF THE THIRD UNITED NATIONS CONVENTION ON THE LAW OF THE SEA, 1982.

Indian Ocean Littoral and Island States
Table of Signatures and Ratifications of the Convention and Final Act of the UN Conference on the Law of the Sea

States	Final Act Signature	Convention Signature	Ratification
Australia	*	*	—
Bahrain	*	*	30.5.85
Bangladesh	*	*	—
Comoros	—	6.12.84	21.6.94
Djibouti	*	*	8.10.91
Egypt	*	*	26.8.83
Ethiopia	*	*	—
France	*	*	—
India	*	*	—
Indonesia	*	*	3.2.86
Iran	*	*	—
Iraq	*	*	30.7.85
Israel	*		—
Kenya	*	*	2.3.89
Kuwait	*	*	2.5.86
Madagascar	—	25.2.83	—
Malaysia	*	*	—
Maldives	*	*	—
Mauritius	*	*	—
Myanmar	*	*	—
Oman	*	1.7.83	17.8.89
Pakistan	*	*	—
Papua New Guinea	*	*	—
Qatar	—	27.11.84	—
Saudia Arabia	—	7.12.84	—
Seychelles	*	*	16.9.91
Singapore	*	*	—
Somalia	*	*	24.7.89
South Africa	—	5.12.84	—
Sri Lanka	*	*	—
Sudan	*	*	23.1.85
Tanzania	*	*	30.9.85

Thailand	*	*	—
United Arab Emirates	*	*	—
United Kingdom	*	—	—
Yemen	*	*	21.7.87

Those states which signed the Convention on 10 December 1982 are indicated by a '*'. Those which signed at a later date are indicated by that date.

Source: *Law of the Sea Bulletin*, No. 6, UN Publication, New York, 1985, 1–5.

APPENDIX E

NATIONAL LEGISLATION CITED

Australia
Continental Shelf Proclamation, 11 September 1953
Pearl Fisheries Act 1952–53, 12 October 1953
Continental Shelf (Living Natural Resources) Act, 1968
Fisheries Act 1952–73
Whaling Act 1960–73
Petroleum (Submerged Lands) Act No. 118, 22 November 1967
Fisheries Act 1975
Territorial Sea and Continental Shelf Act 1970
Fisheries Amendment Act No. 99 of 1978
Whaling Amendment Act 1978

Bangladesh
Territorial Waters and Maritime Zones Act, No. XXVI of 1974

Burma
Territorial Sea and Maritime Zones Law, No. 3, 9 April 1977

Comoros
Ordinance No. 76-038/CE Specifying the Limits of Comoran Territorial Waters and the Establishment of an Exclusive Economic Zone of 15 June 1976

Djibouti
Law 52/AN/78, 9 January 1979

Kerguelen Island — France
Decree of 9 February 1978

Tromelin Islands, Glorius Archipelago, Juan de Nova and Europa Bassas — France
Decree of 12 February 1978

India
Proclamation of September 30, 1967
Territorial Waters, Continental Shelf, Exclusive Economic Zone and other Maritime Zones Act, 28 May 1976

Indonesia
Law No. 4, 18 February 1960
Declaration on the Exclusive Economic Zone, 21 March 1980

Iran
Law on the Continental Shelf, 19 June 1955
Act Amending the Act of 15 July on the Territorial Waters and the Contiguous Zone (1959)

Iraq
Official Proclamation Concerning the Continental Shelf
Law No. 71 of 1958 Delimiting the Iraqi Territorial Waters

Jordan
Fisheries Act No. 25 of 1943

Kenya
Presedential Proclamation, 28 February 1979

Kuwait
Proclamation of the Sheikh of Kuwait with Respect to the Sea-bed and Subsoil of the High Seas of the Persian Gulf, 1949
Decree Regarding the Delimitation of the Breadth of the Territorial Sea, 17 December 1967

Madagascar
Ordinance No. 73-060, 28 September 1973
Ordinance No. 85-013 Establishing the Limits of the Maritime Zones, the Territorial Sea, the Continental Shelf and the Exclusive Economic Zone, 1985

Malaysia
Continental Shelf Act, 28 July 1966
Petroleum Mining Act No. 58 of 1966
Proclamation of 25 April 1980

Maldives
Law No. 30/76 Relating to the Exclusive Economic Zone, 5 December 1976
Law 32/76 Relating to the Navigation and Passage by Foreign Ships and Aircraft through the Airspace, Territorial Waters, and the Economic Zone, 5 December 1976

Mauritius
The Maritime Zones Act, 31 May 1977

Mozambique
Decree Law No. 31, 19 August 1976

Oman
Royal Decree of 17 July 1972
Royal Decree No. 44 of 16 June 1977
Decree No. 15/81 of 20 February 1981

Papua New Guinea
Fisheries (Declared Fishing Zone) Act 1977
Tuna Resources Management (National Seas) Act (1977)
Continental Shelf Act No. 5, 1966
National Seas Act (1977)
Offshore Seas Proclamation 1978

Pakistan
Territorial Waters and Maritime Zones Act, 1976
Exclusive Fishery Zone (Regulation of Fishing) Act, 1975

Qatar
Proclamation with respect to the Sea-bed and the Subsoil of the High Seas of the Persian Gulf
Declaration Concerning the Exclusive Sovereign Rights of the State of Qatar in the Zones Contiguous to the Territorial Sea, 2 June 1974

Saudi Arabia
Royal Pronouncement Concerning the Policy of the Kingdom with Respect to the Subsoil and Sea-bed in the Persian Gulf, 1945
Decree No. 33 on the Territorial Waters, 1959
Decree Relating to the Ownership of Red Sea Resources of September 1968
Declaration Concerning the Limits of the Exclusive Fishing Zones of Saudi Arabia in the Red Sea and the Arabian Gulf of 1974

Seychelles
Marine Zones Act, No. 15, 1977
The Exclusive Economic Zone Order 1978

Somalia
Law No. 37 on the Territorial Sea and Ports, 10 September 1972

South Africa
Territorial Waters (Amendment) Act, 1977

Sri Lanka
Maritime Zones Law No. 22, 1 September 1976
Presidential Proclamation, 15 January 1977 in Pursuance of Law No. 22

Tanzania
Presidential Proclamation Extending Tanzania's Territorial Waters, 7 September 1973

Thailand
Proclamation Establishing the Economic Zone, 21 February 1980

United Arab Emirates
Proclamation on the Status, Breadth, and the Delimitation of the Exclusive Economic Zone, 25 August 1980
Abu Dhabi — Proclamation with respect to the Sea-bed and Subsoil of the Persian Gulf, 10 June 1949
Ajman —Proclamation with respect to the Sea-bed and the Subsoil of the High Seas of the Persian Gulf, 20 June 1949
Dubai —Proclamation with Respect to the Sea-bed and Subsoil of the High Seas of the Persian Gulf, 14 June 1949
Ras al-Khaymah —Proclamation with Respect to the Sea-bed and Subsoil of the High Seas of the Persian Gulf, 17 June 1949
Sharjah —Proclamation with Respect to the Sea-bed and Subsoil of the High Seas of the Persian Gulf, 16 June 1949

Yemen Arab Republic
Decree No. 16 Concerning the Continental Shelf, 30 April 1967
Fisheries Law, 1977

Yemen Democratic Republic
Act No. 45 of 1977 Concerning the Territorial Sea, Exclusive Economic Zone, Continental Shelf and other Marine Areas

APPENDIX F

MARITIME DELIMITATION AGREEMENTS CITED:

Indian Ocean Littoral States

1928
Malaysia/Singapore
Territorial Sea Boundary in the Strait of Johore, 3 Aug 1928.

1958
Bahrain/Saudi Arabia
Agreement Concerning Delimitation of the Continental Shelf, 22 February 1958.

1968
Abu Dhabi/Dubai
Agreement on the Offshore Boundary, 18 February 1968.

Iran/Saudi Arabia
Agreement Concerning the Sovereignty over the Islands of Al-' Arabiyah and Farsi and the Delimitation of the Boundary Line Separating the Submarine Areas, 24 October 1968.

1969
Abu Dhabi/Qatar
Agreement on Settlement of Maritime Boundary Lines and Sovereign Rights over Islands, 20 March 1969.

Iran/Qatar
Agreement Dividing the Continental Shelf in the Persian Gulf, 20 September 1969.

Indonesia/Malaysia
Agreement on the Continental Shelf Boundaries, 27 October 1969.

1970
Indonesia/Malaysia
Treaty on the Delimitation of the Boundary Line of the Territorial Waters at the Strait of Malacca, 17 March 1970.

1971
Australia/Indonesia
Agreement Establishing Certain Seabed Boundaries, 18 May 1971.

Bahrain/Iran
Agreement Concerning the Delimitation of the Continental Shelf, 17 June 1971.

Indonesia/Thailand
Agreement on the Delimitation of a Continental Shelf Boundary in the Northern Part of the Strait of Malacca and in the Andaman Sea, 17 December 1971.

Indonesia/Malaysia/Thailand
Agreement Relating to the Delimitation of the Continental Shelf Boundaries in the Northern Part of the Straits of Malacca, 21 December 1971.

Australia/Indonesia
Agreement Establishing Certain Seabed Boundaries in the Area of the Timor and Arafura Seas, 9 October 1971.

1973
Australia/Indonesia
Agreement Concerning Certain Seabed Boundaries in the Area of the Timor and Arafura Seas, 12 February 1973.

Indonesia/Singapore
Agreement Stipulating the Territorial Sea Boundary Lines, 25 May 1973.

1974
Sudan/Saudi Arabia
Agreement Relating to the Joint Exploitation of the National Resources of the Sea-bed and Sub-soil of the Red Sea in the Common Zone, 16 May 1974.

India/Sri Lanka
Agreement on the Boundary in Historic Waters, 26-28 June 1974.

Iran/Oman
Agreement Concerning Delimitation of the Continental Shelf, 25 July 1974.

India/Indonesia
Agreement Concerning Delimitation of the Continental Shelf, 8 August 1974.

Iran/United Arab Emirates
Agreement on the Boundary Line Dividing Parts of the Continental Shelf, 13 August 1974.

1975
Indonesia/Thailand
Agreement Relating to the Delimitation of the Sea-bed Boundary in the Andaman Sea, 11 December 1975.

1976
India/Sri Lanka
Agreement on the Maritime Boundary in the Gulf of Manaar and the Bay of Bengal and Related Matters, 23 March 1976.

Kenya/Tanzania
Exchange of Notes between the United Republic ofTanzania and Kenya Concerning the Delimitation of the Territorial Waters Boundary, 9 July 1976.

India/Maldives/Sri Lanka
Agreement Concerning the Determination of the Tri-junction Point between the Three States in the Gulf of Manaar, 31 July 1976.

India/Sri Lanka
Supplementary Agreement on the Extension of the Maritime Boundary in the Gulf of Manaar from the Position 13 m to the Trijunction point between India, Sri Lanka and Maldives, 22 November 1976.

India/Maldives
Agreement on the Delimitation of Maritime Boundary in the Arabian Sea, 28 December 1976.

1977
India/Indonesia
Agreement Relating to the Extension of the 1974 Continental Shelf Boundary in the Andaman Sea and the Indian Ocean, 14 January 1977.

1978
India/Thailand
Agreement Relating to the Delimitation of the Sea-bed in the Andaman Sea, 22 June 1978.

India/Indonesia/Thailand
Agreement Concerning the Determination of the Trijunction Point and the Delimitation of the Related Boundaries of the Three Countries in the Andaman Sea, 22 June 1978.

Australia/Papua New Guinea
Treaty Concerning Sovereignty and Maritime Boundaries in the Area between the Two States, including the Area known as Torres Strait, 18 December 1978.

1979
Malaysia/Thailand
Continental Shelf Boundary Agreement, 24 October 1979.

1980
France/Mauritius
Convention on the Delimitation of the French and Mauritian Economic Zones between the Island of Reunion and Mauritius, 2 April 1980.

Burma/Thailand
Agreement on the Delimitation of the Maritime Boundary in the Andaman Sea, 25 July 1980.

Indonesia/Papua New Guinea
Continental Shelf Boundary Delimitation in the Arafura Sea, 13 Dec 1980.

1981
Australia/Indonesia
Establishment of a Provisional Fisheries Enforcement and Surveillance Line in the Timor and Arafura Seas, 29 Oct 1981.

1982
Australia/France
Continental Shelf Boundary between Heard and Kerguelen Islands 4 January 1982.

1987
Burma/India
Continental Shelf Boundary in the Andaman Sea, 14 Sep 1987.

1988

Tanzania/Mozambique

Determination of the Maritime Boundary between the two states, 28 Dec 1988.

1989

Australia/Indonesia

Establishment of a Zone of Cooperation in the Timor Sea, 11 Dec 1989.

1993

Iraq/ Kuwait

Land boundary demarcated and maritime boundary delimited by the U.N. Iraq–Kuwait Boundary Demarcation Commission (IKBDC). On 21 May 1993 (S25811). Accepted by Kuwait, but challenged by Iraq on 6 June 1993. However, Iraq has subsequently (14 October 1994) announced that it would recognise the common border and Kuwait's sovereignty.

APPENDIX G

MARITIME BOUNDARY AGREEMENTS BETWEEN INDIAN OCEAN LITTORAL STATES

The following maritime boundary agreements, or adjudications, are in force unless followed by an asterisk (*) indicating that the agreement has been signed only. Unless otherwise indicated the delimitation creates a maritime boundary separating all applicable maritime jurisdiction permitted under international law, including the territorial sea, fishing, continental shelf, and other rights permitted in the exclusive economic zone. Boundaries separating other specific types of jurisdiction are noted as follows: TS = territorial sea; CZ = contiguous zone; CS = continental shelf; F = fishing zone.

The date that the agreement or adjudication entered into force, or was signed, is in parenthesis.

Australia (Heard/McDonald Islands) – France (Fr. Southern and Antarctica Lands – (9 Jan 1983)
Australia – Indonesia (2 boundaries; CS; 8 Nov 1973)
Australia – Indonesia (F; 1 Feb 1982)
Australia – Indonesia (CS; 11 Dec. 1989)
Australia – Papua New Guinea (2 boundaries; 15 Feb 1985)
Bahrain – Iran (CS; 14 May 1972)
Bahrain – Saudi Arabia (CS; 26 Feb 1958)
Burma – India (CS; 14 Sept 1987)
Burma – Thailand (CS; 12 Apr 1982)
France (Reunion) – Mauritius (CS; 2 Apr 1980)
India – Indonesia (CS; 17 Dec 1974 and 15 Aug 1977, two agreements)
India – Indonesia – Thailand (CS; 2 Mar 1979 – tripoint agreement)
India – Maldives – Sri Lanka (CS; 31 July 1976 – tripoint agreement)
India – Maldives (CS; 8June 1978)
India – Sri Lanka (CS; 8 July 1974 and 10 May 1976, two agreements)
India – Thailand (CS; 15 Dec 1978)
Indonesia – Malaysia (CS; 7 Nov 1969)
Indonesia – Malaysia (TS; 8 Oct 1971)
Indonesia – Malaysia (2 boundaries; CS; 7 Nov 1969 and 16 July 1973, two agreements)
Indonesia – Malaysia – Thailand (CS; 16 July 1973 – tripoint agreement)
Indonesia – Papua New Guinea (2 boundaries; TS; 26 Dec 1974)
Indonesia – Papua New Guinea (CS; 10 July 1982)
Indonesia – Singapore (TS; 29 Aug 1974)
Indonesia – Thailand (CS; 16 July 1973 and 15 Dec 1978, two agreements)
Iran – Oman (CS; 28 May 1975)
Iran – Qatar (CS; 10 May 1970)
Iran – Saudi Arabia (CS; 29 Jan 1969)
Iran – United Arab Emirates (Dubai) * (CS; 31 Aug 1974)

Kenya – Tanzania (9 July 1976)
Malaysia – Singapore (TS; 3 Aug 1928)
Malaysia – Thailand (TS; 15 July 1982)
Malaysia – Thailand (CS; 16 July 1973 and 15 July 1982, two agreements)
Mozambique – Tanzania * (28 Dec 1988)
Qatar – United Arab Emirates (Abu Dhabi – CS; 20 Mar 1969)

APPENDIX H

MARITIME BOUNDARY AGREEMENTS: BY TYPE

The numbering pertains to the number of boundaries that have been created by the agreement(s) or adjudications. Boundary delimitations are in force unless noted by an asterisk (*). For dates of signature or of entry into force refer to Appendix G.

MARITIME BOUNDARIES
Australia – (Heard/McDonald Islands) – France (Fr. Southern and Antarctica Lands)
Australia – Papua New Guinea (2)
Burma – India
Burma – Thailand
France (Reunion) – Mauritius
India – Maldives
India – Sri Lanka (2 agreements)
Kenya – Tanzania
Mozambique – Tanzania *

CONTINENTAL SHELF BOUNDARIES
Australia – Indonesia (2; 2 agreements)
Australia – Indonesia *
Bahrain – Iran
Bahrain – Saudi Arabia
India – Indonesia (2 agreements)
India – Indonesia – Thailand (tripoint)
India – Maldives – Sri Lanka (tripoint)
India – Thailand
Indonesia – Malaysia (3; 2 agreements)
Indonesia – Malaysia – Thailand (tripoint)
Indonesia – Papua New Guinea
Indonesia – Thailand (2 agreements)
Iran – Oman
Iran – Qatar
Iran – Saudi Arabia
Iran – United Arab Emirates (Dubai) *
Malaysia – Thailand (2; and joint development zone)
Qatar – United Arab Emirates (Abu Dhabi)

TERRITORIAL SEA BOUNDARIES
Indonesia – Malaysia
Indonesia – Papua New Guinea (2)
Indonesia – Singapore
Malaysia – Singapore

Malaysia – Thailand (2)

FISHING BOUNDARIES
Australia – Indonesia

JOINT DEVELOPMENT ZONES OR SIMILAR COOPERATIVE APPROACHES
Australia – Indonesia
Bahrain – Saudi Arabia
Kuwait – Saudi Arabia
Sudan – Saudi Arabia
Malaysia – Thailand

APPENDIX I

MARITIME BOUNDARIES BY COUNTRY

The following list provides information on both resolved (either by negotiation or by adjudication) and potential maritime boundaries of the world's coastal states. One asterisk (*) indicates a boundary agreement has been signed only; two asterisks (**) signifies the agreement is in force. Date of signature or date agreement enetered into force is given in parenthesis.

Unless otherwise indicated, the cited agreement creates a boundary that separates all applicable maritime jurisdiction permitted under international law, including the territorial sea, fishing, continental shelf, and any other rights permitted in the exclusive economic zone. Agreements separating other specific types of sovereignty or jurisdiction are noted as follows: TS = territorial sea; CZ = contiguous zone; CS = continental shelf; F = fishing zone.

AUSTRALIA (10)
France (New Caledonia) ** (9 Jan 1983); Indonesia ** (2; CS – 8 Nov 1973); Indonesia**(F; 1 Feb 1982); Indonesia * (CS; 11 Dec 1989); New Zealand (2); Papua New Guinea **(2; 15 Feb 1985); Solomon Islands * (13 Sept 1988)

AUSTRALIA(Heard and McDonald I) (1)
France (Kerguelen I) ** (9 Jan 1983)

BAHRAIN (3)
Iran ** (CS; 14 May 1972); Qatar; Saudi Arabia ** (CS; 26 Feb 1958).

BANGLADESH (2)
Burma; India.

BURMA (3)
Bangladesh; India ** (14 Sept 1987); Thailand ** (12 Apr 1982)

COMOROS (6)
France (Mayotte); France (Reunion); Madagascar; Mozambique; Seychelles; Tanzania

DJIBOUTI (3)
Ethiopia; Somalia; Yemen.

EGYPT (10)
Cyprus; Greece; Israel (2); Jordan; Libya; Saudi Arabia; Sudan; Turkey; UK (Sovereign Base Areas, Cyprus).

FRANCE (7)
Australia; Comoros; Madagascar; Mauritius; Mozambique; Seychelles.

INDIA (9)
Bangladesh; Burma** (14 Sept 1987); Indonesia** (CS; 17 Dec. 1974 & 15 Aug 1977); Indonesia & Thailand** (CS; 2 Mar 1979); Maldives** (8 June 1978); Maldives & Sri Lanka** (CS; 31 July 1976); Pakistan; Sri Lanka** (8 July 1974 & 10 May 1976); Thailand ** (CS; 15 Dec 1978 & 2 Mar 1979).

INDONESIA (19)
Australia** (2; CS; 8 Nov 1973); Australia** (F; 1Feb 1982); Australia* (CS; 11 Dec 1989); India** (CS; 17 Dec 1974 & 15 Aug 1977); India & Thailand** (CS; 2 Mar 1979); Malaysia ** (TS; 8 Oct 1971); Malaysia** (3; CS; 7 Nov 1969 & 16 July 1973); Palau; Papua New Guniea** (2; TS; 26 Nov 1974); Papua New Guinea** (CS; 10 July 1982); Philippines; Singapore** (TS; 29 Aug 1974); Thailand** (CS; 16 July 1973 & 18 Feb 1978); Vietnam.

IRAN (11)
Bahrain** (CS, 14 May 1972); Iraq; Kuwait; Oman** (CS, 28 May 1975); Pakistan; Qatar** (CS, 10 May 1970); Saudi Arabia** (CS, 29 Jan 1969); United Arab Emirates (Dubai)* (CS, 31 Aug 1974); United Arab Emirates.

IRAQ (2)
Iran; Kuwait.

ISRAEL (5)
Cyprus; Egypt (2); Jordan; Lebanon.

JORDAN (3)
Egypt; Israel; Saudi Arabia.

KUWAIT (3)
Iran; Iraq; Saudi Arabia.

MADAGASCAR (5)
Comoros; France(Mayotte); France(Réunion); Mozambique; Seychelles.

MALAYSIA (14)
Brunei (2);Indonesia** (TS; 10 Mar 1971); Indonesia** (3; CS; 7 Nov 1969 & 16 July 1973); Indonesia & Thailand** (CS; 16July 1973); Philippines; Singapore** (TS; 3 Aug 1928); Singapore; Thailand** (2; CS; 16 July 1973 & 15 July 1982); Thailand** (2; TS; 15 July 1982); Vietnam.

MALDIVES (3)
India** (8 June 1978); India & Sri Lanka** (31 July 1976); United Kingdom (British Indian Ocean Territory).

MAURITIUS (2)
France (Réunion)** (2 Apr 1980); Seychelles.

MOZAMBIQUE
Comoros; France (Réunion); Madagascar; South Africa; Tanzania* (28 Dec 1988).

OMAN
Iran; Pakistan; United Arab Emirates; Yemen.

PAKISTAN (3)
India; Iran; Oman.

PAPUA NEW GUINEA (7)
Australia** (15 Feb 1985); Fed. States of Micronesia; France (New Caledonia); Indonesia** (2; TS; 26 Nov 1974); Indonesia** (CS; 10 Jul 1982); Solomon Islands* (25 Jan 1989).

QATAR (4)
Bahrain; Iran** (CS; 10 May 1970); Saudi Arabia; United Arab Emirates** (CS; 20 Mar 1969)

SINGAPORE (3)
Indonesia** (TS; 29 Aug 1974); Malaysia** (TS; 3 Aug 1928); Malaysia.

SOMALIA (3)
Kenya; Yemen

SRI LANKA (2)
India** (8 July 1974 & 10 May 1976); India & Maldives** (CS; 31 July 1976).

SUDAN (3)
Egypt; Ethiopia; Saudi Arabia.

TANZANIA (4)
Comoros; Kenya** (9 July 1976); Mozambique* (28 Dec 1988); Seychelles.

THAILAND (11)
Burma** (12 Apr 1982); Cambodia; India** (CS; 15 Dec 1978 & 2 Mar 79); India-Indonesia** (CS; 2 Mar 1979); Indonesia**(CS; 16 July 73 & 18 Feb 78); Indonesia & Malaysia** (CS; 16 July 1973) Malaysia** (2; CS; 15 July 1982); Malaysia** (2; TS; 16 July 73 & 15 July 1982); Vietnam.

UNITED ARAB EMIRATES (6)
Iran* (CS; 31 Aug 1974); Iran (2); Oman (2); Qatar** (CS; 20 Mar 1969).

YEMEN (5)
Djibouti; Oman; Saudi Arabia; Somalia; Ethiopia.

BIBLIOGRAPHY

Academy of Sciences (1975) *Geological and Geophysical Atlas of the Indian Ocean*, Main Administration of Geodesy and Cartography, USSR, Moscow.

Agoes, E. R. (1990) Recent National Developments on the Law of the Sea Issues, Paper presented at the SEAPOL International Conference, Bali, Indonesia.

______ (1991) Rules of Joint Development: The Timor Gap Treaty, Paper presented at the ICLOS — NILOS Seminar, Bandung, Indonesia.

Albinski, H. S. (1981) Australia and the Indian Ocean, in Bowman, L. W., and Clark, I. (eds.) *The Indian Ocean in Global Politics*, Westview Press, Boulder, Colorado, 59–86.

Alexander, L. M. (1968) Geography and the Law of the Sea, *Annals of Association of American Geographers*, 57, 177–197.

______ (1977) Regional Arrangements in the Ocean, *American Journal of International Law*, 71, 84–109.

______ (1986) The Delimitation of Maritime Boundaries, *Political Geography Quarterly*, 5, 1, 19–24.

Anon, (1988) Keeping up Appearances, in Pemberthy, J. (ed.), *Time* 3, 39, 17.

Appleyard, R. T. (1988) Human Resources, in Appleyard, R. T. and Ghosh, R. N. (eds.), *Indian Ocean Islands Development*, National Centre for Development Studies, Australian National University, Canberra, 11–43.

Appleyard, R. T. and Ghosh, R. N. (1988) Overview, in Appleyard, R. T. and Ghosh, R. N. (eds.), *Indian Ocean Islands Development*, National Centre for Development Studies, Australian National University, Canberra, 1–2.

Attard, D. J. (1987) *The Exclusive Economic Zone in International Law*, Clarendon Press, Oxford.

Attorney-General's Department, Australia (1980) *Offshore Constitutional Settlement*, Australian Government Publishing Service, Canberra.

______ (1988) *Australia's territorial sea baseline*, Australian Government Publishing Service, Canberra.

Armstrong, P. (1987) Claim and Conflict, Cooperation and Conservation: Land, Ocean and Resources South of Latitude 45° South, in McPherson, K. (ed.), *Oceans and Violence*, Centre for Indian Ocean Regional Studies, Perth, 21–36.

Auburn, F. M. (1971) The International Seabed Area, *The International and Comparative Law Quarterly*, 20, 7, 173–194.

______ (1991) Dispute Settlement Under the Antarctic System, Proceedings of Scientific World Seminar on an International court for the Environment, Florence, Italy.

Auburn, F. M. and Forbes, V. L. (1991) The Timor Gap Treaty and The Law of the Sea Convention, Paper presented at the SEAPOL Workshop, Chiang Mai, Thailand.

Auburn, F. M., Forbes, V. L., and Scott, J. (1991) "Comparative Oil and Gas Joint Development Regimes, Paper presented at the Second International Boundaries Research Unit Conference, Durham University, Durham, England.

Autery, C. B. (1982) Indian Ocean Defence, in *Report of the 1982 Nothern Australian Development Seminar*, Northern Australia Development Council, 44–47.

Australian Customs Service (1991) Annual Report 1990–91, Australian Government Publishing Service, Canberra.

Barnes, J. (1984) Increasing the Global Perspective, *Marine Policy*, Butterworth, London, 171–197.

Barrett, E. C and Curtis, L. F. (1977) *Environmental Remote Sensing 2: Practices and Problems*, Crane Russak, New York.

Barston, R. P. and Birnie, P. W. (1980) Introduction, in Barston, R. P. and Birnie, P. (eds.), *The Maritime Dimension*, George Allen and Unwin, London, 1–7.

______ (1980) The Marine Environment, in Barston, R. P. and Birnie, P. (eds.), *The Maritime Dimension*, George Allen and Unwin, London, 108–127.

Barston, R. P. (1980) The Law of the Sea Conference: The Search for New Regimes in Barston, R. P. and Birnie, P. (eds.), *The Maritime Dimension*, George Allen and Unwin, London, 154–168.

Beazley, K. C. (1981) The October War, the 1973–1974 Arab Oil Embargo, and US Policy on the Indian Ocean, in Bowman, L. W. and Clark, I. (eds.), *The Indian Ocean in Global Politics*, Westview Press, Boulder, Colorado, 107–130.

Beazley, K. C. (1988) The Two Ocean Navy, in Bruce, R.H. (ed.), *Australia and the Indian Ocean: Strategic Dimensions of Increasing Naval Involvement*, Centre for Indian Ocean Regional Studies, Perth, 9–18.

Beazley, K. C. and Clark, I. (1979) *The Politics of Intrusion*, Alternative Publishing Cooperative Ltd, Sydney.

Beckman, R. C. (1991) Singapore and the Law of the Sea, Paper presented at the SEAPOL Workshop, Chiang Mai, Thailand.

Bernaerts, A. (1988) *Bernaerts' Guide to the Law of the Sea*, Fairplay Publications Ltd, Coulsdon.

Berthon, S. and Robinson, A. (1991) *The Shape of the World*, George Philip Ltd, London.

Bird, E. C. F. (1964) *Coastal Landforms*, Australian National University, Canberra.

______ (1985) *Coastal Changes*, Wiley-Interscience, Chichester.

Bird, E. C. F. and Schwartz, M. L. (1985) *The World's Coastlines*, Van Nostrand Rheinhold, New York.

Birnie, P. W. (1980) Contemporary Maritime Legal Problems, in Barston, R. P. and Birnie, P. (eds.), *The Maritime Dimension*, George Allen and Unwin, London, 169–189.

______ (1980) The Law of the Sea Before UNCLOS I and UNCLOS II, in Barston, R.P. and Birnie, P. (eds.), *The Maritime Dimension*, George Allen and Unwin, London, 8–26.

Birtles, T. G. (1988) The Indian Ocean Region: Conflict and Stability, Paper presented at 26th International Geographical Congress, Sydney.

Boggs, S. W. (1930) Delimitation of the Territorial Sea, *American Journal of International Law*, 24, 541–555.

______ (1937) Problems of Water Boundary Definitions, Geographical Review, 27, 451–456.

______ (1961) Delimitation of Seaward Areas Under National Jurisdiction, *American Journal of International Law*, 48, 240–266.

Borgese, E. M. (1976) *Drama of the Oceans*, H. N. Abrams, Inc, New York.

______ (1978) *Seafarm*, H. N. Abrams, Inc, New York.

______ (1985) *The Mines of Neptune*, H. N. Abrams, Inc, New York.

Bowman, L. W. (1981) African Conflict and Superpower Involvement in Western Indian Ocean, in Bowman, L. W. and Clark, I. (eds.), *The Indian Ocean in Global Politics*, Westview Press, Boulder, Colorado, 87–106.

______ (1981) Introduction in Bowman, L. W. and Clark, I. (eds.), The Indian Ocean in Global Politics, Westview Press, Boulder, Colorado, 1–6.

______ (1991) *Mauritius: Democracy and Development in the Indian Ocean*, Westview Press, Boulder.

Blake, G., Dewdney, J. and Mitchell, J. (1988) *Atlas of Middle East and North Africa*, Cambridge University Press, Cambridge.

Bramwell, Martyn (ed.) (1977) *Atlas of the Oceans*, Macmillan, Melbourne.

Braun, D. (1981) New Patterns of India's Relations with Indian Ocean Littoral States, in Bowman, L. W. and Clark, I. (eds.), *The Indian Ocean in Global Politics, Westview Press*, Boulder, Colorado, 21–40.

Brown, E. D. (1984) From UNCLOS to PrepCom, *Marine Policy*, Butterworth, London, 151–164.

______ (1984) *The Areas Within National Jurisdiction*, Volumes I and II, Graham and Trotman Ltd., London.

Bruce, R. H. (1989) Implications for International Security: Observations on the Security Dilemma and the Nature of Concerns Provoked by Indian Naval Expansion, in Bruce, R. H. (ed.), *The Modern Indian Navy and the Indian Ocean* Centre for Indian Ocean Regional Studies, Curtin University, Perth and Australian Institute of International Affairs, Canberra, 109–118.

Bruce, R. and McPherson, K. (1991) India's Military and South Asian Regional Politics: Psychology of Power, India: Prospects for the Future, *IOCPS Briefing Paper No 1*, The Indian Ocean Centre for Peace Studies, University of Western Australia.

Bruntland, G. H. (ed.) (1990) *Our Common Future* The World Commission on Environment and Development (this edition includes a Chapter with special reference to A Sustainable Future for Australia, Lyuba Zarsky (ed.), Oxford University Press, Melbourne. First Published 1987.

Buchholz, H. J. (1987) *Law of the Sea Zones in the Pacific Ocean*, Institute of Southeast Asian Studies, Singapore.

Burmester, H. (1982) The Torres Strait Treaty: ocean boundary delimitation by agreement, *American Journal of International Law*, 76, 2, 321–349.

______ (1990) *Timor Gap Treaty Seminar*, Allen, Allen and Hemsley, Sydney.

Calder, Nigel (1972) *Restless Earth*, Angus and Robertson, Sydney.

Caldwell, J. C. (1981) Population and development in the Indian Ocean Region, in Kerr, A. (ed.), *The Indian Ocean Region*, University of Western Australia Press, Perth.

Canby, T. Y. (1991) After the Storm, *National Geographic*, National Geographical Society, Washinton, 180, 2, 2–35.

Carter, R. W. G. (1988) *Coastal Environments*, Academic Press Ltd., London.

Chaliand, G. and Rageau, J.-P. (1983) *Strategic Atlas*, Penguin, Harmondsworth, Middlesex.

Charnock, H. (1984) Organizing the study of the oceans, *Marine Policy*, April, 120–136.

Chen Degong (1991) Perspects [Prospects] of the United Nations Convention for the Law of the Sea, Paper presented at the SEAPOL Workshop, Chiang Mai, Thailand.

Chia, Lin Sien (1981) The Straits of Malacca and Singapore: Navigational, Resource and Environmental Considerations, in Chia, L. S. and MacAndrews, C. (eds.), Southeast Asian Seas, Mcgraw-Hill, Singapore.

______ (1990) Ship Generated Marine Pollution Issues in Southeast Asia, Paper presented at the SEAPOL International Conference, Bali, Indonesia.

Churchill, R., Simmonds, K. R. and Welch, J. (1973) *New Directions in the Law of the Sea*, the British Institute of International and Comparative Law, Volume III, Oceana Publications Inc, New York.

Clark, I. (1981) Soviet Arms Supplies and Indian Ocean Diplomacy, in Bowman, L. W. and Clark, I. (eds.), *The Indian Ocean in Global Politics*, Westview Press, Boulder, Colorado, 149–172.

Claval, P. (1981) Methodology and Geography, *Progress in Human Geography*, 5: 97–103.

Cohen, S. B. (1964) *Geography and Politics in a Divided World*, New York.

Coker, R. E. (1962) *This Great and Wide Sea*, Harper and Brothers, New York.

Cole, P. J. (1963) *Geography of World Affairs*, Penguin, Hammondsworth.

Commission for the Future (see Bruntland, G. H., above)

Commonwealth Group of Experts (1984) *Ocean Management: A Regional Perpective*, The Commonwealth Secretariat, London.

Conforti, B. and Francalanci, G. (1979) *Atlante Dei Confini Sottmarini,* Dott A. Giuffre Editore, Milaño.

Cool, J. C. (1981) Authoritarianism and development: the search for alternatives, in Kerr, A. (ed.), *The Indian Ocean Region,* University of Western Australia Press, Perth.

Coquia, J. (1991) Does the Archipelagic Regime Depend Upon Entry into Force of the Convention, Paper presented at the SEAPOL Workshop, Chiang Mai, Thailand.

Corlett, E. (1981) *The Ship: The Revolution in Merchant Shipping 1950–1980,* Her Majesty's Stationery Office, London.

Cotter, C. H. (1965) *The Physical Geography of the Oceans,* Hollis and Carter Ltd., London.

Couper, A. D. (1972) *The Geography of Sea Transport,* Hutchinson University Library, London.

______ (1983) *The Times Atlas of the Oceans,* Times Book Ltd., Van Nostrand Reinhold, New York.

Crow, Ben, *et al.* (1983) *Third World Atlas,* Open University Press, Milton Keynes.

Cuyvers, Luc (1984) *Ocean Uses and Their Regulation,* John Wiley and Sons, New York.

Dalziel, I. W. D. *et al.* (1987) Extensional tectonics and the fragmentation of Gondwanaland, in Coward, M. P. *et al.* (eds.), *Continental Extensional Tectonics,* Blackwell, Cambridge, 433–441.

Daus, R. (1989) *Portuguese Eurasian Communities in Southeast Asia,* Institute of Southeast Asian Studies, Singapore.

Davies, J. L. (1972) *Geographical Variation in Coastline Development,* Oliver and Boyd, Edinburgh.

Denman, D. R. (1984) *Markets under the Sea?,* The Institute of Economic Affairs, London.

de Lestang, J. N. (1988) The Fisheries of Seychelles, in Appleyard, R. T. and Ghosh, R. N. (eds.), *Indian Ocean Islands Development,* National Centre for Development Studies, ANU, Canberra, and Centre for Migration and Development Studies, University of Western Australia, Perth, 172–185.

Department of Primary Industries and Energy (1987) *Report on Aerial Littoral Surveillance and Northern Australian Quarantine Strategy,* Australian Government Publishing Service, Canberra.

______ (1988) *Australian Quarantine Requirements for the Future,* Australian Government Publishing Service, Canberra.

Dewey, J. F. (1972) Plate Tectonics, reprinted from *Scientific American,* W. H. Freeman, San Francisco.

Diraputra, S. A. (1991) Disputes Settlements Under the Law of the Sea Convention of 1982 : Issues and Propects Relevant to Indonesia, Paper presented at the SEAPOL Workshop, Chiang Mai, Thailand.

Doyle, W. (1978) *The Old European Order 1600–1800,* Oxford University Press, Oxford.

Driver, P. A. (1980) International Fisheries, in Barston, R.P. and Birnie, P. (eds.), *The Maritime Dimension,* George Allen and Unwin, London, 27–53.

Drysdale, Alasdair (1991) The Gulf of Aqaba coastline: An evolving border landscape, in Rumley, D. and Minghi, J.V. (eds.) *The Geography of Border Landscapes,* Routledge, London, 203–216.

du Castel, Andre (1981) Sugar in the Indian Ocean countries — a prospective study, in Kerr, A. (ed.), *The Indian Ocean Region,* University of Western Australia Press, Perth.

du Toit, A. L. (1937) Our Wandering Continents: An Hypothesis of Continental Drifting, Hafner Publishing Co., Inc., New York.

Eccles, P. (1982) Coastal Surveillance Policies and Practices, in *Report of the 1982 Nothern Australian Development Seminar,* Northern Australia Development Council, 60–65.

El-Hakim, Ali A. (1979) *The Middle Eastern States and the Law of the Sea,* Syracuse University Press, New York.

Fagoone, I. (1983) Why is the Indian Ocean considered less productive? Manuscript at International Union for Conservation of Nature and Natural Resources, Gland.

Fairbridge, R. W. (1952) Preliminary Review of Limits of the Indian Ocean, Paper prepared for the Pan-Indian Ocean Science Association, Perth.

______ (1960) The changing level of the sea, reprinted from *Scientific American*, W. H. Freeman and Company, San Francisco.

Feld, W. J., Jordan, R. S. and Hurwitz, L. (1983) *International Organisations*, Praeger Publishers, New York.

Feliciano, F. P. (1991) Some Aspects of the Dispute Settlement Provisions of the 1982 United Nations Convention of the Law of the Sea, Paper presented at the SEAPOL Workshop, Chiang Mai, Thailand.

Fisher, C. A. (1966) *South-East Asia: A Social, Economic, and Political Geography*, Methuen, London.

Fleurieu, C. F. Claret de (1798–1800) Observations sur la division hydrographique du globe, et changements proposes dans la nomenclature generale et particuliere de l'hydrographie. In Marchand, E. (ed.), *Voyage autour du Monde*, Vol. 4, 1–74.

Food and Agriculture Organisation (1990) *Yearbook of Fishery Statistics*, Vol. 60, United Nations, Rome.

Forbes, V. L. (1980) *Marine Meteorology 1*, Technical Publications Trust, Perth.

______ (1984a) Law of the Sea: Maritime Jurisdictions — the need for up-to-date nautical charts and the delineation of maritime boundaries, Paper presented at the Second International Conference on Indian Ocean Studies, Perth.

______ (1984b) Global Choke Points of the Indian Ocean: Narrow Seaways 1 and 2, in McPherson, K. (ed.), *Indian Ocean Newsletter*, Perth, 5, 2, 8–10.

______ (1985) Palk Strait: Narrow Seaway No. 3, in McPherson, K. (ed.), *Indian Ocean Newsletter*, Perth, 6, 1, 8–10.

______ (1985) Limits in the Indian Ocean, in McPherson, K. (ed.), *Indian Ocean Newsletter*, Perth, 6, 2, 6–7.

______ (1986a) Strait of Malacca: Narrow Seaway No. 4, in McPherson, K. (ed.), *Indian Ocean Newsletter*, Perth, 7, 1, 8 and 9.

______ (1986b) Maritime Jurisdiction in the Timor Sea: The Need for an Early Settlement, in McPherson, K. (ed.), *Indian Ocean Newsletter*, 7, 2, 8–10.

______ (1987a) The Law of the Sea and Its Implications in the Indian Ocean Context, in McPherson, K. (ed.), *Oceans and Violence*, Centre for Indian Ocean Regional Studies, Curtin University, Perth, 53–79.

______ (1987b) Australian Perspectives on Ocean Development and International Maritime Law: nautical charts, bathymetric maps, and the delineation of maritime boundaries. Paper presented at the Second SEAPOL International Conference, Bangkok.

______ (1987c) Exclusive Economic Zones of the Southwest Indian Ocean, in McPherson, K. (ed.), *Indian Ocean Newsletter*, Perth, 8, 2, 7–9.

______ (1987d) Maritime Boundaries: The Persian Gulf, Strait of Hormuz and Gulf of Oman, in McPherson, K. (ed.), *Indian Ocean Newsletter*, Perth, 8, 3, 14–16.

______ (1988a) Maritime Limits off the Western Australian Coastline, Paper presented at the Border Landscapes Conference, IGU Study Group S3, Perth.

______ (1988b) Claimed Waters (Economic Zone) in the Bay of Bengal, in McPherson, K. and Wardrop, J. (eds.), *The Indian Ocean Review*, Perth, 1, 1, 12–13.

______ (1988c) Of Sea Lanes, Straits and (Military) Services: Indian Ocean Region, in McPherson, K. and Wardrop, J. (eds.), *The Indian Ocean Review*, Perth, 1, 2, 12–13.

______ (1988d) The Idyllic Islands of the Indian Ocean: The Maldives, in McPherson, K. and Wardrop, J. (eds.), *The Indian Ocean Review*, Perth, 1, 4, 12–13.

______ (1989a) The Settlement of a Maritime Boundary in the Coco Channel, Andaman Sea and bay of Bengal, in McPherson, K and Wardrop, J. (eds.), *The Indian Ocean Review*, Perth, 2, 1, 12, 13 and 26.

______ (1989b) Fisheries Resources of the Indian Ocean, in McPherson, K. and Wardrop, J. (eds.), *The Indian Ocean Review*, Perth, 2, 2, 14–15.

______ (1989c) The Timor Gap Issue: No longer a Gap but a Zone of Cooperation, in McPherson, K. and Wardrop, J. (eds.), *The Indian Ocean Review*, Perth, 2, 3, 14–18.

______ (1989d) Singapore's Maritime Jurisdiction, in McPherson, K. and Wardrop, J. (eds.), *The Indian Ocean Review*, Perth, 2, 4, 13–18.

______ (1990a) Prevention and Control of Oil Pollution in the Marine Environment: A Western Australian Perspective'. Paper presented at Third SEAPOL International Conference, Bali, Indonesia.

______ (1990b) Timor Gap Treaty: A Geographical Perspective, Paper presented at Workshop on Managing Offshore Hydrocarbons Operations, Bali, Indonesia.

______ (1990c) Maritime Delimitation of Economic Zones in the Mascarene Basin, Southwest Indian Ocean, in McPherson, K. and Wardrop, J. (eds.), *The Indian Ocean Review*, Perth, 3, 1, 8–9.

______ (1990d) Temporary Territorial gains by Iraq: The Iraqi Occupation of Kuwait, in McPherson, K. and Wardrop, J. (eds.), *The Indian Ocean Review*, Perth, 3, 3, 13–16.

______ (1990e) Maritime Limits in the Gulf of Aden, in McPherson, K. and Wardrop, J. (eds.) *The Indian Ocean Review*, Perth, 3, 4, 14–17.

______ (1991a) Australia's Offshore Boundaries and Policies, Paper presented at the SEAPOL Workshop, Chiang Mai, Thailand.

______ (1991b) A Geo-political Appraisal of a Joint Development Regime, Paper presented at the Institute of Strategic and International Studies, Malaysia.

______ (1991c) 'The Maldives and the Sea Level Change Debate', in McPherson, K., (ed.), *The Indian Ocean Review*, Perth, 4, 1, 15–18.

______ (1991d) 'Safer Ships — Cleaner Seas' and 'Report on the SEAPOL Workshop', in McPherson, K. (ed.) *The Indian Ocean Review*, 4, 3, 14–19 and 21–23.

______ (1991e) Implementation and Ratification of UNCLOS III: A Regional Commentary, in McPherson, K. (ed.), *The Indian Ocean Review*, Perth, 4, 4, 14–19.

______ (1992) British Indian Ocean Territory: Chagos Archipelago, in McPherson, K. (ed.), *The Indian Ocean Review, Perth*, 5, 1, 16–19.

Forbes, V. L. and Auburn, F. M. (1991) The Timor Gap Zone of Cooperation, *Boundary Briefing No. 9*, International Boundaries Research Unit, Durham.

Forbes, V. L. and Yasmeen, Samina (1988) The Shatt Al' Arab — Iran and Iraq, in McPherson, K. and Wardrop, J. (eds.), *The Indian Ocean Review*, Perth, 1, 3, 12–13.

Francalanci, G., Raman, D. and Scovazzi, T. (eds.) (1986) Atlas of Straight Baselines, Dott. A. Giuffr Editore, Milano.

Frank, W. T. and Ghosh, R. N. (1981) Some aspects of economic relations between Australia and South and Southeast Asia, in Kerr, A. (ed.), *The Indian Ocean Region*, University of Western Australia Press, Perth.

Frankel, E. G. (1984) Redefining functions, *Marine Policy*, Butterworth, London, 165–170.

Gabbay, R. (1988) Tourism, in Appleyard, R. T. and Ghosh, R. N. (eds.), *Indian Ocean Islands Development*, National Centre for Development Studies, Australian National University, Canberra, 205–226.

Galtung, J. (1991) On the way to Superpower Status: India and the EC Compared, *Occassional Paper, No. 2*, Indian Ocean Centre for Peace Studies, Perth.

Gamboa, E. P. and Laroza, V. C. (1990) Service Contract: Assumption and Distribution of Risks in Oil Exporation in The Philippines, Paper presented at the Workshop on Managing Hydrocarbon Operations in Southeast Asia, Bali, Indonesia.

Gaspart, C. (1981) The Comoro Islands since independence: an economic appraisal, in Kerr, A. (ed.), *The Indian Ocean Region*, University of Western Australia Press, Perth.

Gates, M. (1990) The Exxon-Valdez Oil Spill, Paper presented at the Workshop on Managing Hydrocarbon Operations in Southeast Asia, Bali.

Gentilli, J. (1948) The Indian Ocean: A Background to History, *The Australian Outlook*, Sydney, 167–176.

Geographer, The — (refer Limits Series in Bibliography supplement below)

George, M. (1991) Ratification of the Law of the Sea Convention 1982: A Malaysian

Perspective, Paper presented at the SEAPOL Workshop, Chiang Mai, Thailand.

Ghosh, R. N. (1988) Macroeconomic Policy and Structural Change in Mauritius, in Appleyard, R. T. and Ghosh, R. N. (eds.), *Indian Ocean Islands Development*, National Centre for Development Studies, Australian National University, Canberra, 75–96.

Gibbs, I. J. (1982) Coordinating Our Resource Development with Security in Mind, in *Report of the 1982 Nothern Australian Development Seminar*, Northern Australia Development Council, 22–26.

Glassner, M. I. (1986) The New Political Geography of the Sea, *Political Geography Quarterly*, Butterworths, Guildford, 5, 1, 6–8.

______ (1990) Neptune's Domain, Unwin Hyman, Boston.

Gold, E. (1990) Offshore Hydrocarbon Operations in Southeast Asia: Liability and Compensation for Environmental Damage, Paper presented at the Workshop on Managing Hydrocarbon Operations in Southeast Asia, Bali.

Gomane, J. P. (1981) France and the Indian Ocean, in Bowman, L. W. and Clark, I. (eds.), *The Indian Ocean in Global Politics*, Westview Press, Boulder, Colorado, 189–206.

Gottman, J. (1982) 'The Basic Problem of Political Geography: The Organization of Space and the Search for Stability', *Tijdschrift voor Econ. Soc. Geografie*, 73, 6, 340–349.

Gourlay, K. A. (1989) *Poisoners of the Seas*, Zed Books, Toronto.

Gresswell, R. K. (1957) *Beaches and Coastlines*, Halton Educational Publications, Andover.

Gulland, J. A. (1984) Looking beyong the golden age, *Marine Policy*, Butterworth, London, 137–150.

Ha T. N. (1990) Recent Development in Vietnam in the Law of the Sea Issue, Paper presented at the SEAPOL International Conference, Bali.

Hall, D. G. E. (1981) *A History of South East Asia*, Methuen, London.

Hamzah, B. A. (1990a) *The Spratlies: What can be Done to Enhance Confidence*, Institute of Strategic and International Studies (Malaysia), Kuala Lumpur.

______ (1990b) Conflicting Claims in the Spratly Islands : Some Tentative Remarks on the Need to Adopt Confidence-Building Measures, Paper presented at the SEAPOL International Conference, Bali, Indonesia.

______ (1991) The 1982 Law of the Sea Convention: A Non-Ratifiers Perspective — The Case of Malaysia, Paper presented at the SEAPOL Workshop, Chiang Mai, Thailand.

Hardjasoemantri, K. (1990) Problems of Land-Based Pollution in Southeast Asia, Paper presented at the SEAPOL International Conference, Bali.

Harris, A. (1988) Fisheries, in Appleyard, R. T. and Ghosh, R. (eds.), *Indian Ocean Islands Development*, National Centre for Development Studies, ANU, and Centre for Migration and Development Studies, UWA, 186–204.

Harrison, Brian. (1954) *South-East Asia — A Short History*, Macmillan, London.

Harrison, R. (1982) Offshore Gas Developments — Production Security, in *Report of the 1982 Nothern Australian Development Seminar*, Northern Australia Development Council, 36–41.

Harrison, R. J. (1990) Public and Private Responsibilities in Environmental and Safety Regulations, Paper presented at the Workshop on Managing Hydrocarbon Operations in Southeast Asia, Bali, Indonesia.

Hayman, C. (1980) International Shipping, in Barston, R.P. and Birnie, P. (eds.), *The Maritime Dimension*, George Allen and Unwin, London, 128–141.

Heezen, B. (1956) The origin of submarine canyons. Reprinted from *Scientific American*, W. H. Freeman and Company, San Francisco.

Heezen, B. and Tharp, M. (1964) Physiographic diagram of the Indian Ocean. Geological Society of America, New York.

______ (1965) Descriptive sheet to accompany physiographic diagram of the Indian Ocean. Geological Society of America, New York.

Heirtzler, J. R. (1968) Sea Floor Spreading, *Scientific American*, W. H. Freeman, San Francisco, 219: 66–69

Herschel, J. (1875) *Physical Geography of the Globe*, Boyd and Oliver, Edinburgh.

Higgens, B. and Dung, N. T. (1981) Dualism, dependency and continuing underdevelopment, in Kerr, A. (ed.), *The Indian Ocean Region*, University of Western Australia Press, Perth.

Hirono, R. (1981) Industrialization and technology transfer in Southeast Asia — case of Japanese subsidiaries overseas, in Kerr, A. (ed.), *The Indian Ocean Region*, University of Western Australia Press, Perth.

Hudson, H. (1988) *Northern Approaches*, Department of Transport and Communications, Australian Government Publishing Services, Canberra.

Hydrographic Department (1991) *Annual Summary of Admiralty Notices to Mariners*, Hydrographic Department, Royal Navy, Taunton.

Hydrographic Service (1991) *Annual Australian Notices to Mariners*, Royal Australian Navy, Sydney.

Indonesia National Study Team (1987a) Indonesia and the Protection of the Marine Environment, *Seapol Studies No. 6(b).*

______ (1987b) Passage through waters within National Jurisdiction: Indonesian Perspective', in *Seapol Studies No. 6(a),*

Inman, D. L. and Nordstrom, C. (1971) On the tectonic and morphological classsifications of coasts, *Journal of Geology*, 71, 1–22.

International Hydrographic Bureau (1953) *Limits of Oceans and Seas* Special Publication No. 23, IHB, Monaco.

Jacob, T. K. and Vellios, Jim (1987) *Southland: the Maritime Exploration of Australia*, Ministry of Education, Perth.

Jagota, S. P. (1985) *Maritime Boundary*, Martinus Nijhoff Publishers, Dordrecht.

Jayakumar, S. (1981) The Third UN Conference on the Law of the Sea: Proposals, Issues and Trends Relevant to Southeast Asia, in Chia, L. S. and MacAndrews, C. (eds.), *South Asian Seas*, McGraw-Hill, Singapore, 267–301.

Jayewardene, H. W. (1990) *The Regime of Islands in International Law*, Martinus Nijhoff, Dordrecht.

Joerg, W. L. G. (1930) Brief history of Polar Exploration since the introduction of flying — to accompany a physical map of the Antarctic and a bathymetric map of the Arctic, *American Geographical Society*, Special Publication No. 11, Washington.

Johnston, D. M. (1987) An Overview on the New Law of the Sea in Southeast Asia: Problems and Prospects of Implementation, *SEAPOL Studies No. 1.*

______ (1988) *The Theory and History of Ocean Boundary-Making*, McGill-Queen's University Press, Kingston.

______ (1990) Maritime Boundary Delimitation: The Widening Spectrum, Paper presented at the SEAPOL International Conference, Bali, Indonesia.

Johnson, D. M. and Letalik, N. G. (1984) *The Law of the Sea and Ocean Industry: New Opportunities and Restraints*, Proceedings, Law of the Sea Institute, 16th Annual Conference, Halifax, Nova Scotia.

Johnston, D. M. and Saunders, P. M. (1988) *Ocean Boundary Making: Regional Issues and Developments*, Croom Helm, Beckenham.

Johnston, D. W. (1919) *Shore Processes and Shoreline Development, John Wiley and Sons Ltd., New York.*

Joo-Jock, L. (1979) *Geo-Strategy and the South China Sea Basin*, Singapore University Press, Singapore.

Jukes, G. (1981) Soviet Naval Policy in the Indian Ocean, in Bowman, L. W., and Clark, I. (eds.), *The Indian Ocean in Global Politics*, Westview Press, Boulder, Colorado, 173–188.

Kaikobad, K. (1989) *The Shatt-Al-Arab Boundary Question: A Legal Appraisal*, Clarendon Press, Oxford.

Kapoor, D. C. and Kerr, A. J. (1986) *A Guide to Maritime Boundary Delimitation.* The Carswell Company, Ltd, Toronto.

Kapur, A. (1981) Carter's Diplomacy and the Indian Ocean Region, in Bowman, L. W. and

Clark, I. (eds.), *The Indian Ocean in Global Politics*, Westview Press, Boulder, Colorado, 131–148.

Keegan, John and Wheatcroft, Andrew (1986) *Zones of Conflict: An Atlas of Future Wars*, Simon and Schuster, New York.

Keerawella, G. (1991) Some Observations on Post — Rajiv Gandhi Scenarios, India: Prospects for the Future, *IOCPS Briefing Paper No 1*, The Indian Ocean Centre for Peace Studies, University of Western Australia.

Kent, G. and Valencia, M. (1985) *Marine Policy in Southeast Asia*, University of California, Berkeley.

King, C. A. M. (1962) *Oceanography for Geographers*, Edward Arnold, London.

Kodikara, S. (1979) *Strategic Factors in Interstate Relations in South Asia*, The Strategic and Defence Studies Centre, The Australian National University, Canberra.

Koesoebiono and Dahuri, R. (1990) Sustainable Utilization on the Coastal Environment and Its Resources: The Challenge of Coastal Resource Management in Indonesia, Paper presented at the SEAPOL International Conference, Bali, Indonesia.

Koh, T. (1982) *Straits in International Navigation*, Oceana Publications, London.

Komar, P. D. (1976) *Beach Processes and Sedimentation*, Prentice-Hall, Englewood Cliffs.

Kossinna, E. (1921) 'Die Tiefen des Weltmeeres', *Veroffentlich, d. Institute f. Meeresk*, Berlin, N. F. (Ser. A) 9, 70.

Kotov, L. V. and Yegorov, I. (1970) *Militant Solidarity, Fraternal Assistance*, Progress Publishers, Moscow.

Krey, J. (1973) Primary production in the Indian Ocean, in Zeitzschel, B. and Gerlach, S. A. (eds.), *The Biology of the Indian Ocean*, Springer-Verlag, Berlin.

Krey, J. and Babenerd, B. (1976) *Phytoplankton Production: Atlas of the International Indian Ocean Expedition*, Institut fr Meereskunde an der Universität Kiel, UNESCO, Paris.

Kriangsak, Kittichaisaree (1987) *The Law of the Sea and Maritime Boundary Delimitation in Southeast Asia*, Oxford University Press, Singapore.

______ (1990) Semi-Enclosed Southeast Asian Seas Regime Building in the 1990s, Paper presented at the SEAPOL International Conference, Bali, Indonesia.

______ (1991a) Current Problems and Issues for Thailand, a Non-Ratifier of the 1982 United Nations Convention on the Law of the Sea, Paper presented at the SEAPOL Workshop, Chiang Mai, Thailand.

______ (1991b) Semi-Enclosed Southeast Asian Seas Regime Building in the 1990s, Paper presented at the SEAPOL Workshop, Chiang Mai, Thailand.

______ (1991c) The Missing Signatures: The US and the Law of the Sea An Anecdote, Paper presented at the SEAPOL Workshop, Chiang Mai, Thailand.

Knoke, K. H. (1978) Law of the Sea Conference — Geneva Session, *Aussen Politik* (English Edition) 26, 4, 413–433.

Krmmel, O. (1897) Handbuch der Ozeanographie, Stuttgart, 2 vols, (2nd ed. 1907).

Krutskikh, A. (1986) *US Policies in the Indian Ocean*, Progress Publishers, Moscow (English Edition).

Kwaitkowska, B. (1988) Equitable Maritime Boundary Delimitation — A Legal Perspective, *International Journal of Estuarine and Coastal Law*, 13, 4, 287–304.

______ (1989a) 'Equitable Maritime Boundary Delimitation — A Legal Perspective', *International Journal of Estuarine and Coastal Law*, 3, 4, 287–304.

______ (1989b) *The 200 Mile Exclusive Economic Zone in the New Law of the Sea*, Martinus Nijhoff Publishers, The Hague.

______ (1990) Regional Cooperation in Marine Affairs in Southeast Asia Through International Organisations, Paper presented at the SEAPOL International Conference, Bali, Indonesia.

______ (1990c) Some Problems of Integrated Coastal and Ocean Management at the National Level, Paper presented at the SEAPOL International Conference, Bali, Indonesia.

Kwiatkowska, B. and Soons, A. H. A. (1991) The Law of the Sea Convention and

Extra-Regional Powers — The Case of the European Economic Community, Paper presented at the SEAPOL Workshop, Chiang Mai, Thailand.

La'Cassie, Marguerite (1990) Responsibility and Regulations in Offshore Safety, Paper presented at the Workshop on Managing Hydrocarbon Operations in Southeast Asia, Bali, Indonesia.

Lagoni, Rainer (1984) Arrangements for Joint Development Pending Resolution of Boundaries, *American Journal of International Law*, 78, 2, 345–368.

Lammers, J. G. (1986) The Present State of Research Carried out by the English-speaking Section of the Centre for Studies and Research, *Transfrontier Pollution and International Law*, Kluwer Academic Publishers, Dordrecht.

Langeraar, W. (1984) *Surveying and Charting of the Seas*, Elsevier, Amsterdam.

Lapidoth-Eschelbacher, R. (1982) *The Red Sea and The Gulf of Aden*, Martinus Nijhoff Publishers, The Hague.

Larus, J. (1981) India's Nonalignment and Superpower Naval Rivalry in the Indian Ocean, in Bowman, L. W., and Clark, I. (eds.), *The Indian Ocean in Global Politics*, Westview Press, Boulder, Colorado, 41–58.

______ (1989) India and Its Ocean: The Atypical Relationship Ends, in Bruce, R. H. (ed.) *The Modern Indian Navy and the Indian Ocean*, CIORS, Perth, 55–68.

Laughton, A. (1989) The Oceans, *Royal Society of Arts Journal*, CXXXVII, 5390, 88–102.

Lauterpacht, E. *et al.* (1991) *The Kuwait Crisis: Basic Documents*, Grotius Publications Limited, Cambridge.

Lee Yong Leng (1980) *Southeast Asia and the Law of the Sea: Some Preliminary Observations on the Political Geography of Southeast Asian Seas*, Singapore University Press, Singapore.

______ (1986) The Colonial Legacy in Southeast Asia: Maritime Boundary Problems, *Contemporary Southeast Asia*, 8, 2, 129.

______ (1988) Access to Southeast Asian Waters by Naval Powers: Some Problems and Ambiguities, *Contemporary Southeast Asia*, 10, 2, 135.

______ (1989) The Malaysian-Philippine Maritime Dispute, *Contemporary Southeast Asia*, Singapore, 11, 1, 61–74.

Lim Joo-Jock (1979) *Geo-Strategy and the South China Sea Basin*, Singapore University Press, Singapore.

Linklater, A. (1991) Internationalism in the Modern World, *Occasional Paper No. 5*, Indian Ocean Centre for Peace Studies, Perth.

Livesley, K. (1991) The Timor Gap Treaty: an update. Paper presented at the Australian Mining and Petroleum Law Association Conference, Darwin.

Lotilla, R. P. M. (1991) Philippine Implementation of the UNCLOS: Issues, Problems and Prospects, Paper presented at the SEAPOL Workshop, Chiang Mai, Thailand.

MacDonald, C. G. (1980) *Iran, Saudi Arabia, and the Law of the Sea*, Greenwood Press, Westport, Connecticut.

Maloringan, T. M. (1990) Offshore Hydrocarbon Development and Marine Pollution, Paper presented at the SEAPOL International Conference, Bali, Indonesia.

Mankabady, S. (1978) *Collision at Sea*, North-Holland Publishing Co., Amsterdam.

Mankabady, S. (1984) *The International Maritime Organisation*, Croom Helm Ltd., Beckenham, Kent.

Marchant, L. (1982) *France Australe*, Artlook Books, Perth.

Mayer, P. (1991) Which way does the wind blow in a Cyclone? Longer term trends in rural India!, India: Prospects for the Future, *IOCPS Briefing Paper No. 1*, The Indian Ocean Centre for Peace Studies, University of Western Australia.

McDorman, T. L., *et al*, (1983) *Maritime Boundary Delimitation: An Annotated Bibliography*, DOSP, Lexington.

McGill, J. T. (1958) Map of Coastal Landforms of the World, *Geographical Review*, 48: 402–405.

McKenzie, D. P. and Sclater, J. G. (1974) The Evolution of the Indian Ocean, in Press, F. and Siever, R. (eds.), *Planet Earth*, W. H. Freeman and Company, San Francisco.

McKenzie, and Richter, (1976) Convection Currents in the Earth's Mantle, in Bolt, B. A. (ed.) *Earthquakes and Volcanoes*, W. H. Freeman and Company, San Francisco.

McKinley, M. (1988) From Dante to Shannon: The Indian Ocean in Australia's Strategic Environment, in Bruce, R.H. (ed.), *Australia and the Indian Ocean*, Centre for Indian Ocean Regional Studies, Perth, 21–40.

______ (1989) Indian Naval Developments and Australian Strategy in the Indian Ocean, in Bruce, R.H. (ed.), *Australia and the Indian Ocean*, Centre for Indian Ocean Regional Studies, Perth, 131–168.

McPherson, K. (1991a) *A History of the Indian Ocean Region to the 16th Century*, Paradigm Press, Perth.

______ (1991b) The Indian Ocean: A History of the People and the Sea, unpublished manuscript, Perth.

McPherson, K. and Reeves, P. D. (1987) The Modern Maritime and Strategic Dimensions of the Indian Ocean Region: a Foundation Analysis, in McPherson, K. (ed.), *Oceans and Violence*, Centre for Indian Ocean Regional Studies, Perth, 1–19.

______ (1989a) The Foundations of Indian Naval Power, in Bruce, R. H. (ed.), *The Modern Indian Navy and the Indian Ocean*, Centre for Indian Ocean Regional Studies, Perth, 69–94.

______ (1989b) The Islands of the Indian Ocean in an Historical Context, Paper presented at the Indian Ocean Islands Development Workshop, Perth.

Melamid, A. (1957) The Political Geography of the Gulf of Aqaba, *Annals of Assoc of American Geographers*, 47, 231.

______ (1959) Legal Status of the Gulf of Aqaba, *American Jour. of Int. Law*, New York, 53, 412.

Mendelsohn, O. (1991) Is there a New Politics Trying to be Born in India? India: Prospects for the Future, *IOCPS Briefing Paper No 1*, The Indian Ocean Centre for Peace Studies, University of Western Australia.

Mendis, V. L. B. (1991) *SAARC* Origins, Organisation and Prospects, Indian Ocean Centre for Peace Studies, *Monograph No. 3*, Perth.

Mensah, T. A. (1984) International approaches, *Marine Policy*, Butterworth, London, 95–119.

Miller, L. H. (1990) *Global Order*, Westview Press, Boulder.

Minghi, J. V. (1963) Boundary Studies in Political Geography, *Annals of the Association of American Geographers*, 53, 407–428.

Mochtar Kusuma-Atmadja (1990) Regional Marine Environmental Protection in the Southeast Asian Seas: An Analysis of the Legal Framework of Part XII on the Protection of the Marine Environment, Paper presented at the SEAPOL International Conference, Bali, Indonesia.

Modelski, G. and Thompson, W. R. (1988) *Seapower in Global Politics*, 1494–1993, Macmillan, Houndsmills.

Mohd, Ibrahim Hj. Mohamed (1990) Implementation of the Law of the Sea Convention in the 1990s: National Managment of Fisheries, Paper presented at the SEAPOL International Conference, Bali, Indonesia.

Molner, P. and Tapponnier, P. (1980) The Collision between India and Eurasia, in Bolt, B. A. (ed.), *Earthquakes and Volcanoes*, W. H. Freeman and Company, 62–83.

Maloney, G. J. (1990) The Delimitation of Maritime Boundaries in the Timor Sea, *Australian Yearbook of International Law*, 7, 72–86.

Moorehead, F. J. (1963) *A History of Malaya*, Longmans, Kuala Lumpur.

Morgan, J. and Valencia, M. J. (1983) *Atlas for Marine Policy in Southeast Asian Seas*, University of California, Berkeley.

Muni, S. D. (1980) *Arms Build-up and Development: Linkages in the Third World, Research School of Pacific Studies, The Australian National University, Canberra.*

Munk, Walter (1955) The circulation of the oceans. Reprinted from *Scientific American*, W. H. Freeman and Company, San Francisco.

Mureithi, L. P. (1981) Patterns of industrialization in the countries of the Indian Ocean region, in Kerr, A. (ed.) *The Indian Ocean Region*, University of Western Australia Press, Perth.

Murray, J. (1888) On the height of the land and the depth of the ocean, *Scottish Geographical Magazine*, 4, 1–41.

Murray, J. and Hjort, J. (1912) *The Depths of the Ocean*, Macmillan, London.

Nailor, P. (1980) The Contemporary Use of Maritime Power, in Barston, R. P. and Birnie, P. (eds.), *The Maritime Dimension*, George Allen and Unwin, London, 142–153.

Naim, A. M. and Samuel, L. (1990) Offshore Petroleum Development in Indonesia: Facts and Challenges, Paper presented at the SEAPOL International Conference, Bali, Indonesia.

Nakhleh, E. A. (1991a) The Arab World After the Gulf War: Challenges and Prospects, *Occasional Paper No. 1*, Indian Ocean Centre for Peace Studies, Perth.

______ (1991b) The West Bank and Gaza Recent Developments and Future Prospects, *Occasional Paper No. 3*, Indian Ocean Centre for Peace Studies, Perth.

Natkiel, R. and Preston, A. (1986) *Atlas of Maritime History*, Weidenfeld and Nicholson, London.

Nayoan, G. A. S. and Achmad, Z. (1990) *Identifying Possible Cooperation in Developing Hydrocarbon Resources Within Offshore Border Areas in Southeast Asia*, Pertamina, Java.

Nelson, L. D. M. (1987) Keynote Address to the SEAPOL's Second International Conference, Bangkok.

______ (1991) Renewing the Dialogue, Paper presented at the 15th Annual Seminar Sponsered by the Centre for Oceans Law and Policy, Washington.

Ngantcha, F. (1989) *The Right of Innocent Passage and the Evolution of the International Law of the Sea*, Pinter Publishers, London.

Nicholl, P. (1988) Macroeconomic Policies in Seychelles since 1975, in Appleyard, R. T. and Ghosh, R. N. (eds.), *Indian Ocean Islands Development*, National Centre for Development Studies, Australian National University, Canberra, 44–54.

O'Connor, D. C. (1982) A Practical Approach to the Defence of Northern Australia, in *Report of the 1982 Nothern Australian Development Seminar*, Northern Australia Development Council, 113–128.

Odell, P. R. (1970) *Oil and World Power*, Penguin, Hammondsworth.

______ (1980) Offshore Resources : Oil and Gas, in Barston, R. P. and Birnie, P. (eds.), *The Maritime Dimension*, George Allen and Unwin, London, 76–107.

Ogley, R., (1984) *Internationalizing the Seabed*, Gower Publishing, London.

Ohshima, George (1991) Coastal islands on an international boundary: Dauan and Parma in the Torres Strait, in Rumley, D. and Minghi, J.V. (eds.) *The Geography of Border Landscapes*, Routledge, London, 169–188.

Olson, H. F. and Morgan, J. R. (1985) Enforcement of Maritime Jurisdictions, in Kent, G. and Valencia, M.J. (eds.), *Marine Policy in Southeast Asia*, University of California Press, Berkeley, 341–364.

Onorato, W. T. and Valencia, M. J. (1990) International Cooperation for Petroleum Development: The Timor Gap Treaty, Paper presented at the Workshop on Managing Hydrocarbon Operations in Southeast Asia, Bali, Indonesia.

Opeskin, B. R. and Rothwell, D. R. (1991) Australia's Territorial Sea: International and Federal Implications of Its Extension to 12 Miles, *Ocean Development and International Law*, 22, 395–431.

Osborne, Milton (1990) *Southeast Asia An Illustrated Introductory History*, Allen and Unwin, North Sydney.

Pachusanond, C. (1987) Thailand and the Settlement of Dispute in the 1982 Law of the Sea Convention, in Seapol Studies, No. 2(c).

______ (1990) Thailand and the Sea Law Implementation: Marine Environment Protection, Paper presented at the SEAPOL International Conference, Bali, Indonesia.

Panikkar, K. M. (1959) *Asia and Western Dominance,* George Allen and Unwin Ltd, London.

Parry, J. H. (1966) *Europe and a Wider World 1415–1715,* Hutchinson, London.

Pham Hao (1991) Current Problems and Issues for Non-Ratifiers, Paper presented at the SEAPOL Workshop, Chiang Mai, Thailand.

Phillips-Birt, Douglas (1971) *The History of Seamanship,* Doubleday and Company, New York.

Piyakarnchana, Twesukdi (1990) Implementation of the Montreal Protocol on Land-Based Pollution in Southeast Asia, Paper presented at the SEAPOL International Conference, Bali, Indonesia.

Poll, J. J. K. (1990) Timor Gap Seminar, *Australian Petroleum Exploration Association Journal,* 56, 55–57.

Powell, C. McA. *et al.* (1981) The early Cretaceous break-up of Eastern Gondwanaland, the separation of Australia and India, and their interaction with Southeast Asia, in Keast, A. (ed.), *Edcological Biogeography of Australia,* Dr W. Junk bv Publishers, The Hague, 15–29.

Prescott, J. R. V. (1975) *The Political Geography of the Oceans,* David and Charles, Newton Charles.

______ (1980) The Deep Seabed, in Barston, R. P. and Birnie, P. (eds.), *The Maritime Dimension,* George Allen and Unwin, London, 54–75.

______ (1981) Maritime Jurisdiction in Southeast Asia: A Commentary and a Map, *EAPI Research Report No. 2,* East-West Centre, Honolulu.

______ (1982) An agenda of political maritime issues for Australia, in Bateman, W. S. G. and Ward, M. W. (eds.), *Australia's Maritime Horizons in the 1980s,* Occasional Papers in Maritime Affairs 1, Canberra, 51–65.

______ (1985a) *The Maritime Political Boundaries of the World,* Methuen, London.

______ (1985b) Australia's Maritime Boundaries, *Canberra Studies in World Affairs, No. 16,* ANU, Canberra.

______ (1985c) Maritime Jurisdictional Issues, in Kent, G. and Valencia, M.J. (eds.), *Marine Policy in Southeast Asia,* Uni. of California Press, Berkeley, 58–97.

Prescott, J. R. V., Collier, H. J. and Prescott, D. F. (1977) *Frontiers of Asia and Southeast Asia,* Melbourne University Press, Melbourne.

Purwaka, T. H. (1990) National Mangement of Fishery Resources: Factors for Consideration in the Preparation of Establishing MSC System for Fisheries Management in Indonesia, Paper presented at the SEAPOL International Conference, Bali, Indonesia.

Rais, R. B. (1988) US Military Build-up in the Persian Gulf: Limitations and Risks, in Bruce, R. H. (ed.), *Australia and the Indian Ocean,* Centre for Indian Ocean Regional Studies, Perth, 103–118.

______ (1989) Indian Naval Developments: Implications for Pakistan, in Bruce, R. H. (ed.), *The Modern Indian Navy and the Indian Ocean,* Centre for Indian Ocean Regional Studies, Perth, 119–129.

Rakisits, C. G. P. (1988) Australia and the Persian Gulf Conflict: The Public Perception of the War, in Bruce, R.H. (ed.), *Australia and the Indian Ocean,* Centre for Indian Ocean Regional Studies, Perth, 122–138.

Ramazani, R. (1979) *The Persian Gulf and the Strait of Hormuz,* Sijthoff and Noordhoff, Alphen aan den Rijn, The Netherlands.

______ (1981) The Strait of Hormuz: The Global Chokepoint, in Bowman, L.W. and Clark, I. (eds.), *The Indian Ocean in Global Politics,* Westview Press, Boulder, Colorado, 7–20.

Ratzel, F. (1897) *Politische Geographie,* Oldenbourg, Munich.

______ (1901–2) *Die Erde und das Leben,* Leipzig and Wien.

Raychaudhuri, G. S. and Gupta, A. K. (1981) Plantation agriculture in South and Southeast Asia, in Kerr, A. (ed.), *The Indian Ocean Region*, University of Western Australia Press, Perth.

Reedy, N. B. K. (1981) The emerging geopolitical patterns of the Indian Ocean region, in Kerr, A. (ed.). *The Indian Ocean Region*, University of Western Australia Press, Perth.

Reeves, P. D. (1991) The Assassination of Rajiv Gandhi, the Congress Party and the Future of India, India: Prospects for the Future, *IOCPS Briefing Paper No 1*, The Indian Ocean Centre for Peace Studies, University of Western Australia.

Reitsma, H-J. A. (1983) Boundaries as Barriers — the Predicament of Land Locked Countries, in Kloit, N. and Waterman, S. (eds.), *Pluralism and Political Geography*, Croom Helm, Canberra, 259–269.

Rice, R. J. (1977) *Fundamentals of Geomorphology*, Longman, London.

Roach, J. A. (1991) Compilance with the 1982 Law of the Sea Convention: A Tentative Appraisal, Paper presented at the 15th Annual Seminar Sponsored by the Center for Oceans Law and Policy, Washington.

Robertson, A. J. (1988) The 1987 Defence White Paper — A Maritime Perspective, in Bruce, R.H. (ed.), *Australia and the Indian Ocean*, Centre for Indian Ocean Regional Studies, Perth, 47–64.

Ronquillo, I. (1987) Philippines Marine Living Resources and the 1982 United Nations Convention of the Law of the Sea, *Seapol Studies No. 5(b).*

Rumley, Dennis (1991) Society, state and peripherality: The case of the Thai-Malaysian border landscape, in Rumley, D. and Minghi, J.V. (eds.), *The Geography of Border Landscapes*, Routledge, London, 129–151.

Russ, P. and Tanner, L. (1978) *The Politics of Pollution*, Widescope International Publishers, Pty Ltd, Camberwell.

Saisunthorn, Jumpot (1990) EEZ Delimitation Under the United Nations Convention on the Law of the Sea and The Southeast Asian States' Practice, Paper presented at the SEAPOL International Conference, Bali, Indonesia.

Samson, E. D. (1985) Fisheries, in Kent, G. and Valencia, M.J. (eds.), *Marine Policy in Southeast Asia*, University of California Press, Berkeley, 101–154.

Samuels, M. S. (1982) *Contest for the South China Sea*, Methuen, New York.

Sand, P. H. (1986) *Marine Environment Law in the United Nations Environment Programme*, Tycooly Publishing, London.

Schott, G. (1935) *Geographie des Indischen und Stillen Oceans*, Boysen, Hamburg, 413.

Schweinfurth, U. (1978) Australia's Foreign Policy, *Aussen Politik*, 26, 4, 470–482.

Senftleben, W. (1976) 'Political Geography of the South China Sea', *Philippine Geographical Journal*, 20, 4, 163–175.

Sewell, R. B. Seymour (1940) The Indian Ocean, *Association d'Oceanogr. Phys., Publication No. 8*, 81–86.

Shepherd, G. W. Jr. (1981) Demilitarization Proposals for the Indian Ocean, in Bowman, L. W. and Clark, I. (eds.), *The Indian Ocean in Global Politics*, Westview Press, Boulder, Colorado, 223–248.

Sinclair, I. (1982) Australian Defence and Security, *in Report of the 1982 Nothern Australian Development Seminar*, Northern Australia Development Council, 50–57.

Smith, J. E., (1970) *'Torrey Canyon' Pollution and Marine Life*, Cambridge University Press, Cambridge.

Smith, R. W. (1990) National Claims to Maritime Jurisdiction, *Limits in the Seas*, No. 36, 6th Revision, Office of Ocean Law and Policy, Washington.

Soeriaatmadja, R. E. (1990) Analysis of Impacts Upon the Environment as a part of Decision-Making Processes for a Proposed Development Plan in Indonesia, Paper presented at the Workshop on Managing Hydrocarbon Operations in Southeast Asia, Bali, Indonesia.

Sparks, B. W. (1964) *Geomorphology*, Longmans Green and Co. Ltd., London.

Stalport, N. (1990) Decommissioning Offshore Production Platforms : Legal and Technical

Issues, Paper presented at the Workshop on Managing Hydrocarbon Operations in Southeast Asia, Bali, Indonesia.

Starke, J. G. (1984) *Introduction to International Law,* 9th. Ed. Butterworths, London.

Stetson, H. C. (1955) The continental shelf. Reprinted from *Scientific American,* W. H. freeman and Company, San Francisco.

Subrahmanyam, K. (1988) Strategic Developments in the Indian and South Pacific Ocean Regions, in Bruce, R. H. (ed.), *Australia and the Indian Ocean,* Centre for Indian Ocean Regional Studies, Perth, 79–95.

Suess, E. (1906) *The Face of the Earth,* (translated by H. B. C. Sollas), Macmillan, New York.

Sugandhy, Aca (1990) Issues, Problems and Basic Thinking of Marine and Coastal Zone Management: Indonesia's Case, Paper presented at the SEAPOL International Conference, Bali, Indonesia.

Sverdrup, H. U., Johnson, M. W. and Fleming, R. H. (1942) The Oceans; their Physics, Chemistry, and General Biology, Prentice-Hall, New York.

Tangsubukul, P. (1982) *ASEAN and the Law of the Sea,* Institute of Southeast Asian Studies, Singapore.

Tanja, G. J. (1990) *The Legal Determination of International Maritime Boundaries,* Kluwer Law and Taxation Publishers, Deventer.

Tarling, D. H. and M. P. (1971) *Continental Drift,* G. Bell and Sons, London.

Taylor, M. L. (1985) The Pearling Industry of Western Australia 1850–1985, *Fisheries Publication* No. 3, Department of Fisheries and Wildlife, Perth.

Taylor, P. J. (1985) *Political Geography: World Economy, Nation State and Locality,* Longmans, London.

Tellis, A. J. (1989) Securing the Barrack: The Logic, Structure and Objectives of India's Naval Expansion, in Bruce, R. H. (ed.), *The Modern Indian Navy and the Indian Ocean,* Centre for Indian Ocean Regional Studies, Perth, 5–53.

Terfloth, K. (1975) The Future of the Indian Ocean, *Aussen Politik,* 26, 4, 463–469.

The Philippine National Study Team (1987) Conflicts and Dispute Settlement Under the Law of the Sea, Seapol Studies No. 5(a).

Thomas, R. G. C. (1989) The Sources of Indian Naval Expansion, in Bruce, R. H. (ed.),*The Modern Indian Navy and the Indian Ocean,* Centre for Indian Ocean Studies, Perth, 95–107.

Tin Choo Hick (1987) Paper on Singapore: Law of the Sea, Seapol Studies No. 4.

Tooley, R. V. (1990) *Maps and Map-Makers,* Dorset Press, New York.

Torell, M. (1987) Thai Fisheries and Fishing Industry: Its Development and Prospects with Regards to the 1982 UN Law of the Sea Convention, *Seapol Studies* No. 2(b).

Towle, P. (1987) The United Nations Ad Hoc Committee on the Indian Ocean: Behind Alley or Zone of Peace?, in Bowman, L. W. and Clark, I. (eds.), *The Indian Ocean in Global Politics,* Westview Press, Boulder, Colorado, 207–222.

Townsend-Gault, Ian (1990a) Offshore Hydrocarbon Development and Marine Pollution, Paper presented at the SEAPOL International Conference, Bali, Indonesia.

______ (1990b) The Impact of Joint Development Zone on Previously Granted Interests, Paper presented at the Workshop on Managing Hydrocarbon Operations in Southeast Asia, Bali, Indonesia.

Ulfstein, Geir (1988) The Conflict between Petroleum Production, Navigation and Fisheries in *International Law, Ocean Development and International Law,* Taylor and Francis, 19, 229–262.

United Nations (1983) *United Nations Convention on the Law of the Sea: Official Text and Final Act,* United Nations Publications, New York.

United Nations (1987a) *The Law of the Sea: A Select Bibliography,* United Nations Publications, New York.

______ (1987b) *Current Developments in State Practice,* United Nations Publications, New York.

______ (1987c) *Rights of Access of Land-locked States to and from the Sea and Freedom of Transit,* United Nations Publications, New York.

______ (1988) *The Law of the Sea: A Select Bibliography*, United Nations Publications, New York.

______ (1989a) *The Law of the Sea: A Select Bibliography 1988*, United Nations Publications, New York.

______ (1989b) *National Legislation, Regulations and Supplementary Documents on Marine Scientific Research in Areas Under National Jurisdiction*, United Nations Publications, New York.

______ (1989c) *Baselines: National Legislation With Illustrative Maps*, United Nations Publications, New York.

______ (1989) *The Law of the Sea – Baselines: An Examination of the Relevant Provisions of UNCLOS*, United Nations Publications, New York

______ (1991) *The Law of the Sea: A Select Bibliography 1990*, United Nations Publications, New York.

United Nations Environment Programme (1982) The Health of the Oceans, *UNEP Regional Seas Reports and Studies* No. 16.

______ (1985) Marine mammals: global plan of action, *UNEP Regional Seas Reports and Studies*, No. 55.

______ (1985) Cooperative programmes sponsored by UNEP for the protection of the marine and coastal environment in the wider Indian Ocean region, *UNEP Regional Seas Report and Studies* No. 58.

______ (1985) Management and conservation of renewable marine resources in the Indian Ocean region: Overview, *UNEP Regional Seas Reports and Studies*, No. 60.

U.S. Bureau of the Census (1990) *Statistical Abstract of the United States: 1990*, Department of Commerce, Washington.

Valencia, M. J. (1981) Southeast Asian Seas: National Marine Interests, Transnational Issues, and Marine Regionalism, in Chia, L. S. and MacAndrews, C. (eds.), *Southeast Asian Seas*, McGraw-Hill, Singapore, 302–355.

______ (1985) Oil and Gas Potential, Overlapping Claims and Political Relations, in Kent, G. and Valencia, M. J. (eds.), *Marine Policy in Southeast Asia*, University of California, Berkeley, 155–187.

Valencia, M. J. and Kent, G. (1985) Cooperation: Opportunities, Problems, and Prospects, in Kent, G. and Valencia, M.J. (eds.), *Marine Policy in Southeast Asia*, University of California, Berkeley, 365–382.

Valencia, M. J. and Miyoshi, M. (1986) Southeast Asian Seas: Joint Development of Hydrocarbons in Overlapping Claim Areas? *Ocean Development and International Law*, 16, 3, 211–254.

Vallaux, C. (1933) *Gographie gnrale des Mers*, Alcan, Paris.

Vanden Driesen, I. (1988) Agriculture, in Appleyard, R. T. and Ghosh, R. N. (eds.), *Indian Ocean Islands Development*, National Centre for Development Studies, Australian National University, Canberra, 115–159.

______ (1988) Industry, in Appleyard, R. T. and Ghosh, R. N. (eds.), *Indian Ocean Islands Development*, National Centre for Development Studies, Australian National University, Canberra, 160–171.

Van Zandt, F. K. (1976) *Boundaries of the United States and the Several States*, United States Geological Survey, Professional Paper 909, Washington.

Vascianne, S. C. (1990) *Land-Locked and Geographically Disadvantaged States*, Claredon Press, Oxford.

Vaughan, T. W. (1938) Recent additions to knowledge of the bottom configuration of the southern oceans, *Comptes Rendus, Congress International Geogra.*, Amsterdam, 2, 160–174.

Vaughan, T. W. *et al.* (1940) Report of the Committee on the criteria and nomenclature of the major divisions of the ocean bottom, *Association d'Oceanogr. physique*, Liverpool, publ. sci. no. 8.

Veenstra, C. (1984) Mapping the Australian Continental Shelf, *Proceedings of the 12th International Cartographic Association Conference*, Vol. I, Perth, 411–421.

Veevers, J. J. *et al.* (1991) Review of seafloor spreading around Australia. I. Synthesis of the patterns of spreading. *Australian Journal of Earth Sciences*, 38, 373–389.

Vicziany, M. (1991) An Assessment of the Effects of Political Uncertainty on the Indian Economy, India: Prospects for the Future, *IOCPS Briefing Paper* No. 1, The Indian Ocean Centre for Peace Studies, Perth.

Vongvissesomjai, Suphat (1990) Some Problems of Integrated Coastal and Ocean Management at the National Level, Paper presented at the SEAPOL International Conference, Bali, Indonesia.

Wade, S. O. (1986) 'A Proposal to Include Tunas in U.S. Fishery Jurisdiction' in *Ocean Development and International Law*, 16, 3, 255–304.

Waters, J. F. (1975) *The Continental Shelves*, Abelard-Schuman, New York.

Wegener, A. L. (1915) *Die Entstehung der Kontiente und Ozeane*, Friedr. Vieweg and Sohn, Braunschweig.

Wegener, A. L. (1967) *The Origin of Continents and Oceans* (trans. J. Biram), Methuen, London.

Weil, P. (1989) *The Law of Maritime Delimitation-Reflections*, translated from the French text by M. MacGlashan, Grotius Publications Ltd., Cambridge.

Wilheim, E. (1989) Australia-Indonesia Seabed Boundary Negotiations: Proposals for a Joint Development Zone in the Timor Gap, *Natural Resources Journal*, 29, 821–834.

Wilson, J. T. (1963) Continental Drift reprinted from *Scientific American*, W. H. Freeman and Company, San Francisco.

Wong, A. (1988) Comoros and Maldives: an overview of Macro economies, in Appleyard, R. T. and Ghosh, R. N. (eds.), *Indian Ocean Islands Development*, National Centre for Development Studies, Australian National University, Canberra, 97–114.

Wyrtki, Klaus (1988) *Oceanographic Atlas of the International Indian Ocean Expedition*, The National Science Foundation, Amerind Publishing Co. Pvt. Ltd., New Delhi.

Yusof, H. (1987) The United Nations Convention on the Law of the Sea in Southeast Asia: Problems of Implementation, in *Seapol Studies*, No. 3.

BIBLIOGRAPHY-SUPPLEMENT

United States Department of State. *Limits in the Seas Series*.
Formerly (up to 1987) produced by The Geographer, Bureau of Intelligence and Research.
Cited in this study under The Geographer and/or *Limits*.
Now compiled and produced by the Office of Ocean Law and Policy. Bureau of Oceans and International Environment and Scientific Affairs.
Principal analyst: Dr Robert W. Smith.

No. 1 Continental Shelf Boundary: Indonesia/Malaysia, 21 Jan 1970.
No. 2 Continental Shelf Boundary: Norway/Sweden, 22 Jan 1970.
No. 3 Straight Baselines: Ireland, 23 Jan 1970.
No. 4 Straight Baselines: Mexico, 24 Jan 1970.
No. 5 Straight Baselines: Dominican Republic, 25 Jan 1970.
No. 9 Continental Shelf Boundary: Italy/Yugoslavia, 20 Feb 1970.
No. 10 Continental Shelf Boundary: The North Sea, 2 Mar 1970.
No. 11 Continental Shelf Boundary: Trinidad and Tobago/Venezuela, 6 Mar 1970.
No. 12 Continental Shelf Boundary: Bahrain/Saudi Arabia, 10 Mar 1970.
No. 14 Straight Baselines: Burma, 14 Mar 1970.
No. 15 Straight Baselines: Madagascar, 16 Mar 1970.
No. 16 Continental Shelf Boundary: Finland/Sweden, 25 May 1970.
No. 17 Continental Shelf Boundary: Norway/Soviet Union, 27 May 1970.
No. 18 Continental Shelf Boundary: Abu Dhabi/Qatar, 29 May 1970.
No. 19 Straight Baselines: Denmark, 21 Dec 1978.
No. 24 Continental Shelf Boundary: Iran/Saudi Arabia, 6 Jul 1970.
No. 25 Continental Shelf Boundary: Iran/Qatar, 9 Jul 1970.
No. 26 Territorial Sea Boundary: Denmark/Sweden, 16 Jul 1970.
No. 27 Straight Baselines: Portugal, 20 Sep 1970.
No. 28 Straight Baselines: Angola, 10 Nov 1970.
No. 29 Straight Baselines: Mozambique, 12 Nov 1970.
No. 30 Straight Baselines: Portuguese Guinea, 13 Nov 1970.
No. 31 Straight Baselines: Thailand, 24 Mar 1971.
No. 34 Straight Baselines: Iceland, (revised) 1 Jul 1974.
No. 35 Straight Baselines: Indonesia, 20 Jul 1971.
No. 36 National Claims to Maritime Jurisdictions, 6th Revision, 3 Jan 1990.
No. 41 Straight Baselines: Mauritius, 7 Mar 1972.
No. 45 Maritime Boundary: Mexico/United States, 11 Aug 1972.
No. 49 Territorial Sea Boundary: Cyprus/Sovereign Base Areas (UK), 10 Nov 1972.
No. 50 Territorial Sea Boundary: Indonesia/Malaysia, 10 Jan 1973.
No. 53 Straight Baselines: Syria, 10 Oct 1973.
No. 55 Continental Shelf and Territorial Sea Boundaries: Poland/Soviet Union, 19 Oct 1973.
No. 56 Continental Shelf Boundary: (Northeastern Baltic) Filand/Soviet Union, 19 Oct 1973.

No. 57 Territorial Sea Boundary: Canada/St. Pierre and Miquelon, 12 Sep 1974.
No. 58 Continental Shelf Boundary: Bahrain/Iran, 13 Sep 1974.
No. 59 Territorial Sea Boundary: Soviet Union/Turkey, 9 Oct 1974.
No. 60 Territorial Sea Boundary: Indonesia/Singapore, 11 Nov 1974.
No. 62 Continental Shelf Boundary: India/Indonesia, 25 Aug 1975.
No. 63 Continental Shelf Boundary: Iran/UAE (Dubai), 30 Sep 1975.
No. 64 Continental Shelf Boundary: Argentina/Uruguay, 24 Oct 1975.
No. 65 Continental Shelf and Territorial Sea Boundaries: German Democratic Republic/Poland, 28 Nov 1975.
No. 66 Historic Waters Boundary: India/Sri Lanka, 12 Dec 1975.
No. 67 Continental Shelf Boundary: Iran/Oman, 1 Jan 1976.
No. 68 Territorial Sea and Continental Shelf Boundaries: Guinea-Bissau/Senegal, 15 Mar 1976.
No. 69 Maritime Boundary: Colombia/Ecuador, 1 Apr 1976.
No. 71 Continental Shelf Boundary: Finland/Sweden, 16 Jan 1976.
No. 72 Continental Shelf Boundary: Canada/Denmark (Greenland), 4 Aug 1976.
No. 73 Maritime Boundary: Brazil/Uruguay, 30 Sep 1976.
No. 74 Maritime Boundary: Federal Republic of Germany/German Democratic Republic, 5 Oct 1976.
No. 75 Continental Shelf Boundary and Joint Development Zone: Japan/Republic of Korea, 2 Sep 1977.
No. 77 Maritime Boundary: India/Sri Lanka, 16 Feb 1978.
No. 78 Maritime Boundary: India/Maldives, 24 Jul 1978.
No. 79 Maritime Boundaries: Colombia/Panama, 3 Nov 1978.
No. 80 Straight Baseline: Chile (addendum). 12 May 1980.
No. 81 Maritime Boundaries: Indonesia/Malaysia/Thailand, 12 May 1970.
No. 83 Territorial Sea and Continental Shelf Boundaries: France/Spain, 12 Feb 1979.
No. 84 Maritime Boundary: Colombia/Costa Rica, 15 Feb 1979.
No. 85 Maritime Boundary: The Gambia/Senegal, 23 Mar 1979.
No. 86 Maritime Boundary: Chile/Peru, 2 Jul 1979.
No. 87 Territorial Sea and Continental Shelf Boundaries: Australia/Indonesia/Papua New Guinea, 20 Aug 1979.
No. 88 Maritime Boundary: Ecuador/Peru, 2 Oct 1979.
No. 89 Continental Shelf Boundary: Italy/Tunisia, 7 Jan 1980.
No. 90 Continental Shelf Boundary: Italy/Span, 14 May 1980.
No. 91 Maritime Boundary: United States/Venezuela, 16 Dec 1980.
No. 92 Territorial Waters Boundary: Kenya/Tanzania, 15 May 1981.
No. 93 Continental Shelf Boundaries: India/Indonesia/Thailand, 17 Aug 1981.
No. 94 Continental Shelf Boundaries: The Persian Gulf, 11 Sep 1981.
No. 95 Maritime Boundary: France (Reunion)/Mauritius, 16 Apr 1982.
No. 96 Continental Shelf Boundary: Greece/Italy, 6 Jun 1982.
No. 97 Maritime Boundaries: Costa Rica/Panama 6 Dec 1982.
No. 98 Archipelagic Straight Baseline: Sao Tome and Principe, 1 Nov 1983.
No. 100 Maritime Boundaries: United States/Cook Islands and United States/New Zealand (Tokelau), 30 Dec 1983.
No. 101 Fiji's Maritime Claim, 30 Nov 1984.
No. 102 Maritime Boundary: Burma/Thailand, 30 Jan 1985.
No. 103 Straight Baselines: Colombia, 30 Apr 1985.
No. 104 Maritime Boundary: Cuba/Mexico, 10 Sep 1985.
No. 105 Maritime Boundary: Colombia/Dominican Republic and Netherlands (Neth. Antilles)/Venezuela, 22 Jan 1986.
No. 106 Developing Standard Guidelines for Evaluating Straight Baselines, 31 Aug 1987.
No. 108 Maritime Boundaries of the World, 30 Nov 1990.

No. 109 Continental Shelf Boundary: Turkey/USSR, and Straight Baselines: USSR (Black Sea), 29 Sep 1988.
No. 110 Maritime Boundary: Cuba/United States, 21 Feb 1990.
No. 112 United States Responses to Excessive National Maritime Claims, 9 Mar 1992.
No. 113 Straight Baseline Claims: Djibouti and Oman, 22 April 1992.

United Nations, Office for Ocean Affairs and the Law of the Sea.
Law of the Sea Bulletins. (LOS Bull.)
United Nations Publications, New York.

No. 1 Law of the Sea Bulletin Sep 1983.
No. 2 Law of the Sea Bulletin Dec 1983.
No. 3 Law of the Sea Bulletin Mar 1984.
No. 5 Law of the Sea Bulletin Jul 1985.
No. 6 Law of the Sea Bulletin Oct 1986.
No. 7 Law of the Sea Bulletin Apr 1986.
No. 8 Law of the Sea Bulletin Nov 1986.
Special Issue I (Status of UNCLOS) Mar 1987
No. 9 Law of the Sea Bulletin Apr 1987.
No. 10 Law of the Sea Bulletin Nov. 1987.
Special Issue II (Registration of Pioneer Status) Apr 1988.
No. 11 Law of the Sea Bulletin Jul 1988.
No. 12 Law of the Sea Bulletin Dec 1988.
No. 13 Law of the Sea Bulletin May 1989.
No. 14 Law of the Sea Bulletin Dec 1989.
No. 15 Law of the Sea Bulletin Jul 1990.
No. 16 Law of the Sea Bulletin May 1991.
Special Issue III (Registration of Pioneer Status) Sep 1991.

INDEX

The following abbreviations are employed for this index. f = figure, ff = following pages, m = map, t = table.